The 'shepheards nation'

Jacobean Spenserians and Early Stuart Political Culture, 1612–1625

MICHELLE O'CALLAGHAN

CLARENDON PRESS · OXFORD

OXFORD
UNIVERSITY PRESS

Great Clarendon Street, Oxford, OX2 6DP
Oxford University Press is a department of the University of Oxford.
It furthers the University's objective of excellence in research, scholarship,
and education by publishing worldwide in
Oxford New York
Athens Auckland Bangkok Bogotá Buenos Aires Calcutta
Cape Town Chennai Dar es Salaam Delhi Florence Hong Kong Istanbul
Karachi Kuala Lumpur Madrid Melbourne Mexico City Mumbai
Nairobi Paris São Paulo Singapore Taipei Tokyo Toronto Warsaw
and associated companies in Berlin Ibadan

Oxford is a registered trade mark of Oxford University Press
in the UK and certain other countries

Published in the United States
by Oxford University Press Inc., New York

British Library Cataloguing in Publication Data

Data available

Library of Congress Cataloging in Publication Data

Data available

ISBN–0–19–818638–x

1 3 5 7 9 10 8 6 4 2

Typeset by Regent Typesetting, London
Printed in Great Britain
on acid-free paper by
Biddles Ltd,
Guildford and King's Lynn

Acknowledgements

THIS book was originally written as a doctoral thesis and I would like to thank David Norbrook who supervised the thesis at Oxford and also helped to get the publication of the book moving again after it seemed to have stalled. Thanks should also go to Mike Braddick, Martin Butler, Anthony Milton, and Sue Wiseman who offered comments on sections of the book. A number of friends and colleagues shared ideas, work, or offered much-needed help and advice, in particular: Tim Armstrong, Julie Hanson, Margaret Kean, Andrew McRae, Jane Milling, Nicole Pohl, Paul Salzman, Erica Sheen, and Ros Smith.

Nene-University College Northampton funded research awards that enabled me to complete the book. But I am especially grateful for the supportive working environment that I found amongst my colleagues in English at Nene which made life that little bit easier.

Thanks must go to my family for letting me take them for granted. Finally, this book is dedicated to the ever-patient Mathew Thomson and to Grace who arrived in time to see the book through the press.

An earlier version of Chapter 1 first appeared in *The Seventeenth Century* 12 (1988), and a version of Chapter 2 has appeared in *The Historical Journal* 41 (1998). I would like to thank the Bodleian Library, University of Oxford, for permission to reproduce the woodcut to the 'October' eclogue from Spenser's *The Shepheardes Calender* (4° F 2 Art. Bs. Part II) 39r.

Contents

Introduction

Colin's gone home, the glorie of his clime.[1]

When Spenser died in 1599, he achieved recognition as the nation's poet: he was buried alongside Chaucer in Westminster abbey, and Elizabeth ordered a monument to his memory, although it was never erected. Spenser left succeeding generations with the question of what it means to speak for the nation. His own answer to this question, particularly in his later writings, was troubled by tensions between an imperative to project a unified national community and a recognition of growing divisions.[2] The 'Spenser' that emerged after his death assumed an unsettling doubleness: he was simultaneously the laureate poet gloriously serving his monarch and the oppositional poet, the persecuted critic of the corrupted times. Under James, the epic poet of *The Faerie Queene* often modulated into the poet of complaint. The 1596 edition of *The Faerie Queene* had ended with the poet complaining that 'some wicked tongues' had brought his 'homely verse' 'into a mighty Peres displeasure', and this provided the basis for an early seventeenth-century narrative pattern which has Spenser hunted from the court and exiled to the 'country', the home of 'the shepheards nation' in *Colin Clouts Come Home Againe*.[3] Subsequent writers engaged with Spenser in order to define their own identities and, just as importantly, to define a community. Spenser's volume of elegies for Sidney, *Astrophel*, and *Colin Clouts Come Home Againe* offered a pattern for a textual community that could itself provide a centre for a native humanist literary culture. In 1614 and 1615, William Browne,

[1] John Weever, 'In obitum Ed. Spencer Poetae prestantis', *Epigrammes in the oldest cut, and newest fashion* (London, 1599), G3r.
[2] On Spenser's divided position as national laureate, see: Andrew Hadfield, *Literature, Politics and National Identity: Reformation to Renaissance* (Cambridge: Cambridge University Press, 1994), 173–81.
[3] Edmund Spenser, *The Faerie Qveene*, ed. A. C. Hamilton (London and New York: Longman, 1977), 709; *Colin Clovts Come Home Againe*, in Spenser, *Poetical Works*, ed. J. C. Smith and E. De Selincourt (London, New York, Toronto: Oxford University Press, 1912; 23rd edn. 1969), 536.

George Wither, and Christopher Brooke came together to revive
Spenser's 'shepheards nation' in the collaborative eclogues, *The
Shepheards Pipe* and *The Shepherds Hunting*. This is a study of
the ways in which these writers represented themselves as a distinctive oppositional community in the years 1613 to 1625, and
took up Spenser's question of what it means to speak for the
nation.

Such a study of the dissemination of Spenser's works across a
group of writers offers a different angle on poetic influence to a
patrilineal model that traces the line of descent from strong
fathers to rebellious sons, and tends to focus on individual
writers. This type of model has marginalized these 'minor'
Jacobean Spenserians, who are dismissed as late 'Elizabethans',
a hangover from the 'degenerate' literary culture of the 1590s,
and attention has turned instead to the individual talents of
Donne and Jonson, the founders of new poetic lines.[4] Grundy
complained in the late 1960s, 'Our map of the period is
curiously empty: one gets the impression that the only choice
for readers of the day was between Donne and Jonson and
their respective followers.'[5] Norbrook's study of Jacobean
Spenserianism did much to redress this imbalance. His model of
early seventeenth-century culture as sharply contested, rather
than unproblematically dominated by the court and its poets,
Donne and Jonson, gave the Spenserians a new centrality and
they were identified with the emergence of a poetic 'opposition'
that would culminate in the English republic.[6] Recent studies
interested in nationalism have also given Spenserians, such as
Drayton, a decisive voice in their view of the early modern
period.[7] However, on the whole, New Historicism's trans-

---

[4] Edmund Gosse, *The Jacobean Poets* (London: John Murray, 1894), 2–3, 44,
67; Hugh Kenner (ed.), *Seventeenth-Century Poetry: The Schools of Donne and
Jonson* (New York: Holt, Rinehart, and Winston, 1964), p. xxx.

[5] Joan Grundy, *The Spenserian Poets: A Study in Elizabethan and Jacobean
Poetry* (London: Edward Arnold, 1969), 4.

[6] David Norbrook, *Poetry and Politics in the English Renaissance* (London:
Routledge and Kegan Paul, 1984), chapters 8 and 9.

[7] Richard Helgerson, *Forms of Nationhood: The Elizabethan Writing of England*
(Chicago and London: University of Chicago Press, 1992), chapter 3; Jane Tylus,
'Jacobean Poetry and Lyric Disappointment', in Elizabeth D. Harvey and Katherine
Eisaman Maus (eds.), *Soliciting Interpretation: Literary Theory and Seventeenth-
Century English Poetry* (Chicago and London: University of Chicago Press, 1990),
174–98; Claire McEachern, *The Poetics of Nationhood, 1590–1612* (Cambridge:
Cambridge University Press, 1996), chapter 4.

formation of the map of Renaissance culture has tended to leave the Spenserians on the margins of seventeenth-century studies once more. This is partly due to the 'regicentric model of new historicist enquiry', in the words of Loewenstein, that has resulted in an 'attentuated political nexus' which largely con fines the study of power to 'the institutional grid of monarchy, family, court or church'.[8] A model of cultural politics that draws attention to the relations between writers and the institutions that enable textual communities can provide a perspective for studying early modern culture that does not find its primary point of reference in the court, but explores other models of cultural interaction and production, and simultaneously provokes questions about the circulation of ideas and cultural transmission that are inhibited by an author-centred study.

I am using the term 'textual communities' in the broad sense of arenas of discursive interaction produced through the exchange and circulation of texts in manuscript or print. This model follows Harold Love's concept of 'scribal communities' which draws attention to the way that the exchange of texts in manuscript functions to give figurative, social, and sometimes political representation to a community. Patterns of manuscript transmission are determined by pre-existing communities, and yet these communities are themselves simultaneously constituted through the exchange of texts and accompanying fictions of sociability.[9] Material and symbolic relationships are therefore mutually reinforcing. This book is particularly interested in how these processes of representation and the relations that they describe are reconfigured and transformed when they take place in print. The group of Spenserian poets that is the subject of this study can productively be described as a print community. The continuity between a manuscript and a print culture in this period should not be ignored, yet print did transform modes of sociability.[10] Relationships between writers and their readers in

---

[8] Joseph Loewenstein, 'For a History of Literary Property: John Wolfe's *Reformation*', *English Literary Renaissance*, 18 (1988), 394.

[9] Harold Love, *Scribal Publication in Seventeenth-Century England* (Oxford: Clarendon Press, 1993), 177–81.

[10] Elizabeth Eisenstein, *The Printing Press as an Agent of Change: Communications and Cultural Transformations in Early Modern Europe*, 2 vols. (Cambridge: Cambridge University Press, 1979), i. 132, 226–43; Benedict Anderson, *Imagined Communities: Reflections on the Origin and Spread of Nationalism*

both a manuscript and print culture were dependent on the construction of common traditions and fictions of sociability and community. Love has pointed to the way that the exchange of texts within scribal communities served to foster collective values and to enhance personal allegiances, 'bonding groups of like-minded individuals into a community'. When this process of exchange takes place in print, the community constitutes itself in a public rather than a private form. Love argues that in contrast to the scribal community, a print community is characterized by its relative openness and gives the impression that it is formed through the 'public sharing of knowledge'.[11] This distinction does need qualifying since one could argue that the scribal communities that flourished in the early seventeenth century did take on such public forms and historians have pointed to the formative role of manuscript culture in fostering public political debate.[12] That said, print does give a certain orientation to a concept of the public by enabling the articulation of an ideal of inclusiveness. Because of its qualities of reproducibility which permitted wider dissemination, print was central to the expression of more abstract concepts of community—imagined communities—whereby individuals were able to relate to others outside their immediate social environment. This potential for wider dissemination made it possible for fictions of community to be loosened from their particular social and cultural milieu and to make claims to an idealizing universality. Print, in this sense, is central to the formation of national communities. In the words of Anderson, print 'made it possible for rapidly growing numbers of people to think about themselves, and to relate themselves to others, in profoundly new ways'.[13]

(London: Verso, 1983), 40–2; Roger Chartier, 'Introduction: Print Culture', in Roger Chartier (ed.), *The Culture of Print: Power and the Uses of Print in Early Modern Europe*, trans. Lydia G. Cochrane (Princeton: Princeton University Press, 1989), 1–8.

[11] Love, *Scribal Publication in Seventeenth-Century England*, 177, 183–4.

[12] Alastair Bellany, ' "Raylinge Rymes and Vaunting Verse": Libellous Politics in Early Stuart England, 1603–28', in Kevin Sharpe and Peter Lake (eds.), *Culture and Politics in Early Stuart England* (Basingstoke and London: Macmillan, 1994), 285–310; Thomas Cogswell, 'Underground Verse and the Transformation of Early Stuart Political Culture', in Susan D. Amussen and Mark A. Kislansky (eds.), *Political Culture and Cultural Politics in Early Modern England* (Manchester and New York: Manchester University Press, 1995), 277–300.

[13] Anderson, *Imagined Communities*, 16, 40–4.

The model for a print community that I am offering does, in many ways, look like a microcosm of the public sphere. This comparison has its uses. The Spenserian print community that made its first public appearance in the collaborative volumes of eclogues, *The Shepheards Pipe* and *The Shepherds Hunting*, participated in a process that gave rise to new languages of citizenship and publicness. It does appear to anticipate the new modes of sociability and the idealizing social discourse that characterize Habermas's model of a bourgeois public sphere in more specific terms. Through civic fictions, this community of writers claimed autonomy from the court, projected an idealized social space that was relatively open and accessible, and thereby promoted a social ideal of free intellectual debate that resembles the open dialogue between private citizens that characterizes the public sphere.[14] There are limits, however, to the analytical usefulness of Habermas's model for understanding this early seventeenth-century print community. Not only does he emphasize that the bourgeois public sphere is a concept historically specific to developments in the eighteenth and nineteenth centuries, but there are problems with the model itself.[15] Lacking in the earlier period is 'the specifically bourgeois dialectic of inwardness and publicness' that defines the bourgeois public sphere and is structurally dependent upon capitalism.[16] However, the way that private forms, such as pastoral and friendship, were invested with a public relevance by these Spenserian poets could be seen as part of a process whereby the private sphere became the basis of publicness. Habermas's historical model is developmental and it is possible to see in these texts the emergence of idealizing civic fictions and models of communication that will be realized later in the century. More fundamental reservations arise in relation to Habermas's

[14] Jürgen Habermas, *The Structural Transformation of the Public Sphere: An Inquiry into a Category of Bourgeois Society*, trans. Thomas Burger and Frederick Lawrence (Cambridge, Mass.: MIT Press, 1989), 30–1.

[15] Habermas has spoken of his 'doubts about how far we can push back the very notion of the public sphere into the sixteenth and seventeenth centuries without somehow changing the very concept of the public sphere to such a degree that it becomes something else' ('Concluding Remarks', in Craig Calhoun (ed.), *Habermas and the Public Sphere* (Cambridge, Mass.: MIT Press, 1992), 465). However, he is characteristically unclear about the precise nature of these reservations.

[16] Jürgen Habermas, 'Further Reflections on the Public Sphere', in Craig Calhoun (ed.), *Habermas and the Public Sphere* (Cambridge, Mass.: MIT Press, 1992), 426–7.

model of the bourgeois public sphere itself which is frequently
criticized for being idealized and idealizing. Nancy Fraser sees
it as limited because of its singularity, 'its claim to be *the*
public arena', and instead argues for a 'plurality of competing
publics'.[17] When reconsidering this model, Habermas himself
has moved in this direction and admits the 'pluralization of the
public sphere in the very process of its emergence'.[18] Habermas's
public sphere is valuable for the way it draws attention to
historical processes of modernization, but perhaps it should be
seen less as an authoritative model than as a spur to further
reconceptualizations.

   This pluralization of the public sphere gives it a structural and
ideological flexibility that may help in the formulation of a
model of pre-bourgeois public spheres. Although Habermas
does acknowledge earlier concepts of the public sphere, they
remain shadowy and their relationship to a bourgeois public
sphere is unclear. The origins of the bourgeois public sphere are
traced to a court society and the urban corporations of the early
modern town. The literary public sphere, the precursor to the
political public sphere, often appears in *The Structural Transformation of the Public Sphere* to be a transitional form that
belongs to an earlier period. 'The heirs of the humanistic-
aristocratic society', according to Habermas, 'in their encounter
with the bourgeois intellectuals (through sociable discussions
that quickly developed into public criticism), built a bridge
between the remains of a collapsing form of publicity (the
courtly one) and the precursor of a new one: the bourgeois
public sphere.'[19] However, at other points, the literary public
sphere is located firmly in the late seventeenth and eighteenth
centuries. Moreover, his historical model of sixteenth- and
seventeenth-century England is hampered by a reductive model
of absolutism which centralizes culture within the court. Early
modern culture was not synonymous with the court, but heterogeneous and multi-centred. Such hierarchical, stratified societies

---

[17] Nancy Fraser, 'Rethinking the Public Sphere: A Contribution to the Critique of
Actually Existing Democracy', in Craig Calhoun (ed.), *Habermas and the Public
Sphere* (Cambridge, Mass.: MIT Press, 1992), 121–2. See also: Geoffrey Eley,
'Nations, Publics, and Political Cultures: Placing Habermas in the Nineteenth
Century', in Craig Calhoun (ed.), *Habermas and the Public Sphere* (Cambridge,
Mass.: MIT Press, 1992), 303–6.
[18] Habermas, 'Further Reflections on the Public Sphere', 426.
[19] Habermas, *Structural Transformation of the Public Sphere*, 30.

could accommodate a range of differentially empowered publics.[20] At the same time, the concept of publicness in the sixteenth and seventeenth centuries was undergoing significant transformations. Classical humanist models of the public, for example, such as the concept of *vita activa*, were being transformed both within a print and manuscript culture, through impact of the Reformation, the emergence of a bureaucratic class at court, the developing role of parliament as a consiliar institution, and, in broader terms, through ongoing religious, social, and economic changes.[21] Civic humanism had fostered new forms of communication and a new type of intellectual who demanded an active role in the commonwealth. These new intellectuals flourished by establishing communities, relational networks, that enabled intellectual exchanges and debates. Although these communities often functioned in the service of the court, they were also assuming a relative autonomy and sometimes using the resources of a print culture to do so.[22] This, however, does not imply a polarity between court culture and pre-bourgeois public spheres. Discourses of citizenship were being explored in early modern communities that were not always autonomous from the court, while patronage relationships could coexist with a process of professionalization that typically characterizes the public sphere.[23]

The concept of a plurality of publics and an accompanying focus on textual communities does help to shed light on points of contact between the 'court-centred' Donne and Jonson and the 'anti-court' Spenserians by shifting the line of enquiry away from these writers' relationship to the centre and towards other social networks and cultural environments. Donne and Jonson inhabited a complex set of social and literary relationships that are often obscured by the tendency to view patronage, particularly royal patronage, as the dominant cultural institu-

---

[20] Fraser, 'Rethinking the Public Sphere', pp. 121–2.
[21] See Arthur B. Ferguson, *The Articulate Citizen and the English Renaissance* (Durham, NC: Duke University Press, 1965).
[22] Eisenstein, *The Printing Press as an Agent of Change*, i. 136–45; Henri-Jean Martin, *The History and Power of Writing*, trans. Lydia G. Cochrane (Chicago and London: University of Chicago Press,1988), 367–8.
[23] Melanie Hansen, 'Identity and Ownership: Narratives of the Land in the English Renaissance', in William Zunder and Suzanne Trill (eds.), *Writing and the English Renaissance* (London and New York: Longman, 1996), 90–1.

tion to the exclusion of all others.[24] Writers could occupy different institutional situations simultaneously; the resulting tensions were not disabling, but were experienced creatively and productively. Donne and Jonson were affiliated with the court through patronage relationships and moved within London tavern 'clubs' and political circles—social and discursive arenas where they came into contact with Spenserian poets. Donne and Christopher Brooke were lifelong friends, Lincoln's Inn men, and fellow members of a London tavern 'club' that specialized in the production and circulation of political satires. Jonson was moving in the same London circles as Donne and Brooke and was a leading light of the tavern 'clubs', also frequented by William Browne and George Wither, that met at the Mermaid, Mitre, and Devil and St Dunstan taverns. These 'clubs' fostered the exchange of verses, and Jonson contributed poems to Brooke's *The ghost of Richard the third* (1614) and Browne's *Britannia's Pastorals* (1616). Browne and Jonson seem to have had a mutual respect, and by 1616 they shared a patron in William Herbert, Earl of Pembroke. Norbrook has rightly pointed to an ideology of style in the period and suggested how Jonson's classicism was ultimately ideologically hostile to the apocalypticism of seventeenth-century Spenserianism.[25] Yet, Jonson's classicism had a political flexibility that enabled him to reconcile criticism with panegyric, while his masques indicate a complex negotiation of court politics.[26] Jonson's politics in the early decades of the seventeenth century were not straightforward and he did move between different factional groupings. Nor was he hostile to all forms of Spenserianism: he began, but did not complete, a pastoral drama *The Sad Shepherd*, and his annotations to his copy of *The Faerie Queene* reveal a strong interest in Spenser's neo-Platonic 'House of Alma'.[27] Yet,

[24] For the complexity of Donne's political affiliations, see: David Norbrook, 'The Monarchy of Wit and the Republic of Letters: Donne's Politics', and Annabel Patterson, 'All Donne', in Elizabeth D. Harvey and Katherine E. Maus (eds.) *Soliciting Interpretation: Literary Theory and Seventeenth-Century English Poetry* (Chicago and London: University of Chicago Press, 1990), 3–36 and 37–67 respectively.

[25] Norbrook, *Poetry and Politics in the English Renaissance*, 199–200.

[26] Cf. Martin Butler, 'Ben Jonson and the Limits of Courtly Panegyric', in Kevin Sharpe and Peter Lake (eds.), *Culture and Politics in Early Stuart England* (Basingstoke and London: Macmillan, 1994), 91–115.

[27] See James A. Riddell and Stanley Stewart's highly flawed, if interesting, *Jonson's Spenser: Evidence and Historical Criticism* (Pittsburgh: Duquesne University Press, 1995).

Jonson's reading of Spenser differed from that of Browne, Brooke, and Wither: he was attracted to a 'conservative' ceremonial and courtly Spenser and, unlike these writers, he did not have any sympathy with an apocalyptic Spenser.

Relations between writers were not static but responded to a changing political climate. Jonson attacked Wither in the early 1620s when literary and political culture was becoming more sharply divided. The Jacobean court in the 1610s was heterogeneous and home to competing factions centred around royal favourites, the earls of Northampton and Suffolk, and 'patriot' peers, such as the Earl of Pembroke who attracted the Spenserians as well as Jonson.[28] Moreover, political languages throughout this period had a polyvalency that cannot 'be reduced to a simple ideological programme' so that political positions and ideological distinctions will not always be clear cut.[29] These ambiguities meant that generic and stylistic choices were often determined or rather over-determined by a complex interaction of discursive positions. Jonson's 'country house' poem, 'To Penshurst', for example, has a number of points of contact with a Spenserian 'country' pastoral, and yet, at the same time, Spenserians and contemporary readers, such as Richard Brathwaite, did oppose their 'country' pastoral to a court poetics that found one of its foremost representatives in Jonson. Similarly, although a language of friendship and fellowship is both shared between the Spenserian community, the tavern 'clubs', and the later 'Tribe of Ben', it is differently articulated within these circles, in a way that is suggestive of ideological differences, as I will argue in Chapter One. The fluidity of political discourses does not mean that we cannot talk about ideological motivations and differences in the period but it does advise us to look closely at the immediate historical and generic situation of texts in order to plot the often shifting ideological terrain.

[28] Malcolm Smuts sees the Stuart court as a multi-centred, heterogeneous cultural environment (*Court Culture and the Origins of a Royalist Tradition in Early Stuart England* (Philadelphia: University of Pennsylvania Press, 1987), 4). See also D. H. Sacks's review of studies of the Stuart court, 'Searching for "Culture" in the English Renaissance', *Shakespeare Quarterly*, 39 (1988), 465–88.

[29] Kevin Sharpe and Peter Lake, 'Introduction', in *Culture and Politics in Early Stuart England* (Basingstoke and London: Macmillan, 1994), 13–15.

These writers are usually studied under the broad banner of a Spenserian tradition. 'Spenserian' can be a loose term and is often applied to a range of writers working in various forms and from different cultural perspectives. Yet, as a critical category it does enable us to trace the wider circulation of particular readings of Spenser and to think about associations between writers in stylistic as well as ideological terms. The 'Spenserian' label, in this case, does point to an ideology of style that distinguishes this particular print community from other contemporary textual communities and helps to map broader patterns of cultural transmission that can themselves provide a context for these writers' readings of Spenser. These writers were engaged in processes of literary exchange not only amongst themselves but with past and contemporary writers. The older Elizabethan poet, Michael Drayton, was often identified with this community, although he did not appear in *The Shepheards Pipe* and *The Shepherds Hunting* volumes, perhaps due to their social basis in the Inns of Court.[30] Browne and Drayton were closely associated throughout this period, while Brooke and Drayton seem to have been acquainted through the London tavern 'clubs'—Brooke had contributed a verse to his *Legend of Great Cromwell* (1607). These writers looked to Drayton as a poetic father: Drayton had placed a verse before *Britannia's Pastorals* (1613) in which he passed the mantle of successor to Sidney and Spenser onto the younger poet, and his 1606 *Pastorals* exerted a strong influence over these writers' versions of pastoral community. The older Spenserian John Davies of Hereford did contribute an eclogue to *The Shepheards Pipe*. However, although he had literary and political affinities with this community in 1614, he does seem to be on its margins and less committed to its processes of textual exchange. Writers within this community clearly admired Samuel Daniel as well as Drayton, but Daniel moved in different circles from these poets: his social and cultural environment was that of the court, and he did not divide the court along the same political lines as Browne, Brooke, and Wither, who were uniformly hostile to his patron, Robert Carr, Earl of Somerset. Daniel and these poets shared an interest in a cultural and political tradition of civic

---

[30] Grundy identified Drayton as the leading figure in this Spenserian community (*The Spenserian Poets*, 5).

humanism associated with Sidney and Spenser, and Browne, in particular, engaged with the civic pastoralism of Daniel's *Queenes Arcadia* in Book I of *Britannia's Pastorals* at a time when he was exploring a court poetics. Daniel's cultural sympathies may have been close to Browne's in 1613, but he would not share these writers' often aggressive apocalypticism or Wither's populist tendencies.[31] There were closer ideological ties with the lesser-known Spenserian Richard Niccols. He too can be described as a 'patriot' and was developing a politically charged Spenserianism; while there is no evidence of acquaintance, there are strong indications that these writers were reading his works.

The 'Spenserian' label is appropriate in a more specific sense in that it was Spenser who provided these writers with a model for a print community. E.K.'s notes to *The Shepheardes Calender* emphasized the communal contexts of literary production. As he says in the prefatory letter to Gabriel Harvey, his commentary on the eclogues resulted from his friendship with the author whereby 'I was made priuie to his counsell and secret meaning in them, as also in sundry other works of his.'[32] E.K.'s commentary on Spenser's eclogues sets up a model of dialogue between author and reader and between fellow writers in which meaning is produced collectively through such acts of collaboration. The reader is encouraged by E.K.'s glosses to identify the various shepherds that inhabit the eclogues with a circle that has gathered around Spenser and Gabriel Harvey, who are said to appear under the names of Colin and Hobbinol, 'As also by the names of other shepheardes, he couereth the persons of diuers other his familiar freendes and best acquayntance' (p. 455). The conventional motif of pastoral friendship is amplified to give the impression that there is a pre-existing community on which it depends. Yet, E.K.'s glosses are not intended to render the allegory transparent but rather to invite speculation. The secrecy that often shrouds figures in the eclogues and problematizes such acts of interpretation also has the effect of politicizing this community. Pastoral friendship in *The Shepheardes Calender* is shaped by these dual imperatives

---

[31] On the differences within Spenserianism, see: Norbrook, *Poetry and Politics in the English Renaissance*, 198–9.
[32] Spenser, *Poetical Works*, 418.

of secrecy and openness and gives representation to a semi-private space in which like-minded friends could meet and speak to each other freely in a hostile environment under the cover of pastoral metaphor.[33]

The pastoral community of *The Shepheardes Calender* culminates in *Colin Clouts Comes Home Againe* and Spenser's volume of elegies for Sidney, *Astrophel*, which were published jointly in 1595. Dennis Kay has said that with *Astrophel* 'Spenser invented Spenserian poetry', however, this honour arguably belongs to the 1595 collection as a whole.[34] In *Colin Clouts Come Home Againe*, the shepherd-poet was part of a community of like-minded individuals that came together to form a literary commonwealth. 'The "New" English, as the "shepherdes nation" ', Andrew Hadfield argues, 'are cast in the role of guardians of a tradition of English public poetry which is able to stand outside and by-pass the constraints of a purely courtly culture.'[35] The 'shepheards nation' of *Colin Clouts Come Home Againe* is complemented by the elegiac pastoral community of *Astrophel*. In both texts, the print community is dependent on the agency of the poet and brings the private and the public, the aristocratic and the professional into a transformative dialectic. *Colin Clouts Come Home Againe* transforms patronage relationships into a humanist dialogue to give the impression of cultural as social equality: the governing principle is virtue which is not necessarily dependent on social status. In *Astrophel*, the poet acts as editor, gathering together and organizing the other elegies in the collection.[36] Once more patronage relationships are transformed as Sidney's family and friends join with Spenser to create a community of readers and writers that is united through the kinship of grief, thus eliding social differences.

The Spenserian concept of community increasingly took on a satiric anti-court stance in the early seventeenth century and the shepherd-poet took on the identity of an alienated Meliboeus. Spenser's 'shepheards nation' in *Colin Clouts Come Home Againe* was simultaneously a place of exile, a 'waste, where I

---

[33] Patterson, *Pastoral and Ideology*, 127–8, 133–4.
[34] Dennis Kay, *Melodious Tears: The English Funeral Elegy from Spenser to Milton* (Oxford: Clarendon Press, 1990), 65–6.
[35] Hadfield, *Literature, Politics, and National Identity*, 189.
[36] Kay, *Melodious Tears*, 54.

was quite forgot' (l. 183), and land of 'libertie' (l. 55). Subsequent Spenserian poets fixed on this association between the marginality of exile and liberty: Spenserian exile from the court to the country resulted in a privileged marginality which made possible the critique of systems of authority, the redefinition of public poetry, and the fashioning of a professional identity within new textual communities.[37] When Drayton revised his *The Shepheardes Garland*, first published in 1593, in his *Poemes. Lyrick and pastorall* (1606), he politicized his eclogues by changing Rowland's love lament into an expression of alienation from a corrupt court.[38] Sidney, the original shepherd-poet, in the sixth Eclogue has turned satirist, 'laughing euen Kings, and their delights to skorn | and all those sotts them idly deify'.[39] Drayton parodied the Stuart pastoral trope of Britain as earthly paradise: rather than bringing a prosperous and rejuvenating peace, James is the 'cold northern breath' (F1r) blasting the English pastoral landscape. Consolation was located in a community of poets surrounding Samuel Daniel and Sir William Alexander who maintained Sidney's virtues in such adverse times: 'Men from base enuy and detraction free, | of vpright harts and of humble spirit' (F1v).

A new impetus was given to re-readings of Spenser by the 1609 edition of *The Faerie Queene*, which included the as yet unpublished 'Mutabilitie Canto', and the 1611 edition of Spenser's complete works—an event which coincided with the founding of Henry's court. But it was Henry's death in 1612 that provoked the strongest expression of a politically-charged Spenserianism. The Spenserian elegies tended to combine an aggressive Protestantism and a prophetic, apocalyptic poetics with veiled criticism of the current court regime. Consolation, in the sense of perpetuation of the memory of the dead, became dependent in these elegies on the survival of Spenserian communities which in turn became microcosms of the virtuous

---

[37] Helgerson, *Forms of Nationhood*, 33.

[38] For the political significance of these revisions, see: Drayton, *The Works*, ed. J. Hebel, 5 vols. (Oxford: Basil Blackwell, 1941), v. 183–7; Richard Hardin, *Michael Drayton and the Passing of Elizabethan England* (Lawrence, Manhattan: The University Press of Kansas, 1973), 82–3; Grundy, *Spenserian Poets*, 78–9; Norbrook, *Poetry and Politics in the English Renaissance*, 197.

[39] Drayton, *Poemes. Lyrick and pastorall* (London, 1606), STC 7225.5, F1r.

commonwealth once embodied in Henry and his court.[40] Spenserian symbolism took on a particular political direction in the years following Henry's death.[41] The republication of satiric beast fable *Mother Hubberds Tale* in 1612/13, with its coded criticism of William Cecil, Lord Burghley, and his son, Robert, gave further definition to an oppositional Spenser that was taking shape in the writing of Spenserian poets, such as Browne, Wither, Brooke, Drayton, and Richard Niccols.[42] Protestant allegory was employed in the denunciation of Spanish popery and criticisms of the Jacobean peace, while Spenser's *Complaints* were revived in laments for the decline of a martial aristocratic culture and bitter satires denouncing the *regnum Cecilianum* and its Stuart legacy.

The print community that was consolidated in *The Shepheards Pipe* appropriately had its origins in the volume, *Two elegies, consecrated to . . . Henry Prince of Wales*, jointly published by Browne and Brooke. The *Two elegies* used the resources of the elegy and print to give voice to a politicized community.[43] The volume was dedicated to the prince's now dissolved court and great care and expense went into the printing, including an elaborate title-page and a fold-out copy of William Hole's engraving of the hearse.[44] Brooke's brother Samuel had been appointed chaplain to the prince in September 1612 and a number of his political associates were connected with Henry's

---

[40] Kay, *Melodious Tears*, 125–43.

[41] Norbrook, *Poetry and Politics in the English Renaissance*, 202–13.

[42] Bernard Davies, 'The Text of Spenser's *Complaints*', *Modern Language Review*, 20 (1925), 21–2. John Weever's reference to *The Ruines of Time* being 'cal'd in' in his elegiac epigram for Spenser has been taken as evidence for the suppression of these poems (*Epigrammes in the oldest cut, and newest fashion*, G3r).

[43] Kay argues that the volume has 'a sharper political edge' in comparison with other poems on the Prince's death and is critical of James's pacific neo-Augustanism (*Melodious Tears*, 168).

[44] William Hole's work was closely related to Henry's court: Roy Strong, *Henry, Prince of Wales and England's Lost Renaissance* (London: Thames & Hudson, 1986), 130; T. V. Wilks, 'The Court Culture of Prince Henry and his Circle, 1603–1613', 2 vols. D.Phil. thesis (Oxford, 1987), i. 107. In this period Hole provided engraved title-pages for Davies's *The Muses Sacrifice* (London, 1612), Drayton's *Poly-Olbion* (London, 1612), and Browne's *Britannia's Pastorals* (London, 1613) (A. Forbes Johnson, *A Catalogue of Engraved and Etched English Title-Pages* (Oxford: Oxford University Press, 1934), 26–7).

household in some way.[45] Given Browne's literary aspirations, it is likely that he had looked to the prince for patronage.[46] For Brooke and Browne, the court's dissolution was a repudiation of the Protestant martialism embodied by Henry.[47] The twinned elegies sought to reassemble the fragmented court by offering alternative visions of community: Browne called to sympathetic poets to perpetuate the memory of Henry, to 'Erect a new *Parnassus* on his graue', asserting the value of the poetic community that will continue to promote the ideals of Henry's court and the elegy ended with this community 'all in MOVRNING'.[48] Brooke's collaboration with Browne on the *Two elegies* seems to have encouraged this lawyer-MP to embark upon a poetic career and his Spenserian qualifications were confirmed by his inclusion along with Browne as the two new poets in the second edition of the Elizabethan miscellany *Englands Helicon* (1614).

Since this Spenserian community finds its primary public expression through print it is possible to trace continuing associations through the exchange of commendatory verses and acts of literary collaboration. *The Shepheards Pipe* community was revived later in the year in Wither's sequel *The Shepherds Hunting* where Wither, Browne, and Brooke were joined by William 'Alexis' Ferrar. Davies did not appear amongst this circle but he did renew his relationship with Browne in 1616

[45] Wilks, 'Court Culture of Prince Henry and his Circle', i. 8, 11–12. A number of Brooke's fellow 'Sireniacs' (see Chapter 2) were members of Henry's household: Thomas Coryate, Richard Connock, Sir Robert Phelips, and Inigo Jones (I. A. Shapiro, 'The "Mermaid Club" ', *Modern Language Review*, 45 (1950), 8).

[46] Late 1608 a payment of five pounds to a 'Mr. Browne for a book given to his highnes' was recorded in the statement of accounts for Henry's household and it is possible that this 'Mr. Browne' was William Browne and the book an early manuscript version of *Britannia's Pastorals* (Leila Parsons, 'Prince Henry (1594–1612) as a Patron of Literature', *Modern Language Review*, 47 (1952), 503). This would mean that Browne began composing Book I at 16 or 17 years of age—in *Britannia's Pastorals*, Book I, Song 5 he claims to have been less than 20 when he completed the work.

[47] Kay points to the oppositional significance of the Horatian epigraph to the volume, 'whose application is that the dissolution of Henry's court parallels the destruction of traditional Roman values by accumulated private sinfulness' (*Melodious Tears*, 168).

[48] *Two elegies, consecrated to the neuer-dying memorie of the most worthily admyred; most hartily loued; and generally bewayled Prince; Henry Prince of Wales* (London, 1613) STC 3831, E1v–2r. For an incisive reading of these elegies, see: Kay, *Melodious Tears*, 168–72, and 'The English Funeral Elegy in the reigns of Elizabeth I and James I, with Special Reference to Poems on the Death of Prince Henry (1612)' D.Phil. thesis (Oxford, 1982), 245–50.

when he contributed a commendatory verse to Book II of
Britannia's Pastorals. Wither published his *Fidelia* in 1615 with
the encouragement of his unnamed 'friends': the poem is
answered by Browne's 'Fido: An Epistle to Fidelia' which
remained in manuscript form, suggesting that this circle
exchanged verses in manuscript as well as print. Movement into
print was often a response to moments of heightened political
tension. Browne and Brooke contributed companion verses to
*Sir Thomas Ouerburie His Wife with new Elegies vpon his (now
knowne) vntimely death*: these new elegies were gathered at the
beginning of the volume and collectively gave representation to
a politicized textual community that had joined together to
expose court corruption.[49] Wither contributed a commendatory
verse to the second instalment of Browne's *Britannia's Pastorals*
in the same year, but he was not joined by Brooke. *The
Shepheards Pipe* community however is gathered together in the
volume: in the second Song, Browne invoked a native English
literary community that had its father in Sidney and its contemporary representatives in Chapman, Drayton, Jonson, Daniel,
Brooke, who received extensive praise, Davies of Hereford, and
Wither.[50] Literary friendships continued amongst these writers
in the early 1620s. In 1622, Wither and Browne contributed
verses to the second part of Drayton's *Poly-Olbion*. The
framing narrative of Wither's *Fair-Virtue*, published in the same
year as *Poly-Olbion*, deliberately echoes the topographical
pastoralism of Drayton's poem and Browne's *Britannia's
Pastorals* and, in fact, can be read as a response to the end of
the third Song where Willy–Browne ends his song to greet
Roget–Wither who is accompanied by a shepherdess that
closely resembles Fair Virtue, 'the louely herdess of the dell |
That to an oaten quill can sing so well' (II. iii. 84). Wither was

---

[49] Among the elegies are two consecutive elegies signed 'C.B.' and 'W.B. Int.
Temple'. Malone in his copy of the text (Bodleian Library, Oxford, Malone MS
483) identified 'W.B.' with William Browne and the poem was published in
Goodwin's edition of Browne's poems. Edward Rimbault has identified 'C.B.' with
Christopher Brooke. Other contributors identified by Rimbault are: William
Shipton, Bernard Griffin, Thomas Gainsford, John Ford, Richard Carew, Edmund
Gayton, and John Fletcher (Sir Thomas Overbury, *The Miscellaneous Works
in Prose and Verse*, ed. Edward Rimbault (London: John Russell Smith, 1856),
279).
[50] Browne, *Britannia's Pastorals. The second booke* (London, 1616), STC
3915.5, 36–8.

the only poet to contribute a commendatory verse to Brooke's funeral poem in memory of Sir Arthur Chichester; this poem was prepared for the press but not printed and it may have circulated in manuscript. By the mid-1620s, Browne and Wither had taken different paths: Wither was committed to a print culture, while Browne became involved in scribal communities at Exeter College, Oxford, and at the country houses of the Herbert circle from the 1620s until his death in the early 1640s. Brooke dies in 1628, and he had effectively retired from public life around 1626. The early 1620s do not see a revival of a print community in such a cohesive form as *The Shepheards Pipe* and *The Shepherds Hunting*, however, textual friendships amongst these writers do persist and by tracing these relationships we can explore the conditions for writing and publication in the 1620s, and how they differ from the earlier period of collaboration.

This print community was also structured by material and professional relationships with the book trade. There is a general pattern to be found in these writers' loyalty to particular sets of printers and booksellers. From 1613 to 1616, George Norton was the favourite printer and bookseller of Browne and Wither, publishing *The Shepheards Pipe* (1614), *Britannia's Pastorals* (1613, 1616), *Abuses stript, and whipt* (1614), and *The Shepherds Hunting* (1615) as well as Davies's *The Muses Sacrifice* (1612). In the 1620s, Drayton and Wither work with the booksellers John Grismond and John Marriot who published *Poly-Olbion* (1622) and *Wither's Motto* (1621) and his *Fair-Virtue* (1622). Grismond and Marriot seem to have sought out provocative material; they published *Wither's Motto* without a licence incurring a fine, and in the same year put out Lady Mary Wroth's controversial *Urania*.

Eisenstein has drawn our attention to the importance of the print shop in the intellectual ferment of the Renaissance; in early modern London, the stationers' shop was part of a network of environments, including the Inns of Court, the taverns, and St Paul's, where news and gossip was exchanged and current issues were debated. This Spenserian print community is in many ways a product of early modern London and had one of its main social bases in an Inns of Court culture which was characterized by a high level of political education and collective literary activity.[51] Browne, Brooke, and Wither were Inns of Court men in the 1610s. The transition from university to London brought with it proximity to Westminster and to the book trade and St Paul's, a public arena where information was traded and 'news' circulated.[52] The Inns themselves provided a meeting place for a range of early modern communities—legal, intellectual, and parliamentary—and constituted an important social space for intellectual exchange. They did have affiliations with the court, but this did not prevent them from providing a forum for political debate that often reflected critically on the crown. Inns of Court men were avid, productive readers and writers of libellous political verses, while the culture, traditions, and educational programme of the Inns valued political independence and freedom of speech.[53] The tavern societies that the culture of the Inns supported were, in some ways, similar to the coffee houses later in the century in that they provided arenas of discussion and debate that were not organized around a patron and they were institutionalized through their own rituals, banquets, and rules. However, these societies were more socially exclusive than the later coffee houses and, although there were regular meetings, they lacked the continuity of a coffee house culture.

It is possible to identify a common political outlook that unites these writers and gives this print community a particular ideological colouring. They can collectively be described as 'patriots': they are hispanophobes; they represent themselves as defenders of traditional liberties and oppose corruption at court; and they advocate an 'Elizabethan' revival which is equated with the reform of patronage systems, naval and colonial expansion, and a return to an aristocratic martialism.[54] Religion tends to be viewed in political and geopolitical terms, rather than on a personalized basis: John Davies of Hereford, who contributed an eclogue to *The Shepheards Pipe*, was a

[51] Arthur Marotti, *Manuscript, Print, and the English Renaissance Lyric* (Ithaca, NY, and London: Cornell University Press, 1995), 35.

[52] Love, *Scribal Publication in Seventeenth-Century England*, 193–4.

[53] John Finkelpearl, *John Marston of the Middle Temple: An Elizabethan Dramatist and his Social Setting* (Cambridge, Mass.: Harvard University Press, 1969), 66–8, 79–80.

[54] Thomas Cogswell gives a brief history of this term in his *Blessed Revolution: English Politics and the Coming of War, 1621–24* (Cambridge: Cambridge University Press, 1989), 84–99.

Catholic, but he was also a 'patriot' and his loyalty to the memory of Essex and Sidney brought him into sympathy with his Protestant friends, Browne, Wither, and Brooke.[55] Although 'patriot' politics did not set these writers apart individually from many of their contemporaries, it was central to the way that they defined themselves collectively and, in particular, their claim to represent a broader national community. From this perspective, the terms 'patriot' and 'country' can be seen as interchangeable. I should point out that by drawing attention to a language of the 'country' in these texts, I am not attempting to revive a Whiggish model of the court and country, rather I am interested in the way that a discourse of the 'country' functions rhetorically to provide a language for articulating ideological differences and shared interests.[56] Peter Lake has set out this distinction with admirable clarity: 'to observe that the division between the court and the country . . . does not match the structure of contemporary politics as it has been discerned by historians, does not mean that such a dichotomy operating at the level of ideology was not of crucial importance to contemporaries in their attempts to understand events'.[57] A 'country' discourse did constitute a 'common language of political debate concerning the *polis*' and was not confined to particular political groupings.[58] Yet, at the same time, it did have a polyvalency and within this common language one can trace a variety of traditions and formulations that were taking on different ideological connotations. The 'country' could be viewed from an aristocratic perspective which produced a decentralized view of the nation 'as a patchwork of manorial estates' and defended aristocratic independence.[59] Further along the political spectrum was the centralizing absolutist vision of

[55] Davies commemorated Essex and Sidney in his *The Scourge of Folly* (London, 1611), STC 6341, 88, 213, and *Microcosmos. The discovery of the little world, with the government thereof* (Oxford, 1603), STC 6333, Mm3v.

[56] For a much-criticized model of a court–country opposition, see: Perez Zagorin, *The Court and the Country: The Beginnings of the English Revolution* (London: Routledge and Kegan Paul, 1969).

[57] Peter Lake, 'Constitutional Consensus and Puritan Opposition in the 1620s: Thomas Scott and the Spanish Match', *The Historical Journal*, 25 (1982), 825.

[58] Kevin Sharpe, *Criticism and Compliment: The Politics of Literature in the England of Charles I* (Cambridge: Cambridge University Press, 1987), 14.

[59] Andrew McRae, 'Husbandry Manuals and the Language of Agrarian Improvement', in Michael Leslie and Timothy Raylor (eds.), *Culture and Cultivation in Early Modern England* (Leicester and London: Leicester University Press, 1992), 35.

the 'country' that is familiar from Leah Marcus's studies of early Stuart pastoral.[60]

When these Spenserian poets spoke of the 'country', they were drawing on a concept of the godly commonwealth that derived from the complex interaction of discourses of the ancient constitution, the elect nation, and civic humanism.[61] This godly commonwealth could at times merge with a view of the 'country' that upheld parliamentary privileges and defended the liberties of the subject. Such a rhetoric of the 'country' was a language of political responsibility, and the 'country' from the late sixteenth century began to be associated with concepts of political representation and citizenship.[62] A liberated 'country' in these Spenserian texts presupposed an oppressive and tyrannical 'court'. To speak for and from the 'country' was to denounce the corruption of the 'court', represented by the stock figures of unworthy favourites and evil counsellors, and to uphold the rights and liberties of the freeborn 'countryman'. In this way, the conventional satiric opposition between 'court' and 'country' became part of a language of court corruption that, in the words of Linda Levy Peck, provided 'a discourse of political conflict' and 'clothed attacks on the diplomatic, religious, and financial policies of James I and Charles I'.[63] The source of court corruption tended to be located in weak monarchical government, itself the product of the Jacobean peace.

The term 'country' in the sixteenth and seventeenth centuries was semantically complex, referring simultaneously to a physical environment, a rural as opposed to an urban landscape, to the nation and to the county. This complexity gives the term added critical value when discussing the formation of national communities by making it possible to suggest how

[60] Leah Marcus, *The Politics of Mirth: Jonson, Herrick, Milton, and Marvell, and the Defense of Holiday Pastimes* (Chicago and London: University of Chicago Press, 1986), 19.

[61] J. G. A. Pocock, *The Machiavellian Moment: Florentine Political Thought and the Atlantic Republican Tradition* (Princeton: Princeton University Press, 1975), 337–47.

[62] Richard Cust and Ann Hughes, 'Introduction: After Revisionism', in Cust and Hughes (eds.), *Conflict in Early Stuart England: Studies in Religion and Politics, 1603–1642* (London and New York: Longman, 1989), 19–20.

[63] Linda Levy Peck, *Court Patronage and Corruption in Early Stuart England* (Boston: Unwin Hyman, 1990), 185, 203.

these communities were taking particular cultural and ideological forms. Richard Helgerson has, in fact, argued that the early modern nation was constituted through the Spenserian-style division between 'court' and 'country' which he elaborates through a series of conceptual oppositions between state/nation, king/people, and sovereign/subject.[64] This formulation does raise problems, as Claire McEachern has pointed out, in that it implies that an authentic national consciousness can only be expressed outside the structures of the state when, arguably, a national consciousness may be expressed through, rather than in opposition to, these institutions. Rather, McEachern argues that the early modern nation was 'founded in the ideological affiliation of crown, church, and land' which was made possible by the Reformation and the docrine of the ancient constitution.[65] Yet, it is this very affiliation that was the site of dispute in this period and Helgerson is surely right to argue for a plurality of nationalist discourses traversing several discursive communities.[66] The imaginative space of the nation in this period was radically open-ended and contested as different communities competed for the authority to speak for the nation. Spenserian poems on national themes, such as *Britannia's Pastorals* and *Poly-Olbion*, become generically heterogeneous in the effort to give expression to the land.

There is a complex interaction between genre and politics in these Spenserian texts. Genres, in these poets' hands, were political languages and modes of dialogue, and they were attracted to forms that had 'patriot' affiliations. Pastoral, in particular, became their trademark as 'country' poets, and they turned to a native tradition deriving from Tudor reformist pastoral satire and Elizabethan political pastoral. Marcus has argued recently that early seventeenth-century pastoral was closely tied to Stuart policy in a way which 'exerted a decided ideological pull upon the pastoral as a whole', and sees Spenserian pastoral as an oppositional reaction to this dominant form of royalist pastoral.[67] However, Butler has suggested

[64] Helgerson, *Forms of Nationhood*, 130, 295–6.
[65] McEachern, *Poetics of English Nationhood*, 6–21.
[66] Helgerson, *Forms of Nationhood*, 300.
[67] Leah Marcus, 'Politics and Pastoral: Writing the Court on the Countryside', in Kevin Sharpe and Peter Lake (eds.), *Culture and Politics in Early Stuart England* (Basingstoke and London: Macmillan, 1994), 140.

that such an ideological realignment of pastoral did not take place until the 1620s with Jonson's *Pan's Anniversary*, the 'text which first fully appropriated the pastoral mode in the service of the court's ideological needs'.[68] Arguably, it was the Spenserians who dominated pastoral poetry in the earlier period.[69] Drayton's 1606 *Pastorals*, the pastoral tragicomedies of Daniel and Fletcher, Browne's *The Shepheards Pipe* and *Britannia's Pastorals*, and Wither's *The Shepherds Hunting*, were all taking pastoral in a particular ideological direction in the first two decades of the seventeenth century. The vitality of a tradition of Elizabethan political pastoral in this period was demonstrated by the appearance of a second edition of the Elizabethan pastoral anthology *England's Helicon* in 1614. Native pastoral satire still had a political currency and circulated in populist forms: Henoch Clapham appended 'A Pastorall Epilogue, betweene Hobbinoll, and Collin Clout' to his *Errour on the Left Hand* (1608) and used the native homely form of the Spenserian eclogue to continue his anti-Catholic polemic in another key, while the early Tudor reformist pseudo-Chaucerian *The Ploughmans Tale* was republished in 1606 in the wake of the Gunpowder plot with new notes explaining its topicality, the satire on Rome, and its affinities with Spenser's *The Shepheardes Calender*.[70] Neglect of this pastoral tradition in studies of the genre is part of a tendency to define pure, 'true' pastoral in terms of a poetics of enclosure that is generically conservative and emphasizes values of retirement, leisure, and ease.[71] S. K. Heninger speaks of pastoral becoming perverted in

[68] Martin Butler, 'Ben Jonson's *Pan's Anniversary* and the Politics of Early Stuart Pastoral', *English Literary Renaissance*, 22 (1992), 382–95.

[69] W. W. Greg's *Pastoral Poetry and Pastoral Drama; a Literary Inquiry with special reference to the Pre-Restoration Stage in England* (London: A. H. Bullen, 1906); William B. Hunter (ed.), *The English Spenserians: The Poetry of Giles Fletcher, George Wither, Michael Drayton, Phineas Fletcher, and Henry More* (Utah: University of Utah Press, 1977), 1.

[70] Henoch Clapham, *Errour on the Left Hand through Frozen Securitie* (London, 1608); *The Plough-mans Tale. Shewing by the doctrine and liues of the Romish Clergie, that the Pope is Antichrist and they his Ministers* (London, 1606). Norbrook, 'Panegyric of the Monarch', 241–2.

[71] Andrew Ettin, *Literature and the Pastoral* (New Haven and London: Yale University Press, 1984); Renato Poggioli, *The Oaten Flute: Essays on Pastoral Poetry and the Pastoral Ideal* (Cambridge, Mass.: Harvard University Press, 1975). Exceptions include Greg's *Pastoral Poetry and Pastoral Drama*, Annabel Patterson's *Pastoral and Ideology: Virgil to Valery* (Oxford: Clarendon Press, 1988), and Helen

the Renaissance when the eclogue is employed for satiric and professional purposes, turning pastoral from its proper function of panegyric to critique. Pure pastoral thus took refuge in the enclosed and subjective form of the lyric.[72] Such defences of the privileged, exclusive space of pure pastoral can be traced to Renaissance attacks on Guarini's pastoral tragicomedy *Il Pastor Fido* for its breach of decorum and, implicitly, its legitimation of other forms of transgression, both social and political.[73]

The Spenserian poets eschewed a poetics of enclosure to bring pastoral into dialogue with public modes such as satire, georgic, and epic which resulted in a politically-engaged form of pastoral capable of addressing civic, 'country' concerns. This form of pastoral was not the pastoral of aristocratic leisure and retirement but responded to the the lessons of Sidney's *Arcadia* and Spenser's pastoral romance, Book VI of *The Faerie Queene*, in which the shepherd-knight must confront issues of political responsibility.[74] The Spenserian shepherd-poet similarly donned the spiritual and political armour of the questing knight to become a militant defender of Truth against error and detraction. For their 'country' pastoral, the Spenserians also turned to *The Shepheardes Calender*, which brought together a native early Tudor tradition of pastoral georgic satire and classical and continental models to produce a distinctly English and Protestant version of the pastoral eclogue.[75] Like Spenser, they recovered native genres and traditions in order to define a self-authorizing national literary culture. At the same time, the resulting dialogue between literary modes opened up new ideological possibilities within pastoral.

Browne, Brooke, and Wither turned to other genres, alongside pastoral, to give expression to the 'country'. Spenser offered these writers a standard for public poetry and a complex generic

Cooper's *Pastoral: Mediaeval into Renaissance* (Ipswich: D. S. Brewer; Totowa: Rowman and Littlefield, 1977).

[72] S. K. Heninger Jr, 'The Renaissance Perversion of Pastoral', *Journal of the History of Ideas*, 22 (1961), 254–61.

[73] Jane Tylus, 'The Myth of Enclosure: Renaissance Pastoral from Sannazzaro to Shakespeare', Ph.D. thesis (Johns Hopkins University, 1985), 49–60, 326–9.

[74] Norbrook, *Poetry and Politics in the English Renaissance*, 145.

[75] John N. King, 'Spenser's *Shepheardes Calender* and Protestant Pastoral Satire', in Barbara Kiefer Lewalski (ed.), *Renaissance Genres: Essays on Theory, History, and Interpretation* (Cambridge, Mass. and London: Harvard University Press, 1986), 369–72.

system for addressing issues to do with community and nation-hood. They inherited a form of dialogism from Spenser, who brought genres together in a process of 'dialectic progression' in order to force an ideological re-evaluation in line with reformed humanism.[76] Brooke set up a dialogue between various literary modes and conventions in *The ghost of Richard the third* in order to fashion a new politicized poetics that would 'startle' the reader into interpretive action, his '*sences* in *security* fast bound'.[77] The poem brings together a *Mirror for Magistrates* tradition and Elizabethan Senecan tragedy to produce a 'country' poetic able to address issues of political representation. In Book II of *Britannia's Pastorals*, Browne entered into a critique of Stuart neo-Augustanism through a complex process of generic renegotiation. The heterogeneity of the poem as a whole is itself symptomatic of Browne's search for a national poetics—a search that takes the form of an unending romance quest and results in a radically decentred and open text that expresses the contested space of the nation in the early seventeenth century. Wither was highly eclectic in his use of genre and attracted to genre that enabled expression of the 'I'. Thomas Calhoun sees Wither as the father of a 'loose' poetics that privileges individual experience and perception. A 'loose' style was the product of Renaissance anti-classicism and eschews ornament for the 'naturalness' of self-expression. It differed from a plain style in that it also rejected formal constraints.[78] Robert Burton parodied a 'loose' style in Democratus Junior, 'a loose, plain, rude writer, *ficum voco ficum et ligonem ligonem* [I call a fig a fig and a spade a spade], and as free, as loose, *idem calamo quod in mente* [what my mind thinks my pen writes]'.[79] Wither's interest in a 'loose' style was ideological. He tended to align his defence of his '*free discourse*' unconstrained by the '*strict rules as* Arts-men *vse*' with nonconformist traditions of free speech and it simultaneously provided a flexible and

[76] John N. King, *Spenser's Poetry and the Reformation Tradition* (Princeton: Princeton University Press, 1990), 184.

[77] Christopher Brooke, *The ghost of Richard the third* (London, 1614), STC 3830, B2r.

[78] Thomas Calhoun, 'George Wither: Origins and Consequences of a Loose Poetics', *Texas Studies in Language and Literature*, 16 (1974), 263–4.

[79] Robert Burton, *The Anatomy of Melancholy*, ed. Holbrook Jackson. 3 vols. (London and Toronto: Dent; New York: Dutton, 1932), i. 31; also quoted in Calhoun, 'Origins and Consequences of a Loose Poetics', 263.

responsive form for addressing issues of agency.[80] Wither used a 'loose' style to open out established genres to new ideological influences. His *Wither's Motto* is a radical reorientation of satire in which he himself becomes 'news' and an emblem of the commonwealth.

This book is primarily a study of a literary community in the first decades of James's reign. That said, all three writers are given their own chapters partly for the practical reason of studying their major works in detail, thus enabling me to elaborate common themes and poetic strategies, and relatedly because these writers and their poems have been neglected and so require sustained analysis. The first chapter concentrates on the use of print and pastoral to define a literary commonwealth in *The Shepheards Pipe* and *The Shepherds Hunting*, and argues that these eclogues break new ground in pastoral. Chapter Two is a study of the MP and poet Christopher Brooke and his *The ghost of Richard the third* as a companion text to *The Shepheards Pipe* that stages a literary intervention in contemporary parliamentary debates. Chapter Three is devoted to Browne's *Britannia's Pastorals* and its search for a national poetics, and builds on the study of pastoral and community in the first chapter. Wither's early career is the subject of the fourth chapter which studies his construction of a social self and his economic and political investment in a print culture. I will return to the concept of a Spenserian community in the early 1620s in the final chapter to assess the continuities and changes in these writers' responses to the crises of the early 1620s.

[80] *Faire-Vertue, the mistress of Phil'Arete* (London, 1622), STC 25903, C2v.

I

The 'shepheards nation': William Browne, *The Shepheards Pipe* (1614) and George Wither, *The Shepherds Hunting* (1615)

SOME time after May 1614, William Browne published his collection of pastoral eclogues *The Shepheards Pipe* together with other eclogues supplied by Christopher Brooke, George Wither (currently in the Marshalsea), and John Davies of Hereford. Browne, Brooke, and Wither feature throughout the eclogues under the pastoral guises of 'Willy', 'Cuddy', and 'Roget' respectively.[1] These poets were reunited later in the year in Wither's sequel, his prison eclogues *The Shepherds Hunting* (1615), where the Marshalsea is transformed into a pastoral landscape and his visitors in his 'country' exile are his shepherd friends from *The Shepheards Pipe*, 'Willy' Browne and 'Cuddy' Brooke, who are joined by William 'Alexis' Ferrar.[2] The collaborative energies that generated these volumes suggest a concerted effort on the part of the contributors to identify themselves as a distinctive print community. One can find differences between the writers gathered in these volumes but the volumes themselves resist such division and instead work to consolidate a community united by common poetic and political principles.

'FREE ARE MY LINES': PASTORAL SATIRE AND THE 'SHEPHEARDS NATION'

The Shepheards Pipe and *The Shepherds Hunting* consciously set out to revive the genre of pastoral satire in 1614. The very

---

[1] Wither will change his name to 'Philarete' in the 1620s.
[2] *The Shepherds Hunting* was entered in the Stationers' Register on 8 October 1614, but the publication date on the title-page is 1615.

title of *The Shepherds Hunting* drew attention to its mixed genre status and Wither's by now controversial satire, *Abuses stript, and whipt* (1613), is a strong presence in the volume. He drew attention to his reputation for satire in the second eclogue, reminding the reader that until now he 'was not noted for *Shepheards layes*' but for 'hunting *Foxes, Wolues,* and *Beasts of Pray*',[3] and in this eclogue and the next he is accompanied by his 'hunting dogs' named after his satiric essays, Love, Lust, Hate, Envy, Revenge, and so on. For these writers, a 'Satiricke reed' was demanded by the times.[4] The Somerset marriage on 26 December 1613 had occasioned a fresh outpouring of court masques and epithalamia following the marriage of Elizabeth and Frederick earlier in the year. Yet, the Somerset marriage also attracted criticism since it was made possible by the controversial divorce of Frances Howard and Robert Devereux, the third Earl of Essex. The contrast between the two events provoked complaints about the current abuse of poetry: such 'unworthy' subjects as the Earl and Countess of Somerset crystallized 'the deep-seated problems of panegyric or epideictic art'.[5] Browne's dedicatory poem addressed to Lord Edward Zouche made it very clear that he was not one of those poets who engaged in undiscriminating flattery since 'I scorne to flatter but the men I hate' (A2r). The debasing relationship between patronage and poetry is a recurrent theme in the work of these poets, although they were careful to distinguish 'worthy' courtiers, such as Zouche, from the unworthy. Liberty is the condition in which true poetry flourishes and it is contrasted with court tyranny. Richard Brathwaite in his *A Strappado for the Diuell* (1615) was similarly scornful of those poets 'Who write not for respect, or due esteeme, | Had to their own profession, but to gaine | The fauour of a great one'. To exemplify the few remaining worthy poets, he turned to the Spenserian community of *The Shepheards Pipe* and *The Shepherds Hunting*:

[3] *The Shepherds Hunting: being, certaine eglogs written during the time of the authors imprisonment in the Marshalsey* (London, 1615), STC 25920, C3v.
[4] Browne, *The Shepheards Pipe* (London, 1614), STC 3917, D2r.
[5] David Lindley, 'Embarrassing Ben: the Masques for Frances Howard', *English Literary Renaissance*, 16 (1986), 348–9.

And long may Englands *Thespian* springs be known
'*By louely Wither and by bonny Browne*,
Whilest solid *Seldon*, and their *Cuddy* too,
Sing what our (Swaines of old) could neuer doe.
Yea I do hope, sith they so well can write,
Of Shep-heards sport, and of the fields delight
That when they come to take a view of th'Court,
(As some haue done) and haue bin mew'd vp for't,
They'l tell her freely, (as full well they may)
That in their Iudgements, after due suruay,
Of th'Court & th'Cottage, they may well maintain,
Vices in the Court, but vertues in the Swaine.[6]

By 1615, Browne, Brooke ('Cuddy'), and Wither were recognizable as a distinct group of poets that offered a reforming satiric alternative to court panegyric. Brathwaite does not see these poets as nostalgically clinging to the past but as a new purifying force in English poetry.

Brathwaite placed these poets at the forefront of a broader cultural movement. And, in fact, these volumes were not alone in promoting pastoral satire as an alternative to a debased and debasing court panegyric in this period. The publication of *The Shepheards Pipe* coincided with the appearance of the second edition of the Elizabethan pastoral anthology *Englands Helicon* in 1614 and, interestingly, Browne and Brooke were the only new Jacobean poets to be represented in the volume. While the inclusion of Browne is not surprising, given his recent publication of the first book of *Britannia's Pastorals*, Brooke's presence is—his only other work in print, apart from his eclogue appended to *The Shepheards Pipe*, was the *Two elegies*, jointly published with Browne. Since Richard More, the editor of this second edition of *Englands Helicon*, had published the *Two elegies* it is possible that there was some type of working relationship between More and Browne and Brooke. More may have commissioned the pieces from the two poets, while they in turn may have had a direct influence on the new direction that the second edition took. Both *The Shepheards Pipe* and the second edition of *Englands Helicon* promoted a native tradition of pastoral satire in which pastoral took on a political and

---

[6] Richard Brathwaite, *A Strappado for the Diuell. Epigrams and Satyres alluding to the time, with diuers measures of no lesse Delight* (London, 1615), STC 3588, pp. 23–4.

generic suppleness as its ideological ties to the court were loosened.[7] The new motto to the second edition of *Englands Helicon* took an aggressively 'anti-court' tone and located English pastoral in a virtuous commonwealth that was defined by its independence from the court: 'The Court of Kings heare no such straines | As daily lull the Rusticke Swaines.'[8] Whereas the Latin motto to the first edition had stressed the pure classical origins of pastoral, this new motto gives voice to the plain-speaking shepherd of a native tradition of pastoral satire who also presides over *The Shepheards Pipe*.[9] The new patron, Elizabeth Cary, had Spenserian connections through her tutors, Drayton and Davies of Hereford, and may have been chosen as the fit successor to Mary Herbert, Countess of Pembroke, whose circle at Wilton had been praised by Drayton as an alternative court, a refuge for virtue in corrupt times.[10]

The anti-court tone adopted by this 1614 print community was given a contemporary edge through Wither's imprisonment which provided the immediate occasion for the gatherings in *The Shepheards Pipe* and *The Shepherds Hunting* and served to symbolize the highly volatile political situation in 1614. Wither had gained a reputation for political outspokenness by 1614; when *The Shepheards Pipe* was entered in the Stationers' Register, he had been in the Marshalsea for almost two months, incarcerated on the order of the Privy Council.[11] Although there

[7] See also Jane Tylus on the possible collaboration between More and Browne and Brooke and the anti-court stance of this volume which she has related to a new semi-autonomous print culture ('Jacobean Poetry and Lyric Disappointment', in Elizabeth D. Harvey and Kathleen E. Maus (eds.), *Soliciting Interpretation: Literary Theory and Seventeenth-Century Poetry* (Chicago and London: Chicago University Press, 1990), 182–3).

[8] *Englands Helicon, or, the muses harmony* (London, 1614), STC 3192, π1r.

[9] 'Casta placent superis, pure cum veste venite, | Et manibus puris sumite fontis aquam.' The original motto is taken from the elegies of Tibullus. *England's Helicon 1600, 1614*, ed. H. E. Rollins, 2 vols. (Cambridge, Mass.: Harvard University Press, 1935), ii. 80.

[10] Cary had recently published her Senecan closet drama *Tragedie of Mariam* (1613) which revived a French political Seneca current in the Countess of Pembroke's circle and had provided this circle with a medium for dramatizing political conflicts. Davies of Hereford encouraged Cary to publish *Tragedy of Mariam* during a time when he was involved in a campaign for the release of his patron, the Earl of Northumberland, a 'victim' of James's 'tyranny', and could have read a similar political intent in Cary's complex treatment of tyranny and liberty of conscience.

[11] On Wither's career and imprisonments, see: J. M. French, 'George Wither in Prison', *PMLA* 45 (1930), 959–66, and 'George Wither', Ph.D. thesis (Harvard, 1928).

are no records of what the offence was, it appears to have had
something to do with the continuing popularity of his satire
Abuses stript, and whipt, first published in 1613 but going into
a sixth edition in 1614, and the topicality of certain passages,
which became even more provocative in early 1614 with the
preparations for a new parliament, and may have prompted one
of the satire's more visible targets, the Earl of Northampton, to
take action. Wither had been moving in the same Inns of Court
circles as Browne and Brooke and had produced an elegy
lamenting Henry's death, but Browne and Brooke also appear
to have been eager to capitalize on a public association with a
now controversial poet, and he contributed a verse to Brooke's
The ghost of Richard the third in the same year. Wither's
presence in *The Shepheards Pipe*, in particular, added to the
public visibility and topicality of the volume. Such an alliance
enabled both Browne and Brooke to champion his cause in
defence of freedom of speech—an area that would prove to be
particularly sensitive in the 1614 'addled' parliament. Another
contributor to *The Shepheards Pipe*, John Davies of Hereford
also had reason to add his voice to campaign against an 'unjust'
imprisonment: his patron Henry Percy, Earl of Northumberland, was under harsh sentence in the Tower for supposed
complicity in the Gunpowder plot. Northumberland was
thought to have been the victim of Salisbury's machinations,
and he also counted the Lord Treasurer, Thomas Howard,
among his political enemies. From 1609 to 1614 Davies took
part in the campaign for his release: his dedication of *Humour's
Heau'n on Earth* (1609) to the Earl was suppressed, but the
poem itself remained critical of James's harsh treatment of
Northumberland, and was followed by an epigram addressed
to the Earl in the Tower in *The Scourge of Folly* in 1611.[12]

---

[12] The poem was eventually dedicated to Davies's pupil, the Earl's son, Algernon,
Lord Percy (Steven Clucas, ' "Noble virtue in extremes": Henry Percy, ninth Earl of
Northumberland, Patronage, and Stoic Consolation', *Renaissance Studies*, 9 (1995),
273–87; G. A. Wilkes, 'The "Humours Heav'n on Earth" of John Davies of Hereford, and a Suppressed Poem', *Notes and Queries*, 6 (1959), 209–10). His defence
of aristocratic independence in these poems may coincide with an interest in
republican writings: he may have owned a copy of Buchanan's *De Jure Regni*
(David Norbrook, 'Panegyric of the Monarch and its Social Context under
Elizabeth I and James I', D.Phil. thesis (Oxford, 1978), 245). Algernon Percy held
anti-monarchist views, was his nephew's patron, the republican Algernon Sidney,
and took the Parliamentary side in the Civil Wars (Jonathan Scott, *Algernon Sidney*

Davies had other patronage ties that Browne, Brooke, and Wither would have found politically congenial: he had been Master of Penmanship to Prince Henry and, from the last years of Elizabeth's reign until his death in 1618, he received the patronage of the Herbert family.[13]

Various forms of disaffection drew these writers together in 1614. Brooke was an MP in the 1614 'addled' parliament and actively involved in the conflict over impositions which led to its dissolution. A strong sense of disillusionment with James's failure to embrace 'patriot' policies and advance 'worthy' men ran throughout Browne's poetry and these principles seem to have dictated his choice of patrons: he addressed his work first to the zealous 'patriot' Lord Edward Zouche, a man noted more for his hatred of Spain and opposition to the Howards than his interest in poetry, and then to Pembroke, who combined literary patronage with 'patriot' politics.[14] As Norbrook makes clear the poets typically described as 'Spenserians', Daniel, the Fletcher brothers, Drayton, Browne, Brooke, and Wither, were not 'a monolithic, ideologically coherent group'.[15] However, some coherency can be ascribed to this particular community of Spenserian poets, especially in 1614. These writers employ common political languages and were motivated by common causes. This gives *The Shepheards Pipe* and *The Shepherds Hunting* a similar political cast and the poets involved in these volumes present themselves as a united front against a court 'tyranny'. Perhaps not surprisingly they present their criticisms of certain elements of the court as principled opposition rather than personal dissatisfaction. Their sense of alienation does appear to have been moral and political and not merely the product of a failure to secure royal favour.

---

and the English Republic, 1623–1677 (Cambridge: Cambridge University Press, 1988), 43–48).

[13] Michael Brennan, 'The Literary Patronage of the Herbert family, Earls of Pembroke, 1550–1640', D.Phil. thesis (Oxford, 1982), 203–6.

[14] Zouche did not attract many dedications of poetry apart from Browne and his cousin, Richard Zouche, who dedicated his Spenserian *The Dove* to him in 1613, STC 26130. Related dedications include: Henry Lok, *Ecclesiastes: abridged and dilated in English poesies* (London, 1597), STC 16696; and Francis Markham, *Fiue decades of epistles of warre* (London, 1622), STC 17332.

[15] David Norbrook, *Poetry and Politics in the English Renaissance* (London: Routledge and Kegan Paul, 1984), 198.

'OUR FELLOW SWAINES': A SPENSERIAN PRINT COMMUNITY

With *The Shepheards Pipe*, Browne took over the role of Spenser in *Astrophel* to act as the Spenserian poet–editor, gathering together his own eclogues with those of his friends, Brooke, Wither, and John Davies of Hereford, and shaping this collection into a textual community. His credentials as spokesman for this community were confirmed by his pastoral elegy for Thomas Manwood which clearly echoes Spenser's *Astrophel*. Browne's pastoral elegy is not only structurally the centrepiece of the volume, being the fourth eclogue of seven, it also encapsulates the Spenserian concept of community. Spenser's volume of elegies for Sidney provided his followers with a model of a community united by shared aesthetic, political, and religious values.[16] Browne, like Spenser before him, brings patron and poet together through the kinship of grief. Thomas was the second son of Sir Peter Manwood who had a reputation for enlightened patronage and the works dedicated to him reveal extensive literary, religious, antiquarian, and political interests.[17] The eclogue is followed by a pattern poem addressed to Manwood's sisters in the form of an altar consecrated to Thomas's memory. Browne and the Manwoods are united in mourning before this altar constructed through his poetic expertise.

Browne also follows Spenser in the way that he transforms the ostensible subject of the elegy, Manwood, into an emblem of community. Manwood is largely absent in the main pastoral elegy which unusually does not include digressions on the life of

[16] Dennis Kay, *Melodious Tears: The English Funeral Elegy from Spenser to Milton* (Oxford: Clarendon Press, 1990), 65–6.

[17] Peter Clark, *English Provincial Society from the Reformation to Revolution: Religion, Politics, and Society in Kent 1500–1640* (Sussex: Harvester Press, 1977), 217–19; R. B. Wernham, 'The Public Records in the Sixteenth and Seventeenth Centuries', in Levi Fox (ed.), *English Historical Scholarship in the Sixteenth and Seventeenth Centuries* (London and New York: Oxford University Press, 1956), 25–6. Sir Peter was a friend of Zouche, Browne's current patron, and a member of the 1614 parliament for Kent. This election was beset by rumours of packing and undertaking to favour the candidate of James's favourite, Robert Carr, and resulted in the estrangement of the Kent county governors from the court (John Chamberlain, *The Letters*, ed. Norman E. McClure, 2 vols. (Philadelphia: The American Philosophical Society, 1939), i. 515–16; Clark, *English Provincial Society*, 315).

the deceased, typical to the form of the obituary elegy.[18] It is only through ship imagery that an obscure reference to his death by drowning in France is made. The pastoral elegy is used instead for vocational purposes. Browne fashioned a role for himself in relation to the literary community projected in the elegy and claimed laureate status by nominating himself as the heir to Spenser and Sidney. Laureateship, in these terms, is no longer dependent upon royal favour but based solely upon the poet's relationship with his literary forebears. It was arguably a model for Milton's *Lycidas* in the way that pastoral elegy is individuated to figure the emerging prophetic powers of the youthful poet.[19] Browne's pastoral elegy offers a prophetic vision of a literary community. Manwood takes on a Christlike form, his 'second birth | His brightnesse blindes the sun', and his prophetic powers are transferred to the poet and the poetic community—with his apotheosis as they are urged to 'inwards turne your light, | Behold him there' (D6v). Spenserian prophecy projects a literary community, past, present, and future, that gives meaning to the individual voice. The elegy operates within a dialectic of exile and community so that loss is countered by the consecration of friendship in poetry:

> Looke on the place where we two heretofore
> With locked arms have vowd our loue,
> (Our loue which time shall see
> In shepheards song for euer moue,
> And grace their harmony)
> It solitary seemes.   (D2r)

The inset completes the double movement of the elegy both recording loss and figuring the potential for renewal and continuity through the power of art. The poet rejects all other manifestations of sorrow for the comfort of his own elegy, while material, earthly forms of grief are revealed to be vain attempts at eternity and emptied of any immortalizing power, as 'ended, turne to nought'. Outlasting these transient emblems is the

---

[18] Francis White Weitzmann, 'Notes on the Elizabethan *Elegie*', *PMLA* 50 (1935), 439–40.

[19] J. H. Hanford argues, unconvincingly, that Browne's elegy is too conventional to be a source for *Lycidas* ('The Pastoral Elegy and Milton's *Lycidas*', in C. A. Patrides (ed.), *Milton's 'Lycidas': the Tradition and the Poem* (New York: Holt, Rinehart, Wilson, 1961), 53–4).

poet's own 'truest cause | Of sorrow' which will 'firmly stay' (D7v).

If *The Shepheards Pipe* looked to *Astrophel*, then *The Shepherds Hunting* has strong affinities with *Colin Clouts Come Home Againe*. Fictions of self dominate *Colin Clouts Come Home Againe*; Spenser's relations with the 'New English' community in Ireland, with his patron Raleigh, and at court are translated into pastoral fictions. In *The Shepherds Hunting*, Wither took over the identity of the exiled Colin Clout and his prison experiences provided the narrative thread that links the individual eclogues: each eclogue consists of a dialogue between Roget and one or more of his friends, his visitors in his prison exile. More fundamentally, both *Colin Clouts Come Home Againe* and *The Shepherds Hunting*, by making the poet's personal history the subject of the poem, foreground poetic agency and the poet emerges as an historical actor. In this sense, *Colin Clouts Come Home Againe* shaped the print communities represented by both Browne's *The Shepheards Pipe* and Wither's *The Shepherds Hunting*. At the centre of both volumes is Spenser's 'shepheards nation' and these volumes devoted much of their energy to developing a model of collective cultural production and historical agency on which this concept of a national community depends.

These companion volumes offer a model of authorship that is insistently communal. They are sequels and so presented not so much as the discrete products of individuals authors as part of an ongoing process of intellectual exchange amongst a group of poet friends. *The Shepheards Pipe* and *The Shepherds Hunting* even share eclogues: the eclogue that Wither contributed to Browne's *The Shepheards Pipe* reappeared as the fourth eclogue of his *The Shepherds Hunting*. As this suggests, the eclogues of *The Shepheards Pipe* and *The Shepherds Hunting* can appear interchangeable; the volumes have very similar titles and their eclogues are frequently populated by the same group of shepherd-poets—Willy, Roget, and Cuddy. Social exchanges dominate the eclogues to project an homogeneous literary community within which the volumes were produced. Although they take their model for the pastoral eclogue from *The Shepheardes Calender*, Colin's love laments are replaced by politicitized complaints and they tend to favour the form of the dialogue between poet friends represented by the 'October' eclogue. This prioritizing of friendship over love means that the poetic voice gains meaning not through introspection and the solitary anxieties of love, but through the processes of dialogue. Friendship, in fact, structures these communal eclogues so much so that they have been called 'familiar epistles dramatized'.[20] In *The Shepheards Pipe*, Browne dedicated his fifth eclogue to Brooke, while Brooke, Wither, and Davies addressed their eclogues to Browne, and, in *The Shepherds Hunting*, Wither dedicated eclogues to Brooke, Browne, and William Ferrar. A complex process of ventriloquism characterizes exchanges in these eclogues: 'Friends write speeches for friends—Browne for Wither, Wither for Browne, Brooke for Browne, Browne for Brooke, and so on—and it is sometimes difficult to remember afterwards whether a poet actually said something, or simply had it attributed to him by another.'[21] With this extensive use of *prosopopeia*, voices lose their individual distinction and merge into a collective, corporate voice. *Prosopopeia*, in this form, is a form of rhetoric appropriate to the expression of friendship: the classical concept of friendship as 'one soul in bodies twain' posits a relationship between self and other that is structured by identification rather than difference.[22] Identity is thus always collective and relational, determined by the community represented by the volume as a whole.[23]

The cohesiveness achieved by this print community in 1614 and 1615 was largely made possible by the relatively stable social and cultural environment provided by the Inns of Court. The politicized fictions of community that these poets employed were grounded in, if not identical to, the type of social exchanges that the Inns of Court fostered. *The Shepheards Pipe* advertised itself as an Inns of Court publication: it was prefaced by verses from Edward Johnson and John Onley who signed their poems 'Int. Temp.', and included an elegy for a fellow

[20] Joan Grundy, *Spenserian Poets: A Study in Elizabethan and Jacobean Poetry* (London: Edward Arnold, 1969), 83.

[21] Ibid., 80–1.

[22] Horst Hutter, *Politics as Friendship: The Origins of Classical Notions of Politics in the Theory and Practice of Friendship* (Waterloo, Ont.: Wilfred Laurier University Press, 1978), 9–11.

[23] Jane Tylus also points to the way there is an 'emphasis on the communal contexts of cultural production' in Spenserian texts ('Jacobean Poetry and Lyric Disappointment', 175).

Inner Templar, Thomas Manwood. Brooke was from Lincoln's
Inn and Wither the Middle Temple, while William Ferrar, who
appeared in *The Shepherds Hunting*, was Browne's fellow Inner
Templar. All three, Brooke, Wither, and Ferrar, had contributed
verses to Browne's *Britannia's Pastorals* (1613), and the other
verses, on the whole, were from Inner Templars: John Selden,
his close friend Edward Heyward, Francis Dynne, Francis
Oulde, and Thomas Gardiner. Browne looked to the Inns of
Court to launch his career as the successor to Spenser and
Sidney, and he seems to have been the quasi-official poet for
the Inner Temple in these years, providing the masque for the
1614/15 Christmas festivities. Brooke, a practising lawyer,
maintained close ties with his Inn, and, in the first decades of the
seventeenth century, he was part of a politicized 'scribal community' drawn largely from the Lincoln's Inn and the Middle
Temple, that included his close friend John Donne and fellow
MPs Richard Martin, John Hoskyns, and Robert Phelips.
Wither transferred from a minor inn to the Middle Temple in
1615. His account of his friendship with William Ferrar in *The
Shepherds Hunting* suggests that he was on the edges of these
Inns of Court circles from around 1613. In another eclogue, he
claimed to have met Browne and Brooke at a gathering of Inns
of Court men to hear Browne read from *Britannia's Pastorals* at
the Devil and St Dunstan tavern in Fleet Street, later made
famous by Ben Jonson. John Davies of Hereford, a resident of
St Dunstans-in-the-West, frequented these tavern 'clubs' where
he could have met Browne and the other contributors to *The
Shepheards Pipe*.

The energies of *The Shepheards Pipe* and *The Shepherds
Hunting* are directed towards establishing communities and
investing these communities with a collective agency. The
resulting fictions of community project an idealized social space
where friends meet to exchange ideas freely and to discuss contemporary cultural and political issues. At the same time, these
conversations between friends are grounded in a recognizable
social environment that evokes their Inns of Court haunts
around Fleet Street and vividly illustrates this print community's
material basis in early modern London culture. Wither in his
eclogue dedicated to Browne, printed in both *The Shepheards
Pipe* and *The Shepherds Hunting*, cited the Devil and St

Dunstan tavern in Fleet Street as the place where their friendship first began:

> For it is not long agoe,
> When CUDDY, *Thou*, and I,
> Each the others' skill to try,
> At Saint *Dunstanes* charmed Well,
> (As some present there can tell)
> Sang upon a sudden theame,
> Sitting by the Crimson streame.[24]

Similarly in the fifth eclogue of *The Shepherds Hunting* dedicated to William Ferrar, their friendship is said to have had its
origins in a gathering at 'that Shepheards Coate' in Browne's
honour (G4r), once more gesturing to an Inns of Court
social occasion where verses were read and exchanged. These
references suggest that this Spenserian Inns of Court community
actively participated in an early seventeenth-century tavern
'club' culture and similarly had a degree of ritualized formality
and regularity expressed through these tavern performances and
also through literary exchanges, possibly in manuscript, but
most importantly through print. These volumes simultaneously
give this 'club' culture a particular idealized civic function that
in many ways anticipates the role of the coffee shop later in the
century. Browne in his eclogue addressed to Brooke praised his
recently published *The ghost of Richard the third* (1614), and,
seemingly alluding to one of the Inns of Court tavern, bade him
to 'sing it to our Swaines next holy-day' (E4v): the tavern 'club'
in the context of this eclogue is transformed into a civic space,
a gathering of educated men to discuss poetry and politics outside the constraints of court culture.

  The tavern 'club' is, however, typically identified with a conservative, ultimately royalist culture that will crystallize in the
mid-century 'cavaliers', and opposed to a reforming Protestant
political culture.[25] Similarly, it is argued that a vocabulary of
fellowship and holiday pastimes 'became part of the symbolic

---

[24] This eclogue was reprinted as the fourth eclogue of Wither's *The Shepherds
Hunting*, F2v–3r.

[25] William Hunt, 'Spectral Origins of the English Revolution: Legitimation Crisis
in Early Stuart England', in Geoff Eley and William Hunt (eds.), *Reviving the
English Revolution: Reflections and Elaborations on the Work of Christopher Hill*
(London and New York: Verso, 1988), 315.

language of Stuart power'.[26] The evidence provided by this
Spenserian community suggests that we should be wary of
setting up such structural and ideological polarities within early
seventeenth-century culture. The composition of the tavern
'clubs' in the early part of the century indicates that they were
relatively open and drew Inns of Court men, merchants, MPs,
courtiers, and professional writers, amongst others. Moreover,
it is difficult to distinguish the companies that met at the Mitre
and the Mermaid taverns in terms of membership, suggesting
that these societies were defined by their fluidity rather than
through rigid sets of affliliations.[27] Jonson's verses over the door
of the Apollo Room at the Devil and St Dunstan tavern
described a sociable openness, 'Welcome, all who lead or
follow, | To the Oracle of Apollo', while the '*Leges Convivales*',
the rules for the Apollo, admitted all 'learned, civil, merry
men'.[28] The date of these verses and rules is uncertain, and it is
possible that Jonson was describing the type of gathering that
Wither, Browne, and Brooke were attending from around 1612
to 1614, and may have also been celebrated in Drayton's 'The
Sacrifice to Apollo' in his *Odes* (1619). Yet, Jonson's rules, by
their very nature, also suggest that such conviviality was taking
on an exclusivity that characterized the later 'Tribe of Ben',
which can be distinguished from these earlier, more fluid
societies through its stronger sense of hierarchy and ritualized
paternalism centred on Jonson.[29] The combative exclusivity of
the 'Tribe of Ben' was symptomatic of the heightened political
tensions of the 1620s and 1630s and can be contrasted with the
relative openness of tavern societies in the earlier period.

[26] Leah Marcus, *The Politics of Mirth: Jonson, Herrick, Milton, and Marvell, and
The Defense of Holiday Pastimes* (Chicago and London: University of Chicago
Press, 1986), 5.

[27] As Baird Whitlocke argues 'It is not always possible to keep the groups
separate, nor is it ever possible to establish them as essentially the same society'
(*John Hoskyns, Serjeant-at-Law* (Washington: University Press of America, 1982),
381). Timothy Raylor's argument that there are three distinct tavern 'clubs' identi-
fied with particular taverns is difficult to sustain given the degree of overlap
(*Cavaliers, Clubs, and Literary Culture: Sir John Menzies, James Smith, and the
Order of Fancy* (Newark: University of Delaware Press; London, and Toronto:
Associated University Presses, 1994), 72–3).

[28] Ben Jonson, *Works*, ed. C. H. Hereford, Percy Simpson and Evelyn Simpson,
11 vols. (Oxford: Clarendon Press, 1925–52), viii. 657; *Ben Jonson*, ed. Ian
Donaldson (Oxford: Oxford University Press, 1985), 511–12.

[29] Cf. Thomas Randolph, 'A gratulatory to Mr. Ben. Johnson for adopting of him
to be his Son'. I am grateful to Martin Butler for this point.

There are, however, as I am suggesting, distinctions to be drawn between the Spenserian community and some of the other textual communities frequenting the tavern 'clubs'. The witty 'Sireniac' satires, the verses ribbing Thomas Coryate, and the style prescribed by Jonson, for example, are marked by 'a tension between competition and bonding within the group' that characterizes classical groups.[30] Verses often take the form of a contest of wit that serves to set up an internal hierarchy within the group that is a microcosm of a wider social hierarchy. By contrast, internal conflict is deliberately minimized in the Spenserian exchanges. *The Shepheards Pipe* and *The Shepherds Hunting* subordinate individual competition between shepherd-poets, conventionally displayed through the song contest, to the ideal of community. The songs of the shepherd-poets that inhabit these volumes are communal and collective, sung for their 'fellow swaines', rather than individualized through virtuoso displays of wit. Social ties are similarly strengthened through the overriding emphasis on shared cultural and political interests and conflict is always directed outwards to reinforce the integrity of the group. It would therefore appear that these early seventeenth-century textual communities were structured by differing models of fellowship and these differences may have an ideological dimension. The textual community gathered by Coryate and the 'Tribe of Ben' were primarily indebted to classical *convivium* and show a stronger regard for hierarchy and social status. By comparison, social relations within this Spenserian textual community are governed by an ideal of equality that derives from a humanist tradition of friendship.[31]

This particular Spenserian community has its precursors in humanist textual communities that were fashioning a new role for the intellectual in the early modern period. Friendship in *The Shepheards Pipe* and *The Shepherds Hunting* takes on a civic form. The Ciceronian ideal of *amicitia* was a relationship cultivated amongst virtuous men for the public good. Friendship, in this sense, could offer an alternative organization of political

---

[30] Raylor, *Cavaliers, Clubs, and Literary Culture*, 72.

[31] Cf. Jonson, 'An Epistle Answering One that Asked to be Sealed of the Tribe of Ben', *Underwoods*, 47 (Works, viii. 218–20). Raylor, *Cavaliers, Clubs, and Literary Culture*, 72. However, Jonson does draw on a humanist ideal of friendship in a similar way to these poets in verses such as 'Inviting a friend to supper'.

space to the court that had associations with republican liberty.[32] The equality described by friendship was contrasted with the subservience of courtiership, while kingship itself was thought to preclude friendship by requiring the subordination of subjects. Friendship described the relationship between free citizens within the *polis* and was at the basis of the Republic of Letters which gained its intellectual and political strength through the mutual bonds of friendship expressed through the exchange of texts, through literary correspondence.[33] In this humanist form, friendship can be seen as a language of sociability that anticipated the discourses of citizenship and publicness that constituted the early modern public sphere. It is an idealizing language that projects a social space where social status is subordinated to the imperatives of dialogue and there-fore gives the appearance of being accessible and inclusive rather than exclusive. In civic terms, friendship results in a public of private individuals who gather together for the good of the commonwealth. *The Shepheards Pipe* and *The Shepherds Hunting* locate their fictions of community in this idealized civic space constituted by the equality of friendship. Friendship functions within an anti-court rhetoric in these volumes and is contrasted with the sycophancy fostered by the court. Friends replaced the aristocratic patron in *The Shepherds Hunting* and were the focus for the volume's energies: the dedication to his 'Right Vertuous Friends, my Visitants in the Marshalsey' addressed the volume to his fellow poets from *The Shepheards Pipe*, Browne and Brooke, who return in the following pages to constitute an idealized gathering of friends that is opposed to a restrictive and hostile court culture dominated by 'our Ages Fauourites . . . who now flourish with a shew of vsurped *Greatnesse*' (A4v–5r). In this way, this Spenserian textual community is structured by an incipient notion of a representa-tive publicness and, like the early elite manifestations of the public sphere, it fashions itself as a literary commonwealth that

[32] Reginald Hyatte, *The Arts of Friendship: The Idealization of Friendship in Medieval and Renaissance Literature* (Leiden, New York, Cologne: E. J. Brill, 1994), 27–8; Eric MacPhail, 'Friendship as a Political Ideal in Montaigne's *Essais*', *Montaigne Studies*, 1 (1989), 177–87.

[33] On the importance of literary exchange in the constitution of the Republic of Letters, see: Lisa Jardine, *Erasmus, Man of Letters: the Construction of Charisma in Print* (Princeton: Princeton University Press, 1993).

is not only autonomous from the court but defined in opposition to it.

'COURT' AND 'COUNTRY'

The rhetoric of friendship in these volumes promoted idealizing fictions of equality and accessibility, yet the very cohesiveness of this community was itself dependent upon strategies of exclusion. It should be pointed out that this was a relatively elite group of educated and propertied men: Browne and Wither were young gentlemen residing at the Inns of Court, while Brooke came from a merchant family and was a lawyer-MP, part of a new urban professional elite. Louis Montrose sees the Elizabethan metaphor of the shepherd-poet in terms of 'coded performances in which a community of speakers and auditors, writers and readers, participate in a dialectic of inclusion and exclusion, in a process of social signification'.[34] This 'dialectic of inclusion and exclusion' in *The Shepheards Pipe* and *The Shepherds Hunting* was largely played out through a satiric opposition between 'court' and 'country'. The shepherd-poets in these volumes collectively identified themselves as 'countrymen' and the community as a whole was defined by its difference from the 'court'. A 'court'/'country' conflict had a long literary and cultural history and provided a widely recognized form for dramatizing conflict. The particular ideological direction in which it could be taken was flexible and dependent upon the context in which it was deployed. This flexibility was part of its appeal as it meant that this language of 'court'/ 'country' conflict was multidimensional and so enabled writers to construct a set of shared moral, political, and religious values. Through its opposition to the exclusive 'court' within this satiric formula, the 'country' emerges as a loose, collective term that has associations with the concept of a national community. Although this Spenserian community was composed of a relatively elite group of men, it does have the potential for inclusiveness through its claim to represent the 'country'.

The second eclogue of *The Shepheards Pipe* mobilized a

---

[34] Louis Adrian Montrose, 'Of Gentlemen and Shepherds: The Politics of Elizabethan Pastoral Form', *English Literary History*, 50 (1983), 448.

'court'/'country' conflict to give the print community represented in the volume a distinct identity in Jacobean political
culture. The previous eclogue had introduced Willie (Browne)
and Roget (the recently imprisoned Wither) and the dialogue in
this second eclogue between Willie and Jockie would similarly
seem to be invested with a contemporary relevance. Willie and
his friend Jockie want to be rid of an interloper, a swineherd,
who was introduced to Jockie through Weptol, 'Our fellow-
swaine and friend' (D1r). The swineherd does not maintain
'country' principles, but is identified with the conspicuous
consumption of the 'court', and the eclogue closes with the
Spenserian community vowing to produce satires to 'rid him
fro our plaines' (D2r). The eclogue is situated in a London
environment: the swineherd is usually to be found loitering at
the 'Ale-house door' (D1r), suggesting that this figure was a
regular at one of the Inns of Court tavern gatherings. Willy's
friend Jockie, a name which derives from the Scottish for John,
may be the pastoral persona of Browne's fellow Inner Templar,
John Selden, who had placed a verse before his *Britannia's
Pastorals* in the previous year—this identification is supported
by Brathwaite's *A Strappado for the Devil* (1615) which
included 'solid *Seldon*' amongst this community. Jockie's friend
Weptol may be an anagram of John Powlet or Poulett, a student
of the Middle Temple and MP for Somerset in the 1610
and 1614 parliaments.[35] Powlet, along with Brooke and his
fellow 'Sireniac' MPs, such as Robert Phelips, John Hoskyns,
and Richard Martin, had placed verses before *Coryate's
Crudities* (1611). These connections would situate this second
eclogue within the political culture of the Inns of Court.
Kathleen Tillotson has suggested that the swineherd could
allude to Bacon through the play on his name. Bacon was no
friend of Brooke and his fellow MPs: in 1613, when exploring
means of controlling parliament to James's advantage, he had
delighted in the apparent collapse of opposition from the previous 1610 parliament, and prematurely claimed that Brooke

---

[35] The name 'Jockie' has a rustic association, signifying a 'countryman' or man of
the common people (*OED*, 2nd edn., VIII. 251). Selden possibly had connections
with Brooke through the 'Sireniacs', the Virginia Company, and a mutual interest
in parliament as an institution (David Berkowitz, *John Selden's Formative Years:
Politics and Society in Early Seventeenth-Century England* (Washington: Folger
Books, 1988), 22–4, 55–6).

was dead.[36] In the 1614 parliament, he was returned as MP while remaining the King's Attorney General which raised fears in the Commons that the elections had been rigged in order to guarantee support for Crown policies under his leadership. Moreover, Bacon's Inn, Gray's Inn, had recently produced the *Masque of Flowers*, which he sponsored, for the unpopular Somerset marriage. There may have been some tension between the Inns over this event as they seem to have had distinct, if changing, political and factional allegiances: under Elizabeth, Browne's Inn, the Inner Temple, was closely associated with the Earl of Leicester, and in the first half of James's reign, Gray's Inn was supported by the Bacon family and the Cecils.[37] This second eclogue would therefore appear to be playing out divisions in the political culture of Jacobean London in the wake of the scandal surrounding the Somerset marriage and the following build up to the 1614 'addled' parliament.

A 'country' rhetoric extended the boundaries of this community and enabled it to make claims to broader forms of political representation. The Spenserian community was able to represent the interests of the citizen shepherd and those of aristocratic 'countrymen' who ceased to be identified with the 'court' and rather joined the Spenserians in the 'country'. They gained this independence from the 'court' through their embodiment of an aristocratic martialism, and they tended to be 'patriot' peers. These aristocratic 'countrymen' represented a community of honour that united blood with civic virtue and was identified with Sidney and Essex. This community was dedicated to the service of the monarch, but simultaneously was represented within a Spenserian 'country' discourse as excluded from political power by the dominance of unworthy favourites.[38] This exclusion entailed an increasing emphasis on the moral autonomy of this community and the aristocratic martialist represented the interests of the godly commonwealth

[36] Clayton Roberts and Owen Duncan, 'The Parliamentary Undertaking of 1614', *English Historical Review*, 93 (1978), 489. On Bacon's absolutism see: Julian Martin, *Francis Bacon, the State, and the Reform of Natural Philosophy* (Cambridge, Cambridge University Press, 1992), 111–34.

[37] Norbrook, *Poetry and Politics in the English Renaissance*, 83; W. J. Loftie, *The Inns of Court and Chancery* (Southampton: Ashford Press, 1985), 71.

[38] See Mervyn James's study of a Sidneian community of honour in his 'English Politics and the Concept of Honour, 1485–1642' (*Past and Present*, Supplement 3 (1978), 68–73).

in a way that the monarch, under the influence of 'evil counsellors', was failing to do. Within this rhetoric, the aristocratic 'countryman' also stood for a 'baronial' vision of the 'country' which viewed the history of the land as the history of independent gentry and noble families and can be distinguished from a 'royalist' centralizing vision of the countryside that identifies the land with the body of the monarch.[39] Wither's praise for the Earl of Southampton in *Abuses stript, and whipt* interestingly combined county loyalties and local political representation with a baronial 'country' politics. When railing against the current neglect of the navy and military training, he paused to praise the shining example of Southampton and their home county, Hampshire, 'Whom braue *South-hamptons* gouernment hath kept | In war-like order; I doe meane indeed | Our *Hampshire Ilanders*' (H5v). Southampton's government is distinctly baronial, signifying an independent aristocratic martialism. Given his involvement in the Essex rebellion, Wither's praise of the Earl as a true representative of the 'country' could raise some disturbing memories. After a brief period of reconciliation, Southampton had once more fallen out of favour under James and Salisbury tried to ensure that he was not given a position of power at court.

A baronial view of the 'country' similarly informs Browne's responses to aristocratic estates in *The Shepheards Pipe*. Both the dedicatory verse celebrating Zouche's estate, Bramshill, and the third eclogue move within the same symbolic and ideological terrain as the emerging genre of the 'country house' poem. The patron's estate in the country house poem becomes a microcosm of the virtuous commonwealth. Bramshill's 'shades' provide a Virgilian *umbra*, a refuge for the poet and 'country' ideals in adverse times:

> Be pleas'd (great Lord) whe[n] vnderneath the shades
> Of your delightful *Brams-hill*, (Where the spring
> Her flowers for gentle blasts with *Zephir* trades)
> Once more to hear a silly Shepheard sing.   (A2r)

Drayton had praised the Countess of Pembroke's Wilton as a

---

[39] A baronial 'country' is similar to Andrew McRae's concept of a 'country farm tradition' ('Husbandry Manuals and the Language of Agrarian Improvement', in Michael Leslie and Timothy Raylor (eds.), *Culture and Cultivation in Early Modern England* (Leicester and London: Leicester University Press, 1992), 35–57).

pastoral refuge in the eighth ecologue of his 1606 *Pastorals* and Bramshill similarly embodies an aristocratic tradition of enlightened hospitality that was not dependent on the court. Zouche's Bramshill, built in the style of the Elizabethan great house, was completed in 1612 and he had also acquired several other estates in the surrounding area, establishing himself as an important and powerful figure in Hampshire. His estate was visited by the court: Archbishop Abbot consecrated the chapel at Bramshill, and James hunted on the estate in 1620.[40] Yet, his political stance was often at odds with royal policy particularly in relation to Spain: the Spanish ambassador was warned that he was a 'great heretic and hostile to the peace (with Spain)'.[41] During a diplomatic mission to the Scottish court in 1593, his suspicions of the 'King's inward favour to Spanish "instruments"' had led him to act so 'zealously' in his dealings with James's that he incurred the king's hostility.[42] As a member of the Privy Council, Zouche could be counted amongst a loose 'patriot' coalition that included William Herbert, Earl of Pembroke during the 1614 'addled parliament'.[43] Browne had dedicated Book I of his *Britannia's Pastorals* to Zouche in the previous year and in 1613 and 1614 clearly sought to align himself with the political standpoint that Zouche represented at court.

Browne's version of the country house poem in the third eclogue of his *The Shepheards Pipe* sought to dramatize the fate of political communities, represented by peers such as Zouche, that he believed were being marginalized at the Stuart court. The Spenserian shepherds, Piers and Thomalin, tell the story of

[40] Sir William Cope, *Bramshill: Its History and Architecture* (London: H. J. Infield, 1883), 18–38; William Page (ed.), *A History of Hampshire and the Isle of Wight* (London: Constable and Co., 1911), VCH iv. 77–80. Archbishop Abbot accidently fatally wounded a keeper while hunting on the estate in 1621 which precipitated his downfall.

[41] A. Loomie (ed.) *Spain and the Jacobean Catholics*, 2 vols. (Catholic Record Society, 1973), i. 7. As lord president of the Council of Marches, he devoted himself to pursuing recusants amongst the Welsh gentry; his main support came from Sir John Harington of Exton, father of Prince Henry's favourite, who became Zouche's brother-in-law in 1611 (Penry Williams, *The Council in the Marches of Wales under Elizabeth I* (Cardiff: University of Wales Press, 1958), 299, 305).

[42] M. J. Thorpe (ed.) *Calender of State Papers, the Scottish Series, 1509–1606*, 2 vols. (London, 1858), ii. 642, 644–7, 652.

[43] Thomas Moir, *The Addled Parliament of 1614* (Oxford: Oxford University Press, 1958), 25.

Old Neddy, a patron of the pastoral community, who has been
cheated out of his property by his servants and evicted from his
estate. The eclogue gives voice to those symbolic communities
that a Jacobean Augustanism seemed intent on silencing. The
dispossession of Old Neddy has affinities with the fate of
Virgil's Meliboeus, exiled from his lands with the accession of
the new Emperor Augustus. The eclogue inverts the Stuart
Virgilian topos of the social and political harmony ensuing
from the Jacobean peace to figure the marginalization and
exploitation of the 'country' under the new Augustan order.
The identity of 'Old Neddy' is now obscure. John Shelly pro-
posed Spenser which would accord with the myth developing
in this period that Spenser died in poverty through the malice
of Robert Cecil.[44] However, Old Neddy is not a poet but a
'country' patron who represents a paternalistic tradition of
enlightened hospitality and may allude to one of Browne's
fellow 'countrymen'. Old Neddy's estate is situated in Browne's
own West country through local reference points: 'blessing fire'
is identified in a marginal note as a term for '*Midsummer fires
. . . in the West parts of England*' (D3r); 'hyne' (D4v) is a dialect
word used in Devon and Cornwall for 'a bailiff or upper farm
servant'; while the name given to Old Neddy's dairy, 'WILKINS
Cote' (D3v) tantalizingly suggests an actual place.

   The allegory of Browne's third eclogue tells of the destruction
of an 'Elizabethan' godly and independent 'country' order by a
new corrupting materialism at court typically identified in the
writing of the period with James's habit of selling titles and
the displacement of a feudal system of patronage by a new
economic patron–client relationship.[45] It is possible to read this
eclogue and Jonson's country house poem 'To Penshurst',
published two years later in 1616, as offering opposing political
perspectives on the 'country'.[46] Marcus sums up much recent

   [44] See W. C. Hazlitt's notes to *The Whole Works of William Browne, of
Tavistock, and of the Inner Temple; Now first collected and edited, with a memoir
of the poet and notes* (ed. W. Carew Hazlitt, 2 vols. (Roxburghe Library, 1868), ii.
375–6). 'Old Neddy' may allude to Sir Edward Phelips, Master of the Rolls, and
Brooke's fellow 'Sireniac', who fell from favour during the 1614 parliament and
died soon after—his house in Chancery Lane and country estate at Wanstead was
known for its hospitality (Whitlocke, *John Hoskyns, serjeant-at-law*, 386).
   [45] Linda Levy Peck, *Court Patronage and Corruption in Early Stuart England*
(Boston: Unwin Hyman, 1990), 19–20.
   [46] Annabel Patterson has read a similar passage in *Britannia's Pastorals* II. i.

work on the country house poem when she describes the absolutist perspective built into the genre as producing 'an idealised landscape dominated by a single controlling perspective: the interests of the monarch, the landowner, and the poet himself are aligned'.[47] This type of reading, however, does seems to limit the ideological possibilities of the form. Aemilia Lanyer's 'A Description of Cooke-ham', arguably one of the first Stuart country house poems, displays strongs signs of disaffection with the court and offers an alternative if fragile vision of female community. Moreover, Browne and Jonson to some extent shared an aristocratic view of the 'country'. In any case, given that the subject of 'To Penshurst', Sir Robert Sidney, came from a family seen to embody the ideals of an independent aristocracy, the poem's political vision is arguably more complex than a reading in terms of royal absolutism would indicate. Andrew McRae has identified the poem with a 'country farm tradition' in which the basic unit of the country is the independent manorial estate presided over by the paternal and godly landlord, while Isabel Rivers reads 'To Penshurst' in terms of a Stoic aristocratic self-sufficiency, and Melanie Hansen has drawn an instructive comparison with Drayton's *Poly-Olbion*: 'both share with those antiquarian narratives an intense preoccupation with the relationship between the people and the land, offering thereby a "picture" of the gentry or noble family, the estate, the county or the country at local and individualized levels.'[48]

Browne and Jonson had in common a respect for the moral and political values embodied by the Sidney family. It is not possible to draw a sharp dividing line through Jacobean culture that places the Spenserians on one side and Jonson on the other in terms of their perspective on the 'country'. Yet, while the

188–90 as 'a refutation of the idealizing Jacobean countryhouse poem, of which Ben Jonson's 'To Penshurst', published in the same year as this passage, was the supreme example' (*Pastoral and Ideology: Virgil to Valery* (Oxford: Clarendon Press, 1988), 143–4).

[47] Leah Marcus, 'Politics and Pastoral: Writing the Court on the Countryside', in Kevin Sharpe and Peter Lake (eds.) *Culture and Politics in Early Stuart England* (Basingstoke and London: Macmillan, 1994), 142.

[48] McRae, 'Husbandary Manuals and the Language of Agrarian Improvement', 56–7; Isabel Rivers, *The Poetry of Conservatism, 1600–1745: A Study of Poets and Public Affairs from Jonson to Pope* (Cambridge: Rivers Press, 1973), 33–50; Melanie Hansen, 'Identity and Ownership: Narratives of the Land in the English Renaissance', in William Zunder and Suzanne Trill (eds.), *Writing and the English Renaissance* (London and New York: Longman, 1996), 102.

culture of this period was not polarized there are important distinctions to be drawn between Jonson and this group of writers, particularly in terms of their response to court patronage. Jonson actively sought the king's favour and carefully negotiated a discursive position which was able to harmonize or at least accommodate professional independence and integrity and the dependency of patronage relationships.[49] Browne, Brooke, and Wither did address a number of their works to aristocratic patrons. However, their relationship to a Jacobean patronage culture could be considered oppositional. Not only did they avoid royal favourites and the influential Howard family, their identity as a community depended upon an opposition between a system of patronage and their own professional integrity as humanist poets. Wither did not seek the protection of a patron for his *The Shepherds Hunting* and instead dedicated the volume to his friends, thereby invoking the communal contexts of cultural production. Tensions between a patronage culture and the imperatives of a new print culture disrupt the harmonizing 'country' vision of the dedicatory poem to *The Shepheards Pipe*. Browne claimed that with such a patron as Zouche his eclogues would not need to 'seeke applause amongst the common store', but then closed the verse with a populist assertion of his own poetic and political autonomy, 'Free are my lines, though drest in lowly state, | And I scorne to flatter but the men I hate' (A2r). The satiric levelling effect of this closing couplet threatens to undo the very economy which underpins the dedicatory verse. The contradictions that disrupt the poem are symptomatic of the uneven transition between a patronage culture and the literary marketplace.

TRANSFORMING PASTORAL

Criticism has often been levelled at the immediacy and familiarity of these eclogues. For Mallette, Browne, and Wither used the eclogue merely 'as an elegant disguise to present (their)

---

[49] For tensions within Jonson's use of panegyric see: Butler, 'Ben Jonson and the Limits of Courtly Panegyric', 91–115; Martin Butler and David Lindley, 'Restoring Astraea: Jonson's Masque for the Fall of Somerset', *English Literary History*, 61 (1994), 807–27.

professional problems before the public' and so failed to maintain the idealizing distance of pastoral from the contemporary
world, to speak of greater things in a lowly form.[50] Yet, this
'professionalization' of pastoral is precisely the innovative
feature of these volumes. These eclogues are not inadequate,
overly literal readings of Spenser's 'October' eclogue, but rather
engage with Spenser's own speculations about a literary profession. The 'October' eclogue staged a debate on poetry as a
vocation, whether poetry belonged to the court and the patron
or whether it could transcend the court, circumventing its constraints. The resolution of this dilemma seems to be provided in
the form of the eclogue itself, in the cultural space defined by the
conversation between the two poets, Piers and Cuddy.[51] The
Spenserians sought to realize this cultural space in their own
dialogic eclogues but, in doing so, the eclogue begins to mutate
into another form. Bakhtin speaks of a 'familiarization of styles'
as having a transformative role in destroying 'official styles and
world views' and opening literature to new ideological
influences.[52] Wither in his postscript to *The Shepherds Hunting*
recognized that his pastorals could be criticized for 'erring
from the true nature of an *Eglogue*' (H5v) because of their
familiarity, their basis in his own experience, but insisted that
this immediacy actually validated the form of his eclogues.[53]

The eclogues of *The Shepheards Pipe* and *The Shepherds
Hunting* begin to move towards the form of the pamphlet in the
way that they provided a flexible form for addressing contemporary events. Both volumes attempted to achieve a
political currency and used print to transform themselves into
events, situating themselves at the centre of contemporary
debates. The publication of *The Shepheards Pipe* coincided with
Brooke's *The ghost of Richard the third* that warned of the

[50] Richard Mallette, *Spenser, Milton and Renaissance Pastoral* (Lewisburg:
Bucknell University Press, 1981), 43–4.

[51] Roland Greene, '*The Shepheardes Calender*, Dialogue, and Periphrasis',
Spenser Studies, 8 (1987), 25.

[52] M. M. Bakhtin, *Speech Genres and Other Late Essays*, ed. Caryl Emerson and
Michael Holquist, trans. Vernon W. McGee (Austin: University of Texas Press,
1996), 97.

[53] Drayton, in his preface to his 1619 *Pastorals*, also presented his *Pastorals* as a
new departure in the form: 'but he who hath almost nothing Pastorall in his
Pastorals, but the name (which is my Case) deales more plainly' (Drayton, *Works*,
iv. 517). See also: Rosemary Laing, 'The Disintegration of Pastoral: Studies in
Seventeenth-Century Theory and Practice', D.Phil. thesis (Oxford, 1982), 34–6.

dangers posed by a new 'tyranny'. Brooke, the MP for York in the 1614 'addled' parliament, wanted to ensure that the prerogative powers of the Crown did not undermine parliamentary privileges. The publication of all three volumes seems to have been timed to capitalize on these heated 1614 parliamentary sessions which ended in the dissolution of parliament and the imprisonment of a number of MPs. In a practical sense, parliament provided these writers with a politicized audience since MPs came into London from their counties and were able to frequent the bookshops around St Paul's. James may have agreed to a new parliament as a means of improving his weak financial position, but others clearly saw it as a means of redressing grievances and opening areas of policy to public debate. In the pages of *The Shepheards Pipe* and its sequel *The Shepherds Hunting* a group of politically-motivated writers came together to form a virtuous commonwealth which claimed the authority to engage in public debate on issues of politics and culture.

The civic structure of this community moves pastoral out from the semi-private space of the cabinet and into the public domain.[54] The eclogues of *The Shepheards Pipe* and *The Shepherds Hunting* exploit the resources of pastoral to set up structures of dialogue and debate. Pastoral has a flexibility in these eclogues and they possess an actuality and immediacy which arguably is their defining feature. 'Willy' is William Browne, 'Cuddy' is Christopher Brooke, and 'Roget' is George Wither.[55] The correspondence between the Marshalsea and the pastoral landscape of Wither's *The Shepherds Hunting*, where he has 'nothing to conuerse with but a *Rocke* | Or at least *Outlawes* in their *Caues* halfe pin'd' (B3r), translates his prison experiences into a pastoral fiction so loose that it is almost redundant. Above all, these eclogues are remarkable for the way that they often present themselves as records of actual conversations. There is a conversational informality to

---

[54] Annabel Patterson has argued that 'as a direct result of the policies of the early Stuarts and their reincarnation under late ones, the Virgilian code and the ideological possibilities it represented passed out of the cabinet of the lone intellectual, isolated and beseiged, into the terrain of politics proper and became widely disseminated as a public language' (*Pastoral and Ideology*, 134).

[55] As Grundy points out, 'The writers are not here projecting themselves into an imaginary pastoral world; rather, they are realizing their own lives in pastoral terms' (*Spenserian Poets*, 81).

Browne's and Wither's use of pastoral: these are unrefined plain-speaking shepherds, who avoid the ornate diction of their Italianate counterparts, and both poets employed an irregular seven-syllable line that reinforces the vernacular informality of the verse. In this way, the verse could be said to be modelled on speech genres rather than formal genres thereby enabling these poets to dramatize the social processes of dialogue and debate. The allegorical dimension of pastoral, its ability to speak of politically sensitive issues under cover, is situated firmly within the present. The eclogues themselves take their occasions from contemporary events and the insistent use of 'we' and 'our' situates the speaker and his audience within a contemporary social space. Topical readings are encouraged in both volumes. The unidentified shepherds populating Browne's *The Shepheards Pipe*, for example, send the reader in search of analogues amongst contemporary figures and Browne's personal acquaintances.

Wither insisted on such speculative reading practices with the 'autobiographical' beast fable that runs across the second and third eclogues of *The Shepherds Hunting* and is used to emplot the 'conspiracy' that has resulted in his imprisonment. Roget (Wither) in the second eclogue tells his story to Willy (Browne) and Cuddy (Brooke) and in the third eclogue they are joined by Alexis (William Ferrar). Roget's shepherd friends act as a type of readership, a microcosm of a larger public that is eager for 'news' of Wither's fate. Roget urges Cuddy to tell him what the public is saying is the cause of his imprisonment, 'how doth the *Rumour* goe' (C2r), even though he does not care for 'What the vnsteady common-people deemes' (C2v). This provides the context for Roget's following beast fable which extensively dramatizes the reception of his satire, *Abuses stript, and whipt*, and his subsequent trial and imprisonment after being falsely accused of defaming a peer. The use of the beast fable is strategic. In the hands of Spenser, Drayton, and Richard Niccols, it was an encoded form that educated the reader in the identification of beasts with prominent figures at court and with particular sets of abuses, such as popery, ambition, treason, and corruption. Wither encouraged his readers to adopt such reading practices and to identify his persecutors, those who 'Keep Foxes, Beares, and Wolues, as some great treasure: | Yea, many get their liuing by them to' (D6r), with contemporary courtiers who were reputed to either protect recusants or to be in the pay of Spain. Yet, these two eclogues are remarkable not for the beast fable as such, but for the way that they dramatize the circulation of rumour and a public eager for information about the latest scandal or, in Wither's case, 'cause'. By turning the satiric essays of *Abuses stript, and whipt* into hunting dogs, Wither animates his text, attributes to it an agency and gives it a material presence in the culture of early modern London.

Wither, as this suggests, responded eagerly to an expanding market for controversial political material. Political verse libels and satires circulated widely through manuscript and informal performances, both in private and in public spaces such as St Paul's Yard, and provided an important form of political education by disseminating political gossip and information amongst a relatively broad section of the populace, so much so that they had been described in terms of an ' "underground" media'.[56] The first eclogue of *The Shepherds Hunting* invoked restrictions on free speech that would have taken on an added topicality following the imprisonment of MPs and the burning of their papers in the wake of the dissolution of the 1614 'addled' parliament. This first eclogue takes the form of a dialogue between Roget and Willie (Browne) in which Wither constructs his imprisonment as a form of political exile resulting from a tyrannical regime. Willie assures Roget that 'thou may'st speak freely' as 'there's none heares | But he whom I doe hope thou do'st not doubt' (B5r), to which Roget responds:

> True; but if *dores* and *walles* haue gotten *eares*,
> And *Closet-whisperings* may be spread about:
> Doe not blame him that in such *causes* feares
> What in his *Passion* he may blunder out:
> In such a *place*, and such strict *times* as these,
> Where what we speak is tooke as *others* please.   (B5v)

This evocation of a state of surveillance locates his volume in an

---

[56] Thomas Cogswell, 'Underground verse and the transformation of early Stuart political culture', in Susan D. Amussen and Mark A. Kirlansky (eds.), *Political Culture and Cultural Politics in Early Modern England* (Manchester and New York: Manchester University Press), 284; see also: Alastair Bellany, ' "Raylinge Rymes and Vaunting Verse": Libellous Politics in Early Stuart England', in Kevin Sharpe and Peter Lake (eds.), *Cultural Politics in Early Stuart England* (Basingstoke and London: Macmillan, 1994), 285–310.

environment in which public discourse is severely restricted, yet those 'Closet-whisperings' which 'may be spread about' also gesture to the other side of censorship in a flourishing market for subversive political material. Like verse libels, the eclogues of Browne and Wither often encourage the reader to search for topicality which gives the eclogue a political currency that is often associated with the pamphlet literature of the 1620s. In *The Shepherds Hunting*, Wither depicted his own situation as particularly 'newsworthy'. At the beginning of the second eclogue, he had Cuddy inform the reader that not only were his close friends talking about him and the political issues that his imprisonment raised, but his cause was also being spread abroad through the mechanisms of rumour, so that 'at all meet-ings where our *Shepheards* be, | Now the maine Newes that's extant is of thee' (C2r). His cause is no longer a private concern but 'Newes' circulating in the public domain through rumour and, implicitly, texts such as *The Shepheards Pipe*, *The Shepherds Hunting*, and his defence *A Satyre: dedicated to his most excellent maiestie* (1615).

The seventh eclogue of Browne's *The Shepheards Pipe* similarly engaged with this market for libellous satire and invited a topical application to the divorce of the third Earl of Essex and Frances Howard, and her remarriage to the royal favourite, the Earl of Somerset. As early as 1614, prior to the trial of the couple for the murder of Sir Thomas Overbury, this controversial marriage was viewed as emblematic of court corruption by many political Protestants, particularly those loyal to the memory of the second Earl of Essex.[57] The eclogue relates Palinode's attempts to dissuade his friend, Hobinoll, from marriage with Phillis, and has a satiric sharpness and specificity that calls for contemporary analogues. Palinode lists the number of men Phillis has used 'to sate her lust' (E8r): a goatherd, a figure associated in Spenser's *July* with the reprobate and the proud, ambitious courtier; Cladon, who is a virtuous figure, chosen 'To bee the mate | Vnto our Lady of the gleesome May' (F1r), and recently abandoned by Phillis (possibly an allusion to Howard's first husband, the third Earl of Essex); and himself. Phillis's sexual duplicity is defined

---

[57] On the politics of Frances Howard's marriages and trial, see: David Lindley, *The Trials of Frances Howard* (London: Macmillan, 1996).

specifically in terms of adultery which is in turn associated with courtly intrigue—'her seruants' and 'her fauourites . . . waite her husbands issuing at dore' (F1v). The misogyny of this eclogue and its theme of sexual betrayal invites a comparison with Hoccleve's misogynist complaint against women published in the first eclogue, particularly since Hoccleve's tale of sexual corruption is offered as a model for contemporary satire.[58] The Somerset marriage generated a number of politically-charged verse libels and *Sir Thomas Overbury, His Wife* was published posthumously possibly as part of a campaign vilifying the marriage—it was entered in the Stationers' Register just ten days before the Somerset wedding. Overbury, a friend of Carr, like the shepherd Palinode in Browne's eclogue, opposed the marriage and was eventually committed to the Tower, where he died on 15 September, 1613;[59] Browne and Brooke will contribute elegies to the 1616 volume *Sir Thomas Ouerburie His Wife with new Elegies vpon his (now knowne) vntimely death* condemning the leniency shown to the Earl and Countess of Somerset following their conviction for Overbury's murder. In all these verses, sexual corruption had connotations of moral, political, and religious corruption. James's implication in the scandal surrounding his favourite suggested that corruption had its source at the very heart of the court.[60]

Browne's eclogue functions in a similar fashion to the verse libels by opening the divorce and marriage to public speculation. Aristocratic marriages enabled James to manage his court and to promote fictions of a harmonious and cohesive society. The Somerset marriage tested this strategy: James tried to unite the court behind the marriage, but the relatives of Essex and a number of those opposed to the Howards refused to attend, the Lord Mayor had to be coerced by James into providing entertainment, and only one Inn of Court, Gray's Inn, provided

---

[58] Hoccleve's prologue to 'The *Gesta* tale of Jonathas and Fellicula' frames it as a warning against prostitutes (Hoccleve, *Works*, ed. F. J. Furnival, 3 vols. *Early English Text Society* (London: Kegan Paul, Trench, Trubner, 1892–7), ii. 216–18).

[59] Neil Cuddy, 'The revival of the entourage: the Bedchamber of James I, 1603–25', in David Starkey *et al.* (eds.), *The English Court: from the Wars of the Roses to Civil War* (London: Longman, 1987), 207–14; P. R. Seddon, 'Robert Carr, Earl of Somerset', *Renaissance and Modern Studies*, 14 (1970), 52–63; and *The 'Conceited Newes' of Sir Thomas Overbury and his Friends*, ed. James E. Savage (Gainesville, Fla.: Scholar's Facsimiles and Reprints, 1968), xv–xvi.

[60] Bellany, 'Libellous Politics in Early Stuart England', 196.

a masque. Entertainments and verses written for the Somerset marriage had difficulties in preventing political pressures from disrupting their hymeneal fictions.[61] Browne's eclogue deliberately inverted these harmonizing symbolic strategies by taking the form of an anti-epithalamium: it takes place on the morning of the marriage, the conventional starting point of the epithalamium, but then relates the reasons why this marriage should not take place.[62] Differences between Spenserian responses to the Somerset marriage and the wedding of Elizabeth and Frederick in early 1613 are striking. Wither's *Epithalamia* celebrated the royal marriage as an occasion for unity between 'court' and 'country': the national rivers pay homage to the 'Watrie Court' 'by consent all, naught against their wills'.[63] By 1614, this rhetoric of consensus was under severe pressure.

The concept of public political debate itself is a central concern in the eclogues produced by this group of poets. The self-conscious way that these poets approached this subject is evident in the fifth eclogue of Browne's *The Shepheards Pipe*. This eclogue was dedicated to Brooke and is a continuation of the ongoing exchange between poet friends that structures the volume. The eclogue is offered as a record of an actual conversation between Browne and Brooke and its chosen theme, the relationship between poetry and counsel, moves this private discussion between friends into the realms of public debate. The subject of the eclogue is public poetry: in the words of the argument '*Willy incites his friend to write | Things of a higher frame*' (E2r). Browne is ostensibly encouraging Brooke to publish his *The ghost of Richard the third*, to set it before the public. Yet, the eclogue is primarily a reflection of what this

---

[61] Lindley, 'Embarrassing Ben', 347; Heather Dubrow, *A Happier Eden: The Politics of Marriage in the Stuart Epithalamia* (Ithaca and London: Cornell University Press, 1990), 130–3, and ' "Sun on the Water": Donne's Somerset Epithalamium and the Poetics of Patronage', in Heather Dubrow and Richard Strier (eds.), *The Historical Renaissance: New Essays on Tudor and Stuart Literature and Culture* (Chicago and London: University of Chicago Press, 1988), 201–13.

[62] See the section on the anti-epithalamium in Virginia Tufte's *The Poetry of Marriage: The Epithalamium in Europe and its Development in England* (Los Angeles: Tinnon Brown, 1970), 37–8). Brooke's 'An Epithalamium' published in *Englands Helicon* suggests a similar disillusionment with the harmonizing role of marriage in the Jacobean court, although Heather Dubrow has read the poem as a straightforward celebration of a marriage (*A Happier Eden*, 153, 181–96).

[63] Wither, *Epithalamia: or Nuptiall Poemes* (London, 1612), STC 25901, B1r.

might mean in 1614. Pastoral on its own is too limited a form to address these issues and so Browne introduced a georgic note to bring pastoral into the public domain. Like Spenser before him, he took a georgic view of poetry which sees it as a redemptive, cultivating labour akin to a humanist concept of counsel. His use of pastoral georgic to frame the conversation between the two friends portrays them as 'countrymen': the politicized georgic language of husbandry translates the shepherd-poet into a citizen actively tending the political landscape of the commonwealth.[64] The dawn of the labouring day unfolds to reveal hardworking godly shepherds, who have their forefathers in the Reformation ploughman, vigilantly tending their flocks. The eclogue uses the occasion of Brooke's publication of his *The ghost of Richard the third* to stage a debate about issues of freedom of speech that were also engaging Brooke in parliament. The idealized public sphere that would enable such free debate is constituted in relation to a concept of tyranny. In the eclogue, Browne has 'Cuttie' Brooke speak of the dangers now confronting poets who delve into state affairs: 'Who 'gainst the Sun (though weakned by the morne) | Would vie with lookes, needeth an Eagles eye' (E3r). Brooke, in his companion eclogue dedicated to Browne in the same volume, defended intellectual freedom within a context of political repression: 'Thought hath no prison and the minde is free | Vnder the greatest King and tyrannie' (F6r). Willy's response to tyranny in the fifth eclogue is to enthusiastically insist on the ethical and political autonomy of the poet, boldly advising Brooke that 'Thou canst giue more to kings then kings to thee' (E3v) and 'if ther's none deserves what thou canst doe, | Be then the Poet and the Patron too' (E4r). The poet, released from the constraining structures of court culture, assumes an autonomy that qualifies him as a cultural spokesman.

Wither used a concept of slander in a similar way. Slander was akin to tyranny in that it was a condition of a corrupted court and perverted the humanist ideal of counsel, of public language serving the common good.[65] Slander was particularly pertinent in Wither's case. There is strong evidence that the

[64] Patterson, *Pastoral and Ideology*, 133–4.

[65] Anne Lake Prescott, 'Evil Tongues at the Court of Saul: The Renaissance David as a Slandered Courtier', *Journal of Medieval and Renaissance Studies*, 2 (1991), 169.

charge that led to his imprisonment was that of *scandalum magnatum*, libelling a peer or officer of state. Defamation was a particularly unstable offence and to a certain extent reversible in that those accused could claim to have been themselves the victim of a slander by insisting that their words were true or misrepresented and that the charge against them was itself motivated by malice.[66] Wither presented the charge against him as a part of a campaign to undermine public poetry by slanderously misreading it as libellous.[67] In many ways, to become a victim of slander was to become a Spenserian poet. Wither, like other Spenserians, was attracted by the ending of Book IV of *The Faerie Queene* where the poet and his 'homely verse' fall prey to slander. His own slanderer in *The Shepherds Hunting* is a 'man-like *Monster*', a version of Spenser's Blatant Beast, and identified as an evil counsellor, an abuser of public language, and an unregenerate servant of the papist Antichrist. In response, he carefully constructed a poetics of persecution that defended the poets' rights to discuss political issues. His Roget takes on the appearance of a slandered and anti-courtly David from the *Psalms*. Protestant reformers placed a new emphasis on slander in their depiction of David as a prophetic anti-court poet and victim of court tyranny. Wither himself was a careful Protestant reader of the *Psalms* and went on to publish *A Preparation to the Psalter* (1619) and *Exercises upon the first Psalme* (1620).[68] In *The Shepherds Hunting*, he identified with a politicized David of the *Psalms*, who 'in his troubles eas'd the bodies paines | By measures rais'd to the soules rauishing' (B8v) and he read the *Psalms* as an historical and personal drama, involving the persecution of the godly under a court tyranny, that was currently being played out in his own imprisonment.

Roget's situation also has strong affinities with Colin Clout's Ovidian exile in *Colin Clouts Come Home Againe*. In Ovid's case, exile was both a punishment for political transgression and created an enabling space for the construction of a new

[66] M. Lindsay Kaplan, *The Culture of Slander in Early Modern England* (Cambridge: Cambridge University Press, 1997), 16.

[67] For further discussion of the connection between libel and public political debate, see Chapter 4.

[68] Prescott, in her lucid account of a Renaissance David, describes the David of these latter works as 'an anticourt poet, and his heavenly court precisely opposes the one where the psalmist was so infamously treated' ('Evil Tongues at the court of Saul', 164–5, 185).

authorial identity.[69] Wither's prison exile, 'quite beyond the *Desearts* here confin'd' (B3r), similarly results in a higher liberty, 'since I truly finde my *conscience* free' (B3v). In this way, Spenser's 'libertie' is translated into a Foxean freedom of conscience. Wither saw himself as a Protestant martyr, the righteous and godly victim of a 'criminal' state: '*Tyrants* may boast they to much *power* are borne, | Yet he hath more that *Tyrannies* can scorne' (B4v). His imprisonment resulted from placing the health of the commonwealth above his own personal safety, 'I suffer, cause I wish'd my Countrey well' (G7v). Foxe's *Acts and Monuments* provided Wither with a dramatic structure that enabled him to mediate between an inward self and history and to privilege an oppositional subjectivity centred in the nonconformist principle of liberty of conscience:[70]

> My *mind's* more pretious freedome I so weigh
> A thousand wayes they may my *body* binde,
> In thousand *thralls*, but ne're my minde betray.   (B4r–v)

Roget's 'prisoners *Lay*', a hymn to the transcendent liberty of the soul, turns Wither's imprisonment into a providential trial and gives a georgic inflection to the pastoral landscape. Pastoral georgic in *The Shepherds Hunting* takes a Protestant reformist rather than a Virgilian form: pastoral is the locus for spiritual truth and the shepherd poet is assimilated to the godly husbandman battling against tyranny and error. Wither's poetics of exile is informed by the enthusiasm of prophetic engagement so that pastoral in this eclogue does not result in an enclosed landscape of retirement and ease, but in a providential drama of spiritual and political conflict.

Brooke's eclogue appended to *The Shepheards Pipe* similarly rejected Italianate pastoral ease for a reforming visionary pastoral. His paean addressed to Browne in 'praise of Shepheards and of thee their King' (F5v) is modelled on Spenser's Mount of Contemplation in Book I of *The Faerie*

[69] Julia Reinhard Lupton, 'Mapping mutability: or, Spenser's Irish plot', in Brendan Bradshaw *et al* (eds.), *Representing Ireland* (Cambridge: Cambridge University Press, 1994), 106; 'Home-Making in Ireland: Virgil's Eclogue I and Book VI of *The Faerie Queene*', *Spenser Studies*, 7 (1990), 119–27.

[70] On this Foxean drama, see: John Knott, *Discourses of Martyrdom in English Literature, 1563–1694* (Cambridge: Cambridge University Press, 1993), 7.

Queene. Brooke's Contemplation fuses a Christian mystical contemplation with Neoplatonism. The spiritual and philosophical ascent of the shepherd-poet figures a spiritual and generic conversion of pastoral into a higher form. In these terms, the reforming pastoral of Browne's *The Shepheards Pipe*, according to Brooke, is able to mediate between the lowly pastoral and the Christian epic:

> Thou low thou seem'st thy *Genius* mounts the Hill
> Where heauenly *Nectar* doth from *Ioue* distill;
> Where *Bayes* still grows (by thunder not struck down)
> The Victors-Garland; and the Poets-Crowne.   (F6r)

Brooke carefully followed Spenser's negotiations between pastoral georgic and epic romance in the Mount Contemplation episode: 'the Shepheard' is 'a true figure | Of Contemplation' who undertakes a purified and internalized epic romance journey, in which the shepherd-poet's 'discoursive thought, do'st range as farre | Nor canst thou erre', that opens the pastoral to a visionary historical perspective.[71] This visionary intellectual space is politicized through the expression of a transcendent liberty of conscience that Wither will find so compelling in *The Shepherds Hunting*: 'Thought hath no prison and the mind is free | Vnder the greatest king and tyrannie.' The scene of Contemplation, 'Truthes discouery', offers an apocalyptic if secularized historical vision in which present 'errors' are redeemed in 'future times' and prompts a utopian humanist vision of learning where 'dignity with safety do combine | Pleasure with merite make a louely twine' (F6r). The active and the contemplative are aligned in line with Spenser's Contemplation, but the heroic action of the shepherd-poet is located within an intellectual rather than martial, epic framework: 'All monuments of Armes and Power decay, | But that which liues to an Eternall day, | Letters preserue' (F6v). Visionary pastoral finds its true domain in the world of letters.

Wither's sense of his prophetic calling radicalized his pastoral eclogues in both political and generic terms. He systematically reached towards a prophetic strain that only appears fleetingly in *The Shepheards Pipe* in the Manwood elegy. Poetic

---

[71] See King's study of the generic strategies of the Mount Contemplation episode (*Spenser's Poetry and the Reformation Tradition*, 217–20).

authority in *The Shepherds Hunting* is located within the divinely inspired self and not in a literary tradition or patron. The poet possessed by *furor poeticus* is a regular feature of Wither's eclogues and makes an appearance in the description of his satire's progress in the third eclogue:

> Stretching their *musicke* to the highest strains
> That when some Thicket hid them from mine eye,
> My eare was rauish'd with their melody.   (D3v)

The increasingly frantic and eventually unrestrained movement of the hunt becomes a metaphor for his own 'liberated' poetic practice, his use of a 'loose' poetics. Like Milton a generation later, he insisted on his literal rather than figurative possession by the prophetic spirit.[72] *Furor poeticus* demonstrates the limits of language and genre and the possibility of their transcendence and functions as a 'mode of physical dissolution' that signals the desire to ascend to an apocalyptic union with the divine origin.[73] At the close of the ecstatic hymn to divine poesy in the fourth eclogue, Wither had Willy interrupt Roget to remind him of the limits of his pastoral location:

> The kinde flames of Poesy
> Haue now borne thy thoughts so high,
> That they vp in Heauen be
> And haue quite forgotten mee.   (F8r)

This interruption self-consciously echoes the moment in Spenser's *Colin Clouts Come Home Againe* when Cuddy recalls Colin from his poetic flight in praise of Cynthia–Elizabeth; Drayton also imitated this device in the fifth eclogue of his 1606 *Pastorals* after his panegyric to Idea to point out that the pastoral was too low a mode for his divine subject and that he was in danger of breaking the decorum of pastoral (E4v–6v). Wither reworked this trope to concentrate on the tension between the prophetic poet's soaring imagination and the restrictions of generic form and the figure of the patron is tellingly absent. Amongst his fellow Spenserians, Wither seems to have had the greatest investment in a Protestant prophetic tradition. In the years following the publication of *The*

---

[72] Milton, *Paradise Lost*, ed. Alistair Fowler (Essex and New York: Longman, 1986), 359.
[73] Calhoun, 'Origins and Consequences of a Loose Poetics', 278.

Shepherds Hunting, he will devote himself to work on the *Psalms*, publishing his *Exercises upon the first Psalme* in 1620 and *The hymnes and songes of the Church* in 1623.[74]

The *Shepheards Pipe* and *The Shepherds Hunting* are important reorientations of pastoral. These communal, collaborative eclogues extend the Renaissance pastoral of vocation to dramatize a literary commonwealth and to promote a generic inclusiveness that accommodates pastoral to more public modes such as satire and georgic. Loosened from a court culture, pastoral is assimilated to a complex 'country' ideology and simultaneously naturalized as a representative English genre. Browne signalled his own commitment to Spenser's nationalistic project of founding a 'kingdom of our own language' by publishing a modernized version of Thomas Hoccleve's 'The *Gesta* Tale of Jonathas and Fellicula' in the first eclogue of *The Shepheards Pipe*.[75] Wither in the fourth eclogue of *The Shepherds Hunting*, when encouraging Browne to return to work on his *Britannia's Pastorals*, similarly offered an English 'country' vision of pastoral festivities in defence of the new Spenserianism, invoking may-games and dreams of 'Strawberries and Creame' (E6v). This desire to literalize pastoral in the English countryside, to have it speak 'plainly' was already present in Drayton's Cotswold sheep-shearing festival in the revised ninth eclogue of his 1606 *Pastorals* which had redefined pastoral for the Spenserians as a native 'country' mode.[76] Yet, while both *The Shepherds Hunting* and *The Shepheards Pipe* transform the pastoral eclogue, Wither did take this process further and continually dramatized the limits of pastoral and rehearsed the conditions for its transformation. Even in his defence of Spenserian pastoral in the fourth eclogue, there is a strong sense that he was representing a form that was already

---

[74] His friendship with William Ferrar, the younger brother of John and Nicholas who later established the religious community at Little Gidding, may have been part of an attempt to gain support for these projects (A. L. Maycock, *Nicholas Ferrar of Little Gidding* (Grand Rapids, Mich.: Eerdams, 1980), 7).

[75] On Spenser's nationalism, see: Richard Helgerson, *Forms of Nationhood: The Elizabethan Writing of England* (Chicago and London: Chicago University Press, 1992), 1–18.

[76] For the 'country' associations of this eclogue, see: Drayton, *Works*, v. 186–7; Richard Hardin, *Michael Drayton and the Passing of Elizabethan England* (Lawrence, Manhattan: University Press of Kansas), 103–5; Tylus, 'Jacobean Poetry and Lyric Disappointment', 185–6.

completed in the pastorals of Drayton, Browne, and others, and signalling a new beginning for English poetry in his own prophetic verse. *The Shepherds Hunting* is a highly skilful combination of 'Newes' and a prophetic strain. The iconoclasm of Wither's 'loose' poetics opens established genres, such as pastoral, to new institutions and transformative ideologies. *The Shepherds Hunting* locates the pastoral eclogue within a new print culture, but in doing so expands its boundaries almost beyond recognition, and looks forward to the radically novel *Wither's Motto* (1621).

2

Tyranny, Parliament, and the 'Country': Christopher Brooke's *The ghost of Richard the third* (1614)

THE *ghost of Richard the third* was in many ways a companion text to *The Shepheards Pipe*: the two poems were entered in the Stationers' Register on consecutive days, Browne's fifth eclogue dedicated to Brooke united these texts in their resistance to tyranny, and his commendatory verses before *The ghost of Richard the third* portrayed the two poets collaborating on a new politicized 'country' poetics:

> Nor shall thy buskind Muse be heard alone
> In stately Pallaces; the shady woods
> By me shall learn't, and Eccho's one by one
> Teach it the hils, and they the siluer floods.[1]

The figure of echo embodies Spenserian praxis, the solitary voice gives way to a plurality of voices to describe the inter-dependency of the poetic voice on prior communities. Wither also joined Browne in placing commendatory verses before Brooke's poem, once again renewing *The Shepheards Pipe* community. Yet, Brooke's *The ghost of Richard the third* also had strong links with other early seventeenth-century London communities. Brooke, an MP in the 1614 'addled' parliament, was part of a loose grouping of MPs opposed to impositions whose long-standing friendships dated back to their youth at the Inns of Court and had continued through their parliamentary careers and the London tavern 'clubs'. The way that *The ghost of Richard the third* moves between various com-

[1] *The ghost of Richard the third*, A3r. Brooke's poem has attracted little interest from literary critics, with a few notable exceptions, see: David Norbrook, *Poetry and Politics in the English Renaissance* (London: Routledge and Kegan Paul, 1984), 210–11; and Dennis Kay, 'The English Funeral Elegy in the reigns of Elizabeth I and James I, with Special Reference to Poems on the Death of Prince Henry (1612)', D.Phil. thesis (Oxford, 1982), 246–7.

munities illustrates the importance of these type of relational networks in the transmission of ideas. The discourse of tyranny and court corruption that Brooke draws on in *The ghost of Richard the third* was influenced by his fellow Spenserian poets and also shaped by contemporary parliamentary debates over issues of political representation. Early seventeenth-century political culture was not marked by a sharp divide between print and scribal communities. Brooke's poem both enabled parliamentary debates to enter the public realm of print and participated in a sphere of political debate evident in the manuscript circulation of political separates and satires. Parliamentary speeches, including Brooke's own speeches in the 1610 and 1614 parliaments, circulated widely within Inns of Court and parliamentary communities and have been described as 'an important form of political activism'.[2] The fluidity of Brooke's social and textual alliances is indicative of a dynamic culture that facilitated these type of exchanges.

Brooke himself is an instructive figure. The courtier who combined a political career with literary activity is now a familiar figure in Renaissance studies, but Brooke's career offers a less well-known pattern, that of a lawyer-MP who was committed to publishing his poetry and used the media of poetry and print to continue parliamentary debates. His career accords with the humanist ideal of *vita activa*, fulfilling the role of counsellor to the commonwealth through his combined parliamentary and poetic activity. A practising lawyer, he was MP for York from 1604 to 1626, sitting in all of James's parliaments. He did not gain his seat through aristocratic patronage but through his merchant and civic background.[3] He came from a merchant family prominent in the civic government of York: his father Robert Brooke served two terms as Lord Mayor of York, and represented the city in the 1584 and 1586 parliaments. York's civic government under the Tudors and the Stuarts was dominated by merchants.[4] Brooke's consistent opposition to

[2] Harold Love, *Scribal Publication in Seventeenth-Century England* (Oxford: Clarendon Press, 1993), 9–19; Wallace Notestein and Frances Relf (eds.), *Commons Debates for 1629* (Minneapolis: University of Minnesota, 1921), xv–lxv.

[3] He dedicated *The ghost of Richard the third* to Sir John Crompton, a fellow MP in the 1614 parliament, and his wife Lady Frances Crofton, members of a prominent Yorkshire family.

[4] P. M. Tillot (ed.), *A History of Yorkshire, The City of York* (London: Oxford University Press, 1961), 179, 186.

impositions in the 1610 and 1614 parliaments may have been partly influenced by these interests. Due to its strong merchant civic presence, York was hostile to economic measures which threatened trade and in the 1597 to 1598 and 1601 parliaments campaigned against monopolies.[5] There was probably a similar hostility towards impositions given the bitter confrontation between the crown (headed by Salisbury) and merchants in the Bate's case, put forward by the crown as the test-case for impositions.[6] York apparently was pleased with Brooke's performance in the 1610 parliament: his claim for wages was met in full and he was re-elected without a contest for the rest of his life.[7] Brooke's poetry operated within this civic and parliamentary context and consistently engaged with debates in the Commons. His *The ghost of Richard the third* and the eclogue he contributed to Browne's *The Shepheards Pipe* were published either during or soon after the 1614 'addled' parliament and shared with his parliamentary speeches a concern that the traditional liberties of the subject were being eroded in and outside parliament. Similarly, his *Poem on the Late Massacre in Virginia* (1622) and his elegy for Sir Arthur Chichester, which was refused a licence for printing in 1625, continued his criticism of Jacobean foreign policy in the 1621 and 1624 parliaments through the medium of poetry.[8]

The ghost of Richard the third is an eclectic, mixed genre work which is composed of a loose mix of Machiavellian, Tacitean, and Senecan discourses, and combines the didactic form of the *Mirror for Magistrates* with the style of the politicized Elizabethan Senecan tragedy. Like other Spenserian texts, the poem's eclecticism was strategic: Brooke incorporated forms and themes that had taken on certain political and cultural resonances and he was attracted to genres with Protestant 'patriot' associations. The strong Senecan flavour of the poem deliberately recalled an Elizabethan politicized Seneca current in the tragedies produced within the Countess of

[5] David Dean, 'Pressure Groups and Lobbies in the Elizabethan and Early Jacobean Parliaments', *Parliaments, Estates and Representation*, 11 (1991), 150.

[6] Pauline Croft, 'Fresh Light on Bate's Case', *The Historical Journal*, 30 (1987), 523–39.

[7] *A History of Yorkshire*, 196; Unpublished biography, *History of Parliament*, 790, 1, 12. I would like to thank the History of Parliament Trust for access to this document.

[8] See Chapter 5 for discussion of these poems.

Pembroke's circle. There appears to have been a revival of Elizabethan Senecan tragedy in response to the conflicts within the political elite and between king and Commons in the first half of James's reign. In 1609 during the build-up to the 1610 parliament, a revised version of Greville's Elizabethan Senecan tragedy, *Mustapha*, was published. While the earliest version of the play was imbedded in the ideological and factional conflicts of the mid-1590s, the publication of a revised version on the eve of the 1610 parliament suggests the perceived re-emergence of a comparable political dilemma under James. *Mustapha* addressed contemporary fears of an incipient 'absolutism' with the evil favourites and counsellors in the play encouraging the king to adopt an increasingly tyrannical position towards his subjects.[9] The later Jacobean version incorporated passages discussing the validity of resistance together with warnings of the dangers resulting from kings extending their prerogative beyond the bounds of law: 'Where kings too oft vse their prerogatiue | The people do forbeare, but not forgiue.'[10] Brooke similarly drew on an Elizabethan Seneca to express his dissatisfaction with the current state of court politics. Seneca is viewed through Machiavelli to produce a politically cynical view of the court, particularly in the early treatment of Richard's rise to power.

The political currency of the evil counsellor and the associated language of tyranny and corruption, evident in the writings of Wither and Browne, pointed Brooke towards the history of Richard III in 1614. Pauline Croft has drawn attention to the 'remarkable chronological relationship between Cecil's career and the popularity of histories of King Richard III' while Margaret Hotine has argued for the topicality of Shakespeare's *Richard III* in relation to Sir Robert Cecil and his political schemes.[11] The rhetoric of tyranny in histories of

---

[9] R. A. Rebholz, *The Life of Fulke Greville, First Lord Brooke* (Oxford: Clarendon Press, 1971), 101–3.

[10] Fulke Greville, *The Tragedy of Mvstapha* (London, 1609), STC 12362, D2v. J. G. A. Pocock has pointed to the ambiguity and moral pessimism of Greville's justification of absolutism in *A Treatise of Monarchy* (*The Machiavellian Moment: Florentine Thought and the Atlantic Republican Tradition* (Princeton: Princeton University Press, 1975), 352–3).

[11] Pauline Croft, 'The Reputation of Robert Cecil: Libels, Political Opinion and Popular Awareness in the Early Seventeenth Century', *Transactions of the Royal Historical Society*, 1 (1991), 43–69; Margaret Hotine, '*Richard III* and *Macbeth*— Studies in Tudor Tyranny?' *Notes and Queries*, 236 (1991), 480–6.

Richard III was available for an attack on Cecil not merely because of the equation of physical and moral deformity (Cecil like the legendary Richard was stunted) but also because it offered a complex critical humanist language for discussing issues of state and the failure of counsel. A humanist discourse of tyranny provided Brooke with an encoded political language for tacitly airing contemporary concerns over the relations between king and Commons and the health of the commonwealth in general. This particular concept of tyranny had its source in the Tudor histories of Richard III which form the basis of *The ghost of Richard the third*. A humanist discourse of tyranny had found its most important formulation in Sir Thomas More's *History of Richard III* which reworked the classical concept of tyranny based on perverted royal will to incorporate the novel sense of tyranny arising out of a failure of counsel. More set up a series of causal relationships between imperial ambitions, faction, the breakdown of conciliar institutions, and tyranny: 'Ambition sowed the seed of tyranny, which failure of counsel (especially in the king's council) and faction nourished.'[12] To curb princely imperial ambitions, More upheld the role of the Commons and advocated institutional reform of the Privy Chamber.[13] A critical humanist concept of tyranny as resulting from a failure of counsel informed Francis Seager's epistle to the tragedy of Collingbourne which prefaced his tragedy of Richard III. It was not usurpation but the failure of the king and his counsellors to listen to the complaints of the people, rather than sycophants, and to respond by reforming royal policy, that was the cause of his downfall.[14] An emphasis on the contractual bonds between kings and subjects led Seager to extend the *de casibus* theory of kings' accountability to God to a more radical concept of the accountability of kings to the people: '*Vox populi, vox dei.*'[15] *The Encomium of Richard III*, originally written by Sir William Cornwallis the younger, was

[12] T. F. Mayer, 'Tournai and Tyranny: Imperial Kingship and Critical Humanism', *The Historical Journal*, 36 (1991), 258, 271. Dermot Fenlon also reads More's concept of tyranny in terms of failure of counsel ('Thomas More and Tyranny', *Journal of Ecclesiastical History*, 32 (1981), 476).

[13] Mayer, 'Tournai and Tyranny', 273–6.

[14] Andrew Hadfield, *Literature, Politics and National Identity: Reformation to Renaissance* (Cambridge: Cambridge University Press, 1994), 107.

[15] L. B. Campbell (ed.), *The Mirror for Magistrates* (Cambridge: Cambridge University Press, 1938), 359.

reworked in the late 1590s or early 1600 by members of Essex's circle as part of propaganda which preceded the Essex rebellion. Although Cecil was the main political target, arguments drawn from resistance theory were incorporated which take the critical humanist discourse of the evil counsellor in a radical direction, implicating the monarch in court corruption and advocating a purge of the body politic.[16] The political solution posed by this revised *Encomium of Richard III* accorded with the construction of Tacitus within the Essex circle. As the epistle 'A.B. to the Reader' which prefaced Henry Saville's translation of Tacitus states: 'In Galba thou maiest learne, that a good Prince gouerned by euill ministers is as dangerous as if hee were euill himselfe.'[17]

The figure of the evil counsellor can be seen as a marker of a breakdown in the bonds of counsel between the sovereign and the political elite, and the crown and parliament. When Cecil died in 1612, Henry Howard, Earl of Northampton inherited his reputation as the archetypal evil counsellor.[18] Significantly, the Howards had been ennobled under Richard III and sponsored Sir George Buck's defences of Richard written in the early seventeenth century.[19] Northampton was an important

[16] This version was dedicated to Sir Henry Neville by a 'Hen. W.', possibly either Henry Wotton, secretary to Essex, or Essex's close associate Henry Wriothesly, Earl of Southampton. Editors of the text have argued that it was presented to Neville to persuade him to take a more active role in the uprising, including hostile measures against his relative, Cecil, who is extensively attacked in this version as an ambitious tyrant (William Cornwallis (the younger), *The Encomium of Richard III*, ed. A. N. Kincaid (London: Turner and Devereaux, 1977), pp. v–viii, 18–19). Brooke probably had access to the first version of the *Encomium* as Cornwallis dedicated it to Donne in the period that Donne and Brooke were sharing chambers.

[17] Tacitus, *The Ende of Nero and Beginning of Galba. Fower Bookes of the Histories of Cornelius Tacitvs. The Life of Agricola*, trans. Henry Saville (London, 1591), π3r.

[18] Peter Lake, 'Anti-Popery: the structure of a prejudice', in Richard Cust and Ann Hughes (eds.), *Conflict in Early Stuart England: Studies in Religion and Politics 1603–1642* (London and New York: Longman, 1989), 88.

[19] Buck's *History of King Richard the Third* published in 1619, although begun at an earlier date, was dedicated to Thomas Howard, Earl of Suffolk. Buck had previously championed Richard III in his historical pastoral poem, *Daphnis Polystephanos*, published in 1605 for James's coronation, and dedicated to Northampton (Sir George Buck, *The History of King Richard the Third (1619)*, ed. A. N. Kincaid (Gloucester: Alan Sutton, 1979), pp. xiii–iv). His defence of the Howards also informed his censorship of *The Second Maiden's Tragedy*, licensed by him as Master of the Revels on 31 October 1611, which cut passages that would undermine the sanctity of royal authority, while the part of Helvetius, easily identifiable with Northampton, is censored extensively (Anne Lancashire (ed.), *The*

patron of Continental absolutist theory in England and one of James's principal spokesmen in the 1604 and 1610 parliaments.[20] It was widely rumoured in 1614 that he had a hand in plots to undermine parliament and alienate James from the Commons.[21] There is a strong similarity between Brooke's Richard III and Wither's 'man-like *Monster*': the commendatory verse Wither placed before *The ghost of Richard the third* praises the poem as having 'character'd the condition | The life and end, of a meere polititian'. Just as the evil counsellor in *Abuses stript, and whipt* is both the product and the cause of the Jacobean peace, so too Richard III's rise to power is facilitated by a state weakened by peace and internal conflict.

Brooke maintained a Sidneian and 'patriot' political perspective in *The ghost of Richard the third*, combining a political Protestantism and critical reformed humanism. Within this political framework, the weak checks on the imperial and tyrannical ambitions of the monarch were symptomatic of a state corrupted by peace. 'Patriot' politics informed his reworking of the conventional Senecan tyrant feminized by his enslavement to his passions. Rather than lust and political ambition coalescing in the tyrant figure, these destabilizing desires are dispersed, becoming a condition of the court. A sexualized language of tyranny is employed to depict the degeneration of the masculine martial nation into a feminized corruption. The opening satire attacks the contemporary court and courtier as luxurious and effeminate. Strong emphasis is placed on the sexual ambivalence of the court. The courtier is derided for his political and sexual mutability, like '*Cameleons* in your Change of gaudy Sights' and 'wanton *Salmasis*, with Lust impure' (B1v). The reference to the hermaphrodite Salmacis in the context of the anti-court satire works within the early modern language of sodomy, bringing together the sexual, moral, and political, to produce an image of court corruption that implicates James and

Second Maiden's Tragedy (Manchester: Manchester University Press, 1978), 71, 104–13, 276–8).

[20] Linda Levy Peck, 'The Mentality of a Jacobean Grandee', in Linda Levy Peck (ed.), *The Mental World of the Jacobean Court* (Cambridge: Cambridge University Press, 1991), 148–68.

[21] Clayton Roberts and Owen Duncan, 'The Parliamentary Undertaking of 1614', *English Historical Review*, 93 (1978), 491.

his policies.[22] The corruption at the centre infects the nation as
a whole. The luxurious effeminacy of the court is a product of
Jacobean peace and has resulted in a national passivity and the
decline of heroic martial virtues. Whereas Jacobean pane-
gyricists viewed peace as bringing prosperity to the country,
Spenserian writers saw appeasement of Spain in terms of decay
in the countryside and the decline of national energies. The
history of Richard III was offered as a corrective, designed to
'startle' the English nation 'from their sleepe, | Their *sences* in
security fast bound' (B2r). Brooke's support for a Sidneian
political agenda and his 'patriot' opposition to Spanish appeas-
ment informed his idealization of the war which results in the
defeat of Richard. He mystified war as an instrument of divine
providence, 'since Warre (in heauens iust lawes) | Is euer sway'd
by Iustice of the cause'. War becomes the primary means of
purging the nation of corrupting influences for in a state of
war 'not presumption then, but truth preuailes' (K3v). This
apocalyptic view of war carries with it a concept of national
reform through the active role of citizens in a strong military
state.[23]

   Brooke's 'patriot' critique of the Jacobean peace has its most
detailed expression in the description of Edward's court:

> Yet now (secure) *Edward* enioy'd the Crowne,
> Warres sterne *Alarums* heere began to cease;
> Bankes, turn'd to Pillowes; Fields to Beds of Downe,
> And Boystrous Armes, to silken Robes of Peace;
> Warres Counsellor resum'd the *States-mans* Gowne,
> And welcom'd Blisse grew big with all encrease,
>   Wealth follow'd Peace, and Ease succeeded Plenties,
>   And needfull Cates, were turn'd to wanton Dainties.
>
> Now *Mars* his Brood, were chain'd to Womens Lockes;
> Surgeons, and *Leaches*, vs'd for *Venus* Harmes:
> They that erst liu'd by Wounds now thriue by'th Pox,
> For smoothest Pleasure, still ensues rough Armes;
> Whiles I, gryn'd like a Woolfe, lier'd like a Fox,
> To see soft Men, turn'd swine, by *Cyrces* Charmes,

---

[22] Alan Bray, 'Homosexuality and the Signs of Male Friendship in Elizabethan
England', *History Workshop Journal*, 29 (1990), 1–19.
[23] Pocock argues that the concept of the English apocalypse and the doctrine of
the Elect Nation becomes a mode of national and civic consciousness in the early
seventeenth century (*Machiavellian Moment*, 337, 342–7).

And being not shap't for *Loue*, employd my Wits,
In subtile Wiles, t'exceede these hum'rous Fits.   (D3v–4r)

This passage departs from More's *History of Richard III*, where Edward's peaceful reign is described in positive terms, and rather is a close imitation of Richard Niccols's depiction of Edward's reign in his 'Tragicall Life and Death of King Richard the Third' in his 1610 edition of *A Mirror for Magistrates*.[24] Brooke's conscious imitation of Niccols foregrounds the currency of a 'patriot' discourse within the wider phenomenon of Spenserianism. Brooke closely followed Niccols in representing the Jacobean peace seducing the nation into the security of 'easefull pride' in contrast with the 'patriot' ideal of military vigilance. Niccols's 'patriot' politics similarly incorporated a model of active citizenship. His *Londons Artillery*, published in 1616, praised the London citizen and argued for a city militia, drawing on civic humanist writers, such as Machiavelli.[25] Praise is coupled with criticism; the current decline of the nation into a peaceful inertia is equated with the fall of Republican Rome and described in language reminiscent of his tragedy of Richard III. London is where 'Now French-sicke Syrens, and Lewd Circe's dwell' (4). Niccols's revised edition of the *Mirror for Magistrates* was part of a broader Spenserian revival of political poetic traditions in this period. His tragedy of Richard III is included in a section entitled *A Winter Nights Vision* which is headed by an Induction highly critical of James and dominated by the image of a Jacobean winter blasting the English pastoral landscape.[26] He followed the Jacobean *Winter Nights Vision* with *Englands Eliza*: a nationalist Protestant vision which represented Elizabeth's reign as an heroic period of naval supremacy and domestic harmony. Significantly, Cecil was excluded from this vision, while the verse closed without the conventional paean to the peaceful accession of James.[27]

[24] Sir Thomas More, *The History of King Richard III*, in *The Complete Works*, ed. R. S. Sylvester, 15 vols. (New Haven and London: Yale University Press, 1963), ii. 4; Richard Niccols, *A Mirour for Magistrates* (London, 1610), STC 13446, 53–4.
[25] 'euery state or commonwealth should rather imploy and traine vp their owne natiue people in martiall discipline for their defence, then strangers' (*Londons Artillery* (London, 1616), A4r–v).
[26] Niccols, *A Mirour for Magistrates*, 555–60.
[27] Niccols originally dedicated *Winter Nights Vision* to Prince Henry. This dedication was suppressed, possibly because of Niccols's call to the youthful prince to assume an interventionist role in continental politics and thus oppose his father's

Brooke's poem gives this Spenserian 'patriot' discourse a further political dimension. *The ghost of Richard the third* was, in part, a response to the parliamentary conflicts of 1614 and Brooke drew on a critical humanist discourse of tyranny and court corruption to formulate and to talk about the threat from a new 'absolutism'. James I was not an absolutist monarch.[28] However, the Bate's case was seen by contemporaries as setting a dangerous precedent for the introduction of new and troubling absolute powers, and it is in MPs' responses to impositions that James Daly has identified a pejorative 'absolutist' definition of the absolute prerogative.[29] While Brooke recognised the absolute powers of the crown within well-defined spheres, the judges' decision seemed to be defining these powers in an 'absolutist' way to circumvent common law and so infringe upon the subjects' property rights; according to Bodinian absolutism, kings should rule by law and obtain their subjects' consent to taxation, however they could rule outside it according to their discretion, particularly in cases of public necessity.[30]

policy of appeasement (Percy Dobell, 'Note on Sales', *TLS* (22 Sept. 1921), 616; Niccols, *A Mirour for Magistrates* (Bodleian Library, Oxford, Arch A e. 116), 551). The verse to the prince was replaced by a safer, though still militaristic dedication to Charles Howard, Earl of Nottingham recalling his role in Essex's successful Cadiz expedition (*A Mirour for Magistrates* (Bodleian Library, Oxford, Malone 269), 551).

[28] Glenn Burgess has argued that 'Genuine absolutism existed, at best, only on the margins of English political thought' in his *Absolute Monarchy and the Stuart Constitution* (New Haven and London: Yale University Press, 1996), 90, and his *The Politics of the Ancient Constitution: An Introduction to English Political Thought, 1603–1642* (London and Basingstoke: Macmillan, 1992), 139–57. For qualifications and criticism of his arguments, see: Anthony Milton, 'Thomas Wentworth and the political thought of the Personal Rule', in J. F. Merritt (ed.), *The Political World of Thomas Wentworth, Earl of Strafford, 1621–24* (Cambridge: Cambridge University Press, 1996), 133–56; Johann Sommerville, 'English and European Political Ideas in the Early Seventeenth Century: Revisionism and the Case of Absolutism', *Journal of British Studies*, 15 (1996), 168–94.

[29] *Proceedings in Parliament 1614*, 95. James Daly, 'The Idea of Absolute Monarchy in Seventeenth-Century England', *The Historical Journal*, 21 (1978), 232–3.

[30] Sommerville discusses the use of 'absolutist' arguments by the chief baron of the Exchequer, Sir Thomas Fleming, in the Bate's case ('English and European Political Ideas', 191). Burgess points out that the crown viewed impositions as beyond the scope of the common law and 'within the sphere of absolute power because they involve *international* commerce' (*Absolute Monarchy*, 83). However, Brooke and his fellow MPs did not view impositions in this way. For their general suspicion of the crown's case on impositions, see: Croft, 'Fresh Light on Bate's Case', 523–39.

In *The ghost of Richard the third*, Richard boasts that he can manipulate the law, 'a mute female judge', for his own politic ends, to 'make a foot-stoole on't for me to rise' (E2r). MPs' unease was compounded by the way that James spoke about his royal powers. 'In the 1610 speech', as Glenn Burgess points out, 'there was an unresolved tension between the claim that the royal office was defined by law (though not subject to it) and the claim that the king possessed a mysterious absolute authority that was essentially undefinable.'[31] This vagueness worried a number of MPs and generated disquiet about the direction of royal policy. Brooke's opposition to the definition of impositions as part of absolute prerogative operates within a different register or genre to his tyrant tragedy. However, the complex humanist language of tyranny did enable him to bring impositions and other areas of political and cultural concern into a critical proximity.[32]

Brooke's parliamentary activities and political views need to be viewed in the context of his involvement with the Inns of Court tavern 'club', the 'Sireniacs', which also included a number of his close colleagues in the 1610 and 1614 parliaments. These gatherings were occasions for political discussion, for 'talking politics'.[33] Thomas Coryate's letters from Ajmere, India, published in 1615, were addressed to 'the right worship-full Fraternitie of Sireniacal Gentlemen, that meet the first Fridaie of euery Moneth, at the signe of the Mere-maide in Bread Street in London', and this company appears to coincide with those who attended a 'Convivium Philosophicum' in Coryate's honour at the Mitre Tavern sometime between 1609 and 1612.[34] The core of the 'Sireniacs' appears to have been

[31] Burgess, *Politics of the Ancient Constitution*, 157.

[32] Norbrook reads Brooke's 'sententious denunciation of tyranny' as an expression of 'his fears that tyranny might become a reality in England in parliament' (*Poetry and Politics in the English Renaissance*, 211).

[33] Annabel Patterson, 'All Donne', in Elizabeth D. Harvey and Katherine E. Maus (eds.), *Soliciting Interpretation: Literary Theory and Seventeenth-Century English Poetry* (Chicago and London: Chicago University Press, 1990), 37–67; Pascal Brioist, 'Que de choses avons nous vues et vécues à la Sirène', *Histoire et Civilisation*, 4 (1991), 89–132.

[34] Shapiro points out that this was not a professional literary society but composed of MPs, members of Prince Henry's household, barristers, and business men ('The "Mermaid Club"', *Modern Language Review*, 45 (1950), 7–10). Members of the 'Sireniacs' included Sir Edward Phelips and his son Robert, Brooke, Donne, Martin, Hoskyns, Holland, Jones, William Hakewill, Ben Jonson, Sir Robert

John Donne, Richard Martin, John Hoskyns, William Hakewill, Christopher Brooke, and Robert Phelips and his father, Sir
Edward, who was a patron of the company. Members were
almost exclusively Lincoln's Inn or Middle Temple men.[35]
Brooke's close lifelong friendship with Donne began when
Donne entered Lincoln's Inn in 1592.[36] The Inns of Court were
the point of social exchange between the Spenserians and the
'Sireniacs' and Brooke seems to have been able to move between
these two communities in a way which gives a view to the
complex social dynamics of London political culture.

The legal and rhetorical culture of the Inns provided a train-
ing ground for a parliamentary career. Finkelpearl suggests that
Cotton, Thomas Bond, George Garrard, Dr Mocket, Robert Bing, and Lawrence
Whitaker. Baird Whitlocke's research into the composition of the 'Sireniacs' indicates its fluidity. To Shapiro's list he adds George Speake, Samuel Purchas, and
William Stansby, and places Coryate, Martin, Hoskins, Brooke, Holland, Jones, the
Phelips family, Donne, Jonson, Hakewill, Garrard, and Bond in the central group,
while the core of the group consisted of Hoskyns, Martin, and the Phelips family
(*John Hoskyns, Serjeant-at-Law* (Washington: University Press of America, 1982),
388–91). R. C. Bald places Brooke's fellow Spenserian poet John Davies of Hereford
at the edge of this circle (*John Donne: A Life* (Oxford: Clarendon Press, 1970),
192).

[35] Brioist, 'Que de choses avons nous vues et véçues à la Sirène', 112–17. The
links between Lincoln's Inn and the Middle Temple were strong, they jointly produced court entertainments, such as George Chapman's *Memorable Maske* for the
marriage of Frederick, Elector Palatine, and Princess Elizabeth, and the entertainment at the barriers to honour Prince Charles's creation as Prince of Wales in 1616.
The Sireniacs involved in the production of the *Memorable Maske* were Sir Edward
Phelips, who sponsored the masque, Inigo Jones, the designer, Martin and Hakewill
who contributed funds, and Brooke who was in charge of expenditure (T. Orbison
(ed.), *The Middle Temple Documents Relating to George Chapman's 'The
Memorable Masque'*, The Malone Society (Oxford: Oxford University Press, 1983),
xii. 4). For Prince Charles's Barriers, Martin and Hoskins organized the armour on
behalf of the Middle Temple, while Brooke and Hakewill acted as senior agents for
Lincoln's Inn (Shapiro, 'Mermaid Club', 14).

[36] Brooke and another Yorkshireman, Edward Loftus, acted as sureties for
Donne. Brooke and Donne shared chambers in the early 1590s and it is in this
period that Donne dedicates 'The Storm', which relates to Donne's service under the
Earl of Essex, and an epistle to Brooke. Christopher and his brother Samuel were
present at Donne's secret marriage to Anne More in 1601; Samuel conducted the
ceremony and Christopher acted as witness. For his part in the marriage,
Christopher was imprisoned in the Marshalsea (Bald, *John Donne*, 53, 55, 62, 128,
135–6). They remained close friends until Brooke's death. His will bequeathed a
painting of Mary Magdalen and an Italian painting of Apollo and the Muses to 'my
deere ancient and worthie freind D [o]c [t]or Dunn the Deane Pawles' (Christopher
Brooke, *The Poems*, ed. A. B. Grosart, *Miscellanies of the Fuller Worthies' Library*,
4 vols. (1872–6), iv. 23). Brooke also had some type of connection with Donne's
patron in this period, Sir Thomas Egerton, as he was present at the funeral of his
son.

a grounding in common law together with the Inn's tradition of liberty of speech and political freedom fostered the political radicalism of Inns of Court men, such as John Hoskyns. Norbrook has also drawn attention to Hoskyn's political use of classical rhetoric to oppose the crown over impositions and to defend the civic interests of parliament.[37] Equally importantly, the Inns of Court fostered a culture of collaboration and conviviality that provided the basis of a working relationship in parliament. Pascal Brioist has suggested that the 'Sireniacs' met on Fridays when parliament was in session and that these meetings provided a forum where parliamentary speeches were informally rehearsed.[38] The 'Sireniacs', Brooke, Hoskyns, Martin, Hakewill, and Phelips, father and son, formed a loose political alliance in James's early parliaments. All were members of the 1604 to 1610 parliaments and, apart from Martin, the 1614 'addled' parliament. Donne also sat in the 1614 parliament for Taunton, Devon, through the patronage of Sir Edward.[39] There appears to have been a working relationship between Brooke, Robert Phelips, Martin, and Hoskyns in these parliaments: they often appeared on the same committees and supported each other in speeches. Martin did not have a seat in the 1614 sessions, but he did appear in the Commons on behalf of the Virginia Company. Brooke forwarded the motion that the business of the Virginia Company be treated and when Martin was censured for presuming to lecture the House on the importance of the colony, Brooke and Phelips spoke in his defence.[40] Although this group did not operate in these parlia-

[37] Philip Finkelpearl, *John Marston of the Inner Temple: An Elizabethan Dramatist and his Social Settling* (Cambridge, Mass.: Harvard University Press, 1969), 66–8, 79–80; David Norbrook, 'Rhetoric, Ideology and the Elizabethan World Picture', in Peter Mack (ed.), *Renaissance Rhetoric* (London and Basingstoke: Macmillan, 1994), 147–54.

[38] Brioist, 'Que de choses avons nous vues et vécues à la Sirène', 125. The interests that held the 'Sireniacs' together, as Shapiro has recognized, were not primarily cultural or literary but rather political ('Mermaid Club', 10; Patterson, 'All Donne', 42).

[39] Bald, *John Donne*, 286. Brioist suggests that Martin may have acted as a parliamentary patron, appointing his 'Sireniac' associates to sub-committees in his frequent role as moderator of the Committee of the whole House ('Que de choses avons nous vues et vécues à la Sirène', 125).

[40] *Proceedings in Parliament 1614*, 257, 276; Whitlock, *John Hoskyns*, 446. Brooke and a number of the 'Sireniacs' had close ties with the Virginia Company. I am grateful to Julie Hanson for this information.

mentary sessions according to a coherent political agenda in the sense of a modern 'party', they do appear to have held common political principles which included opposition to royal control over impositions.[41]

Conviviality was a dominant theme in the writings of the 'Sireniacs'. The verses of Thomas Coryate dramatized the meetings of a distinct group of like-minded men, brought together by a mutual interest in wit, wine, and politics. Friendship in these writings was defined as the medium of writing and political life. For Ben Jonson, who was on the margins of the 'Sireniac' inner circle, friendship in his 'Inviting a Friend to Supper' constituted a semi-private sphere where like-minded men could air political views that were dangerous to voice in public. Jonson, in the spirit of friendship, placed a verse before Brooke's *The ghost of Richard the third*—he had been commissioned to write a play, *Richard Crookback*, a year after the Essex revolt, that was probably part of a satiric campaign against Cecil.[42] The writings produced within and around the 'Sireniacs' constitute a fluid discursive sphere, a space of dialogue and debate. When 'talking politics' the 'Sireniacs' employed a range of forms from parliamentary speeches to Brooke's poetic tragedy, *The ghost of Richard the third*, the satires and paradoxes of Donne, and the witty outpourings of Coryate. Political discourse in this period, as recent studies argue, was not confined to the realms of high political theory but often took the form of satires, libels, and gossip.[43] The liveliness of this political exchange and circulation of texts is suggested by the 'Sireniac' 1606 political and scatalogical satire 'The Censure of a Parliament Fart'. This highly popular satire was a group effort. In a manuscript copy, Hoskyns, Inigo Jones, Martin, and Brooke are named as co-authors and the 1606 parliamentary session included a number of friends of Brooke, Martin, and Hoskyns—Henry Goodyere, Martin's brother Henry, John Harington, Sir Edward Phelips, Ingram, and Hakewill. This type of collaboration continued as

[41] Menna Prestwich has focused on the political inconsistencies in the careers of this group, claiming that they were allied primarily by personal ambition rather than common political principles (*Cranfield: Politics and Profit under the Early Stuarts* (Oxford: Clarendon Press, 1966), 104, 141–6). However, Whitlock has questioned her argument due the inaccuracy of some of the supporting evidence (*John Hoskyns*, 422 n. 35).

[42] Croft, 'The Reputation of Robert Cecil', 56.

[43] Bellany, 'Raylinge Rymes and Vaunting Verse', 285–310.

MPs of subsequent parliaments added to the satire which may have led to the questioning of Hoskyns by the Privy Council in the 1620s.[44] Jonson playfully praised the wit of these poet-MPs in *The Alchemist* (1610).[45] In the verse 'Kit Brooke' censures the fart because it contravenes parliamentary procedure. The authors of 'The Censure of a Parliament Fart', possibly including Brooke himself, affectionately poked fun at his lawyer-like concern with procedure and precedent, however the joke also had a topical, political edge particularly when viewed in terms of the contemporary conflict between the crown and the Commons over the authority of parliament.

Impositions were the primary site of conflict between the crown and the Commons in the 1610 and 1614 parliamentary sessions. The Commons presented two petitions of grievances during the 1610 parliament in which they denied the legality of the new impositions and called for their abolition. Salisbury's defence of the argument that impositions on trade were part of the absolute prerogative did not convince the Lower House.[46] The conflict foregrounded the need to define and to clarify the constitutional relationship between king and parliament. James was careful to acknowledge common law, but he was intellectually indebted to Bodinian theories of sovereignty. From his point of view, parliamentary privileges had their source in the crown and were thus dependent on his good grace. Faced with this response, the Commons attempted to educate their Scottish king in English politics by setting out the traditional rights and privileges of the Commons.[47] MPs opposing impositions in the tumultuous 1610 and 1614 parliaments were not anti-monarchical. Rather, as Jansson has argued, they were concerned to secure mutually compatible and acceptable definitions of the jurisdiction of the crown and the Commons.[48] This need to clarify the relationship between the crown and the

[44] Whitlock, *John Hoskyns*, 284–5. British Library, Additional MSS 4149, 23,299 and 23,339, and MS Stowe 962.

[45] Jonson, *The Alchemist*, II. i. 101–3.

[46] Croft, 'Fresh Light on Bate's Case', 524.

[47] Johann Sommerville, 'James I and the Divine Right of Kings: English Politics and Continental Theory', and Jenny Wormald, 'James VI and I, *Basilikon Doron* and the *Trew Law of Free Monarchies*: The Scottish Context and the English Translation', both in Linda Levy Peck, *The Mental World of the Jacobean Court* (Cambridge: Cambridge University Press, 1991), 55–70, 36–54.

[48] *Proceedings in Parliament 1614*, xix–xx.

Commons suggests that if there was a political consensus, it was extremely fragile.

Brooke in the 1610 and 1614 parliaments was concerned with the questions of procedure and precedent that, according to Jansson, began to define the institutional identity of parliament.[49] He affirmed the authority of parliament within the framework of a balanced constitution and carefully maintained the principle of an indissoluble link between the royal prerogative and the liberties of the subject.[50] The difficulty with the theory of a balanced constitution is foregrounded, however, when there is a conflict between the royal prerogative and the subjects' rights: which takes precedence, the royal prerogative or the liberties of the subject?[51] This conflict became apparent in the debates over impositions. By the end of the 1610 parliamentary sessions, Brooke found it increasingly difficult to maintain the language of balance and sharply responded to the king's criticism of the Common's delay over supply:

> The King told us that the wants of the King must be necessarily relieve(d). If the King make this proposal that howsoever the King will want. If the King will make periods as did thorny Minotaur, no reason that such wants and the like should be relieved.[52]

Although the report from this diarist is very compressed, the minotaur analogy would seem to invoke the political dangers posed by tyrants to the liberty and property of the subject. In the impositions debates in the 1614 sessions, he warned that 'If the King may impose by his absolute power, then no Man certain what he has, for it shall be subject to the King's pleasure.'[53] The minotaur analogy is clarified: if the king is able

[49] One of the recorders of Brooke's speeches in the 1610 Parliament was probably a law student. His entries in his parliamentary diary note points of procedure and privilege suggesting an interest in legal and constitutional issues. While this interest may give his report a certain bias, his detailed account of Brooke's speeches is suggestive. See Elizabeth Read Foster's discussion of the diarist Add. 48119 in *Proceedings in Parliament 1610* (2 vols. (New Haven and London: Yale University Press, 1966), i. p. xlviii).

[50] *Proceedings in Parliament 1610*, ii. 94. For further discussion of Brooke's activities in these parliaments see my ' "Talking Politics": Tyranny, parliament, and Christopher Brooke's *The ghost of Richard the third* (1614)', *The Historical Journal*, 41 (1998), 105–7.

[51] Johann Sommerville, *Politics and Ideology in England, 1603–1640* (London and New York: Longman, 1986), 135.

[52] *Proceedings in Parliament 1610*, ii. 394–5.

[53] *Proceedings in Parliament 1614*, 95.

to impose by his absolute power outside parliament and tax without his subjects' consent then the subjects' liberty and property will be placed in jeopardy. Daly has argued that the widespread use of absolute power as a 'synonym for tyranny' was a product of the 1640s.[54] In the imposition debates, however, 'absolute' power does take on some of the negative connotations associated with this later period, so that the conceptual distance between political 'absolutism' and an older concept of tyranny is narrowed and, at the same time, a language of tyranny is made available for addressing contemporary constitutional and ideological issues raised in parliamentary debates.

The 1610 and 1614 parliamentary debates engaged MPs, such as Brooke, in discussions of political theory. These debates had a lasting impact on successive parliaments and on individuals at home and abroad.[55] A number of the 'Sireniacs' took up these political debates in their writings in a manner which strongly suggests that they were well aware of the constitutional issues and their wider ideological ramifications. Patterson has read the uneasy balance between the prerogative powers of the sovereign and the liberties of the subject in John Donne's paradox *Biathanatos* in this context.[56] His friend, Brooke, responded to political 'absolutism' in *The ghost of Richard the third* through a humanist discourse of tyranny. A suspicion of mystifications of the royal prerogative is suggested by the way that the poem discredited political arguments drawn from an analogy which underpinned divine right theory by placing them in the mouth of a tyrant as part of his justification of the murder of the princes in the tower:[57]

[54] Daly, 'Idea of Absolute Monarchy', 235.

[55] Christopher Thompson points to MPs citing 1614 breaches of parliamentary privileges during the 1621 parliament (*The Debate on Freedom of Speech in the House of Commons in February 1621* (Essex: The Orchard Press, 1985), 15–16). Contemporary ambassadorial reports indicate that 'European rulers were concerned about the implication of two issues debated in England, notably those that touched on monarchy and the prerogative powers of the crown, and the traditional parliamentary control of subsidy' (Jansson, *Proceedings in Parliament 1614*, p. xiv). For a counter-'revisionist' study of this parliament, see: Conrad Russell, *The Addled Parliament of 1614: The Limits of Revision* (University of Reading, 1992).

[56] Annabel Patterson, 'All Donne', 42–60, 'John Donne, Kingsman?', in Peck, *Mental world of the Jacobean court*, 251–72, and *Reading between the lines* (London: Routledge, 1993), 184–7.

[57] See Norbrook's discussion of John Hoskyns' scepticism towards political arguments drawn from analogies in his 'Rhetoric, Ideology and the Elizabethan World Picture' (147–54).

I thought my selfe not absolute instated,
Nor could make free vse of my purchast gaine,
Till without *Riuall*, I might shew my brow,
One King in state, one Sunne the Heauens allow.   (G3r)

This is also the only point in the text where Brooke used the term 'absolute' in a political form. Here, 'absolute' in the neutral sense of independence of external powers, or perfect rule, blends with a perjorative sense of absolute power as arbitrary, beyond the bounds of law and conscience. Absolute power governed by the king's 'sensual will' is contrasted with the rule of reason in an extensive stoic debate:

Reason obiects (to countercheck my pride)
How *Kings* are *natures Idols*, made of clay:
And though they were by mortalls *Deifide*,
Yet in the Graue, Beggers as good as they:
The *Sence* was slauish, and for *man* no *guide*,
That *Reason* should Command and *Will*, obey:
   And that with all worlds pompe and *Fortunes good*,
   We still were nothing else but *flesh* and *blood*.   (E2v)

The stoic dichotomy between reason and will provides the basis for a humanist critique of the divinity of kings which is revealed by the power of reason to be an idolatrous innovation.[58] It is reason's 'Powre onely, could distinguish things; | Shew what was *Reall*, what but Forme, and Fashion' (E2v). The emphasis is placed on individual agency rather than on royal supremacy: '*Reason* infer'd, *Men* in effect were *Kings*, | If they could rule themselues, and conquer *Passion*' (E2v). The question is then posed, to be rejected by the tyrant-king: 'If *Reason* rul'd Men, then what need of *Kings*?' (E3v). The poem subjects the mystification of kingship to a humanist critique which privileges an ideal of citizenship.[59]

[58] The Stoic republican La Boetie in his condemnation of tyranny also attacked the outward show of monarchy as idolatrous, a drug to make the people submissive (Peter Burke, 'Tacitism, Scepticism, and Reason of State', in J. H. Burns and Mark Goldie (eds.), *The Cambridge History of Political Thought* (Cambridge: Cambridge University Press, 1991) 491–2).

[59] Classical Republicans during the mid-seventeenth century viewed politics in terms of a conflict between reason (associated with the rule of law and popular sovereignty) and will (identified with the rule of men and hereditary monarchy) (Blair Worden, 'Classical Republicanism and the Puritan Revolution', in Hugh Lloyd-Jones *et al* (eds.), *History and Imagination: Essays in honour of H.R. Trevor-Roper* (London, 1981), 193–5).

The stoicism that structures this section of the poem is, in many ways, highly conventional. Yet, through its vision of the rule of reason overturned by a tyranny of the will that panders to kings' passions, Brooke does seem to be making a similar point to his contemporaries who complained that channels of counsel were being abused by apologists for absolutism who sought to undermine parliament and find favour with the king through their politic mystification of the royal prerogative. Richard Martin vilified members of the higher clergy for preaching absolutist theories in support of the crown's position on impositions, and warned his fellow MPs of the dangers posed to parliament from those clerics who 'by such base means as the selling the liberty of the people and the laws would seek to prefer themselves'.[60] Brooke was among those MPs in the 1614 parliament who condemned the Bishop of Lincoln's speech that asserted the supremacy of the king and the bishops and denied the authority of parliament to counsel the king on matters of policy.[61] The political dangers posed by the misuse of counsel are condensed in the apologist for tyranny, Dr Shaw, and the accompanying satiric complaint against members of the clergy who exploit their religious position for politic ends:

> Such *Doctors* were (I doe not say there are)
> Whose Breaths scall'd *Heauen*; Harts, clog'd with worlds desire,
> That without Scruple, touch of Shame, or Feare,
> Would wrest the Scripture, to make Truth a Lyer:
> And these like Mercenarie Men appeare;
> That loue the *Word*, for Wealth; the worke, for Hyre;
>   Whose tutor'd tongues, to take off Great Mens Blames,
>   Set stronger Seales on theirs, and their owne Shames.   (F2v)

Such a passage participated in the parliamentary attacks on apologists for absolutism, and, at the same time, added a further dimension to the figure of the evil counsellor in the writings of his fellow Spenserians in that court corruption takes on 'absolutist' connotations associated with the abuse of counsel.

Brooke's *The ghost of Richard the third* developed the Spenserian theme of corruption to produce a language for

---

[60] *Proceedings in Parliament 1610*, ii. 328–9.

[61] *Proceedings in Parliament 1614*, 343–4, 353, 365–6, 368. Daly argues that the clergy's 'greater emphasis on royal authority' prepared 'the way for the later pejorative evolution of the term absolutism' ('Idea of Absolute Monarchy', 234).

addressing a range of contemporary issues from impositions to appeasement of Spain.[62] In Tacitean fashion, the poem stresses the way that court corruption fosters the formation of factions to produce a type of bloodless civil war within the state:

> I saw in *Friendship*, *Vertue* best did suite;
> In Factions, *Powre*, and the most pollitick Head,
> Since it can only plot, not execute;
> With meaner Fortunes, best was seconded;
> Some *Wise*, some *Valiant*, some of base repute;
> And all like seuerall *simple* tempered;
>> Which well prepar'd by a proiecting Braine,
>> Giue *Greatnesse* strength, Ambitious hopes maintaine.   (C3v)

A weak monarchical state dominated by factional self-interest is open to subversion from within and without. Richard in the guise of Machiavellian courtier conspires:

>> To get close Friends about a *Forraine Prince*,
>> To further home designes with Secresie,
>> And (to relieue the priuate *State* Expense)
>> Make publique Purses fill the Treasurie.   (C4r)

A new element was added to the history of Richard III—the secret collaboration of the Machiavellian politician with foreign powers to undermine the state. This passage moves from a general satire on court corruption to a seemingly specific allusion related to contemporary fears that influential courtiers, particularly Northampton and his clients, were collaborating with Spain and so dangerously influencing Jacobean foreign policy. A Tacitean perspective on court politics coloured and reinforced fears of Spanish plots and pensioners at court.[63] Brooke controversially coupled this threat from foreign influences with the highly topical issue of supply derived from public taxation, that is, impositions, as an example of domestic tyranny. Smuts has argued that this type of political critique did

[62] Peck argues that the rhetoric of corruption provided a language of opposition in the period: *Court Patronage and Corruption*, 203, 207–8.

[63] Albert J. Loomie (ed.), *Spain and the Jacobean Catholics*, 2 vols. (Catholic Records Society, 1973), ii. pp. xiv–xvii; L. B. Wright, 'Propaganda against James I's "Appeasement" of Spain', *Huntington Library Quarterly*, 6 (1943), 149; Malcolm Smuts, 'Court-Centred Politics and Roman Historians', in Kevin Sharpe and Peter Lake (eds.), *Culture and Politics in Early Stuart England* (Basingstoke and London: Macmillan, 1994), 36–7.

not emerge until the 1620s with the pamphlets of Thomas Scott where 'mistrust of luxury and corruption caused by peace fused with a conspiratorial interpretation of Spanish politics and acute mistrust of English courtiers in a powerful indictment of James's policies'.[64] A similar fusion of anti-Spanish propaganda and the language of court corruption was active a decade earlier in Spenserian writing and responded to a similar crisis of confidence in James's government. Pauline Croft has argued that the parliamentary conflicts of the 1620s 'were fore-shadowed in the interlocking financial, legal and political issues' raised by impositions.[65] Impositions not only raised constitu-tional issues but also brought together anti-Spanish feeling and the corruption of public office. The introduction of impositions in 1604 was part of the peace negotiations with Spain. The Levant Company, which controlled the lucrative currant trade that was the main target of impositions, was firmly anti-Spanish and had strong Puritan links. Salisbury, who engineered the introduction of impositions had financial interests in the taxes as did the lord chamberlain, Suffolk.[66] Brooke's framing of the abuse of taxes in *The ghost of Richard the third* suggests an awareness of the range of issues raised by impositions.

Criticism of royal policy was compatible with the rhetoric of balanced constitution. Brooke's *Ghost of Richard the third* and his parliamentary activity do not support a straightforward ideological and political polarization between crown and oppo-sition. *The ghost of Richard the third* closed with a panegyric to James I:

> Now *Englands Chaos* was reduc't to order
> By *God-like Richmond*; whose successiue *Stems*,
> The hand of Time hath Branch't in curious Border,
> Vnto the mem'rie of thrice Royall *Iames*:
> An *Angels Trumpe* be his true Fames *Recorder*,
> And may that *Brittaine Phoebus* from his Beames
>   In Glories light his influence extend,
>   His Off-spring, countles; *Peace*, nor Date, nor End.   (L3r)

The continuity established between '*God-like Richmond*' and '*Royall James*' was founded on an idealized model of the

---

[64] Smuts, 'Court-Centred Politics and Roman Historians', 37.

[65] Croft, 'Fresh Light on the Bate's Case', 539.

[66] Ibid. 524–9.

godly judicious king. Yet this praise of 'Royall *James*' existed uneasily alongside the extensive Tacitean and topical satire on court corruption and weak monarchical government and the demystification of divine right forms of sovereignty in the poem. The critical tension between panegyric and satire opened a gap between the ideal and perceived reality which functioned, in the words of Francis Seager in the preface to his tragedy of Richard III, to act as a 'warning for ever, to al in authoritye to beware howe they vsurpe or abuse theyr offices'.[67] *The ghost of Richard the third* is a reformist text. It was highly critical of royal policy and called for reform along 'patriot' lines while maintaining the principle of the mutual obligations binding king and subject. However, although Brooke may have drawn on similar political phrases to apologists for royal policy in the 1610 and 1614 parliaments, this does not necessarily imply they were speaking the same political language. Peter Lake and Kevin Sharpe have argued for the 'relative instability' and fluidity of political discourses in early modern England that would enable, for example, the language of balanced constitution to be deployed to authorize *and* to criticize royal policy. Linda Levy Peck similarly views early Stuart politics in terms of a spectrum of political theories in which contractual shades into balanced constitution which in turn shades into absolutist.[68] The use of a language of a balanced constitution therefore does not preclude the articulation of political differences.

Brooke's *The ghost of Richard the third* renewed the didactic mode of the *Mirror for Magistrates* to provide its own piece of advice in 1614. The advice to this prince by his loyal subject was to listen to the counsel of worthy 'patriots' and his parliaments rather than flattering and dangerous sycophants. Yet this balance between advice and criticism was simultaneously placed under pressure in Brooke's poem, and in the writings of other Spenserians, and became increasingly difficult to maintain. The failure of James to listen to counsel was a continuing concern of these poets throughout his reign and came into sharp focus once more in 1621 when parliament was finally recalled. This

---

[67] *The Mirror for Magistrates*, 359.

[68] Peter Lake and Kevin Sharpe, 'Introduction', in *Culture and Politics in Early Stuart England* (Basingstoke and London: Macmillan, 1994), 14; Peck, *Court Patronage and Corruption*, 208. Sommerville insists on distinct, competing political ideologies in the period in his *Politics and Ideology in England*.

emphasis on counsel in the writings of Brooke and his contemporaries transformed the subject into a citizen. A civic self-image took shape in their work through a range of intersecting discourses deriving from the doctrines of the ancient constitution, classical humanism, political Protestantism, and early Tudor and Elizabethan traditions of didactic literature. Civic consciousness, particularly in the case of Brooke and his fellow 'Sireniac'-MPs, was also formed through parliament which provided practical political experience and a sense of communal and institutional identity. The activity of Brooke and his fellow Spenserians and 'Sireniacs' would suggest that parliament was taking on a distinct political and cultural identity, providing a focus for political and literary activity, and a forum for debate in early Stuart England.

3

'Thus deare Britannia will I sing of thee': William Browne, *Britannia's Pastorals*

What neede I tune the Swaines of *Thessalie*?
Or, bootlesse, adde to them of *Arcadie*?
No: faire *Arcadia* cannot be compleater,
My praise may lessen, but not make thee greater.
My *Muse* for loftie pitches shall not rome,
But onely pipen of her natiue home:
And to the Swaines, Loue rurall Minstralsie,
Thus deare BRITANNIA will I sing of thee.[1]

GREG has described *Britannia's Pastorals* as 'the longest and most ambitious poem ever composed on a pastoral theme'.[2] To set yourself the task of representing Britain in the early Stuart period was to enter into debates over the identity of the nation. The landscape of Britain was the site of competing representations as different communities struggled for the authority to represent the land and its history.[3] The heated debates over sovereignty during the years of union were symptomatic of a heightened national self-consciousness.[4] The 'union of the crowns' brought about by the accession of James defined empire in dynastic terms and reinvigorated a Virgilian Augustanism. However, his pursuit of an Anglo-Spanish alliance increasingly suggested to 'patriots' a reluctance to embrace an older Reformation and apocalyptic form of empire that defined

[1] William Browne, *Britannia's Pastorals* (London, 1613), STC 3914, 2.
[2] W. W. Greg, *Pastoral Poetry and Pastoral Drama: A Literary Inquiry with Special Reference to the Pre-Restoration Stage in England* (London: A. H. Bullen, 1906), 131. See also Leah Jonas, *The Divine Science, the Aesthetic of some Representative Seventeenth-Century English Poets* (New York: Columbia University Press, 1940), 89–91.
[3] Paul Hammond, 'The Language of the Hive: Political Discourse in Seventeenth-Century England', *The Seventeenth-Century*, 9 (1994), 119–33.
[4] Bruce Galloway, *The Union of England and Scotland, 1603–1608* (Edinburgh: John Donald, 1986), 165–7.

English sovereignty in terms of independence from Rome. In Book I, Browne sought to reconcile James with this Protestant vision of empire, however in Book II he begins to dismantle the form of the epic and to look to alternative sources of authority in the land, national communities, and the poetic self.

Nationalist and humanist energies in the early seventeenth century were increasingly orientated towards the representation of the land, often finding their expression in antiquarian projects.[5] The very title of Browne's pastoral epic recalls Camden's *Britannia* (1586) and aligns the poem with the antiquarian impulse to map the country and the nation. Drayton's ambitious chorographical poem, *Poly-Olbion*, is an expression of these energies and similarly provided a precedent for Browne's pastoral epic. The first instalment of *Poly-Olbion* had been published in 1612, the year before Book I of *Britannia's Pastorals*, and both Drayton and Selden, who provided the historical notes to *Poly-Olbion*, contributed commendatory verse to Browne's poem. Like Drayton's *Poly-Olbion*, Browne's *Britannia's Pastorals* is polyphonic and polymorphous, exploring genres and narrative strategies that would enable the representation of the 'country'.

Books I and II of *Britannia's Pastorals* are very different and these differences respond to a changing political culture. Browne's response to the Jacobean court was not one of straightforward opposition. Like the other Spenserian poets, he used genres as political languages and Book I, published in 1613, drew on the resources of pastoral tragicomedy to imagine a consensus between 'court' and 'country' and to celebrate James as the poet's king in the wake of the Gunpowder Plot. 1614 was a turning point for Browne. The experience of producing *The Shepheards Pipe* and the process of collaborating with Brooke and Wither served as a type of political education and with this volume he commited himself to an oppositional poetic. Book II of *Britannia's Pastorals* was published in 1616 in the wake of the trial of the Earl and Countess of Somerset for the murder of Sir Thomas Overbury, which symbolized the degeneration of the court into moral and political corruption,

---

[5] Melanie Hansen, 'Identity and Ownership: Narratives of the Land in the English Renaissance', in William Zunder and Suzanne Trill (eds.), *Writing and the English Renaissance* (London and New York: Longman, 1996), 87–105.

and the poem's vision of the landscape of Britannia is dominated by satire and a romance instability. The Protestant humanist poet wanders in a Spenserian exile and looks to the 'country' for alternative sites of poetic validation.

<h2 style="text-align:center">I BRITANNIA'S PASTORALS, 1613:
ARCADIA REFORMED</h2>

Book I of *Britannia's Pastorals* seeks to translate the newly fashionable dramatic mode, tragicomedy, into a poetic form. The first three·songs of Book I are 'pure pastoral drama' and owe much to Tasso's *Aminta,* Guarini's *Il Pastor Fido,* and Fletcher's *The Faithful Shepherdess.*[6] These Songs trace the loves and misfortunes of shepherds and shepherdesses, the stock-in-trade of pastoral tragicomedy. The shepherdess Marina, spurned by the faithless Celadine, first attempts suicide but is rescued to find briefly her true love in the shepherd Doridon before being abducted by a lustful swain—Marina does not return until the next Book when she is abandoned on the shores of Anglesea only to be captured by Limos (Famine) and imprisoned until the last Song of Book II. Doridon is wounded in the attack and while his physical wound heals, his heart's wound does not and he wanders melancholy, meeting with the good shepherd Redmond and his mistress Fida and her pet deer. Redmond and Fida are also separated in the fourth Song and Redmond and Doridon will wander throughout Book II searching for their mistresses—Fida finally briefly reappears in the last Song.

To mark his entrance into the literary world, Browne may have wanted to display his skill in a new form, particularly one that privileged virtuousity, but tragicomedy also provided a model for organizing diverse genres and styles and, just as importantly, for accommodating different ideological positions. The formal and ideological parameters of tragicomedy in the early seventeenth century resist fixed definition, as recent studies of the form illustrate.[7] At one end of the political

---

[6] For details of Browne's borrowings from these plays, see: Joan Grundy, 'William Browne and the Italian Pastoral', *Review of English Studies,* 16 (1953), 305–16.
[7] Gordon McMullan and Jonathan Hope 'The Politics of Tragicomedy,

spectrum, tragicomedy has been aligned with Stuart 'absolutism', or from a different angle with the Stuart dynasty, while
at the other end it has been identified with individual agency,
and the accommodation between dramatic liberty and formal
genres within tragicomedy likened to a mixed or limited
monarchy,[8] Tragicomedy, it seems, had a pervasive, modal
influence on literature in this period because it was not tied to a
particular political structure and instead had a relative ideological openness.[9] Guarinian tragicomedy licenses generic
trespassing; the constantly shifting generic perspectives reveal
the limitations of earlier forms and open new conceptual possibilities.[10] Since tragicomedy is adept at mediating between
different systems, it is particularly suited to moments of
historical transition. Tragicomedy enabled Browne to respond
to the accession of James I as a Spenserian poet and, in
particular, to negotiate between the nationalist and ethical
imperatives of an 'Elizabethan' reformed humanism and the
new Stuart cultural forms.[11]

Italianate pastoral tragicomedy, a distinct genre within the
broader mode of tragicomedy, had been invested with an
ethical function in the Renaissance that made it attractive to a

1610–50', in McMullan and Hope (eds.), *The Politics of Tragicomedy: Shakespeare
and After* (London: Routledge, 1992), 7.

  [8] Leah Marcus, *Puzzling Shakespeare: Local Reading and its Discontents*
(Berkeley, Los Angeles, and London: University of California Press, 1988), 141–2;
Frances Yates, *Shakespeare's Last Plays: A New Approach* (London: Routledge and
Kegan Paul, 1975), 17–84; David Bergeron, *Shakespeare's Romances and the Royal
Family* (Kansas: University Press of Kansas, 1985), 63; David Norbrook, ' "What
Cares these Roarers for the Name of King?": Language and Utopia in *The Tempest*',
and Erica Sheen, ' "The Agent for his Master": Political Service and Professional
Liberty in *Cymbeline*', both in Gordon McMullan and Jonathan Hope (eds.), *The
Politics of Tragicomedy: Shakespeare and After* (London: Routledge, 1992), 21–54
and 55–76 respectively; Nancy Klein Maguire, 'Towards Understanding
Tragicomedy', in Maguire (ed.), *Renaissance Tragicomedy: Explorations in Genre
and Politics* (New York: AMS Press, 1987), 4.

  [9] McMullan and Hope, 'Politics of Tragicomedy', 14.

  [10] Jane Tylus, 'The Myth of Enclosure: Renaissance Pastoral from Sannazzaro to
Shakespeare', Ph.D. thesis, pp. iii, 17–18; Stephen Greenblatt, 'Sidney's *Arcadia* and
the Mixed Mode', *Studies in Philology*, 70 (1973), 274; Joseph Loewenstein,
'Guarini and the Presence of Genre', in Nancy Maguire (ed.), *Renaissance
Tragicomedy: Explorations in Genre and Politics* (New York: AMS Press, 1987),
40–1.

  [11] On the popularity of Italian literature at the Scottish court, see: R. D. S. Jack,
The Italian Influence on Scottish Literature (Edinburgh: Edinburgh University Press,
1972), 92–142.

poet, like Browne, who laid claim to the cultural inheritance of Sidney and Spenser. The formal practice of *genera mista*, the artistic control over various genres and multiple plots, mirrored in the way that passions are brought under the sway of reason in the action of the play, gave a lesson in temperance that likened the proper rule of the body to the government of the commonwealth.[12] Guarini's sophisticated shepherds move out of the enclosed pastoral world into the public arena and begin to metamorphose into citizens.[13] Pastoral tragicomedy, in this aspect, is compatible with the strenuous pastoral romances of Sidney and Spenser, and when Daniel and Fletcher 'english' the form they do so through Elizabethan political pastoral.[14] Daniel's pastoral tragicomedy for Queen Anne's court, *Arcadia Reformed*, performed in 1605 and published the following year as *The Queenes Arcadia*, opens the pastoral enclosure to forces of corruption and discord through satire, so that pastoral becomes a civic space for the trial of virtue in a situation of adversity. The main vehicles of corruption, Colax (Flattery) and Techne (Art), simultaneously figure the corrupting ambitions of the new nobility and have a self-reflexivity that points to the dangers of undiscriminating court panegyric. Although these figures are exiled in the last act, the play closes not with a compliment but with a warning to the court to guard against abuses.[15] The elder statesmen-like shepherds, Ergasto and Meliboeus, derive from Sidneian pastoral and safeguard the memory of an earlier 'Elizabethan' era; the play opens with their lament for the decline of Arcadia from 'plaine honesty',

---

[12] James J. Yoch, 'The Renaissance Dramatization of Temperance: The Italian Revival of Tragicomedy and *The Faithful Shepherdess*', in Nancy Maguire (ed.), *Renaissance Tragicomedy: Explorations in Genre and Politics* (New York: AMS Press, 1987), 115–23.

[13] Guarini's followers, Giovanni Savio, Orlando Pescetti, and Giovanni Malacreta make explicit connections between shepherds and citizens (Tylus, 'Myths of Enclosure', 59).

[14] As early as 1602, in his verses before the translation of *Il Pastor Fido* by his patron Sir Edward Dymock, Daniel claimed an English 'right' to pastoral tragicomedy which '*now in England can | Speake as good English as Italian*' (Guarini, *Il Pastor Fido: Or The faithfull Shepheard. Translated out of Italian into English* (London, 1602), STC 12415, A3v).

[15] See Johanna Procter's reading of the play in '*The Queenes Arcadia* (1606) and *Hymens Triumph* (1615): Samuel Daniel's Court Pastoral Plays', in J. Salmons and W. Moretti (eds.), *The Renaissance in Ferrara and its European Horizons* (Cardiff: University of Wales Press; Ravenna: Mario Lapucci Edizioni del Girasole, 1984), 88–93.

'vndisguised truth', and 'simple innocence' into disloyalty, delusion, and slander.[16] This georgic, civic aspect of Daniel's 'English' pastoral tragicomedy also characterized Fletcher's *The Faithful Shepherdess*—a play that Browne directly echoed in Book I. Fletcher's pastoral tragicomedy deliberately recalled Elizabethan political pastoral through the transfer of power from Pan to the virgin priestess Clorin.[17] Like Daniel's *The Queenes Arcadia*, the pastoral world is not a secluded place of retirement and leisure but constituted through trial and the active pursuit of virtue and the emphasis is placed firmly on ethical and political responsibility.[18] Shakespeare's tragicomedy, *A Winter's Tale*, has been read by Graham Holderness as a complex subversion of court drama.[19] Pastoral in the play carries with it the georgic strain of native pastoral satire: Perdita's response to the 'court' echoes medieval and early Tudor compaints, 'I was about to speak, and tell him plainly | The self-same sun that shines upon his court | Hides not his visage from our cottage, but | Looks on alike' (IV. iv. 443–6). The recurrent georgic trope of grafting is a figure for tragicomedy itself and equates poetic labour with agency; in the statue scene the wondrous energies of tragicomedy are identified with the artist not as the king's servant but as his conscience.

The Italianate pastoral plots of Book I are filtered through this ethical vision of English pastoral tragicomedy. The drama of the first three Songs is generated by the frustrations of love and emotional disturbances resulting from violent passions, but the treatment of these themes is remarkably chaste. There is a

---

[16] *The Queenes Arcadia*, in *The Complete Works in Verse and Prose*, ed. A. B. Grosart, 5 vols. (London, 1885), iv. 217–19. Queen Anne's court had strong Sidneian and Essexian connections: the Countess of Bedford was her chief lady-in-waiting, Robert Sidney, her Lord Chamberlain, William Herbert, Earl of Pembroke, a long-standing favourite, and his brother, Philip, Earl of Montgomery, married one of the ladies of her court, Susan de Vere. Daniel's patrons, Pembroke and Bedford, may have recommended him to Queen Anne as a writer of masques (Leeds Barroll, 'The Court of the First Stuart Queen', in Linda Levy Peck (ed.), *The Mental World of the Jacobean Court* (Cambridge: Cambridge University Press, 1991), 200–8; Michael Brennan, *Literary Patronage in the English Renaissance: The Pembroke Family* (London: Routledge, 1988), 108–9).

[17] Gordon McMullan, *The Politics of Unease in the Plays of John Fletcher* (Amherst: The University of Massachusetts Press, 1994), 67.

[18] McMullan, *The Politics of Unease*, 68–70.

[19] Graham Holderness et al., *Shakespeare: Out of Court Dramatizations of Court Society* (Basingstoke and London: Macmillan, 1990), 195–235.

paradigmatic revision of *Il Pastor Fido* in the first Song which insists on the sublimation of disruptive erotic energies for the good health of the individual and, by analogy, the commonwealth. The lustful Corsica's soliloquy on the futility of constancy in love in *Il Pastor Fido* is given to the benevolent shepherd Redmond and in this new context becomes part of an ethical imperative to self-government: Redmond intervenes at the request of the water nymph to direct Marina away from her unrequited, self-destructive love for the faithless shepherd Celadine towards reciprocal, generative love.[20] This drive to contain erotic energies governs the response to Marlowe in the poem. Book I contains numerous echoes of *Hero and Leander* which function to Anglicize the Italianate form of pastoral tragicomedy and to evoke psychological states of desire by acting as generic signposts that rely on Marlowe's reputation as the English Ovid.[21] There are clear echoes of Marlowe's Leander in the blazons of Redmond (13–14) and Doridon (31). Both blazons involve the representation of masculine virtue within an amatory as opposed to a heroic context, whereby the feminizing of the male subject describes his susceptibility to love, but these blazons lack the unsettling homoerotic engagement with the masculine subject that characterizes Marlowe's text. Rather his response to Marlowe works within a Spenserian tradition that sought to bring the Ovidian epyllion in line with a reforming temperance.[22] A poetics of temperance has its clearest expression in the episode relating the abduction of Marina at the close of the second Song. A libertine readership is interpellated and then satirized in Spenserian fashion as victims of Circean charms, who 'wallowing lye within a sensuall sincke', while his own verse is distinguished from Ovidian dissimulation, 'Whose fained gestures doe entrap our youth | With an apparancie of

[20] Grundy argues that this is consciously ironic ('Browne and Italian Pastoral', 306).
[21] See Joan Grundy on the influence of Marlowe and Ovidian romance in Book I (*The Spenserian Poets: A Study in Elizabethan and Jacobean Poetry* (London: Edward Arnold, 1969), 143, 147).
[22] See, for example, Drayton's *Endimion and Phoebe* and Chapman's continuation of *Hero and Leander*. Colin Burrow, 'Original Fictions: Metamorphosis in *The Faerie Queene*', and Lawrence Lerner, 'Ovid and the Elizabethans', both in Charles Martindale (ed.), *Ovid Renewed: Ovidian Influences on Literature and Art from the Middle Ages to the Twentieth Century* (Cambridge: Cambridge University Press., 1988), 99–119 and 128–9 respectively.

simple truth' (41). Spenser had used the defeat of Circean Acrasia to defend his Protestant epic against the seductive charms of romance, but in this episode Browne seeks an accommodation between Ovidian romance and a reformed humanist aesthetic.[23] The following moralized romance landscape represents a complex revision of Ovid. The river carrying the swain and the unconscious Marina is anthropomorphized so that it intervenes to thwart the intended rape by unleashing its destructive capacities on the landscape to evoke horror, despair, and guilt. Metamorphosis is transferred from victim to aggressor and internalized within the conscience of the swain to reform lustful desire. Marina's chastity stands in for the integrity of the poet and his text, 'Such are their states, whose soules from foule offence, | Enthroned sit in spotlesse *Innocence*' (44).

There is a dramatic stylistic and generic reorientation in the fourth Song as the Italianate pastoralism that had dominated the first three Songs gives way to a generic heterogeneity that incorporates allegory, epic, medieval estates satire, complaint, the epyllion, and elegy. These polyphonic books follow Spenser's method of incorporating genres in his text through a revisionary 'dialectical progression' whereby genres are tested as they are assimilated. The resulting representational battle between truth and error aims for the revelation of Protestant Truth in history.[24] The revisionary generic heterogeneity of these last Songs opens pastoral to historical process in the form of a Protestant apocalypticism that takes its pattern from Book I of *The Faerie Queene*, where a Reformation history is tied to the Tudor dynasty in Virgilian fashion. Tragicomedy at this point becomes modal and it provides a way of emplotting recent history according to a pattern in which Truth is revealed after a period of wandering in exile. The main plot of these Songs centres on Aletheia–Truth, her exile, and her eventual return to England where she is united with Amintas, or Riot reformed. The death of Prince Henry occurs during her period of exile, while her return and union with Amintas symbolizes the align-

---

[23] John Watkins, *The Specter of Dido: Spenser and the Virgilian Epic* (New Haven and London: Yale University Press, 1995), 139–43.

[24] John N. King, *Spenser's Poetry and the Reformation Tradition* (Princeton: Princeton University Press, 1990), 184.

ment of the Stuart dynasty with a Reformation history in the marriage of Princess Elizabeth and Frederick, Elector Palatine. Historical and generic reformation is initiated by an Ovidian metamorphosis: Fida's deer is murdered by Riot and transformed into Aletheia–Truth. The metamorphic revelation of Aletheia is figured through phoenix imagery popular in epithalamia for the royal couple, where it is used to identify Princess Elizabeth with an Elizabethan imperial revival.[25] Browne's allegory of Truth in these Songs is part of a vogue for apocalyptic representations of Protestant Truth in entertainments such as the unperformed wedding masque for Elizabeth and Frederick, *The Masque of Truth*, and Middleton's Lord Mayor's pageant, *The Triumph of Truth*, performed in the winter of 1613, that resulted from the brief influence of Henry and, following his death, Elizabeth and her husband, on court culture. In the unperformed *Masque of Truth*, possibly sponsored by Henry, Aletheia resides in England under the protection of the zealous Calvinist prince, James I, symbolizing his commitment to a Protestant alliance.[26] The triumph of Protestant Truth, and her defender Zeal, over Error and Envy in Middleton's *Triumph of Truth* ushers in the reign of Perfect Love, a compliment to James's imperial union of the kingdoms and its perfection in the marriage of Elizabeth and Frederick.[27]

The iconography of Truth tended to focus national energies on Elizabeth rather than her father, and she inherited much of the iconography of her namesake to become the embodiment of the godly nation. The emblematic blazon of Aletheia in the fourth Song is patterned on Spenser's iconographical portraits

[25] Yates, *Shakespeare's Last Plays*, 32–4.

[26] David Norbrook, ' "The Masque of Truth": Court Entertainments and International Protestant Politics in the Early Stuart Period', *The Seventeenth Century*, 1 (1986), 81–110.

[27] Thomas Middleton, *The Triumph of Truth* (1613), in *The Works*, ed. A. H. Bullen, 8 vols. (London, 1886), vii. 231–60. S. Williams, 'Two Seventeenth-Century Semi-Dramatic Allegories of Truth the Daughter of Time', *The Guildhall Miscellany*, 11 (1963), 208–16. Norbrook suggests Middleton may have been the author of *The Masque of Truth*. Browne may have had access to the manuscript version of the *Triumph*, which was published around the same time as Book I, since both he and Middleton were acquainted with Richard Fishbourne, a London Mercer, and he had other associations with London Puritan merchants, such as John Browne (Norbrook, ' "The Masque of Truth" ', 94, 109 n. 68; William Browne, *The Poems*, ed. George Goodwin, 2 vols. (London: George Routledge & Sons; New York: Dutton, 1894), ii. 347).

of royal women that located Elizabeth in British history through
the Reformation image of the godly woman:[28]

> Vpon her fore-head, as in glory sate
> Mercy and Maiestie, for wondering at,
> As pure and simple as *Albania's* snow,
> Or milke-white Swannes which stern the streames of *Poe*:
> Like to some goodly fore-land, bearing out
> Her haire, the tufts which fring'd the shoare about.
> And least the man which sought those coasts might slip,
> Her eyes like Starres, did serue to guide the ship.
> Vpon her front (heauens fairest *Promontory*)
> Delineated was, th'Authentique Story
> Of those Elect, whose sheepe at first began
> To nibble by the springs of *Canaan*:
> Out of whose sacred loynes, (brought by the stem
> Of that sweet Singer of *Ierusalem*)
> Came the best Shepheard euer flockes did keepe,
> Who yeelded vp his life to saue his sheepe.   (p. 68)

Aletheia is a compendium of portraits of Elizabeth I: 'Mercy
and Maiestie' associate her with Mercilla, while her purity joins
mercy and majesty with chastity, the defining virtue of
Elizabeth's public and private government; the description of
Aletheia as an island recalls the Ditchley portrait, in which
Elizabeth's chastity stands in for the invulnerability of the
English nation; and finally her body is assimilated to the
history of the Elect nation and, in this aspect, she resembles
Spenser's Una, the embodiment of Reformed Truth, an
exemplum of the faithful queen, and representative of Eliza-
beth's role in the history of the British Church.

   With the revelation of Aletheia, the pastoral framework shifts
from an Italianate to a Protestant scriptural mode. Her story is
related through the Elizabethan and Jacobean iconography of
Veritas Filia Temporis. The awakening of Truth and her
reunion with her father, Time, in Dekker's apocalyptic history
play, *The Whore of Babylon*, performed by the Prince's servants
in 1607, imagined the triumph of Protestant England over the
papist Antichrist in the accession of Elizabeth I and looked
forward to a final defeat in the reign of James I, the 'second

---

[28] King, *Spenser's Poetry and the Reformation Tradition*, 120.

Phoenix'.[29] Browne's 'stately nymph of yore', Verolame, who laments religious martyrdom under Mary I, had appeared in Spenser's *The Ruines of Time*, where she laments the decline of the English empire. This tragic history is reversed in *Britannia's Pastorals* with England's deliverance from the Gunpowder Plot:

> And Riuers dancing come, ycrown'd with Townes,
> All singing forth the victories of *Time*,
> Vpon the Monsters of the Westerne Clyme,
> Whose horrid, damned, bloudy, plots would bring
> Confusion on the Laureate Poets King.   (pp. 72–3)

Celebrations interestingly take on a civic form, with the rivers crowned with towns, that recalls the popular, civic apocalyptic symbolism of Dekker's play and Middleton's *Triumph of Truth*. This is the first and only time that Browne will praise James, the 'Laureate Poets King', while the pageantry of the 'victories of *Time*' imagines a national consensus over the destiny of the Protestant nation.

The story of Truth's exile and persecution looks forward typologically to the restoration of Truth to England under James. Elizabethan imagery of the true Church wandering in the wilderness is intermixed with medieval estates satire reminiscent of early Tudor reformist complaints.[30] Aletheia is refused entry first at an Abbey that symbolizes papist idolatry and religious persecution and where 'hee that lou'd me, or but moan'd my case, | Had heapes of fire-brands banded at his face' (74), then at the court dominated by the prince's 'Seruant *Adulation*' (76), and finally by the town tradesmen, the Miller, Tailor, and Weaver, because of Truth's ability to reveal corruption.[31] Truth's wanderings take her into the Solitary Vale where she provides a sympathetic audience for the laments of Endimion, a 'braue, heroicke, worthy *Martialist*' (80), and a 'learnedst

---

[29] Thomas Dekker, *The Whore of Babylon*, in *The Dramatic Works*, ed. Fredson Bowers, 5 vols. (Cambridge: Cambridge University Press., 1953–61), ii. 497–500.

[30] For Browne's use of medieval satire, see: F. W. Moorman, *William Browne. His Britannia's Pastorals and the Pastoral Poetry of the Elizabethan Age* (Strassburg: Trubner, 1897), 43–5.

[31] Both Moorman and Goodwin claim that the last satire on corrupiton in the trades is heavily influenced by John Day's *Perigrinatio Scholastica, or, Learneinges Pilgrimage* (Moorman, *William Browne*, 50; Goodwin, *Poems of Browne*, ii. 327). However, M. E. Borish has argued from the evidence of the dedications that the text was completed between 1618 and Day's death in 1625 ('A Second Version of John Day's *Peregrinatio Scholastica*', *Modern Language Notes*, 55 (1940), 35–9).

Maide' (82). These laments are veiled accounts of the fall of
Raleigh, Essex, and Arabella Stuart.[32] Both Raleigh and Stuart
were in the Tower in 1613 on James's orders, in fact, Raleigh
had been imprisoned for suspected involvement in a plot to
place Arabella rather than James on the throne. These laments
continue the story of the persecution of the godly and would
seem to be part of a campaign for their release and, in Essex's
case, the recuperation of his memory and political legacy, which
may have gained impetus from the perceived change in royal
attitude suggested by the court entertainments of late 1613. The
laments are introduced by a georgic simile of a farmer releasing
water from a rock to relieve a drought stricken land, 'Whereby
the waters from their prison runne, | To close earths gaping
wounds made by the *Sunne*' (80), which would seem to be
associated with the freeing of poetic expression, and perhaps
Raleigh and Stuart themselves, through a more receptive
political climate. While this episode appears to be a plea for
the restoration of the reputations of these figures, Browne is
codedly critical in his assessment of James's conduct in the case
of Stuart. Her current fate results from 'colde *Winters* rage'
(83), invoking the Spenserian vision of a Jacobean winter, and
Browne would appear to accuse James of heartless tyranny in
the simile of the parents' cruel refusal of their son's desire to
marry a poor but by nature royal maid, 'as a Kings heart left
behinde, | When as his corps are borne to be enshrin'd' (83);
Stuart had been imprisoned following her marriage to William
Seymour, the grandson of the Earl of Hertford, in 1611 without
the permission of James and by 1613 there were reports of her
increasing illness and despair.[33] The fourth Song closes with
'chaste Penelope', the exemplar of heroic female virtue, await-
ing the return of Ulysses.[34]

The crowning lament of the Vale of Woe is the elegy for
Prince Henry that was printed in the same year in *Two elegies,*

[32] David Norbrook, 'Panegyric of the Monarch and its Social Context under
Elizabeth I and James I', D.Phil. thesis (Oxford, 1978), 268, ' "The Masque of
Truth"', 95–6, 109 n. 67. Stuart was also a close friend of Essex (S. J. Steen,
'Fashioning an Acceptable Self: Arabella Stuart', *English Literary Renaissance*, 18
(1988), 82–3).

[33] Steen, 'Fashioning an Acceptable Self', 85–6.

[34] Penelope is the centrepiece of one of the embroideries of her grandmother, Bess
of Hardwick, at Hardwick Hall. I am grateful to David Norbrook for this information.

consecrated to the neuer dying memorie of . . . Henry Prince of Wales. In the fifth Song, the lament is sung by Idya, the personification of the English nation. England's joy in her providential deliverance from 'the Monsters of the Westerne Clyme' with failure of the Gunpowder Plot is premature and Henry's death turns rejoicing into sorrow with the world a 'Stage made for a wofull Tragedie' (89). The Stuart image of England as the fortunate isle that underpins representations of the Jacobean peace is cast in negative geopolitical terms to signify the nation's dangerous isolation from Protestant Europe with the death of Henry: 'England was ne'er ingirt with waues till now; | Till now it held part with the Continent' (91). Henry died at a point when it appeared that he would fulfil the apocalyptic hopes of advocates of militantly Protestant and anti-Habsburg policies.[35] Browne's elegy reinforces this 'patriot' image of Henry; the identification of 'our Heroe (honour'd Essex)' (92) and Henry in terms of the national impact of their deaths would strongly suggest that he is the prince's political father and not James, who is absent from the elegy. The image of Idya mourning the death of Henry recalls Elizabeth's grief for Essex at the close of the fourth Song and evokes other texts that want to recuperate Essex's memory, such as William Harbert's Englands Sorrowe or, A Farewell to Essex (1606) where Britain, 'a mournful Queen', bemoans the loss of Essex, and his death marks the decline of Elizabethan martialism.[36]

Yet, the location of the elegy within a wider tragicomic pattern tempers these disruptive political energies. Whereas the poet could only find relief by joining with a community of like-minded poets when the poem was published in the Two elegies, in this new context consolation is offered in the image of Truth finding refuge in England, as Idya 'knew mee well since I had beene, | As chiefest consort of the Faiery Queene' (94). Elizabeth's reign signifies the triumph of true religion over papist oppression, the 'Free libertie to taste the foode of Heauen' (95); a state that is implicitly restored with the return of Truth from exile. Browne here comes close to the image of Aletheia–Truth

<hr />

[35] On Henry's political projects, see: Norbrook, ' "The Masque of Truth"', 89–91.

[36] William Harbert, Englands Sorrowe or, A Farewell to Essex: With a Commemoration of the famous Liues, and vntimely Deaths of many woorthie Personages which haue liued in England (London, 1606), STC 12582, B2r–3r.

residing in England under the patronage of the Protestant prince James I in the *Masque of Truth*.[37] The reunion of Aletheia and Idya initiates a tragicomic redemptive pattern and it is at this point that the narrative returns to the figure of Riot to tell of his repentance and transformation into the courtly lover Amintas. Once more, metamorphosis signals a process of generic amplification and revision in the effort to produce a reformed court poetics. Riot in the fourth Song had resembled Spenser's Error and the Blatant Beast: he prophaned true religion, desecrated the past, and, like Middleton's Error in his *Triumph of Truth*, he embodied court luxury and corruption and the oppression of the 'country',

> But when he came on carued *Monuments*,
> Spiring *Colosses*, and high raised rents,
> He past them o'er, quicke, as the Easterne winde.   (p. 66)

When Riot returns in the fifth Song, the discourse of court corruption is incorporated into a Spenserian allegory of fallen man. His entry into the House of Repentance identifies him with Spenser's Redcrosse at the House of Holinesse and looks forward to his reunion with Una. Spenser's porter Humility is replaced by the portress Remembrance which, given the political function of the memory of Elizabeth in this Song, implies that true redemption of the court and nation can only be achieved through a return to Elizabethan martialism.

Riot's redemptive metamorphosis is figured through a revisionary intertextuality that brings Spenser, Du Bartas, and Ovid into dialogue. Browne may have looked to Du Bartas for a reformed court poetic not only because he was regarded as the exemplar of the Protestant divine poet, a Christian Homer, but also because of James's admiration for the poet; he had translated parts of his work and offered the poet his patronage following a visit to the Scottish court in 1587. In England, Du Bartas's influence was strongest amongst the Countess of Pembroke's circle and the Spenserian poets.[38] Browne was

---

[37] This would support Norbrook's suggestion that Browne knew of the masque ('"The Masque of Truth"', 95–6).

[38] Davies of Hereford, Charles Fitzgeoffrey, and Daniel contributed verses to Sylvester's translation of *Divine Weeks and Works* (1605). Anne Lake Prescott, 'The Reception of Du Bartas in England', *Studies in the Renaissance*, 15 (1968), 144; Guillaume De Saluste Sieur Du Bartas, *The Divine Weeks and Works*

attracted to Du Bartas's use of 'homely' similes to express divine Truth, for example, the fettering of Riot by Remorse is accompanied by a simile of a blacksmith and his boy attempting to shoe a headstrong horse (98). The resulting textual alliances, however, are sometimes disorienting. Dour Spenserian allegory clashes with an eroticizing Ovidianism when Riot's metamorphosis into Amintas is compared to a young woman disrobing for the night, or when Amintas in his reformed state is described in an eroticized language that echoes Marlowe's *Hero and Leander*. A similar disjunction unsettles the union of Amintas and Aletheia–Truth:

> How often wisht *Amintas* with his hart,
> His ruddy lips from hers might neuer part;
> And that the heauens this gift were them bequeathing,
> To feede on nothing, but each others breathing!   (p. 109)

As Grundy points out, 'Browne has turned Spenser's sober tale into an Ovidian romance, as much in the manner of *Hero and Leander* as of *The Faerie Queene*.'[39] These unsettling textual juxtapositions are symptomatic of the way that Browne often struggles to hold divergent aesthetic and political positions together. Just as an erotic Ovidianism sits uneasily with a moralizing Spenserianism, so too the praise of James I is disturbed by the political sympathies conveyed in the elegy for Henry and by the poet's support for Raleigh and Stuart.

Book I's energies are directed towards accommodation and reconciliation. The union of the pastoral lovers at its close recalls the pattern of reconciliation and renewal that structures the resolution of pastoral tragicomedy. The elegy for Henry which opened the fifth Song is transformed by its epithalamic ending, and the tragic rupture in the dynastic state is healed in the union of Aletheia, Protestant Truth, and Amintas, the reformed courtly lover. Their union is a thinly veiled compliment to Elizabeth and Frederick. Browne calls to Drayton and Chapman, 'Or any one sent from the sacred Well, | Inheriting the soule of *Astrophell*', to add their voice to the glorification of the couple. For his own part, he ends Book I with the hope that

Translated by Josuah Sylvester, ed. Susan Snyder, 2 vols. (Oxford: Clarendon Press, 1979), i. 18–22.

[39] Grundy, *Spenserian Poets*, 146–7.

his own poetry will provide a model for a new court aesthetics able to reconcile the interests of the 'court' and the 'country':

> My *Muse* may one day make the Courtly Swaines
> Enamour'd on the *Musicke* of the Plaines,
> And as vpon a hill shee brauely sings,
> Teach humble Dales to weepe in Christall Springs.   (p. 109)

The political climate of 1613 enabled Browne to look to the court as a national cultural institution that could inspire his 'country' epic. Book I has a coherency that arises out of the use of a tragicomic structure to accommodate differences within a reformed Arcadia. This process of accommodation was, however, fraught with difficulties, and there are strong signs in the last Songs, particularly in the Vale of Woe, of just how fragile this vision of a united Britannia was.

11 *BRITANNIA'S PASTORALS*, 1616

Famine

Riot returns unreformed in Book II in the shape of Limos, the personification of Famine. The consensus that the poet was able to imagine at the end of Book I has been shattered in Book II, published three years later, and a critical, satiric distance has opened between 'court' and 'country'.[40] Arcadia is no longer a refuge for Truth but is blighted by Famine who will only be defeated in the third Song by the collective agency of the 'shepherds nation' in a way that recalls the collaborative eclogues, *The Shepheards Pipe* and *The Shepherds Hunting*. The ambivalences underlying the representation of James in Book I are more pronounced in Book II and sharpen into direct criticism of royal policy. Satire prevails and the poet speaks from the 'country'—an oppositional space on the margins of the dominant culture. The earlier 1613 image of James as the poet's king following England's deliverance from the Gunpowder plot has been replaced by a blinded and distant monarch in the first Song of Book II. This Book is marked by an increasing

[40] J. McClennen, 'William Browne as a Satirist', *Papers of the Michigan Academy of Science, Arts and Letters*, 33 (1947), 355–6.

digressiveness and the shepherds and shepherdesses from Book I retreat into the distance. Marina's capture by Limos in the first Song initiates the satire on the causes of Famine which is then followed by a satire on Avarice and the failure to erect a monument to Spenser. The second and third Songs concentrate on a native pastoral community, the English shepherds, and, at the same time, the poet increasingly turns to his native Devon. A satiric digression on the decay of the navy opens the fourth Song and prefaces the return to the form of pastoral tragicomedy. The satire of Book II is not anti-monarchical, but it does cut close to the bone. Browne invokes the political memory of Elizabeth to figure the fallen state of monarchy and the failure not only of the Jacobean imperial vision but his own vision of national reconciliation and redemption under a reforming king in Book I.

Limos signals the return of the disruptive energies affiliated with court corruption. Like Riot, he desecrates the past and licences the social injustices that have resulted in the oppression of the country. The extensive satiric digression on the effect of Famine on the countryside in the first Song is framed by the progress of the imperial sea goddess, Thetis, the mother of Achilles. The poem sets up a framework of royal government that provides a standard against which James's shortcomings will be measured. Throughout Book II, Thetis evokes the memory of Elizabethan imperialism. Her journey around the coast of Britain in this instance recalls the Elizabethan royal progress and its role in maintaining and reinforcing the bonds between central and county government.[41] In the first Song, Thetis's progress is clearly identified with the political goals of maintaining good government within the nation:

> A iourney, onely made, vnawares to spye
> If any *Mighties* of her Empery
> Oppress the least, and forc'd the weaker sort
> To their designs, by being great in Court.[42]

The reason given for Thetis's arrival in England situates the satire on Famine firmly within the context of the proceedings

---

[41] Malcolm Smuts argues that the royal progress declined under James (*Court Culture and the Origins of a Royalist Tradition in Early Stuart England* (Philadelphia: University of Pennsylvania Press, 1987), 54).

[42] *Britannia's Pastorals. The second booke.* (London, 1616), STC 3915.5, 22.

against the Earl and Countess of Somerset for complicity in the murder of Sir Thomas Overbury in early 1616. Richard Weston, who was found guilty of poisoning Overbury, voiced the hope at his trial that 'they doe not make a nett to catche the little fishes or flyes and lett the greate goe' and it became a catch-phrase in the effort to secure convictions against those 'great in Court', the Earl and Countess of Somerset.[43] This context is reinforced by the reference to the 'diuelish Politician (who) all conuinces, | In murdring Statesmen and in poisning Princes' (23) that heads the catalogue of injustices that James is urged to reform. During the trial, a witness had claimed that the sudden death of Prince Henry resulted from his poisoning by those responsible for the murder of Overbury.[44]

For Browne, the revelations regarding the death of Overbury strike at the very heart of royal government. The following digression on abuses in the countryside describes how corruption at the centre spreads throughout the commonwealth. Browne uses a 'country' narrative of royal favourites exploiting their estates and tenants in order to finance their excesses to uncover a failure of royal husbandry. Patterson has described this digression as 'a parody of the 'happy man' section of the second georgic', but arguably the generic frame of reference is mixed, bringing the georgic theme of political husbandry and the role of the governing classes into dialogue with the medieval genre of the 'advice to princes' and Tudor Reformation satire, which used the plain-speaking plowman as a vehicle for social protest.[45] The Spenserian poet here wishes to instruct his prince by revealing harsh realities and calls on the king to view the activities of his court favourites with a clear sight by taking up a 'glasse prospectiue':

> If Monarchs, so, would take an Instrument
> Of truth compos'd to spie their Subiects drent
> In foule oppression by those high in seate,
> (Who care not to be good but to be great)

[43] Martin Butler and David Lindley, 'Restoring Astraea: Jonson's Masque for the Fall of Somerset', *English Literary History*, 61 (1994), 813.

[44] S. R. Gardiner, *History of England from the Accession of James I to the Outbreak of the Civil War, 1603–1642*, 10 vols., 3rd edn. (London, 1889–94), ii. 344.

[45] Annabel Patterson, *Pastoral and Ideology: Virgil to Valery* (Oxford: Clarendon Press, 1988), 143; John N. King, 'Spenser's *Shepheardes Calender* and Protestant Pastoral Satire', in Lewalski, *Renaissance Genres*, 376.

In full aspect the wrongs of each degree
Would lye before them; and they then would see.   (p. 23)

Browne's reformist satiric vision, his 'Instrument of truth' works against the concept of the masque as a mirror that instructively reflects and magnifies the virtues of the prince and his court. Implicitly, this type of mirror has dazzled and blinded the king and made him susceptible to the manipulative flattery of his favourites. The satiric digression describes the failure of a Stuart imperial vision that offered James the role of the new Augustus who heals the wounds of civil war and presides over a golden age of peace, prosperity, and cultural magnificence. Jonson's *Prince Henries Barriers*, performed in 1612, had presented Henry with the following vision:

> To your first speculation, you may view
> The eye of *iustice* shooting through the land,
> Like a bright *planet* strengthened by the hand
> Of first and warlike EDWARD; then th'increase
> Of trades and tillage, vnder laws and peace,
>
>   .   .   .   .   .   .
>
> These, worthyest Prince, are set you neere to reade,
> That ciuill arts the martiall must precede
> That lawes and trades bring honors in and gayne,
> And armes defensiue a safe peace maintayne.[46]

This 1612 vision of royal good husbandry that reaps the rewards of peace through national prosperity is reversed in Browne's 1616 satire. If the king cared to view the land, he would now see nothing but injustice. When detailing rural oppression, Browne repeatedly draws attention to the practices of engrossing and rack-renting:

> Here should they finde a great one paling in
> A meane mans land, which many yeeres had bin
> His charges life
>
>   .   .   .   .
>
> The *Country Gentleman*, from's neighbours hand
> Forceth th'inheritance, ioynes land to land,
> And (most insatiate) seekes vnder his rent
> To bring the worlds most spacious continent.   (p. 23)

[46] Jonson, *Speeches at Prince Henries Barriers*, in *Works*, ed. C. H. Hereford, Percy Simpson, and Evelyn Simpson, 11 vols. (Oxford: Clarendon Press, 1925–52), vii. 328–9.

Browne aligns his text with contemporary pamphlets attacking the use of these practices by rich and powerful farmers and landlords as they had undermined traditional systems of husbandry and led to rural unemployment and depopulation.[47] The poet becomes the voice for the dispossessed, a new Piers Plowman, while the catalogue of abuses similarly invokes the politics of Reformation satire. The source of rural abuses is to be found in the court and in the corruption resulting from poor royal husbandry.[48]

Browne's satire may contrast markedly with Jonson's 1612 georgic vision of the Stuart peace, but it does have affinities with his masque, *The Golden Age Restored*, performed in early 1616. Butler and Lindley have convincingly argued that the occasion of Jonson's masque is the scandal surrounding the Earl and Countess of Somerset and the factional manoeuvrings at court that helped to bring down the Earl and saw the rise of the new favourite, George Villiers.[49] The purpose of Thetis's journey in Browne's first Song echoes the reason given for the return of Astraea in Jonson's masque:

> JOVE can endure no longer,
>   Your great ones should your less inuade,
>   Or, that your weake, though bad, be made
> A prey vnto the stronger.[50]

There are similarities between Jonson's anti-masque of the Iron Age and Browne's Famine and both can be read as responses to the recently uncovered corruption. These correspondences could be part of an 'Exchange *of* Letters', a term Jonson uses in his poem before Book II of *Britannia's Pastorals*, which he also commends as *'most worthy to be read'*. The texts are also associated through the new dedicatee of Book II, the Earl of Pembroke who presided over the production of Jonson's

---

[47] Joan Thirsk, *The Agrarian History of England and Wales*. iv: *1500–1640* (Cambridge: Cambridge University Press, 1967), 207, 239.

[48] Annotations to this passage in a copy of *Britannia's Pastorals*, that have been ascribed to Milton, 'Poor labour to feed the luxury of the rich', indicate that it was read in terms of class oppression (*The Uncollected Writings of John Milton*, in *The Works*, ed. T. O. Mabbot and J. M. French. 18 vols. (New York: Columbia University Press, 1938), xvii. 339). However, Beal doubts the attribution to Milton (*Index of English Literary Manuscripts*, 2 vols. (London: Mansell, 1980–93), ii. 80).

[49] Butler and Lindley, 'Restoring Astraea', 807–27.

[50] Ben Jonson, *Works*, ed. C. H. Herford, Percy Simpson, and Evelyn Simpson (Oxford: Clarendon Press, 1925–52), viii. 421.

masque as the new Lord Chamberlain following the disgrace of Somerset. Lord Zouche, Pembroke's ally and Browne's early patron, was one of the Commissioners appointed for the trial of the Earl and Countess. The main masque of *The Golden Age Restored* appears to compliment Pembroke and his court allies among the Essex circle and the performance as a whole, in the words of Butler and Lindley, 'could scarcely have been a clearer or more dramatic announcement of the renewal of anti-Spanish, anti-Howard alignments at court'.[51]

When the scandal broke, James had presented himself as the prime agent for 'the discovery of truth', as he put it in a letter to the Commissioners, and his apparent zeal for justice may have encouraged Browne in the belief that he would be receptive to his own 'Instrument of truth'.[52] Even so, Jonson's masque is far more diplomatic in the way that it counsels the king—Browne praises Jonson as surpassing Seneca in the theatre in the second Song (37), perhaps suggesting his skilful negotiation of the dangers that face those who write for a volatile court and king. Jonson's masque distances the king from corruption by representing these forces in the antimasque as a political rebellion against the royal Jove.[53] For Browne, by contrast, the scandal was the direct result of James's empowering of favourites and strikes at the heart of his government. The king's attempt at damage limitation by remitting the death sentence of the Earl and pardoning the Countess, commuting both their sentences into a short imprisonment in the Tower, was greeted by widespread public protest.[54] The elegies that both Browne and Brooke contributed to *Sir Thomas Ouerburie His Wife with new Elegies vpon his (now knowne) vntimely death* criticize royal leniency as a failure to uphold justice. The consolation that Browne offers in his elegy is political: since the trial has revealed the extent of corruption amongst those powerful at court, it may result in reform in Overbury's name, 'The poyson that works upward now, shall striue | To be thy faire *Fames* true *Preseruative*.'[55] Brooke insists that God's justice will triumph in spite of the king's actions and make 'the stately Brow | Bend to

---

[51] Butler and Lindley, 'Restoring Astraea', 816–17.
[52] Quoted in ibid. 811.   [53] Ibid. 821.
[54] Chamberlain, *Letters*, ii. 17; Gardiner, *History*, ii. 361–3.
[55] *Sir Thomas Ouerburie His Wife with new Elegies vpon his (now knowne) vntimely death*, STC 18910, π7r.

the Foot!' (π4v)—a striking image, particularly in view of the way that he had maintained the role of parliament as a check on royal ambitions in the recent debates on impositions.

The figure of Limos, Famine, suggests an even sharper if veiled indictment of James's government. The paintings on the wall of the Cave of Limos constitute a coded political allegory. The first painting displays the 'siege of great *Ierusalem*' from Josephus' *The Lamentable and Tragicall Historie of the Wars and Utter Ruine of the Iewes*.[56] Given the wider allegorical role of Limos, Browne seems to be reading this story through Sylvester's translation of the *Divine Weeks and Works*. Sylvester follows Du Bartas's allegory of Famine with an extensive prophetic digression calling on the English nation to repent: under James's reign of 'Peace and Plentie', the nation has become forgetful of the political memory of Elizabeth, '*his sacred instrument*', who delivered the nation from Spanish oppression, has fallen from the ways of true religion, is divided by faction, and is corrupted by 'Sensual *wallowing in* Lascivious *Riot*'. Sylvester does not directly criticize James and rather offers counsel in the form of an idealized vision of the king, Prince Henry, the nobility, and the Commons governing the nation in harmony.[57] Browne's satire is more pointed: the final painting in the Cave of Limos, '*Erisichthons* case in *Ouids* Song' (20), would appear to damn James himself for desecrating the memory of Elizabeth and fostering corruption. In the Ovidian story, the sacrilegious king, Erysichton, desecrates Ceres's sacred tree in an intentional act of impiety and is condemned by the goddess to become a victim of Hunger, destroying his own kingdom to feed his appetite and finally devouring himself.

Famine parodies the Virgilian language of royal husbandry in Jacobean panegyric and initiates a critique of Stuart Augustanism that will be sustained throughout Book II. The allegory of Famine has a political valency that operates in a similar way to a discourse of corruption by providing a language of opposition that connects corrupt practices with the

---

[56] Josephus, *The Famous and Memorable Workes*, trans. Thomas Lodge (London, 1609), STC 14810, 734. This story seems to have been popular in this period and was retold in John Taylor's *Taylor's Vrania, or His Heauenly Muse with a briefe Narration of the thirteen Sieges, and sixe Sackings of the famous Cittie of Ierusalem* (London, 1615), STC 23806, F1r.

[57] *Divine Weeks and Works*, 160–2.

decay of the state and carries with it a veiled attack on the domestic and foreign policies of the crown.[58] The immediate occasion of the satire in the first Song was the Overbury trial which had implications beyond the innocence or guilt of the Earl and Countess of Somerset and provided a focus for political discontent that prefigured the corruption trials of the 1620s, and enabled connections to be made between corruption, the abuse of privilege and, given James's leniency, the use of the royal prerogative to overrule the law. The biblical overtones of the allegory of Famine carries with it a vision of the godly commonwealth that could be realised if the state were to be reformed, and Browne wanted to reactivate Tudor reformist satiric models to provide this 'country' vision with a native godly and oppositional literary inheritance. In this way, his textual politics are very different from those of Jonson who was hostile to Protestant literary traditions and rather cultivated a neo-Augustanism that may have enabled a critical diplomacy but lacked the political bite of Spenserian satire.

'Exiled Naso'

Browne also turns to Ovid for his critique of a Stuart Augustanism, as his use of the story of Erysichton in the Cave of Limos suggests. Ovid exerts the strongest influence over the structure of Britannia's Pastorals as a whole.[59] A transgressive Ovid, 'exiled Naso', appeared in the fourth Song of Book I and introduced the lament for Essex. This Ovid derives from a reading of his exile as a political punishment for an act of transgression against the Augustan regime and his elegies, Tristia and Ex Ponto, as protest poems. Ovid, for Browne, represented a counter tradition to an Augustan Virgil. The opening of the Metamorphoses speaks of 'bodies changed into other forms' and has been read as a trope for the way that the Ovidian narrative dismantles the form of the Virgilian epic and, in doing so, provides a sophisticated critique of Augustan imperialism.[60]

[58] Linda Levy Peck, Court Patronage and Corruption in Early Stuart England (Boston: Unwin Hyman, 1990), 203.

[59] Carol Marshall has calculated that citations from Ovid outnumber those from works by other poets ('William Browne and Britannia's Pastorals', Ph.D. thesis (Cambridge, Mass., 1951), 90–125).

[60] David Quint, Epic and Empire: Politics and Generic Form from Virgil to

An Ovidian metamorphic narrative has close associations with the form of the romance in that both narrative forms have an openness which undermines epic closure. Ovidian errancy characterizes the structure of Book II of *Britannia's Pastorals* which is marked by an increasing digressiveness and a failure or an unwillingness to find narrative endings or coherency.

As the appellation 'exiled *Naso*' suggests, Ovid provided Browne with a model for the poet marginalized by an arbitrary political regime, akin to the state of tyranny described in the fifth eclogue of *Shepheards Pipe*. An oppositional Ovid was taking shape in other texts of the period, such as Gervase Markham's unpublished 'The Newe Metamorphosis', subtitled 'The Arraignment of Vice', which was completed around 1615.[61] It is possible that Browne knew of this work: he praises Markham's *Tragedy of Sir Richard Grinville* in Book II and Markham's satiric Ovidian figures parallel Riot and Limos, the embodiments of court corruption. Markham's 'The Newe Metamorphosis' continues the Ovidian process of de-forming the epic by reading Ovid's poem as an epic satire. The subject of the last book is British imperial history. The opening catalogue of ancient British kings triumphantly culminates in James's union of the kingdoms and his royal issue, but this is quickly overtaken by a lengthy lament for the death of Prince Henry, the pillar of Protestant chivalry and exemplary royal patron. As in a number of other works, consolation for his death is offered in the marriage of Elizabeth and Frederick, but unusually the marriage festivities do not take place in the reformed court envisioned in the 'Masque of Truth' or by Browne at the close of Book I. There is no Riot reformed, rather the poem ends by satirizing those vices still present at court, Luxury, Avarice, and Prodigality.[62]

Milton (Princeton: Princeton University Press, 1993), 82–3, 139; Watkins, *Specter of Dido*, 31–4; Brook Otis, *Ovid as an Epic Poet*, 2nd edn. (Cambridge: Cambridge University Press, 1970), 343–62.

[61] Gervase Markham, 'The Newe Metamorphosis', British Library, Additional MSS 14824–6. J. H. Lyon, *A Study of the Newe Metamorphosis, written by J.M., Gent, 1600* (New York: Columbia University Press, 1919), 5–6, 29–40, 152–6; Norbrook, ' "The Masque of Truth" ', 96–7. Sandys, glossing the Actaeon story in his 1621 translation of the *Metamorphoses*, said that it showed 'how dangerous a curiosity it is to search into the secrets of Princes' and that 'some such unhappy discovery procured the banishment of our Ovid'.

[62] Additional MS 14826. f. 249–57.

The deaths of Essex and Prince Henry represent the failure of an imperial theme in *Britannia's Pastorals*. Poems on martial themes in the early seventeenth century tend towards the elegiac and often take on a romance instability.[63] An exilic Ovid is intimately associated with Essex in the 'Vale of Woe'. For Browne, Essex is simultaneously the exemplar of Elizabethan chivalry and an oppositional poet in the Ovidian mould: 'Once, as hee sate alone, | He sung the outrage of the lazy *Drone*, | Vpon the lab'ring *Bee*' (i. 80). Essex's song of exile turns his imprisonment into an act of honourable resistance to an arbitrary and corrupt authority. However, Browne avoids criticizing Elizabeth directly and produces a version of the Ovidian story of Cephalus and Procris, a story of mistaken infidelities, involving informers, accidental death, and remorse, to focus on Cecil, who is behind the figure of Envy, as the figure responsible for Essex's fall. Roles are reversed and Essex takes on the role of the accidently murdered Procris and Elizabeth that of her husband Cephalus so that the Queen is absolved of responsibility, rather she is represented as dying of a broken heart. Browne clearly admired Essex with few reservations and may have owned a collection of Essex memorabilia that consisted of copies of documents relating to his imprisonment and execution and included a copy of the verse, 'The buzzeinge Bees complaynt', that is cited in this fourth Song.[64] The verse had been printed in John Dowland's *The Third and Last Booke of Songs or Airs* that went into a fifth edition in 1613.[65] Dowland's collections of songs charted the fortunes of Essex. The second book published in 1600 and dedicated to the Countess of

---

[63] See, for example, William Harbert's *Englands Sorrowe or, A Farewell to Essex*.

[64] Oxford, Ashmole MS 767, ff. 1–68. Steven May suggests that Browne's source for the poem was this manuscript which is currently appended to a manuscript owned by Browne during James's reign (*The Poems of Edward De Vere, Seventeenth Earl of Oxford and of Robert Devereux, Second Earl of Essex*, ed. Stephen May, *Studies in Philology*, 77 (1980), 112). It is impossible to prove definitively that Browne owned this first manuscript because the binding of the volume belongs to Elias Ashmole and therefore the two manuscripts could have been collated by him or by Browne; although the first manuscript is not in Browne's hand, the copies were produced in the early years of James's reign.

[65] John Dowland, *The Third and Last Book of Songs or Airs*, *An English Garner*, ed. E. Arber (1882), iv. 620. The verse has also been attributed to Essex's secretary, Henry Cuffe, and John Lyly (E. H. Fellowes *et al.* (ed.), *English Madrigal Verse, 1588–1632*, rev. and enlarged F. W. Sternfield and D. Greer (Oxford: Clarendon Press, 1967), 741).

Bedford, whose husband was one of Essex's company in the rebellion, takes a melancholy tone that speaks to the political disillusionment and despair of this period. The third book, published three years later in 1603, has a more elegiac tone and the epistle to the reader employs the romance metaphor of the book as a ship tossed upon 'perilous seas' and the satiric motif from the 'Buzzeinge Bees complaynt' to locate the book in a political climate governed by envy and malice.[66] *Britannia's Pastorals* similarly utilizes these romance and satiric motifs to depict an embattled and marginalized poet who speaks for a community whose heroes are dead. The form of elegiac romance that appears in the 'Vale of Woe' and Book II of *Britannia's Pastorals* operates in a similar fashion to what Quint has described as the 'epic of defeat' which 'dismantles teleological narrative structures in the name of a losing political opposition for which nothing is settled and everything remains an open book'.[67]

In *Britannia's Pastorals*, an exilic Ovid is the model for the poet's own estrangement from imperial myths of national destiny. An Ovidian twinning of exile and death works to dismantle the form of the epic in the poem. When the elegy for Henry was originally published in the *Two Elegies* it had been prefaced by a tag from Ovid's *Tristia* that introduces the recurrent motif of exile as death, 'Wherever you had looked was the sound of mourning and lamentation.'[68] The death of Prince Henry continues to haunt Book II through the elegies for 'Alexis' and Spenser in the first Song and marks the poet's exile from his *patria*, the sense of a fatherland invested in the body of the monarch. Before embarking upon his elegy for the prince in Book I, the poet had recalled Virgil's *Aeneid* and Homer's *Iliad* and *Odyssey*, the latter sung by his '*Friend*' (i. 88)—Chapman had begun his translation of Homer under the patronage of Essex and continued the project under Prince Henry. This reinscription of the epic within the elegiac 'Vale of Woe' reorientates the heroic towards narratives of exile. There are

[66] Lillian M. Ruff and D. Arnold Wilson, 'The Madrigal, the Lute Song and Elizabethan Politics', *Past and Present*, 44 (1969), 28–43.

[67] Quint, *Epic and Empire*, 168.

[68] Ovid, *Tristia*, 1.3.21. Betty Rose Nagle, *The Poetics of Exile: Program and Polemic in the 'Tristia' and 'Expistulae ex Ponto' of Ovid* (Brussels: Latomus, 1980), 23, 29–31.

traces of an exiled Odysseus in the images of national and emotional dislocation scattered throughout the elegy, '*though my passions swimme,* | *Yet are they drowned e'er they landed be*', '*O happy! were I hurled* | *And cut off from life as* England *from the world*' (91). Burrow has argued that the nostalgia and loss that structures Chapman's translation of the *Odyssey* 'is intimately linked with the increasingly elegiac tone of the Spenserian view of Jacobean culture. The two work sadly together to portray life as a vale of tears.'[69]

The 'Vale of Woe' and the lament for Spenser at the end of the first Song of Book II are also indebted to Spenser's *Ruines of Time* which reads Ovid's exilic elegies through Du Bellay.[70] The lament of the Roman nymph, Verulame, over the ancient British city, Verulamium, in *The Ruines of Time* fragments an imperial narrative of nationhood into an elegiac narrative that expresses the poet's own sense of internal exile. The native land is filled with the sound of Verulame's laments for the deaths of members of the 'princely' Sidney–Dudley family. This elegiac landscape is reinscribed in the Vale of Woe—a dry, parched landscape, traversed by blocked, choked up rivers and streams, where the only voices heard are laments for Raleigh, Essex, and Arabella Stuart. Browne in 1613 was able to redeem the native land by imagining a cultural renewal through the dynastic epithalamic ending of Book I. However, the 1616 allegory of Famine in the first Song of Book II returns to this Spenserian vision of the *patria* as a cultural wasteland, inhospitable to those who seek inspiration through memory. It is the task of the epic poet to commemorate the dead, but in *Britannia's Pastorals* bodies are missing or monuments are lost. The satire on the causes of Famine in the first Song of Book II is succeeded by an abortive epic cultural *translatio* in which it is Spenser himself

---

[69] Colin Burrow, *Epic Romance: Homer to Milton* (Oxford: Clarendon Press, 1993), 229.
[70] The *Ruines of Time* draw on Du Bellay's *Les Antiquitez de Rome* and *Les Regrets*, which in turn engage with Ovid's exilic elegies (Margaret W. Ferguson, ' "The Afflatus of Ruin": Meditations on Rome by Du Bellay, Spenser, and Stevens', in Annabel Patterson (ed.), *Roman Images* (Baltimore and London: The Johns Hopkins University Press, 1982), 23–39; Jeffrey C. Persels, 'Charting Poetic Identity in Exile: Entering Du Bellay's *Regrets*', *Romance Notes*, 28 (1988), 195–202). Browne is attracted to Spenser's reading of Du Bellay and produces his own 'Visions' which draw on *The Ruines of Time*, 'Visions of the World's Vanity', and 'Visions of Bellay' (Browne, *Poems*, ii. 279–82).

who inspires the elegiac vision. An Elizabethan Thetis makes the conventional journey from classical Greece and Rome to Renaissance Italy and France, finally landing at the 'coast of Britany' to hear Colin Clout perform his epic poem, but he dies before it is completed. Thetis–Elizabeth orders a monument, but Avarice intervenes and 'rob'd our *Colin* of his Monument' (27). Avarice is a version of the Blatant Beast that roams free at the end of Book VI of *The Faerie Queene* and a thinly disguised Cecil. The conflict and sense of historical contingency that dominates the first Song has strong affinities with the bleak, elegiac national vision of Spenser's *Ruines of Time*. The failure to memorialize Spenser is equated with the failure of an imperial *translatio*. Satire now takes the place of epic: the poet calls on the '*English Shepheards*, sonnes of *Memory* | For *Satyres* change your pleasing melody' (27), invoking the collaborative eclogues, *The Shepheards Pipe* and *The Shepherds Hunting*.

Browne's identification of Spenser with the exiled Colin Clout of his late pastorals and complaints, such as the *Ruines of Time*, appears to have been encouraged by the 1609 publication of *The Faerie Queene* with the as yet unpublished and mysterious Ovidian fragment, 'The Mutabilitie Cantos'. The 'Mutabilitie Cantos' foreground rather than resolve the tensions of Book VI: the final canto where the poet is threatened by 'a mighty Peres displeasure' would seem to be confirmed by the fragmentary 'Mutabilitie Cantos', and lent support to the myth that Spenser died in poverty due to Cecil's malice.[71] The Ovidian 'Mutabilitie Cantos' direct *The Faerie Queene* away from epic closure and towards the openness and historical contingency of romance.[72] An ambivalent and wandering Spenser is popular amongst Spenserian writers and structures the way that *The Faerie Queene* is being read in the early seventeenth century. He appears in Richard Niccol's *Winter Night's Vision*, appended to

[71] See Joseph Hall's verse before William Beddell's 'A Protestant Memorial, or the Shepherd's Tale of the Powder-Plott' (Bodleian Library, Oxford, MS Rawlinson poet. 154, ff. 11–24).

[72] Gordon Teskey, 'Mutability, Genealogy, and the Authority of Forms', *Representations*, 41 (1993), 113–17. On romance and Book VI see Patricia Parker, *Inescapable Romance: Studies in the Poetics of a Mode* (Princeton: Princeton University Press, 1979) 106, 109, 113; Clare Regan Kinney, *Strategies of Poetic Narrative: Chaucer, Spenser, Milton, Eliot* (Cambridge: Cambridge University Press, 1992), 73, 84–93.

his 1610 edition of *Mirror for Magistrates*, and his *The Cuckow* (1607), where the Elizabethan Philomel finds her song rejected at the court of Phoebe, a vision of James's court as a Spenserian Bower of Bliss, and is exiled in a bleak winter's landscape. The opening simile of Book II of *Britannia's Pastorals* registers a shift towards romance wandering by mapping the structural and imaginative distance between exile and the return to the homeland. The Odysseian 'Marriner (accounted lost) | Vpon the watry *Desert* long time lost', 'descryes his natiue soyle at last', but is suddenly blown back out to sea (ii. 1–2). This echoes Spenser's image of the 'beaten marinere' spying 'port from farre' (I. iii. 31) that is used to figure Una's misrecognition of the dissembling Archimago for Redcrosse, where the false return or repossession of an original unity initiates a period of wandering in exile. Browne takes this simile in an elegiac direction to record his poem's distance from the epic. Marina wanders, lost on 'rouling trenches, of self-drowning waues' (2) prefiguring the following elegy for 'Alexis' lost at sea. Browne here is drawing on the Odyssean metaphors that are employed throughout Book VI of *The Faerie Queene* to figure the weariness of the poet 'in stormie surges tost' which is mirrored in his hero's desire to rest from his quest. Calidore complains that he is 'tossed'

> With stormes of fortune and tempestuous fate,
> In seas of troubles and of toylesome pain,
> That whether quite from the for to retrate
> I shall resolue, or backe to turne againe.   (ix. 31)

The storm tossed ship is an emblem of Odyssean romance and registers the fall from 'an ordered epic narrative into the aimlessness of romance'.[73]

The speaker in Spenser's late pastorals uses this space of exile to explore alternatives to the Virgilian epic. These alternatives take the form of romance and public lyric which appears in Book VI of *The Faerie Queene* and in *Colin Clouts Come Home Againe*.[74] Public lyric gives the poet a new authority deriving from his ability to initiate a collective voice and so define new textual communities. Book II of *Britannia's Pastorals* begins

---

[73] Quint, *Epic and Empire*, 139.
[74] Paul Alpers, 'Spenser's Late Pastorals', *English Literary History*, 56 (1989), 797, 807.

with an elegy for the poet's friend, 'Alexis', that returns to the community of *The Shepheards Pipe*. The speaker, 'Willy', Browne's pastoral persona, desires to secure the body of his friend who died at sea and whose coffin is now *'toss'd by fish and surges fell'*:

> Great Neptune *heare a Swaine!*
>   *His Coffin take,*
>   *And with a golden chaine*
>   *(For pittie) make*
> *It fast vnto a rocke neere land!*
> *Where eue'ry calmy morne Ile stand*
> *And ere one sheepe out of my fold I tell*
> Sad WILLY's *Pipe shall bid his friend* Farewell.   (p. 8)

Sea tossed 'Alexis' condenses the earlier romance images of exile in the opening passages of Book II. The absence of the body of the dead intensifies the recuperative aesthetic vision of the poet. 'Alexis' is a figure for memory, the creative impulse to recover the body of the past that is generated by a sense of exile. The poet finds consolation not only in his own song, which functions as an aesthetic embodiment of the dead friend, but more significantly through his audience dramatized by Marina's responses to the elegy, 'I doe pitty thee: | For who by death is in a true friend crost, | Till he be earth he halfe himselfe hath lost' (8). Sympathy and pity are emotionally linked with friendship. These priorities are present in Marina's lament to Echo, who 'of all woes, onely speakes the last' (6) which frames the elegy, supplying its interpretive context. Echo is both a metaphor for memory and a figure for those marginalized voices that exist on the borders of official culture.[75] Echo had previously appeared in Browne's commendatory verse before *The ghost of Richard the third* where she embodied a Spenserian poetic and she reappears in Book II in a similar form to prefigure the address to the poet's friends and fellow satirists, the '*English Shepheards*, sonnes of *Memory*'.

---

[75] Joseph Loewenstein, *Responsive Readings: Versions of Echo in Pastoral, Epic, and the Jonsonian Masque* (New Haven and London: Yale University Press, 1989), 80.

'English Shepheards, *sonnes of* Memory'

There is a change in direction in the second Song which is
initiated by this address to the English shepherds at the end of
the first Song and the second and third Songs return to the communities of *The Shepheards Pipe* and *The Shepherds Hunting*.
The shepherds' festivals in Book II are a continuation of the
shepherds' holidays in *The Shepheards Pipe* and function to
express a civic consciousness and to materialize textual relationships within existing social communities. Thetis's progress
in the second and third Songs gives direction to the narrative,
and she loses many of her earlier imperial associations to
function as a muse-like figure that provides the occasion and
inspiration for the literary community symbolized by the
English shepherds.[76] This Arcadian community is an offspring
of Sannazaro's *Arcadia* and Spenser's *Colin Clouts Come Home
Againe*. Sannazaro's Arcadia is a literary landscape that tends
towards the elegiac in its sense of a contemporary culture that
can no longer sustain a humanist poetics.[77] The Arcadian community in the second Song, by contrast, is transformed into an
idealized refuge in which an English humanist poetic tradition
can prosper, and in these terms it is closer to the community of
shepherds in *Colin Clouts Come Home Againe*. These Songs
consciously situate themselves within a tradition of Elizabethan
lyric. In Browne's hands, the lyric signifies his membership of
the educated gentry classes, which in turn allies him with the
community of London and Inns of Court based writers represented by the English shepherds. Membership requires the social
and linguistic refinements associated with courtly lyric, while,
paradoxically, alienation from a court culture becomes an
affirmation of the writer's inclusion within this 'professional'
community.

Rituals and fictions of community are expressed through
festive singing contests. The song contest is a sophisticated form
of gift-giving that bonds the community and simultaneously

[76] Thetis in these Songs has a similar function to Drayton's muse as described by
Helgerson (*Forms of Nationhood: The Elizabethan Writing of England* (Chicago
and London: University of Chicago Press, 1992), 143–5).

[77] William Kennedy, *Jacopo Sannazaro and the Uses of Pastoral* (Hanover and
London: University Press of New England, 1983), 100–48. On the influence of the
Arcadia on *Britannia's Pastorals*, see: Grundy, 'Browne and the Italian Pastoral',
310.

enacts a process of literary exchange. The first song sung in
the second Song by the youthful shepherd-poet, a version of
Browne's pastoral persona, clearly echoes Shakespeare's
epyllion 'Venus and Adonis'. Intertextuality here opens a
creative dialogue with poetic forebears that validates the poetic
'origin' and the poet's own echoic song. Browne's poetic
persona is deliberately composite, put together by assuming the
identity of powerful poetic forebears. Sidney, 'Astrophell', is
claimed as his primary pastoral forefather, 'Sidney began . . . I
sung the Past'rall next; his Muse, my mover' (36). The insistent
intertextuality of Britannia's Pastorals serves to map poetic
lineages, to construct literary communities, and in this sense it
is reminiscent of the collaborative energies of The Shepheards
Pipe. In this second Song, the poet takes over the mantle of an
orphic Ovid from the Elizabethan Ovidian poets with his
audience leaving 'the Thracian for the English Swaine' (33). The
song contest dramatizes the interaction between a writer and his
audience and enables Browne to interpellate a specific readership, situating the processes of literary exchange within a contemporary social environment. Elizabethan Ovidianism was
centred in the universities and Inns of Court and here Browne's
imitative poem dialogically invokes its earlier social conditions
and readership.[78] The following lyric in praise of his mistress
had already gained popularity amongst his Inns of Court
associates; in his commendatory verse to Shepheards Pipe,
Onley had played on the line 'Be she browne, or, faire' (35) in
his 'Fair Muse of Browne'.[79]

Browne's poems in general tended to circulate widely in
manuscript miscellanies, the path of transmission probably
beginning within the Inns of Court and then radiating to
universities and other scribal communities.[80] The verses in
Britannia's Pastorals that proved most popular were the songs
at the end of the third Song of Book I, the elegy for 'Alexis', set
to music by Henry Lawes, and the lyric songs interspersed
throughout Book II. These lyrics enact a process of textual and
intellectual exchange that also characterizes the printed and

[78] William Keach, Elizabethan Erotic Narratives: Irony and Pathos in the
Ovidian Poetry of Shakespeare, Marlowe, and their Contemporaries (Sussex:
Harvester, 1977), 29–40.
[79] Shepheards Pipe, A4v.
[80] Beal, Index of English Literary Manuscripts, i. 115.

scribal miscellany. The exchange of verses recorded in the miscellany gave a textual representation of networks of friends and associates that typically coincided with established social communities from the Inns of Court and the universities to groups of like-minded individuals.[81] The singing festivals of Book II situate themselves within the communities represented in the verses before *Britannia's Pastorals*: Browne's fellow Inner Templars and Inns of Court men; the friends from *Shepheards Pipe*, Brooke, Wither, and John Davies of Hereford; and a professional community of established poets, represented by Drayton and Jonson. The Inns of Court community was not discrete but intersected with other types of community. For example, John Glanville, who provided the opening commendatory verse for Book II, was Browne's fellow countryman, born at Kilworthy near Tavistock, and in the 1614 parliament was the MP for Liskeard in Cornwall, while his brother, Francis, was MP for Browne's birthplace, Tavistock. John was a member of Brooke's Inn, Lincoln's Inn, and the Glanville brothers sat on a number of committees with him in this parliament, and appear to have shared his opposition to the crown over certain key issues.[82] This 'country' community also included court patronage relationships. Browne's dedication of Book II to William Herbert, Earl of Pembroke, who had emerged as the leader of a 'patriot' court grouping in this period, inaugurated a successful patronage relationship with the Herbert family that lasted until Browne's death.[83] The 'country' community projected by *Britannia's Pastorals* has a diverse social basis and should be seen as a network of interconnected communities rather than an ideologically coherent social grouping.

[81] Love, *Scribal Publication*, 79–82.
[82] Browne owned a manuscript that included 'Eight bookes of Poeticall Astrologie written in the form of an Epistle, . . . by John Glanvill of Lyncolnes Inn, gentleman' (Bodleian Library, Oxford, MS Ashmole 45). *Proceedings in Parliament, 1614*, 291, 294, 395, 397; Thomas Moir, *The Addled Parliament of 1614* (Oxford: Oxford University Press, 1958), 129. Glanville continued to have a prominent role in opposition to the crown in the 1620s parliaments, although he ultimately remained loyal to Charles and was impeached in 1643 (*DNB*, xxi. 413).
[83] Brennan, *Literary Patronage of the Herbert family*, 122–39; Simon Adams, 'Spain or the Netherlands? The Dilemmas of Early Stuart Foreign Policy', in Howard Tomlinson (ed.), *Before the English Civil War: Essays on Early Stuart Politics and Government* (London: Macmillan, 1983), 92.

The centrepiece of the second Song is a textual monument that honours Browne's contemporaries. The established poets, Chapman, Drayton, Jonson, and Daniel head the list and are joined by his friends from *Shepheards Pipe*, Brooke, Wither, and John Davies of Hereford. This is a distinctly English literary community led by poets who have surpassed their classical forefathers in the best humanist tradition: Chapman, the English Homer, Drayton, 'our second *Ouid*', and Jonson, the English Seneca (36–7). Browne's panegyric takes the place of the abandoned monument to Spenser in the first Song and fills the cultural vacuum opened by his death. The writers represented are ideologically and poetically diverse: Chapman, Drayton, Daniel, Brooke, Wither, and Davies could *very* loosely all be described as Spenserians, but Jonson is usually identified with a rival literary tradition.[84] Browne unites these poets by representing them as the inheritors of a humanist tradition of public poetry descended from Sidney and Spenser. This English literary community takes a civic form that is reminscent of *The Shepheards Pipe* and is determined by a concept of writers' collective agency in shaping culture and constituting the conditions for writing. The parameters of this literary commonwealth are constituted in opposition to a patronage culture. The conditions which unite these writers are envy and neglect, 'base contempt', and autonomy from the 'bondage' of patronage, 'Nor great in titles make our worth obey, | Since we haue lines farre more esteem'd then they' (38), and later in the fourth Song, 'My free-borne *Muse* will not like *Danae* be | Wonne with base drosse to clip with slauery' (89). Browne and his fellow Spenserians consistently represent patronage as synonymous with court corruption and satirize court poetry as worthless panegyric that debases the humanist ideal. This projected commonwealth of literature, however, exists uneasily alongside the patronage relationships of Chapman, Daniel, Jonson, and Browne himself. Moreover, Chapman, Daniel, and Jonson could easily be candidates for Browne's Danae since they all enjoyed the patronage of the newly-fallen royal favourite, Somerset, and Chapman and Daniel remained loyal to him, although Jonson seems to have

---

[84] See David Norbrook's *Poetry and Politics in the English Renaissance* (London: Routledge and Kegan Paul, 1984), 197–200.

found himself compromised when the scandal broke.[85] Browne's literary commonwealth is a fiction that enables the humanist poet to claim a professional autonomy from the dominant social order. This autonomy is, to a certain extent, illusory. With the 'English shepherds', Browne imagined a professional community that did not as yet have an institutional basis and still had a dependency on a patronage culture.

The fictions of community that structure these Songs find their textual equivalent in the practice of intertextuality. The exquisite rainbow simile in the third Song is a metaphor for the metamorphic intertextuality of *Britannia's Pastorals* as a whole:

> As in the *Rainbowes* many coloured hewe
> Here see wee watchet deepned with a blewe,
> There a darke tawny with a purple mixt,
> Yealow and flame, with streakes of greene betwixt,
> A bloudy streame into a blushing run
> And ends still with the colour which begun,
> Drawing the deeper to a lighter staine,
> Bringing the lightest to the deep'st againe,
> With such rare Art each mingleth with his fellow,
> Like to the changes which we daily see
> About the Doues necke with varietie,
> Where none can say (though he it strict attends)
> Here one begins; and there the other ends:
> So did the Maidens with their various flowres
> Decke vp their windowes, and make neate their bowres.   (p. 62)

The 'rare Art' of the rainbow's 'many coloured hewe' is the art of copia in which variation and transformation are the organizing principles. The variety of colours, 'Where none can say . . . | Here one begins; and there the other ends'—a theme which is elaborated through the use of enjambment—is a poetic figure for the fluid heterogeneity of *Britannia's Pastorals*. The poem's assimilation of a variety of texts and sources is described in terms of a metamorphic, transformational aesthetic in which 'borrowed fragments are naturalized

---

[85] A. R. Braunmuller, 'Robert Carr, Earl of Somerset, as Collector and Patron', in Linda Levy Peck (ed.), *The Mental World of the Jacobean Court* (Cambridge: Cambridge University Press, 1991), 240–6; John Pitcher, *Samuel Daniel: The Brotherton Manuscript* (University of Leeds, 1981), 66–70, 98; David Lindley, 'Embarassing Ben: The Masques for Frances Howard', *English Literary Renaissance*, 16 (1986), 344–5.

('digested') and re-issued as members of a new corpus'.[86] Browne's rainbow itself has its source in the Ovidian story of Arachne where it describes the *intertextos* of Arachnean art, 'the seamless web of changing narrative'.[87] Arachne is Ovid's double and the metamorphic verisimilitude of her tapestry signifies a new aesthetic, represented by the *Metamorphoses* itself, that marks a radical departure from the linearity of the Virgilian epic.[88] Post-structuralist theorizing of intertextuality tends to prioritize the text over the maker—the author—and to delegitimize discussions of agency and the materiality of the writing and reading subject. However, the figure of Arachne, the weaver, describes a theory of intertextuality that is predicated on the agency of the poetic maker.[89] Browne follows Ovid in adopting Arachne for his own aesthetic and he significantly concentrates on her activity as the Lydian weaver, the maker of texts, prior to her disabling and deforming metamorphosis into a spider, and so rescues her from a medieval tradition of *Ovid moralise* in which Arachne the spider is associated with the arts of dissimulation. Browne appropriates weaving as his poetic signature: the rainbow simile is secured in the activity of the maiden's weaving garlands for their bowers which in turn stands in for the virtuousity of the male poet and his metamorphic text.

Intertextuality in these Songs is central to the formation of national communities as it enables the poet to construct common literary traditions. The landscape of Britannia is not defined through families or dynasties, but rather through rivers, natural monuments, and other poets who have given voice and representation to the land. The narrative in the fourth Song

[86] Terence Cave, *The Cornucopian Text: Problems of Writing in the French Renaissance* (Oxford: Clarendon Press, 1979), 278.

[87] Leonard Barkan, *The Gods Made Flesh: Metamorphosis and the Pursuit of Paganism* (New Haven and London: Yale University Press, 1986), 3–5.

[88] Pamela Royston MacFie, 'Text and *Textura*: Spenser's Arachnean Art', in D. Allen and R. White (eds.), *Traditions and Innovations: Essays on British Literature of the Middle Ages and the Renaissance* (Newark: University of Delaware Press, 1990), 89–91, and 'Ovid, Arachne, and the Poetics of Paradise', in Rachel Jacoff and Jeffrey T. Schnapp (eds.), *The Poetry of Allusion: Virgil and Ovid in Dante's 'Commedia'* (Stanford: Standford University Press, 1991), 160–3.

[89] Nancy K. Miller coins the term 'arachnology' to refer particularly to women's agency and a feminist poetics in her 'Arachnologies: The Woman, the Text, and the Critic' in Nancy Miller (ed.), *The Poetics of Gender* (New York: Columbia University Press, 1986), 271.

takes the form of an 'unfolding' of the work of generations of English poets who are vital sources of individual and national inspiration:

On now my loued *Muse*, and let vs bring
Thetis to heare the *Cornish Michael* sing;
And after him to see a Swaine vnfold
The Tragedie of DRAKE in leaues of gold.
Then heare another *Greenvils* name relate,
Which times suceeding shall perpetuate.
And make those two the *Pillers* great of *Fame*,
Beyond whose worths shall neuer sound a Name.   (p. 90)

These monuments to Drake and Grenville are the hagiographies written at the close of Elizabeth's reign, Charles Fitzgeffrey's popular *Sir Francis Drake his Honorable lifes commendation and his Tragicall Deathes lamentation* (1596), and Gervase Markham's *The most Honorable Tragedy of Sir Richard Grinville, Knight* (1596). In the opening stanzas of his own poem, Fitzgeffrey had called on his fellow poets, Spenser, Daniel, and Drayton, to follow him by honouring the memory of Drake and so revive a flagging nationalism.[90] Fitzgeffrey and Markham join a native tradition of public poetry that stretches back to the medieval topographical poets, 'Cornish Michael' and 'aged *Robert*, (who) sung of yore, | In praise of *England*' (90–1): Michael Blaunpayn, Dean of Maestricht around 1250, and Robert of Gloucester, author of the *Metricle Chronicle* and patron of William of Malmesbury, whose chronicles were used by Browne for a number of the historical and topographical references in *Britannia's Pastorals*. The third Song had invoked Joseph of Exeter's poem on the Trojan wars to mark Thetis's arrival at Exmouth. Extracts from these poets were available in Camden's antiquarian work, *Remaines*, first published in 1605 and again in 1614. Woolf has described this work as 'the skeleton of a cultural history of England' and, in a similar fashion to *Britannia's Pastorals*, it offers a national narrative based on the work of the country's poets and works to construct a history of the land out of earlier cultural fictions.[91]

---

[90] Fitzgeffrey, *Sir Francis Drake his Honorable lifes commendation and his Tragicall Deathes lamentation* (Oxford, 1596), STC 10944, B5r.

[91] Daniel Woolf, 'Change and Continuity in English Historical Thought, *c.*1590–1640', D.Phil. thesis (Oxford, 1983), 246. The further revised edition of 1623, the

Browne's own poetry consciously looks back to medieval poets, who in turn are the founding fathers in his canon of '*British Bards*' (91). The process of canon formation, of constructing distinctly nationalistic literary traditions, coincides with the formation of an antiquarian community in the late sixteenth and early seventeenth centuries. Hansen points to the way that this community was shaped by the sharing of knowledge and intellectual exchange; an ideal of dialogue and intellectual friendship that is celebrated by Browne and his fellow Spenserian poets.[92] Browne seems to have become involved in antiquarian circles through the Inns of Court. He had begun acquiring medieval manuscripts in his youth, including a number of volumes from the library of John Stow who died in 1605.[93] He also owned at least one manuscript from the library of Sir Thomas North, the translator of Plutarch, who died around 1601.[94] His antiquarianism coincides with his interest in constructing native poetic traditions. A programme of recovery of medieval writers is evident in *The Shepheards Pipe* where he publishes a modernized version of Hoccleve's 'The Gesta Tale of Jonathas and Fellicula', 'never before imprinted', and informs the reader that 'As this shall please, I may be drawn to publish the rest of his works, being all perfect in my hands.'[95] Hoccleve's *Regement of Princes* was of especial

year of Camden's death, included Browne's unpublished epitaph on the Dowager Countess of Pembroke (STC 4523, 340), and the 1636 edition included his unpublished elegy on Anne Prideaux (STC 4525).

[92] Hansen, 'Identity and Ownership', 90–1.

[93] These volumes include: *Willelmi de Malmesbiria de gestis Regnum Angorum*, Book V (British Library, Add. MS 23,147); a collection of English poems by Chaucer and Lydgate (British Library, Add. MS 34,360); *Chronicle of Brute in English* (British Library, MS Stowe 68); *The Pilgrimage of the Life of Man*, a translation of Guillaume de Deguile Ville's *Pelerinage de la vie humaine* ascribed to Lydgate (British Library, MS Stowe 952); a collection of medieval ballads (Bodleian Library, Oxford, MS Ashmole 59); a collection of Hoccleve's poems (Cathedral Library, Durham, MS Cosin V III.9). Annabel Patterson argues that 'it can be inferred' from his manuscript collections and 'independent historiographical projects . . . that Stow was unusually interested in political protest and resistance' (*Reading between the lines* (London: Routledge, 1993), 123).

[94] *Legenda Sanctorum in Englisshe* (British Library, Add. MS 35,298). This volume of lives of the English saints probably provided the source for his reference to 'holy *Vrsula*' in the fourth Song (91).

[95] This text derives from a manuscript of Hoccleve's poems (MS Cosin V III. 9). He also owned a MS of the works of Lydgate, previously in the library of Sir Thomas Tresham (1543–1605), (Bodleian Library, Oxford, MS Ashmole 46, and a

interest to Browne; he undertook a large amount of restoration work on the volume, replacing missing lines of text and leaves, as well as correcting errors in the transcription.[96] These interests appear to have drawn him to his fellow Inner Templar, John Selden, and the two shared books and information. When restoring the *Regement of Princes*, it is likely that he collated his manuscript with a second volume owned by Selden which included the *Regement* and six *Gesta* tales.[97] In *Britannia's Pastorals*, he often refers the reader to his 'very learned Friend Mr. Selden' (i. 1): in the third Song of Book II, he notes the publication of Joseph of Exeter's poem on the Trojan wars in Germany where it has been 'falsly attributed to *Cornelius Nepos*' and directs the reader to Selden's notes in *Poly-Olbion* for confirmation of this attribution.[98] This type of inter-textuality grounds the text within a material process of intellec-tual exchange and dialogue. His friendship with Selden and Drayton suggests that he was also in contact with the circle that had gathered around Sir Robert Cotton and his library and included William Camden.[99] Antiquarianism had gained a certain prominence around 1614, the year when Cotton, Camden, Sir William Spelman, and Sir John Davies unsuccess-fully attempted to revive the Society of Antiquaries.[100] It was a period that coincided with a renewed interest in topographical poetry, in the fashioning of a poetic that explores the terrain of

MS of a medieval romance, *The Story of the Erle of Tolous*, once owned by Sir William Fitzwilliam (1526–99), lord deputy of Ireland (Bodeleian Library, Oxford, MS Ashmole 45 (W. H. Black, *A Descriptive, Analytical, and Critical Catalogue of the Manuscripts bequeathed unto the University of Oxford by Elias Ashmole* (Oxford: Oxford University Press, 1845), 69–71).

[96] Hoccleve, *The Regement of Princes* (Bodleian Library, Oxford, MS Ashmole 40). This is no firm evidence that his MS was from Stow's library, see: M. C. Seymour, 'The Manuscripts of Hoccleve's *Regiment of Princes*', *Edinburgh Bibliographical Society Transactions*, 4 (1974), 278.

[97] Bodleian Library, Oxford, MS Arch Selden Supra 53.

[98] Drayton, *Poly-Olbion*, 125–6. A similar point is made in Camden's *Britannia: or a Chorographical Description of Great Britain and Ireland, together with adjacent islands* (trans. E. Gibson, 2nd edn. (London, 1722), 40).

[99] Drayton was a friend of Stow, Cotton, and Camden, possibly using Cotton's library for *Poly-Olbion*. Cotton also knew Christopher Brooke through their con-temporary Richard Martin (Kevin Sharpe, *Sir Robert Cotton, 1586–1631, History and Politics in Early Modern England* (Oxford: Oxford University Press, 1979), 198, 206).

[100] J. Evans, *A History of the Society of Antiquaries* (Oxford: Oxford University Press, 1956), 8–13.

Camden's *Britannia*, that is evident in works such as Drayton's *Poly-Olbion* and Browne's *Britannia's Pastorals*.

Although antiquarianism did not necessarily take on an oppositional cast in the early seventeenth century, nor was it free from political interests. Selden's early writings on the history of English institutions supported the authority of parliament and its institutional status in a period when the crown was perceived to be encroaching upon its privileges. Browne's antiquarianism similarly often has a political dimension. He extensively annotates Hoccleve's *Regement of Princes*, a reformist 'advice to princes', and reads the poem politically, marking passages that urge social and religious reform and advise on the good government of princes.[101] The *Regement* is a likely source for his own 'advice to princes' in the allegory of Famine: he notes passages that counsel Henry 'Not to begge pardon for Murderers' (f. 51), 'Avarice ill beseems a Prince' (f. 72), 'Prodigalitie in a Prince beggars the commonwealth' (f. 79), 'Ambition and auarice causeth Civill Warres' (f. 93), and 'Learninge vnrewarded when adulation is well beneficed' (f. 94). The satiric digression on the plight of veteran soldiers in the fourth Song echoes Hoccleve's 'On Avarice' where Browne's annotation, 'Shame to begge' (f. 83) marks a passage on the degradation of the honest poor through begging and calls on Prince Henry to relieve the plight of his soldiers on his accession (ff. 83–4).

Intertexuality is the poetic of community in *Britannia's Pastorals* and enables Browne to stage a dialogue with his literary forefathers and with contemporary communities of writers and intellectuals, ranging from Inns of Court contemporaries to fellow poets and scholarly antiquarian circles. The diversity of these communities suggests the emergence of cultures that were not fully dependent on the court, but were attaining a degree of autonomy exemplified by the antiquaries' attempts to define a society that was not divorced from a patronage culture, yet able to organize itself in terms of its own professional standards and intellectual pursuits.[102]

---

[101] Hoccleve, *The Minor Poems*, ed. F. J. Furnivall and I. Gollancz; rev. J. Mitchell and A. I. Doyle (Oxford: Oxford University Press, 1970), xix.

[102] Hansen, 'Identity and Ownership', 89–91.

'Haile thou, my natiue soile'

James's 'union of the crowns' brought about a shift in the meaning of empire. The Reformation had defined an imperial monarchy, in the words of Thomas Wilson in 1600, as 'held neither of Pope, Emperor nor of any of but God'.[103] With the 'union of the crowns' in 1603, empire took on associations that looked back to the Roman Empire, rather than the Reformation, to describe 'an aggregation of dominions' under the authority of one monarch—as James styled the new state in a 1604 proclamation, 'our imperial monarchy of these two great kingdoms'. The Jacobean union was an imperial and dynastic union, not a 'perfect union', that united the kingdoms in James's person, in his blood, but not in the body politic, as the laws, churches, and political institutions of Scotland and England remained distinct.[104] Widespread enthusiasm had at first greeted the union, however, once the implications began to be explored in parliament and the law courts, it soon became a site for English anxiety over sovereignty and prompted a rethinking of issues relating to monarchy, state institutions, and nationhood. Lawyer's objections had caused James to withdraw his proposal to call the new state 'Greater Britanny', but in the 1604 proclamation he gave himself the title King of Great Britain 'by force of our royal prerogative'.[105]

The Stuart union defined empire regno-centrically and reinvigorated the Virgilian identification between the nation as empire and an ideology of monarchy.[106] Exile functions in Book II to rupture this identification and to redirect attention to other narratives and communities marginalized by this ideology of empire. Fictions of nationhood in Book II are generated by a state of exile.[107] Exile provides a trope that reorientates and

[103] Quoted in Brian Levack, *The Formation of the British State: England, Scotland, and the Union* (Oxford: Clarendon Press, 1987), 2.

[104] Levack, *Formation of the British State*, 1–4; C. H. Firth, 'The British Empire', *The Scottish Historical Review*, 15 (1918), 185–6.

[105] Firth, 'British Empire', 186.

[106] For this ideological encoding of the Virgilian epic, see David Quint, *Epic and Empire: Politics and Generic Form from Virgil to Milton* (Princeton: Princeton University Press, 1993), 7–9.

[107] Exile and nationalism in the early modern period are not conflicting states, although Timothy Brennan views them as 'conflicting poles of feeling that correspond to more traditional aesthetic conflicts: artistic iconoclasm and communal

transforms the relationship between the individual and the native land, and the resulting dislocation is experienced creatively so that the landscape of exile is imagined as a new place. Browne derives his topos of exile from Spenser, in particular, his Irish poems *Colin Clouts Come Home Againe* and 'The Mutabilitie Cantos'. For Spenser, Ireland provides 'home-away-from-home' where the poet claims the freedom to fashion himself, his community, and the 'new' land. In this case, the exilic narrative coalesces with a programme of colonization and the 'new' homeland must be violently cleared in order to be re-imagined.[108] The trope of exile takes a parallel historical path in *Britannia's Pastorals* that converges at points with a narrative of colonization, but is regional rather than global in its orientation. Exile is internalized as the poet turns inward to his birthplace Devon, which is transformed into his *patria* and his *natio*, his native land.

Browne's poetic response to Devon is informed by a range of historical and ideological imperatives. In broad terms, it participates in a new consciousness of the land demonstrated by the increasing interest in patriotic and regional poetry in the seventeenth century.[109] Changing responses to the land were shaped by a new agrarian economics, the professional consolidation of antiquarianism, and the contestation of the political and religious space of the 'country'.[110] Devon functions in a synecdochic relation to the nation in *Britannia's Pastorals* and, like Britannia, is an imagined community made up of a net-

assent, the unique vision and the collective truth' ('The National Longing for Form', in Homi Bhabha (ed.), *Nation and Narration* (London, 1990), 60–1).

[108] Julia Reinhard Lupton, 'Home-making in Ireland: Virgil's Eclogue I and Book VI of *The Faerie Queene*', *Spenser Studies*, 7 (1990), 119–24; 'Mapping Mutability: or, Spenser's Irish Plot', in Brendan Bradshaw *et al.* (eds.), *Representing Ireland* (Cambridge: Cambridge University Press, 1994), 99–105.

[109] Chris Fitter sees the Spenserians as belonging to a sixteenth- rather than seventeenth-century view of the land, but this view does not take into account the ideological dimension of their poetry or the significance of antiquarianism or recognize the generic diversity of *Britannia's Pastorals* (*Poetry, Space, Landscape: Towards a New Theory* (Cambridge: Cambridge University Press, 1995), 270).

[110] Andrew Macrae, 'Husbandry Manuals and the Language of Agrarian Improvement', in Michael Leslie and Timothy Raylor (eds.), *Culture and Cultivation in Early Modern England* (Leicester and London: Leicester University Press, 1992), 35–7; Hanson, 'Identity and Ownership', 85–105; Richard Cust and Ann Hughes, 'Introduction: After Revisionism', in Cust and Hughes, *Conflict in Early Stuart England: Studies in Religion and Politics, 1603–1642* (London and New York: Longman, 1989), 19–20.

work of overlapping and sometimes divergent narratives of nationhood that, as such, do not and cannot cohere into an homogeneous landscape. There are three generically mixed interlocking narrative forms that constitute the landscape of Britannia in the poem: a patriotic regional epic, an Ovidian epyllion, and a lyricized poetics of place. These narrative forms work to disrupt earlier imperial forms, thereby divesting the epic of a monarchical ideology and offering alternative narratives of the land. None of these narrative forms are completed in the poem, rather they are in the process of being fashioned, which contributes to the poem's distinctive formlessness. Alongside the linearity of the epic, *Britannia's Pastorals* appears deformed and deviant, however, this is symptomatic of the way that imperial forms are being dismantled in the poem to produce other, as yet incoherent nationalist narratives.[111]

A patriotic regional epic is glimpsed in the third Song of Book II. Thetis's imperial progress takes her along the '*Kentish, Sussex* shores' to Devon, and inspires the poet's panegyric to his homeland, 'Haile thou my natiue soile! thou blessed plot, | Whose equall all the world affordeth not!' The landscape or rather seascape is imagined through the memory of Devon's Elizabethan naval heroes:

> Time neuer can produce men to o're-take
> The fames of *Greenuil, Dauies, Gilbert, Drake,*
> Or worthy *Hawkins* or of thousands more
> That by their powre made the *Deuonian* shore
> Mocke the proud *Tagus.*   (p. 67)

Memory is central to the formation of national myths and functions to interpellate a collective past.[112] National unity in the past has been achieved through hostility to Spain: the '*Deuonian* shore' is a natural national boundary symbolically constituted through conflict with a rival imperial power. This fiction of nationhood is structured by the Protestant vision of England as the elect nation. Under Elizabeth, this discourse shaped English imperialism and tended to mediate between

---

[111] See Quint on the subversive formlessness of romance (*Epic and Empire*, 34, 41).

[112] Eric Hobsbawn, 'Inventing Traditions', in Eric Hobsbawn and Terence Ranger (eds.), *The Invention of Traditions*, 2nd edn. (Cambridge: Canto, 1992), 1–8.

loyalty to the monarch and loyalty to an abstract concept of the state.[113] The local heroes, Grenville, Davies, Gilbert, and Drake, however, are remembered as instruments of divine justice in the service of the land and not the monarch, subduing the 'boasting *Spaniard*' for the greater honour and fame of Devon. The poet's pride in his native soil is shaped in part by the strong patriotic local identity that had emerged in Devon in the sixteenth century. The county in this period was central to England's economy, military defences, and colonial enterprises— Grenville, Gilbert, and Hawkins had all been involved in the colonization of the Americas and the Indies. By the end of Elizabeth's reign, Devon was also one of the strongest Protestant counties with several key parishes held by Puritan ministers.[114] A monument to Elizabeth was once painted on the wall of the parish church of Tavistock with the following verse inscription:

> This! This was she, that in despight of death
> Lives still ador'd, admired Elizabeth:
> Spain's rod, Rome's ruin, Netherland's relief,
> Heaven's gem, earth's joy, world's wonder, nature's chief.[115]

In a similar fashion to *Britannia's Pastorals*, Elizabeth is remembered in militant Protestant terms, leading the elect nation into battle against Catholicism at home and abroad. Yet, the memory of the dead queen paradoxically disrupts the identification of the current monarch with the nation as this symbolic space is simultaneously already filled and empty, occupied by a ghostly absent presence. Elizabethan nostalgia here enables the poet to reorientate a Protestant nationalist rhetoric towards the land and its people represented by local heroes, such as Drake, Grenville, Gilbert, and Hawkins.

Fitzgeffrey's and Markham's late Elizabethan hagiographies of England's naval heroes, that are invoked in the fourth Song of *Britannia's Pastorals*, underlie Browne's vision of a regional patriotic epic. These hagiographies were structured by an

---

[113] Patrick Collinson, *The Birthpangs of Protestant England: Religious and Cultural Change in the Sixteenth and Seventeenth Centuries* (London: Macmillan, 1988), 2.

[114] Hoskins, *Devon*, 62, 206–8, 237; Thirsk, *Agrarian History*, 73–6.

[115] Quoted from Prince's transcription in A. E. Bray, *A Description of the part of Devonshire bordering on the Tamar and Tavy*, 3 vols. (London: John Murray, 1836), i. 129–30.

aristocratic politics that privileges martial independence, an heroic individualism, and the pursuit of honour.[116] Fitzgeffrey and Markham were associated with Essex's circle: Fitzgeffrey praised Essex as the sole remaining pillar of Elizabethan militancy (D7r), while Markham's *Tragedy of Sir Richard Grinville* was dedicated to Essex's circle, Lord Mountjoy, the Earls of Sussex and Southampton, and Sir Edward Wingfield, and both poems are strongly anti-Spanish and patriotically Protestant.[117] The type of aristocratic politics represented by these volumes is transferred to Devon's naval heroes and the land itself in Book II of *Britannia's Pastorals*. The epic celebration of the English empire through its naval heroes loosens the Virgilian associations between the imperium and the monarchy. The county is the new *patria*, the homeland, and the focus of revitalized nationalistic energies. *Britannia's Pastorals* provided Browne's contemporaries with a model for the patriotic epic. In 1624, William Kidley, an undergraduate at Browne's college, Exeter, consciously styled himself on the older poet and began an heroic chorographical poem, 'Kidley's Hawkins or A Poetical Relation of the Voyage of S[i]r Richard Hawkins Knight', that drew much of its inspiration from Book II.[118]

An heroic Devon in Book II is imagined through its estuaries and rivers which carry traces of the Roman rivers of empire. These imperial rivers brought the furthest reaches of empire to the centre of Rome; the strength and progress of the Tiber symbolized the processes of civilization, the dissemination of Roman *virtú* throughout its colonies. Virgil invested the imperial river with a monarchical politics, tracing in the course of the Tiber a dynastic history that found its fulfilment in Augustus.[119] The rivers of empire in *Britannia's Pastorals* are fragmented into local county rivers and, although they still bear the memory of the earlier form, the new seascape and land-

[116] Mervyn James, 'English Politics and the Concept of Honour, 1485–1642', *Past and Present*, Suppl. 3 (1978), 31.

[117] Markham, *The most Honorable Tragedy of Sir Richard Grinville, Knight* (London, 1596), STC 17385, B4v.

[118] William Kidley, 'Kidley's Hawkins or A Poetical Relation of the Voyage of S[i]r Richard Hawkins Knight vnto Mare Del[A]zore . . . The History of 88 w[i]th other Historical Passages of those Tymes . . .' (British Library, Sloane MS 2024, f. 8).

[119] William Herendeen, *From Landscape to Literature: The River and the Myth of Geography* (Pittsburgh: Duquesne University Press, 1986), 52–7.

scape are loosened from regnal histories. Local patriotism and nationalism are mutually reinforcing and, in many ways, Browne's identification with his 'native soil' is at the centre of the poem's sense of nationhood. Helgerson argues that nationalism 'ultimately justifies' the particularity of the local county chorographies produced in the early seventeenth century: 'the nation, unlike the dynasty, is in turn strengthened by its very receptiveness to such individual and communal autonomy'.[120]

Browne's plans for a regional epic would produce a poem along the lines of Drayton's *Poly-Olbion*. Sovereignty resides in the land and its rivers:

> Ile striue to draw
> The *Nymphs* by *Thamar, Tauy, Ex* and *Tau*,
> By *Turridge, Otter, Ock,* by *Dert* and *Plym*,
> With all the *Nayades* that fish and swim
> In their cleare streames, to these our rising Downes,
> Where while they make vs chaplets, wreaths & crownes,
> Ile tune my Reede vnto a higher key,
> (And haue already cond some of the *Lay*.)   (p. 86)

By the 1620s, Browne had gained a reputation as a distinctively Devon poet amongst the chorographers of the county. Nathaniel Carpenter in his *Geographie Delineated Forth in two Bookes*, first published in 1625 and dedicated to Browne's patron, Pembroke, praised Browne and *Britannia's Pastorals* and, in the section on his 'owne Countrey of *Deuon*', identified him as a native Devon poet, saying that he would leave the writing of Devon's poetic heritage to Browne who 'will easily bee intreated a little farther to grace it, by drawing out the line of his *Poeticke* Auncestors, beginning in *Iosephus Iscarus*, and ending in *himselfe*'.[121] Thomas Westcote published Browne's 'Lydford Law', only available in manuscript form, in his *A View of Devonshire*, and similarly identified him as a local poet.[122] His associate, Tristram Risdon in his *Chorographical Description of Devon*, a work begun in 1605 and completed in manu-

---

[120] Helgerson, *Forms of Nationhood*, 138.

[121] Nathaniel Carpenter, *Geographie Delineated Forth in two Bookes. Containing the Sphericall and Topicall parts thereof*, 2nd edn. (Oxford, 1635), STC 4677, Rr2v–4v.

[122] Thomas Westcote, *View of Devonshire in MDCXXX, with a Pedigree of Most of its Gentry*, ed. Rev. G. Oliver and Pitman Jones (Exeter, 1845), 359–61.

script in 1630, incorporated an anonymous topographical verse, a 'gift from a friend', on the Devon rivers, the Tamar, Torridge, and Ock, in a style strongly influenced by Browne.[123]

National myths are consistently disassociated from the Stuart dynasty thoughout Book II and rather gain their authority from custom and ancient tradition and the process of myth-making itself. The legend of Trojan Brute, for example, had been assimilated to Stuart dynastic fictions and had enabled James to present himself as reinvigorating an ancient British empire.[124] *Britannia's Pastorals* resolutely ignored this Stuart version of the Trojan myth and instead traced the myth to the medieval chroniclers and to the land itself:

> The *Brittish Bards* then were not long time mute,
> But to their sweet *Harps* sung their famous *Brute*:
> Striuing in spight of all mists of eld
> To haue his *Story* more authenticque held.
> Why should we enuy them those wreaths of *Fame*?
> Being as proper to the *Trojan* name
> As the dainty flowres which *Flora* spreads
> Vnto the *Spring* in the discoloured Meads.
> Rather afford them all the worth we may,
> For what we giue to them adds to our Ray. (p. 91)

Browne is echoing Drayton's attack on 'fooles that all Antiquitie defame' because 'some credulous Ages layd | Slight fictions with the truth' (vi. 276–83). In doing so, he enters into the 'friendly discourse and debate' between Drayton and Selden that structures *Poly-Olbion*.[125] Selden's criticisms of medieval chronicles in terms of their credibility as historical sources is part of a broader rejection of the monarchical politics which inform chronicle history.[126] Browne still has a cultural investment in the form of the chronicle history, but his political objectives in revising the Stuart version of the Trojan myth

---

[123] Tristram Risdon, *The Chorographical Description, or, Survey of the County of Devon* (London, 1714), 302–6. I have been unable to identify the author of this verse.

[124] Graham Parry, *The Golden Age Restor'd: The Culture of the Stuart Court, 1603–42* (Manchester: Manchester University Press, 1981), 8–9.

[125] Paul Christianson, 'Young John Selden and the Ancient Constitution, 1610–18', *Proceedings of the American Philosophical Society*, 128 (1984), 284; Anne Lake Prescott, 'Marginal Discourses: Drayton's Muse and Selden's "Story"', *Studies in Philology*, 88 (1991), 307–28.

[126] Woolf, 'Change and Continuity', 250.

are similar. A national rather than a royal readership is inter-
pellated when he addresses his defence of the Trojan myth to
contemporary '*Brittons*' who are invited to find their original
in 'their famous *Brute*' (91). Lineage is conceived not in
dynastic terms but rather through an incipient organic concept
of national character: ancient Trojan ancestry is 'proved'
through the humanist commonplace that true nobility derives
from virtue rather than blood, which in turn is demonstrated by
the valour of contemporary Britons whose 'owne worths
challenge as triumphant *Bayes* | As euer *Troian* hand had powre
to raise' (92).

Browne's Britannia is distinctly Cambro-British. The
medieval incorporation of Wales into an English State did not
effect English sovereignty, and many Englishmen saw Welsh
incorporation as a model for the 'union' of England and
Scotland.[127] The exclusive focus on this older, anglo-centric
form of 'Britishness' marginalizes James's vision of the imperial
union of the two kingdoms of England and Scotland. In the
opening description of Anglesey in the first Song, Browne
evacuates the Trojan myth of its Stuart resonances; in his hands,
the myth only has relevance to the land and the national
character of its peoples: '*Cambria* is a land from whence haue
come | *Worthies* well worth the race of *Ilium*.' This myth
becomes the basis of a reworked narrative of imperial *translatio*
whereby collective *virtù* passes from the national origin, Wales,
to Browne's homeland, his native Devon:

> And though of might *Brute* I cannot boast,
> Yet doth our warlike strong *Deuonian* coast
> Resound his worth, since on her waue-worne strand
> Hee and his *Troians* first set foot on land,
> Strooke Saile, and Anchor cast on **Totnes* shore.   (p. 4)

Geoffrey of Monmouth had popularized the myth that Brute
first landed in Britain at Totness.[128] Ancient British myth
authorizes Browne's own regional epic with the Trojans finding
their descendants in the poet's countrymen, Drake, Grenville,
and Davies. Tristram Risdon, in his *Chorographical Description, or Survey of the county of Devon*, similarly sees the land

---

[127] Levack, *Formation of the British State*, 16–19.
[128] Drayton, *Poly-Olbion*, I.I.311–18; Camden, *Britannia*, 35–36; Risdon, *Chorographical Description of Devon*, 58.

itself as organically forming the character of the Devon descen-
dents of the ancient Britains, 'a puissant People, taking Heart
even of the Soil it self, imbolden'd by the Roughness of the
Country, Inlets of the Sea, and their own Magnanimity'.[129]

British myth coexists with Saxon history in the poem.[130] The
antiquarian energies of Book II focus on the recovery of an
indigenous history from the landscape of Britannia. The new
classical pastoral home within Browne's Britannia is Tavistock,
the poet's birthplace, which provides the original for the
classical *locus amoenus*. This sacred origin is Saxon:

> And thinke that *Ordgar's* *sonne
> (Admonish'd by a heauenly vision)
> Not without cause did that apt fabricke reare,
> (Wherein we nothing now but *Eccho's* heare
> That wont with heauenly *Anthemes* daily ring
> And duest praises to the greatest King)
> In this choise plot.   (p. 86)

Ordulphus

The Saxon noble, Ordulphus, had 'endowed (Tavistock) with so
many Mannors, Rents, and Revenues, that it became a Barony',
and it was where his father Ordgar kept his court 'in the Days
of *Edgar* the first unresisted Monarch of this Land'.[131] Browne's
interest in the Saxon Duke Ordulphus is patriotic and
Protestant; the sacred pastoral source is revealed to be the
origin of the primitive church in all its Saxon purity. Saxon
history provided both antiquarians and Protestants with
foundational cultural fictions that located the origins of an
indigenous national history and church in a Saxon past.[132] But
if Tavistock becomes the sacred national origin, it is also structured by the sense of its loss through the ravages of time. The
sense of the poetic line is broken by the image of the ruins of
Tavistock abbey, where once 'heauenly *Anthemes*' rung 'we
nothing now but *Eccho's* heare'. Here, echo returns to figure
loss, the disembodied voice of memory that records the dis-

[129] Risdon, *Chorographical Description of Devon*, 8.

[130] Rosemund Tuve sees the distinction between the classical and the indigenous
in terms of a polarization between the Ancients and the Moderns emerging in the
seventeenth century ('Ancients, Moderns, and Saxons', *English Literary History*, 6
(1939), 166–82).

[131] Risdon, *Chorographical Description of Devon*, 148, 271–2.

[132] Tuve, 'Ancients, Moderns, and Saxons', 166–9.

location between an epic voice of a collective history and a
fragmentary poetics of exile that still has to establish new sites
of cultural authority. The ruins of Tavistock abbey have a
similar function to ruins in Drayton's *Poly-Olbion* in that they
are markers of the disjunction between past glory and present
memory. At the moment that both poems are involved in
the production of alternative cultural fictions and collective
histories, there is also the sense that a culture can become lost,
forgotten, and irrecoverable.[133]

Browne's epyllion on his local Tavistock rivers, the Tavy and
the Walla, in the third Song is the centrepiece of Book II and has
its source in Spenser's Irish epyllia in the 'Mutabilitie Cantos'
and *Colin Clouts Come Home Againe*. Lupton points to the
way that the mythic space of Spenser's colonized and classicized
'ideal Ireland is insistently punctured by those intransigent
"corners" and "coverts" of locality', by the sense of the spe-
cificity of place.[134] The strong sense of the local, regional
particularity of the landscape of Britannia similarly disrupts the
narrative tendencies towards a mythic, classicizing universality.
In Browne's epyllion this alterity is embraced in the attempt to
produce a genealogy of the land, a seemingly contradictory
mythopoetic local natural history. The native Ovidian landscape of the epyllion is simultaneously classicized and univer-
salized and localized and personalized. The visual disjunction
between myth and realism is prefigured in description of the
Tavy in the Ovidian landscape of Book I where the violent
romance landscape is configured through local geography as the
Tavy flows past local landmarks: the Virtuous Lady Cave, the
ruins of Tavistock Abbey, to the point where it meets the river
Waltham at 'Double Water'.[135] The story of the Tavy and the
Walla in the third Song of Book II has its basis in the Ovidian
story of the nymph Arethusa loved by the river god Alpheus and
her metamorphosis into the Italian stream which provided the
classical model for myths of locality.[136] Once more, allusions

[133] Brink, *Drayton Revisited*, 90–91.
[134] Lupton, 'Mapping Mutability', 102.
[135] Sukanta Chaudhuri also argues for the descriptive realism of the poem
(*Renaissance Pastoral and its English Developments* (Oxford: Clarendon Press,
1989), 335).
[136] Rudolf B. Gottfried, 'Spenser and the Italian Myth of Locality', *Studies in
Philology* 34 (1937), 110.

to native epyllia are introduced to Anglicize this myth into a poetics of place: the introductory blazon of the Walla echoes Marlowe's blazon of Hero, while the wanton nymph's attempted seduction of the Tavy recalls the speeches of Venus in Shakespeare's 'Venus and Adonis'. The epyllion is grounded in Devon through a complex interweaving of Ovidian pastoral modes and geographical description. At points, myth does subsume a local particularity such as in the account of the number of streams that flow into the Tavy which provides the analogy for the mutability, inconstancy, and variety of love in the nymph's seduction speech. However, with the satyr's pursuit of the Walla, the verse becomes more directly topographical. The Victorian chorographer, Mrs A. E. Bray, saw Browne primarily as a Devon 'nature' poet and read the epyllion topographically in her *Description of the part of Devonshire bordering on the Tamar and the Tavy* as both a realistic and a mythopoetic account of the local features of the countryside through which the Tavy flows.[137] The fast-moving flow of the Tavy, overturning 'mighty Rockes', through '*Fords* where pibbles lay secure beforne', and 'Low'd *Cataracts*' (79) describes the natural features of the area surrounding the source of the Tavy under Fur Tor in Dartmoor from where it flows rapidly through the steep, boulder-strewne ravine of Tavy Cleave. The text then traces the movement of the river through cultivated land after leaving the moor, through 'a Vale extended to the North | Of *Tavy's* streame' (80).[138] Mythopoesis is coupled with a descriptive realism: Innescombe or '*Ina's Coombe*' (80) is personified in a Diana-like nymph, a genius of place that also marks the point where the Wallabrook joins the Tavy near Tavistock. The entrapment of the Walla in rocks figures its source just beyond Yar Tor in Dartmoor, while the subsequent grief of the Tavy becomes a local myth that can account for the notoriously violent character of the river, 'Since when he neuer on his bankes appeares | But as one franticke' (84).

Spenser's epyllia on the Irish rivers on his estate are narratives of land ownership and colonization. The colonizing imperative is internalized and aestheticized in *Britannia's Pastorals* to pro-

---

[137] Bray, *A Description of . . . Devonshire*, iii. 2–19.
[138] J. W. Page, *The Rivers of Devon from Source to Sea* (London: Seeley & Co., 1893), 214.

duce a poetics of place and self-possession. Ovid enables these poets to claim a greater lyric autonomy. Browne's identification with the rivers of his birth-place is an act of self-possession that provides the occasion for the lyricizing of the poetic voice noticeable in the numerous inset songs throughout the second and third Songs sung by the poet's youthful pastoral personae. Rivers function as metaphors for the poet's state.[139] The Tavy provides the vehicle for a subjectivity that defines itself in relation to an individualized origin. The poem continually lyricizes the poet's relationship with the rivers of his birthplace, 'I haue beene borne | To take the kind ayre of a wistful morne | Neere *Tauies* voycefull streame' (p. 70), and again in the invocation to the fourth Song, that begins with the Marlovian simile of the lovers' reluctant parting,

> Braue Streame, so part I from thy flowry bancke,
> Where first I breath'd, and (though vnworthy) dranke
> Those sacred waters which the *Muses* bring
> To woo *Britannia* to their ceaselesse spring.   (p. 86)

The river here occupies the same discursive space as the poet's muse in the first Song where the invocation similarly entwines the language of love and prophecy:

> O yee blessed *Muses*!
> Who as a Iem too deare the world refuses!
> Whose truest louers neuer clip with age,
> O be propitious in my *Pilgrimage*!
> Dwell on my lines! and till the last sand fall,
> Run hand in hand with my weake *Pastorall*!
> Cause euery coupling cadence flow in blisses,
> And fill the world with enuy of such kisses.
> Make all the rarest Beauties of our *Clyme*,
> That deigne a sweet looke on my younger ryme,
> To linger on each lines inticing graces
> As on their *Louers* lips and chaste imbraces!   (p. 2)

Prophecy and pastoral combine in the metaphor of the self as text to evoke a sensual visionary love of nature and a lyric self-possession that Romantic poets, such as Keats, were drawn to in Browne's poetry.[140]

---

[139] Herendeen, *From Landscape to Literature*, 163.

[140] Joan Grundy, 'Keats and William Browne', *Review of English Studies*, 21 (1955), 44–52.

The identification of the poet and his birth-place is amplified by the various extended similes seemingly drawn from childhood, particularly schoolboy experiences, such as the simile describing the eagerness of 'two little Lads' to escape their 'carefull *Tutor*' (130) in the fifth Song, that appear to be authentic because they are so mundane and jar with the surrounding Italianate narrative. The return to the place of childhood is a return to an original imaginative 'wholeness'. These invocations, similes, and localized descriptive passages work by accumulation rather than in isolation. When the Romantics praised the organic 'Englishness' of *Britannia's Pastorals* they had in mind passages like the following:

> The Mvses friend (gray-eyde *Aurora*) yet
> Held all the Meadowes in a cooling sweat,
> The milke-white *Gossamores* not vpwards snow'd,
> Nor was the sharpe and vsefull steering goad
> Laid on the strong-neckt Oxe; no gentle bud
> The *Sun* had dryde; the cattle chew'd the cud
> Low leuel'd on the grasse; no Flyes quicke sting
> Inforc'd the Stonehorse in a furious ring
> To teare the passiue earth, nor lash his taile
> About his buttockes broad; the slimy Snayle
> Might on the wainscot, (by his many mazes
> Winding *Meanders* and self-knitting traces)
> Be follow'd, where he stucke, his glittering slime
> Not yet wipt off.   (p. 29)

John Clare wrote of Browne's verses that 'There is a freshness and beauty about them that supprised me & with which I was not acquainted—there is much english landscape about them.' Fitter is right that in such passages 'the local and individual nature in experience is rhetoricized into melodious generality', but by reading these passages in isolation he misses their wider generic role. These 'topocosmic' passages contextualize the passages of localized description in *Britannia's Pastorals* by working to constitute a distinctly 'English' landscape that, as Fitter recognizes, wants to trace its origins to a 'pre-urban, pre-scientific . . . oral and working tradition'.[141] Clare's delight in

---

[141] Quoted in Grundy, *Spenserian Poets*, 4fn9; Fitter, *Poetry, Space, Landscape*, 272.

Browne's poetic landscapes is a response to this process of inventing traditions and cultural fictions.

Critics who privilege a georgic, scientific mode of nature poetry as somehow a more 'authentic' seventeenth-century representation of the land tend to disparage poems like *Britannia's Pastorals*, labelling them Elizabethan and not early modern and viewing the looseness of structure in terms of a failure to realize this new emergent form that will triumph in the eighteenth-century.[142] Browne does not have the talent of Milton or Marvell, however, the 'looseness' of *Britannia's Pastorals* should not be dismissed lightly. As Hansen points out 'there was no one or homogeneous "picture" by which the country and the nation were understood by its citizens during the Renaissance'.[143] This heteroglossia structures *Britannia's Pastorals* and the poem is the unstable locus of a range of divergent and convergent discourses describing the 'country' and the land. The various 'pictures' of the country in *Britannia's Pastorals* do not cohere precisely because the space of the country is in flux, constituted by processes of historical transition. This process of transformation informs the state of exile adopted by the poet, who moves from the centre to an unstable and unformed periphery, 'from organised space invested with meaning to a boundary where the conditions of experience are problematic'.[144]

Politics of Romance

The return to Italianate pastoral tragicomedy gives the last two Songs of Book II a greater narrative coherency.[145] The tendency for pastoral tragicomedy to modulate into romance is pronounced in these Songs: death dominates the pastoral landscape and the vulnerability of the pastoral lovers is heightened. These

[142] Fitter's response to *Britannia's Pastorals* is not atypical, see also James Turner's comparison between the 'intoxicating muddle' of Browne's landscapes and the 'new landscape' represented by Richard Corbett and Denham, which, 'by contrast, is a triumph of management' (*The Politics of Landscape: Rural Scenery and Society in English Poetry, 1630–1660* (Oxford: Basil Blackwell, 1979), 12).

[143] Hansen, 'Identity and Ownership', 104.

[144] Robert Edwards, 'Exile, Self, and Society', in Maria-Ines Lagos-Pope (ed.), *Exile in Literature* (1988), 16–17.

[145] Grundy argues that Browne uses pastoral tragicomedy in the opening and closing songs of the poem as a whole to draw the work together ('Browne and Italian Pastoral', 316).

last two Songs have a narrative self-sufficiency within the Book as a whole. Thetis arrives in Wales to hear the story of Pan and the death of his beloved and the fate of the lovers, Philocel and Caelia, condemned to death for accidently violating the tree consecrated to Pan's dead mistress. There is a distinct difference between the uses of pastoral tragicomedy in Book I, where it is brought into alignment with a dynastic narrative, and in Book II, where it takes on an oppositional function. The second major satiric passage in the fourth Song that prefaces the story of Pan is a critique of Stuart Augustanism that equates the decay of the navy with a failure of royal husbandry, and records the failure of the epic in the nation's fall into a degraded georgic state. The presence of Thetis and 'all her Fleet' (86) at Plymouth Sound invests the home harbour of Drake and Hawkins, the scourge of the Spanish Armada, with an epic status that is simultaneously placed decisively in the past. Royal neglect has succeeded where Spain had failed: under James, 'now our Leaders want, those Vessels lye | Rotting, like houses through ill husbandry' (87). Corn and cornfields had figured English naval supremacy in the preceding epic battle simile, but in the following lament they are reconfigured through a parodic inversion of the first Georgic.[146] Once England's navy had reaped 'What was by *Iberia* sowne', now these ships themselves have become cornfields and soldiers reduced to ploughmen:

> When now as if we wanted land to till,
> Wherewith we might our vselesse Souldiers fill:
> Vpon their Hatches where halfe-pikes were borne
> In euery chincke rise stems of bearded corne.   (p. 87)

Inverse georgic gives way to a plea for the plight of veteran soldiers who are reduced to almshouses, poor houses, and other forms of social degradation that lead Browne to insist that he will never 'respect those times that rather giue him | Hundred to punish then one to relieue him' (88). Fears of renewed Spanish aggression and England's lack of military preparedness were increasing. At the end of 1614, Habsburg forces successfully attacked the Low Countries, raising fears for the safety for Elizabeth and Frederick. Despite the changing balance of power on the Continent, there was no attempt to restore the navy and

---

[146] Patterson, *Pastoral and Ideology*, 142–3.

by 1615 the fleet was literally rotting in the docks.[147] Browne's
lament gestures towards a type of 'epic of defeat'. Patterson has
incisively argued that Drake's name 'functions as the sign of a
generic boundary—of what the poem might have been had
Browne lived a generation earlier'.[148]

Wales once more is the site of a revision of an imperial
ideology, but with a difference. Whereas in the earlier Songs,
Wales was the imperial origin of the warlike Devonians and
incorporated within the form of a regional epic, in the last two
Songs it is the locale of a pastoral tragicomedy that prioritizes
love over war. This dual, contradictory functioning of Wales in
Book II points to the limits of the poem's imperialism. It could
be inferred from Browne's elegy for Henry and the lament for
the decline of the navy in this fourth Song that he, like other
Protestant 'patriots', views an aggressive colonial policy as a
continuation of the military campaign against Spain. The third
Song, with its paean to Devon's colonizing naval heroes,
operates within this political framework, but the closing image
of Devon's enviable self-sufficiency is out of step with the
westward movement of colonial expansion:

> for whose richest spoyle
> The boasting *Spaniard* left the *Indian* soyle
> Banckrupt of store, knowing it would quit cost
> By winning this though all the rest were lost.   (p. 67)

This passage reworks the motif in Daniel's *Tethys' Festival*
which describes the waters of the British Isles as having 'More
treasure, a more certaine riches got | Then all the Indies to *Iberus*
brought' and forms part of his counsel against imperialism.[149] In
Britannia's Pastorals, this type of patriotic anti-imperialism
finds its fullest expression in the extensive digression in the
fourth Song urging '*Brittish* swaines' to 'stay at home':

> And long, and long, for euer may wee rest
> Needlesse of help! and may this *Isle* alone
> Furnish all other Lands, and this Land none!   (p. 109)

---

[147] C. D. Penn, *The Navy under the Early Stuarts and its influence on English History* (London: Cornmarket Press, 1970), 16–26, 31–7.

[148] Patterson, *Pastoral and Ideology*, 142.

[149] Samuel Daniel, *Tethys' Festival*, in *Court Masques*, 59; John Pitcher, ' "In those figures which they seeme": Samuel Daniel's *Tethys' Festival*', in David Lindley (ed.), *The Court Masque* (Manchester: Manchester University Press, 1984), 37–8.

British self-sufficiency, however, is not invoked within a Stuart Virgilian topos to celebrate James's reign of peace and plenty. Rather it is incorporated into a patriotic attack on trade as depleting the naval strength of the nation through the high mortality of sailors on these voyages, since 'Such expert men are spent for such bad *fares*' (109).

This anti-imperialist outburst is prefaced by a Virgilian allusion that gestures to a more wide-ranging critique of the imperial epic. The holy plant consecrated to Pan's dead mistress is likened to that

> golden slip the *Troian wanderer*
> (By sage *Cumaean Sybil* taught) did bring
> (By *Fates* decreed) to be the warranting
> Of his free passage, and a safe repayre
> Through darke *Auernus* to the upper ayre.   (p. 108)

In Book VI of the *Aeneid*, Aeneas descends to the underworld to learn of the destiny of Rome from his father, and it is at this point that an ideology of empire is overtly aligned with Augustus. This episode was also the source of the motto adopted by James as the British Augustus and frequently invoked by court poets.[150] The fourth Song of *Britannia's Pastorals* continually closes down such patriarchal foundational narratives. The Virgilian underworld is shadowed in *Britannia's Pastorals* in the cave that Pan repairs to following the death of his beloved, however, here it changes from a sacred source, where imperial destiny is revealed to the chosen, to a place of irredeemable fallenness holding the body of one whose memory shall not outlive his death, 'Let no man for his losse one teare let fall, | But perish with him his memoriall' (103). This fore-closure of a patrilineal imperial narrative culminates in the childless Pan who

> shall not as other *Gods* haue done
> Glory in the deedes of an heroicke Sonne,
> Nor haue his Name in Countryes neere and farre
> Proclaim'd; as by his Childe the *Thunderer*;

---

[150] 'remember thou, O Roman, to rule the nations with thy sway—these shall be thy arts—to crown Peace with Law, to spare the humbled, and to tame in war the proud', *Virgil* trans. H. Rushton. rev. edn. (Cambridge, Mass.: Harvard University Press (Loeb); London: William Heinemann, 1967), 567. Pitcher, 'In those figures in which they seeme', 36–7.

If *Phoebus* on this Tree spread warming rayes,
And Northerne blasts kill not her tender sprays,
His Loue shall make him famous in repute,
And still increase his Name, yet beare no fruite.   (p. 107)

The poem consciously opposes epic to romance and chooses the latter. The allusion to the 'Northerne blast', that is so often related to James in Spenserian pastoral, suggests that a patriarchal Stuart imperialism simultaneously is being opposed to these 'other' cultural forms.

Pan symbolizes the way that pastoral tragicomedy is taken in a romance direction to produce an alternative to the epic that is energized by love and the accompanying emotions of grief and pity. The narrative focus of the fourth Song is Pan's grief for the death of his beloved and in the fifth Song it is the anguish of the lovers, Philocel and Caelia. Browne chooses the elevated and humanized Pan from Italian pastoral drama over the lusty Greek or Ovidian Pan, but he adds further emotional range and depth by modelling him on Sannazaro's grieving speaker in the eleventh Eclogue of his *Arcadia*.[151] Pan's dream in which the ghost of his mistress appears to tell him of her death conflates the scene from Book II of the *Aeneid* where Creusa's ghost comforts her husband Aeneas, revealing that his long exile will end with a new marriage and dynasty and the episode in Sannazaro's *Arcadia* where the nymph takes the grieving speaker to a cave—a version of the imperial and prophetic river source in the fourth *Georgic*—where his destiny is revealed and he returns to a reinvigorated intellectual community represented by his poet-friends. The trajectory in Browne's poem is very different. The ghost that appears to Pan does not have an overt prophetic function: she tells Pan not to look to man but to the wolf for her killer, however, this does not resolve itself into an anti-Catholic polemic, as one may expect given the papist associations of the animal, instead the narrative is more interested in the emotional impact of sorrow. The conventional political dimension of the ghostly vision does surface in the cave that holds the body of one 'hated now of Shepheards', a Machiavellian figure who 'neuer lent | His hand to ought but to

---

[151] Grundy, 'Browne and Italian Pastoral', 306; Jacopo Sannazaro. *Arcadia and Piscatorial Eclogues*, trans. R. Nash. (Detroit: State University Press, 1966), 133–41.

our detriment' (103). As this figure mirrors Avarice in Book I, the dead body would appear to be that of Cecil, who by this stage had become a symbol of the suppression of an aristocratic martial culture. The cave here is closer to the deathly landscape of the speaker's 'dream of abandonment amidst deserted tombs' in Sannazaro's *Arcadia*, rather than the imperial and prophetic Virgilian river cave.[152] Browne's cave signals the failure of this type of vision; Pan does not return to a revitalized community and instead retires to a self-imposed exile.

Pan is consistently feminized in the fourth Song. Grieving, he is placed under the guidance of a Diana-like nymph who takes him by the hand like 'a kinde mother' (105), and the narrative as a whole has its point of reference in the Elizabethan Thetis, who is the audience to the old shepherd's tale of Philocel and Caelia. Royal female agency is privileged in a similar way to Fletcher's feminizing of pastoral tragicomedy through the chaste and magisterial shepherdess Clorin in *The Faithful Shepherdess*. The portrayal of Pan changes dramatically in the fifth Song as the emotional focus is transferred to the lovers. Pan is remarkable by his absence; the lovers are sentenced by the judges, the 'Substitutes on earth of mighty *Pan*' (130), and the absent Pan is equated with the tyranny of the law. While the shepherd community feels pity and sympathy for the lovers, it is ineffective in the face of the judges' desire to pass sentence and 'cleare themselues from all impunitie' (130); the valorization of love foregrounds the inhumanity of an arbitrary law. It is possible that Pan in the fifth Song carries an allusion to James that prefigures, in a different ideological form, Jonson's association of Pan with a Jacobean 'absolutism' in *Pan's Anniversary*.[153] The absence of Pan is symptomatic of the way that the poem clears a symbolic space that will enable Thetis to intervene and simultaneously feminizes sovereignty and the narrative, replacing the law with pity. Thetis not only rescues the lovers, Philocel and Caelia, but releases Marina from her prison. A triumphant Thetis gestures to the reinvigoration of an

---

[152] Kennedy, *Sannazaro and the Uses of Pastoral*, 140.

[153] See Martin Butler, 'Jonson's *Pan's Anniversary* and the Politics of Early Stuart Pastoral', *English Literary Renaissance*, 22 (1992), 369–97. The punishment of the lovers may, in part, be an encrypted response to the death of Arabella Stuart in the Tower in 1615. A lament for Stuart had been incorporated into the Vale of Woe in Book I.

Elizabethan-style imperialism, to the return of other histories suppressed by the new regime. The optimism conveyed by this ending may be due to the recent rise of Pembroke, the dedicatee of Book II, to a powerful position at court. Yet, this optimism seems provisional and while Thetis's rescue of the lovers and Marina in one swoop may bring the narrative to closure, it is an ineffective and inconclusive form of closure that fails to carry through the tragicomic imperative towards reconciliation. Passions are not brought under the sway of temperance and, since the lovers are innocent victims of an inhumane law, there is a separation between moral cause and effect that emphasizes the arbitrary workings of fortune rather than a redemptive providential pattern.

The weak closure of Book II has affinities with the narrative suspension of romance. The lovers separated in Book I and wandering throughout Book II are not re-united but await a further instalment. Browne's attraction to the form of romance is ideological. Romance works by the 'perpetual displacement of sacred patterns or archetypal myths' and produces prodigal narratives that announce their marginality to the dominant culture.[154] The twin subjects of *Britannia's Pastorals*, as the poet announces at the outset of his poem, are his 'natiue home' and 'Loue rurall Minstralsie' (i. 2) and together they mark a movement away from the form of the imperial epic to the uncharted romance landscape of the 'country'. Pastoral romance rejects patrilineal narratives of the land that invest cultural meaning and identity in the dynasty for prodigal narratives that explore the alterity of exile and open alternative narrative possibilities. Marcus says of the 'broader, cartographic perspective' of Spenserian landscapes that 'royal authority is conspicuous by its absence: the landscape, through its decentralised configuration, subtly undermines the Stuart vision of an England repastoralized from the court through the promulgation of Stuart policies towards the countryside'.[155] Marginality comes at a price, and in the case of *Britannia's Pastorals* it is a disorientating fluidity. As the poem dismantles the form of the

---

[154] Geoffrey Hartman, *Saving the Text: Literature/Derrida/Philosophy* (Baltimore and London: The Johns Hopkins University Press, 1981), 49.

[155] Leah Marcus, 'Politics and Pastoral: Writing the Court on the Countryside', in Kevin Sharpe and Peter Lake (eds.), *Culture and Politics in Early Stuart England* (Basingstoke and London: Macmillan, 1994), 142.

epic, it becomes open to criticism for its lack of unity, and its digressiveness is viewed as a deviation from the end-directed epic narrative. Book II cannot imagine the type of cultural consensus that would enable such an epic narrative, rather its formlessness is a creative response to the proliferation of discourses and ideological possibilities as different communities in the early seventeenth century began to claim the authority to speak for and from the 'country'.

4

George Wither, Citizen Prophet

'I AM Master of my selfe.'[1] Wither's characteristic self-assertion would seem to make him an ideal representative of Renaissance individualism. Yet, individualism cannot fully account for Wither's particular expression of selfhood. In the words of Charles Lamb, 'he seems to be praising another person, under the mask of self' and 'by the self he sometimes means a great deal,—his friends, his principles, his country, the human race'.[2] Lamb's deft analysis of *Wither's Motto* isolates the distinctive nature of the self in Wither's writings: the 'I' is insistently social. Individual identity is achieved through a dialectic between an individual self identity and a collective social identity. Recent criticism on Renaissance selfhood, however, has tended to focus on the former at the expense of the latter, often relegating a collective identity to an earlier mode of selfhood that was superseded by Renaissance individualism.[3] The Renaissance, Foucault has argued, was 'the privileged moment of *individualization*' when the 'author' came into being.[4] This reading of the Renaissance is limiting. Other historical trajectories were being opened at this moment resulting in a pluralization of modes of identity. Wither's poetry offers an alternative account of the self. Introspection frequently turns into a study of the way that the self is constituted through the processes of social interaction. Protestantism and civic humanism merged in his texts to produce a discourse that was able to imagine the self as a social actor within a wider national and apocalyptic drama.

[1] Wither, *Faire-Virtue*, B5v.
[2] Charles Lamb, 'On the Poetical Works of George Wither', *The Prose Works*, 3 vols. (London: Edward Moxon, 1836) i. 218–19.
[3] See, for example: Stephen Greenblatt, *Renaissance Self-fashioning: from More to Shakespeare* (Chicago and London: Chicago University Press, 1980); Catherine Belsey, *The Subject of Tragedy: Identity and Difference in Renaissance drama* (London and New York: Methuen, 1985); Francis Barker, *The Tremulous Private Body: Essays on Subjection* (London: Methuen, 1984).
[4] Michel Foucault, 'What is an Author?', in Josué V. Harari (ed.), *Textual Strategies: Perspectives in Post-structuralist Criticism* (London: Methuen, 1979), 141.

The self that was produced is simultaneously individualized and collective, as Lamb notes. This form of social identity is central to the Spenserian concept of community. *The Shepheards Pipe* and *The Shepherds Hunting* projected a collective identity that is the basis of a discourse of citizenship that in turn structures these communal eclogues. Wither's texts took up the implications of *The Shepheards Pipe* and *The Shepherds Hunting* in relation to a civic self and also in relation to print which, to a certain extent, makes this self possible. Print was fundamental to the creation of new author functions and new publics. Its reproducibility and dissemination held new possibilities for shaping a collective identity.[5] For Wither, print enabled the citizen to take an active role in the godly commonwealth as both reader and writer.

'MY MINDE IS MY KINGDOME'

Wither's texts chart the relationship between individual experience and the public world and project an idealized social self that can function as the medium for civic life in a reformed society. He was attracted to genre that enabled scope for the expression of the 'I'.[6] The main body of *Prince Henries obsequies*, one of Wither's earliest works, consists of a sonnet sequence followed by two echo poems. The sonnet sequence maps the shifting responses of the speaker to the prince's death and, through this process of self-examination, the speaker's experience gradually assumes wider prophetic and national dimensions. The speaker is solitary in the opening sonnets, isolated from his fellow mourners, 'My Soule in publike greefe no pleasure knowes.'[7] In his account of his emotions upon first hearing of Henry's death, the sonnet meets the spiritual autobiography:

[5] On the 'author' and print, see: Martin Elsky, *Authorizing Words: Speech, Writing, and Print in the English Renaissance* (Ithaca, NY, and London: Cornell University Press, 1989); and Richard Helgerson, *Self-Crown'd Laureates: Spenser, Jonson, Milton, and the Literary System* (Berkeley and Los Angeles: University of California Press, 1983).

[6] Thomas O. Calhoun, 'George Withers: Origins and Consequences of a Loose Poetics', *Texas Studies in Language and Literature*, 16 (1974), 266–70.

[7] *Prince Henries obsequies or mournefull elegies upon his death* (London, 1612), STC 25915, A4r.

> When as the first sad rumour fill'd my eare
> Of *Henries* sickenesse; an amazing terror,
> Strucke through my body, with a shuddering feare
> Which I expounded by my frailties error.   (18. 1–4)

This is thinking as writing: the use of enjambment conveys the tensions between the closed form of the sonnet and the rapidly shifting emotions of the speaker. In a similar fashion to the spiritual autobiography, the speaker is brought to understand that this emotional turmoil results from his lack of faith in divine providence, daring in his private grief to 'dispute with God' (25.1). This recognition marks a transition in the sequence: the 'I' begins to give way to 'we' and 'you' and the sonnets gesture to a social self that finds its identity in the elect nation. The speaker moves from the interior space of anguished self-examination to become an observer at the Prince's funeral whereby the flawed solipsism of the earlier sonnets gives way to a renewed engagement with public world. The opening lines of sonnet 29, 'You that beheld it', project a community of experience, while the pictorialism of the description of the funeral procession, which crystallizes in the movement of the prince's horse, 'his dumb Steed, that erst for none would tarry, | Pac'd slow, as if he scarce himselfe could carry' (13–14), has an immediacy that is almost journalistic in its attempt to isolate and to communicate events to a wider audience. This shift from private to public is accompanied by an apocalypticism which dominates the remaining sonnets in the sequence and the following echo poems and provides a language for conceptualizing the self as a social actor. The speaker adopts a more active role and assumes the voice of the divine scourge, warning of an impending Catholic plot and calling for harsher measures against recusants that culminates in demands for a purge at court.

Wither experimented with genre throughout his career in the effort to produce a flexible literary form capable of plotting the dynamics of a social self. His next work, *Abuses stript, and whipt. Or Satirical Essayes* (1613) is an amalgam of satire, sermon, moralized complaint, autobiography, prophecy, and, most interestingly, the essay. The essay was a new genre emerging in the sixteenth century: Bacon's *Essays* were first published in 1597, and John Florio's translation of Montaigne's *Essais* was available from 1603, and a second edition was put out in the same year as *Abuses stript, and whipt*. Bacon described his essays as 'fragments of my conceites' and 'dispersed meditations'.[8] The informality and openness of the essay made it amenable to the 'loose' style favoured by Wither and he presented himself as producing something new in his satirical essays, pioneering a mode of self-representation that contrasts with the formality of 'Spencers, *or* Daniels *well-composed numbers; or the deep conceits of now flourishing* Iohnson'.[9] Wither's dedication of *Abuses stript, and whipt* to himself in the dedicatory epistle introduces an analogy between the book and the self that seems to draw its energy from Montaigne's *Essais*, particularly his epistle to the reader, where he sets out his intention, in Florio's translation, 'to be delineated in mine owne genuine, simple, and ordinary fashion, without contention, arte or studie; for it is my selfe I pourtray . . . Thus gentle Reader my selfe am the ground-worke of my booke.'[10] Like Montaigne's essays, Wither's satirical essays take their topics from personal experience, '*in that I haue so bluntly spoken what I haue obserued*' (B1v), and privilege a plain style as the 'true' language of the self. The reader is encouraged to identify the speaker of the essays with Wither himself. The autobiographical 'Occasion of this Worke', which offers an account of Wither's life from his school days until the publication of *Abuses stript, and whipt*, represents the act of writing as a process that is continuous with the development of the author's personality. The various satirical essays are unified through the agency of the perceiving self who means 'to speake but what I know', so that knowledge is achieved not through imitation or study of the classics, but from self-observation and 'try'd experience' (C7r).

Self-observation has a didactic function in *Abuses stript, and whipt* and serves as the basis for the essays' moralizing observation of man. This method produces an exemplary, generalized self that is representative of a collective, national character. The speaker often translates his personal experience into a wider national and international struggle between the

[8] Francis Bacon, *The Essays*, ed. John Pitcher (London: Penguin, 1985), 238–9.
[9] Wither, *Abuses stript, and whipt. Or satirical essayes* (London, 1613), STC 25891, B1r.
[10] Michel de Montaigne, *The essayes, or morall, politike discourses: done into English by J. Florio* (London, 1603), STC 18041.

godly and the unregenerate; in the early epigram 'To Time', he is a godly witness to '*Romes fall*', 'Yea from my *Cradle* I did still surmize; I I should see *Babell* tumble *Bethell* rise' (B3r). The language of election provided a language for imagining a social self. Pocock speaks of the elect nation as 'a means of conceptualizing, in a complex and particular time-frame, a public realm, at once secular and godly, in which the individual, at once saint and Englishman, is to act'.[11] *Abuses stript, and whipt* is both a humanist mirror and a scourge driving 'sinfull man' (T5r) towards salvation. His satire on the times looked to tradition of Protestant satirical journalism illustrated by pamphlets such as John Wharton's *Wharton's Dreame* (1578), which carried recommendations from John Foxe and Robert Crowley, among others, and combined social realism with the sensational and the apocalyptic in its invective against the practice of usury in London: 'So the couetousnes of London, the pride of London, the wantonnes of London, the ryotousnes of London, both poyson the whole Realme of Englande, and maketh it apte to all wickednesse.'[12] These pamphlets helped to formulate a mode of Protestant counsel which brought together the prophets and 'Cicero, that singular and famous Orator . . . [who] sayeth that letters were the most worthyest things that euer was inuented'.[13] Wither's satirical essays similarly often take on the appearance of secular sermons. One of the main forms of instruction are anecdotes reputedly based on the experiences of the speaker or 'a friend of a friend', and their very banality produces a commonality of experience, hence interpellating a relatively wide readership in terms of social status, although unified by shared religious values. This moderate Protestant readership is implicitly qualified to participate actively in the social and religious life of the nation. The speaker provides just such a model of agency: 'these vngodly and disorder'd times' (M7r) have turned him from a passive

---

[11] J. G. A. Pocock, *The Machiavellian Moment: Florentine Political Thought and the Atlantic Republican Tradition* (Princeton: Princeton University Press, 1975), 37.

[12] John Wharton, *Whartons Dreame* (London, 1578), A4v. See Norbrook on *Abuses stript, and whipt* and a tradition of Protestant satire (*Poetry and Politics in the English Renaissance*, 209).

[13] *Whartons Dreame*, A2r. On the relationship between the sermon and satirical journalism, see: Neil Rhodes, *Elizabethan Grotesque* (London, Boston, and Henley: Routledge and Kegan Paul, 1980), 50–62.

observer into a citizen prophet, and the satirical essays increasingly take on an apocalyptic note that culminates in the closing
essays, 'Of Presumption' and 'The Scourge'. By the end of
Abuses stript, and whipt, the opening book of the self has been
transformed into a manual for the direction of spiritual life of
the nation.

The Protestantism of *Abuses stript, and whipt* is mediated by
civic humanism. Along with his fellow Spenserians, Wither
inherited a reformed humanist tradition of 'commonwealth'
literature—a literature of public discussion in which the godly
citizen poet had a duty to contribute to the flow of counsel on
which the health of the commonwealth depended.[14] Wither
adopted the role of the honest 'countryman' in his satires, his
plain 'Country dish' (V8r). The humanist argument that man
should devote himself to the public good and the accompanying
condemnation of the contemplative life as a form of moral
and national weakness voiced in the essay 'Of Weakness' is
politicized in the essay 'Of Presumption' where he delivered his
sharpest censure of current policy.[15] The recent 'truce with
Spain' (S5r) has weakened the nation through the neglect of
'our former care of *Martiall discipline* | For exercises merely
feminine' (S4v). The political solution he advocated was two-
fold: a process of national remilitarization involving the reform
of abuses in the navy and army, and the training of yeomen and
citizens along the lines of the Hampshire Islanders, under the
command of the Earl of Southampton, praised in the essay 'Of
Feare'; and the summoning of parliament to reform corruption
and to purge the state of pro-Spanish counsellors, in particular
that '*vndermining hand,* | That studies for the ruine of the Land'
(S5r). This vision of national reform is influenced by classical
republicanism in that civic greatness resides in martial discipline
and the citizen is provided with an active role in the commonwealth through arms and through the structures of counsel.[16]
This effectively extends the sphere of political activity from an

[14] Arthur B. Ferguson, *The Articulate Citizen and the English Renaissance*
(Durham, NC: Duke University Press, 1965), pp. xi–xvi.

[15] Markku Peltonen argues that *Abuses stript, and whipt* is 'an ideological attack
on the contemporary political system' (*Classical Humanism and Republicanism in
English Political Thought, 1570–1640* (Cambridge: Cambridge University Press,
1995), 165).

[16] Peltonen, *Classical Humanism and Republicanism*, 175, 216–20.

elite group of counsellors to incorporate the godly citizen. Martialism also has a significant apocalyptic dimension in that the elect nation comes into being through its readiness for battle, that 'fearefull bloudy day' (S6v).

This language of citizenship is virulently masculine, and the feminine is conceived negatively as a degeneration of the martial ideal. Yet, Wither also appropriated the feminine in a positive form in his elaboration of a poetics of citizenship. His *Fidelia*, first published in 1615, used the form of the female-voiced complaint to broaden the humanist language of citizenship to incorporate the interests of the Protestant gentry and middling classes. The preface advertised the text as a type of conduct book for young men and women and borrowed the language of popular Puritan household manuals; these volumes were primarily addressed to the gentry and middling classes and sought to define the proper government of that 'little common-wealth', the family.[17] Fidelia is a domestic model for the Protestant citizen: she is discreet, constant, rational, and above all contemporary. Her social identity is that of a gentlewoman of middling wealth, with a fortune 'Not basely meane, but such as may content'.[18] Wither was careful to ameliorate negative feminine stereotypes in order to safeguard and to strengthen Fidelia's character. Feminine softness signifies women's emotional and spiritual superiority, their 'nobler and more gentle hearts' (A10v), and not necessarily moral weakness. Conventional stereotypes are reversed: it is her absent male lover who is condemned as an exemplar of inconstancy, fickleness, and duplicity, and the reader is presented with a rational, vocal Fidelia who defends her just 'cause', 'Suing for that which is by right my owne' (C4v); not only was feminine thought predominantly defined as weak and illogical in this period, but rhetorical skills were thought to transgress ideals of feminine humility and modesty.[19] The poem constantly validates Fidelia's literary activity in humanist terms: her purpose in writing the

[17] On the household manual, see: Susan D. Amussen, 'Gender, Family and the Social Order, 1560–1725', in Anthony Fletcher and John Stevenson (eds.), *Order and Disorder in Early Modern England* (Cambridge: Cambridge University Press, 1985), 201–3.

[18] *Fidelia* (London, 1615), STC 25905, B9r.

[19] Linda Pollock, ' "Teach her to live under obedience": The Making of Women in the Upper Ranks of Early Modern England', *Continuity and Change*, 2 (1989), 231, 243.

letter is not private revenge but didactic, whereby 'my words may proue a mirror, | Whereon thou looking may'st behold thine error' (A8v).

Fidelia is the innocent victim of male tyranny and, as such, her position is analogous to that of the Spenserian shepherd-poets in *The Shepheards Pipe* and *The Shepherds Hunting*. In fact, there is an explicit identification between Fidelia's suffering and the impassioned marginality of these poets:

> But oh you noble brood, on whom the world
> The slighted burthen of neglect hath hurl'd,
> (Because your thoughts for higher obiects borne,
> Their groueling humors and affections scorne)
> You whom the *Gods*, to heare your straines, wil follow,
> Whilst you do court the sisters of *Apollo*.
> You whom there's none thats worthy, can neglect,
> Or any that vnworthy is, affect:
> Do not let those that seeke to doe you shame,
> Bewitch vs with those songs they cannot frame:
> The noblest of our Sexe, and fairest too,
> Do euer loue and honour such as you.　　(B8r–v)

Such an empathetic identification between a female readership, that has its spokeswoman in Fidelia, and the Spenserian poets serves to ally them as victims of 'male' slander and a patriarchal tyranny and to reinforce their marginality. As in the Spenserian texts of 1614, the denunciation of tyranny carries a critique of Stuart policy. Fidelia is her most assertive during an extensive debate on the question of how far parents should determine the choice of the marital partner that draws its frame of reference from popular Puritan household manuals.[20] Fidelia argues for a voluntary and equal marriage and the weight of the argument is on the side of the children. The extensive denunciation of the social ills attendant upon parental tyranny is complimented by a paean to 'liberty in choice' (C2r) which goes beyond the question of marriage to address *'more weightie Arguments then are (perhaps) expected in such a subiect'* (A8r), and clearly

---

[20] Martin Ingram, *Church Courts, Sex and Marriage in England, 1570–1640* (Cambridge: Cambridge University Press, 1987), 125–42; and Susan D. Amussen, *An Ordered Society: Gender and Class in Early Modern England* (Oxford: Basil Blackwell, 1988), 1–57. John Dod and Robert Cleaver, *A Godly Forme of Householde Gouernement: For the Ordering of Private Families, according to the direction of Gods Word* (London, 1614), STC 5387, H2r–I2r, V5r–6v.

echoes the hymn to liberty of conscience in *The Shepherds Hunting*. Analogies between patriarchal authority within the domestic and the political sphere formed part of the political vocabulary of Stuart England. Wither may not explicitly invoke this analogy, although he cites examples of parental tyranny causing civil war, yet arguably such a resemblance is implied by the subject given the analogy's centrality in household manuals. Moreover, he develops a language of citizenship through the issue of marriage choice. The Puritan household manuals tended to describe the family in terms of a limited monarchy, arguing against arbitrary and unlimited power within the family and, by implication, the state, often emphasizing the relative independence of children, and maintaining the importance of the principle of consent.[21] Fidelia's arguments operate within a similar political framework: they acknowledge the legal and natural duties that children owe to their parents, but they are often aggressively nonconformist in their insistence that disobedience is justified when reason and conscience are under threat from a parental tyranny, then ''Tis lawfull, yea, my duty, to refuse: | Else, how shall I lead so vpright a life' (C1v). The threat to the health of the commonwealth in the private and public realms is not from these rational children/citizens but from wilful, tyrannical parents/monarchs.

Fidelia has a double voice: on the one hand, she speaks a language of citizenship, and on the other, she voices an impassioned lament that enables the male poet to explore states of interiority:

Oh that there were some gentle-minded *Poet*
That knew my heart, as well as now I know it;
And would endeare me to his loue so much,
To giue the world (though but) a slender touch
Of that sad *Passion* which now clogs my heart,
And shew my truth, and thee how false thou art.
That all might know, what is beleeu'd by no man,
Theres ficklenesse in men, and faith in woman.   (B5r)

The dominant poetic value here is empathy which is premised on the fiction that the writer can give voice to another's inner

[21] For Dod and Cleaver 'the rule of Parents over their children, ought to resemble the gouernment of good Princes . . . and not to keepe them vnder a seruile of slauish awe & subiection' (*Godly Forme of Householde Gouernement*, V5r–v).

experiences and private feelings that remain hidden from public view. Like other female-voiced complaints, *Fidelia* is a drama of inwardness that charts the highs and lows of the character's emotional life, her self-reflection on her actions and words, and her attempts to deduce her lover's feelings and intentions—his physical inaccessibility is a marker of his emotional inscrutability that contrasts with her emotional openness. This produces a sense of a continuous, individualized consciousness that has important affinities with the characterization of Wither's persona, Roget, in *The Shepherds Hunting*, and similarly implies a character with a 'life outside the text' and produces a voice that appears to belong to an individuated person rather than to a set of literary conventions. Fidelia's dual roles as citizen and lamenting woman are ultimately complementary: the citizen is invested with an interiority and language of self-expression.

Wither's Motto is the culmination of the representational strategies that Wither had been rehearsing in these earlier texts. He returned to the concept of the book as a self-portrait, describing his *Motto* as a 'Picture of my Minde'.[22] His intention in writing a book of the self, set out in the epistle 'To any body', was 'to draw the true Picture of mine own heart; that my friends, who knew mee outwardly, might haue some representation of my inside also' (A2v). Once more, there is a strong echo of Montaigne's dedication of his *Essais* to 'my kinsfolkes and friends: to the end, that loosing me (which they are likely to do ere long) they may therein finde some lineaments of my conditions and humours'.[23] *Wither's Motto* offers a portrait of the inner man, his motivations, and his character. Yet, this interior self simultaneously has a public aspect and provides a mirror whereby his friends if they 'liked the forme of it they might (wherein they were defectiue) fashion thier [sic] owne mindes thereunto' (A2v–3r). The humanist metaphor of the book as a mirror was applied to those works designed to educate an elite governing class in the principles of *vita activa*. Wither's appropriation of this magisterial metaphor for his own book of the self extended its model of civic government to the private sphere and effectively broadened the class of magistrates to incorporate the godly citizen, represented in his ideal form by Wither him-

[22] *Wither's Motto* (London, 1621), STC 25927, A6v.
[23] Montaigne,'The Author to the Reader', *Essayes*.

self. The godly citizen is therefore, in the full political sense, representative of the commonwealth. *Wither's Motto* itself aims for this type of representativeness. The values that are set out through his extensive explication of what he has not, wants not, and cares not are very generalized and often mundane, giving the impression that they are rooted in everyday personal experience. Taken as a whole they give shape to a collective identity—that of the freeborn Protestant Englishman. The text constructs a character, 'Wither', that is identifiable with a collective body of readers. This character belongs to the moderate Protestant middling to gentry classes—like his Fidelia, Wither claimed to have a fortune 'Not basely meane, but such as may content'.[24] In *Wither's Motto*, Wither created a national character in his own image and, in doing so, began to imagine an 'embryonic' national community and to invest this representative body with a personal life.[25]

The values of this national character are those of Protestant humanism. Election is the guarantee of *vita activa* and the citizen takes on the role of 'Christ's soldier' (C8r). Like *Abuses stript, and whipt*, *Wither's Motto* imagines a simultaneously secular and godly public realm in which the godly citizen is to act. Imprisonment in 1614 had confirmed Wither in his own sense of himself as a central political actor on the public stage and had given a certain direction to his writings. The language of persecution that he had perfected in *The Shepherds Hunting* derived part of its inspiration from John Foxe's *Acts and Monuments*, where he found a precedent for his heroic suffering in the service of Truth. *Acts and Monuments* provided a culturally recognizable dramatic structure which enabled Wither to transform his imprisonment into a drama of martyrdom. The drama continues in *Wither's Motto* where he once more adopted the role of the Foxean martyr: 'And they who loued *Truth* and *Innocence*; | Out of oppression shall aduance their head: | And on the ruines of those *Tyrants* tread' (D2v). Wither becomes the faithful servant of Truth who challenges the powers of corrupt authorities in a way that draws attention to the limitations of the state to control the individual conscience

[24] *Fidelia* (London, 1615), STC 25905, B9r.
[25] On national character as an 'embryonic' nation, see Benedict Anderson, *Imagined Communities: Reflections on the Origin and Spread of Nationalism* (London: Verso, 1983), 32.

and, alongside his constant complaint that he was denied a fair trial, reveals the abuse of power rife in society. Like Foxe's martyr's before him, actions and experiences within this drama are ideologically charged and figure wider social and political issues.[26] The dominance of this model of selfhood in Wither's writings means that they do lack that despairing uncertainty, 'the anxious honing of a sense of identity' that has been identified by John Stachniewski in other Protestant texts that grapple with the question of election.[27] The speaker does draw attention to his spiritual travails as he wanders in the 'Grove of Ignorance', but he has the certainty of his election to comfort him, 'I haue trust, that all my woes to come, | Will bring my Soule, eternall comforts home' (C5v). The emblem and its accompanying motto that make up the frontispiece to the text portray Wither as the embodiment of Christian fortitude, constancy, and self-sufficiency: he lies far above the world, which he rejects, with his gaze fixed on divine redemption, and protected through the divine word from all forms of temporal and spiritual danger. The drama of martyrdom enabled this type of combination of inward stoic resolution with the principles of *vita activa*. In 1625, 'T.G.' published *An Answer to Wither's Motto* in which he attacked the author for his presumption in claiming the role of Old Testament prophet and mocked his self-confidence in his election as an example of complacent self-righteousness. 'T.G.' interestingly seems to trace Wither's self-confidence to the value that is placed on reason in the *Motto*. It is reason that enables the citizen to take an active role in the commonwealth and such certainty in human agency departs from Calvinist doctrines of absolute predestination and man's inherent sinfulness: as 'T.G' reminds Wither 'Can humane wisdome be so prouident | The end of things before hand to preuent?'[28]

The political model implied by this language of godly citizenship would seem to look forward to his later republicanism.[29]

---

[26] John Knott describes *Acts and Monuments* as a 'recapturable mythic drama' in his *Discourses of Martyrdom in English Literature, 1563–1694* (Cambridge: Cambridge University Press, 1993), 7–13.

[27] John Stachniewski, *The Persecutory Imagination: English Puritanism and the Literature of Religious Despair* (Oxford: Clarendon Press, 1991), 88.

[28] T. G., *An Answer to Withers Motto* (Oxford, 1625), STC 11509, C4r.

[29] David Norbrook has argued that Wither in the 1640s preferred a mixed

However, Wither's constant assertions of his independence from secular authority, including that of the king, were often accompanied by declarations of his loyalty to James. Wither was not being politically disingenuous and masking his radical politics through these expressions of loyalty, rather these apparently incompatible political models point to the way that contradictory theories of government could coexist simultaneously. Patrick Collinson speaks of an Elizabethan monarchical republic that was both a legacy of Protestant humanism and a practical response to the problem of succession. The queen and her privy council, he argues, represented 'two somewhat distinct poles of authority' that were equally valid:

Elizabethan government was often government without counsel, or with unorthodox or irregular counsel. But . . . the privy council, with whatever futile consequences on some occasions, was in a position to contemplate the world and its affairs with some independent detachment, by means of its own collective wisdom and with the queen absent.[30]

Wither, like a number of other loyal subjects, was capable both of viewing the king as the ideal head of state and seeing himself as part of an independent body of godly citizens who had a collective responsibility to ensure the health and safety of the commonwealth. The family–state analogy that structures the marriage debate in *Fidelia*, for example, follows through this logic and looks to the collective agency of rational godly citizens to curb the excesses of intemperate and wilful monarchs. Similarly, Brooke recognized the absolute prerogative of the king in some areas, but also maintained the right of parliament to provide independent counsel even, as in 1621, in those areas that James claimed as part of his absolute prerogative.

Wither sought new forms 'to recreate my selfe' (A2r). He rejected formal genres for a 'loose' style able to embody the historical agency that characterizes the godly citizen. The style of *Wither's Motto*, like that of *Abuses stript, and whipt*, corresponds with the open, fluid form of the essay in that the

constitution to a republic ('Levelling Poetry: George Wither and the English Revolution, 1642–1649', *English Literary Renaissance*, 21 (1991), 219).

[30] Patrick Collinson, 'The Monarchical Republic of Queen Elizabeth I', in *Elizabethan Essays* (London and Rio Grande: Hambledon Press, 1994), 42.

narrative is generated by loosely associated thought-processes as
the speaker contemplates what he has not, wants not, and cares
not—as he claimed in his introductory epistle, the '*Method* is
none at all' (A3r). When describing his book of the self, images
are chosen that open the closed form of the book to social
processes, evident in the vision of that 'mighty *Volumne*, which
the *World* we call', and his sense of the dynamics of personal
experience:

> My priuate Actions, seriously oreview'd,
> My thoughts recal'd, and what of them ensu'd:
> Are Bookes, which better farre, instruct me can,
> Then all the other Paper-workes of Man.   (D1r)

The speaker frequently draws attention to the way that his
divinely inspired thoughts exceed language and the closed form
of the book:[31]

> Oh! that my *Lines* were able to expresse,
> The Cause, and Ground, of this my *Carelesnesse*.
> That, I might shew you, what braue things they be,
> Which at this instant are a fire in me.   (E8v)

Wither's book of the self turns out to be an endless text. At its
centre is a self that is radically open-ended and constantly in
process. His account of what he has not, wants not, cares not
therefore gives the impression that it is necessarily incomplete
and that it could be extended indefinitely as new thoughts arise.
The resulting text is so fluid that it does not move towards
closure but leaves itself open to be continued.

Wither saw himself in the 1620s as pioneering a new, distinctive literary style. *Fair-Virtue*, published the year after
Wither's Motto, is in many ways a defence of this new
aesthetic, and he frequently digresses to set out its principles,
claiming that '*Pedants* shall not tye my straines, | To our
Antique *Poets* vaines', but 'Being borne as free as these, | I will
sing, as I shall please' (C3r). His '*free Discourse*' which is not
constrained by the '*strict rules as* Arts-men *vse*' (C2v) has a
precedent in the anti-classicism of a 'loose' style which rejects
tradition and formal control and privileges spontaneous modes

---

[31] See also Norbrook's discussion of Wither's later poetry ('Levelling Poetry',
225–7).

of expression.[32] *Faire-Virtue* is generically and stylistically heterogeneous and the resulting wide variety of metrical structures, as French notes, makes the work appear 'largely experimental'.[33] The main body of the poem is a series of sonnets or elegies interlinked to produce a fluid, continuous narrative and is written in simple heptameter couplets. Lamb described Wither as the master of the seven-syllable line, 'whose darling measure it seems to have been, (and) may shew, that in skilful hands it is capable of expressing the subtilest movement of passion'.[34] Augustan dislike for this metre derives from ideological preference for the rigid closed form of the pentameter couplet. Lamb, by contrast, sees the seven-syllable line as having a flexibility and a spontaneity that makes it appropriate for conveying experience in a seemingly unmediated form.

Wither's anti-classicism took on an ideological dimension in his *Motto*. Tudor reformers pitted the spontaneous words of plain-spoken Protestant martyrs against the corrupt ceremonialism of the Church and State. Anti-classicism in *Wither's Motto* is often articulated within this type of contestatory framework:

> *I care not* who shall fondly Censure it;
> Because it was not, with more *Method* writ:
> Or fram'd in imitation, of the *Straine*,
> In Some deepe *Grecian* or old *Romane* vaine.
>
> .   .   .   .
>
> My *Mind's* my Kingdome; and I will permit
> No others *Will*, to haue the rule of it.
> For I am free; and no mans power (I know)
> Did make me thus, nor shall vnmake me now.
> But, through a Spirit, none can quench in me:
> This *Mind* I got, and this, my *Mind* shall be.   (F1v–2r)

This vigorous self-defence derives from a non-conformist tradition of bold speaking exemplified in the accounts of the trials of Protestant martyrs in Foxe's *Acts and Monuments*. Wither had rehearsed this role in *Abuses stript, and whipt* when, seemingly prophetically, he boldly asserted that 'You were best hang, or clap me into Iaile | To stay my tongue' (N2v).

---

[32] Calhoun, 'Origins and Consequences of a Loose Poetics', 263–4.
[33] J. M. French, 'George Wither', Ph.D. thesis (Harvard, 1928), 223.
[34] Lamb, 'On the Poetical Works of George Wither', i. 226.

'By remaining unmoved by punishment, or even exulting in it,' as Knott points out, 'the victim shows the limitations of the power of the church or state to control the subversive spirit.'[35] In his *Motto*, Wither once again took on the role of Protestant martyr to locate his actions on the wider political stage. The apocalypticism of many passages in the *Motto* portrayed the current times as a period of crisis in which the transformation of society was immanent. The reader is similarly encouraged to see their own experiences in terms of this larger trial of faith. Individual and collective identity is shaped by political events and the subject is envisioned as participating in a very direct way in the political life of the Protestant nation.

'FREEBORNE-LINES': PRINT, POLITICS, AND THE MARKETPLACE

The form of agency that is constructed in Wither's writings is produced through the interaction of a range of discourses circulating in the early seventeenth century and, just as importantly, through the resources of print. The collaborative eclogues, *The Shepheards Pipe* and *The Shepherds Hunting*, demonstrated for Wither the potential of print to reshape the role of the humanist writer. Print became one of the primary modes whereby the citizen poet participated in the commonwealth and transformed the concept of counsel, extending it from an elite body of magistrates within court to the relationship between a writer and his readers within a public sphere. At the same time, the success of his own works, *Abuses stript, and whipt*, *The Shepherds Hunting*, and *A satyre*, made Wither aware of the market for controversial writings and shaped his response to print culture. Recent studies have argued for an '"underground" manuscript trade' in radical political material, particularly libellous verses.[36] Wither in his 1614 verses and in

---

[35] Knott, *Discourses of Martyrdom*, 8.

[36] Thomas Cogswell, 'Underground Verse and the Transformation of Early Stuart Political Culture', in Susan D. Amussen and Mark A. Kirlansky (eds.), *Political Culture and Cultural Politics in Early Modern England* (Manchester and New York: Manchester University Press, 1995), 277–300; Alastair Bellany, ' "Rayling Rymes and Vaunting Verse": Libellous Politics in Early Stuart England' in Kevin Sharpe and Peter Lake (eds.), *Culture and Politics in Early Stuart England*

Wither's Motto envisioned the transformation of this market for news through the resources of print. In *The Shepherds Hunting*, the textual exchanges occasioned by his arrest are characterized as 'Newes', circulating in the public domain, and function to raise awareness of the political ramifications of his imprisonment. Wither recognized the ideological, professional, and economic viability of print. Such an awareness of the demand for contemporary political material simultaneously encouraged him to take an entrepreneurial role in the publication of his texts and he was willing to take risks in order to capitalize on this market. However, he worked to avoid the negative associations of the pot-poet or hack writer by investing the economic motive with a humanist credibility which in turn is extended to the literary marketplace as a whole.

Signs of a more entrepreneurial attitude towards print are evident in *Fidelia* (1615). The history of how the text came to be published set out in the prefatory epistle, 'The Occasion of the Priuate Impression of this Elegie', was unusual for the period and is suggestive of the way that print transformed the relationship between a writer and his work. The preface relates how Wither had incurred substantial losses through his imprisonment in 1614 and took the advice of friends to publish *Fidelia* as a means of remedying this situation and so *'put it out for an aduenture among my acquaintance vpon a certaine consideration . . . I found euery man in who[m] I had any confidence, so voluntarily ready to accept it, that I haue now set it on foote, and hope thereby to make my selfe able to compass that, which shall make both Me, and Them gainers by the bargaine'* (A5r). The term 'adventure', in the context of the passage, suggests a form of speculation, a new and risky commercial enterprise, while 'bargain' similarly denotes a type of financial contract. Wither appears to be describing a form of publishing that is financed by subscriptions and involves a type of contract between an author and his readers that cuts out the middleman, the stationer, and means that the author retains control over copy. Peter Lindenbaum singles out Wither as the author 'who *almost* invented the subscription method of

(Basingstoke and London: Macmillan, 1994), 285–310. See also: Richard Cust, 'News and Politics in Early Seventeenth-Century England', *Past and Present*, 112 (1986), 60–90.

publication' with *Fidelia*.[37] This novel method of publishing provided Wither with an opportunity to reconceptualize the author's economic and intellectual relationship to his work and to his public.

Lindenbaum has argued for two competing modes of literary production in the seventeenth century, one aristocratic, which was dependent on patronage, and the other republican, which found one of its expressions in subscription publishing. Although, as Lindenbaum points out, subscription publishing was more of a commercial venture than a political act and 'did not in itself necessarily spell the end of the aristocratic patronage system and lead to political and moral independence for authors', nonetheless Wither's preface does give it just these types of ideological inflections.[38] When setting out his motivations in the preface to *Fidelia*, Wither opposed subscription publishing to clientage:

> *By this meanes also I shall be sure to be beholding to none, but those that loue* Vertue *or* Mee, *and preserue the vnequald happinesse of a free spirit: Whereas else being forced to accept of some particular bounties, it may be, blinded by seeming courtesies, I might fall into the common basenesse incident to flatterers; and so at length become like those great clergy-men of our times, who dare not vpbraid all sins, for feare they should seeme so saucy as to reprehend their Patrons.* (A5v–6r)

Far from bringing credit, patronage corrupts both patron and author and restricts public discourse. As in other Spenserian satires, patronage is opposed to the principles of freedom of speech and conscience, in the words of Browne, 'My free-borne *Muse* will not like *Danae* be | Wonne with base drosse to clip with slauery.'[39] By contrast, subscription publishing, as set out

---

[37] Peter Lindenbaum, 'John Milton and the Republican Mode of Literary Production', *Yearbook of English Studies*, 2 (1991), 135. John Taylor, who looked to Wither as a literary model, also tried his hand at subscription publishing, see, for example, his: *The pennyles pilgrimage, or the money-lesse perambulation of J. Taylor. From London to Edenborough* (London, 1614), STC 22784; *A new discovery by sea, with a wherry from London to Salisbury* (London, 1623), STC 23778. On Wither and Taylor, see my 'Three Jacobean Spenserians: William Browne, George Wither, and Christopher Brooke' (D.Phil. thesis (Oxford, 1993), 290–2). On Taylor, see: Bernard Capp, *The World of John Taylor the Water Poet* (Oxford: Clarendon Press, 1994).

[38] Lindenbaum, 'The Republican Mode of Literary Production', 123, 135.

[39] *Britannia's Pastorals*, ii. 89.

by Wither in the preface, would secure the author's liberty and moral and political independence. The languages of humanism and the common law coalesce as the citizen author is invested with the rights and liberties of the free-born Englishman. A common law framework enables the text to be viewed as the property of the author to be defended against tyrannical encroachments, while Protestant humanism sees the text as having a productive and transformative role in the cultural economy. Financial profit is consistently translated into cultural profit:

> *I haue vndertaken this, not altogether in hope of profite, but being an honest enterprise I rather attempt it, partly to make tryall who are my friends, and partly to show this Great World, that the* Little World of my Minde *is not so barren, but it can out of it selfe spare somewhat wherewithall to make trafique for others best commodities.* (A5r)

Wither reshaped this humanist language of the profitability of the printed text to loosen its ties to the patronage system and to authorize his own novel method of publishing.[40] Credit does not derive from the author's ability to identify his name with a powerful patron, but from the author's own intellectual labour, his cultivation of '*the* Little World *of my Minde*' in order to make it profitable to others. This is clear when he constrasts his own act of public service with the motivations of others who have their works privately printed, since '*They seek their own commodity, and I, with my particular profit, to be able to do my friends and country good*' (A5v). Publication no longer functions as a mechanism of patronage and instead operates in the service of the author and through him the commonwealth. The ties that bind members of this commonwealth are those of friendship. The preface recalls the 1614 collaborative eclogues in the way that friendship describes a space of economic, intellectual, and social exchange unconstrained by the court. In fact, it is friendship that provides the symbolic and economic basis of subscription publishing.

Subscription publishing, however, does not seem to have been a commercial success for Wither. By the second edition in 1617, the copy had been bought by the stationer, George Norton, who

---

[40] See Lorna Hutson's discussion of this Protestant humanist discourse of profit in her *Thomas Nashe in context* (Oxford: Clarendon Press, 1989), 15–70.

carefully placed a new preface before the work explaining how he gained the author's permission to publish *Fidelia* because Wither

hauing dispersed many, and remembring how farre it would bee from his disposition to lay claime to the proffered gratuities, he wholy repented himselfe of what indeed he neuer well approoued of, and how iustly soever he might haue challenged, more then many would haue lost; yet insteed of beholding, is resolued rather to make those that haue receiued any of his Bookes a little beholding to him, in freely forgiuing them their vnvrged promises.[41]

Norton suggests that Wither was too much of a gentleman to take the money. This account has all the characteristics of the conventional 'stigma of print' reworked to suit the conditions of subscription publishing. It would seem that the project failed because Wither did not have the backing of enough subscribers to make this mode of publishing viable and so sold the copy outright to Norton to offset his losses. Wither's sale of the text to Norton does not seem to have ended his interest in the printed work and this new epistle to the 1617 edition acts as a type of contract between the author and the stationer. Norton states that Wither sold the copy to him on the strict condition that he '*in the imprinting thereof carefully respect his credit*' (A3r–v). Whatever may have been the case, the epistle insists on an agreement between author and stationer whereby the stationer has a responsibility to the author in the printing of his work to respect his 'credit', his intellectual labour that is invested in the quality of the printed text. In the early seventeenth century, a small number of writers were beginning to assert some control over the printed text through a special contract with the publisher. However, this type of contract was rare since it attempted to impose legal limits on the stationers' unlimited rights to reprint.[42]

The epistle prefacing *Faire-Virtue* operates in a similar fashion. John Marriot's letter from 'The Stationer to the

---

[41] *Fidelia* (London, 1617), STC 25906, A3r.

[42] Leo Kirschbaum cites a 1607 contract between Thomas Ford and the stationer John Browne which received official recognition in the Stationers' Register ('Author's Copyright in England before 1640', *Papers of the Bibliographical Society of America* 40 (1946), 77–8). On copyright also see L. R. Patterson, *Copyright in an Historical Perspective* (Nashville: Vanderbilt University Press, 1968), 9–12, 67–76.

Reader' was in fact ghost-written by Wither as he admitted at its close. This type of ventriloquism is reminiscent of the textual exchanges in *The Shepheards Pipe* and *The Shepherds Hunting* and similarly sets up a close collaborative and professional relationship between stationer and author. In fact, Marriot and Wither did seem to have had a good working relationship and had co-operated in the illegal publication of *Wither's Motto* in the previous year. The literary text is similarly characterized in this epistle as the intellectual labour of the author, bearing 'so much resemblance of the Maker' that the stationer is obliged to recognize the author's interest in the text. At first Marriot

got it authorised, according to Order: intending to publish it, without further inquiry. But attaining by chance a more perfect knowledge to whom it most properly belonged: I thought it fitting to acquaint him therewithall. And did so; desiring also, both his good will to publish the same, and leaue to passe it vnder his *Name*.[43]

The stationers' copyright did recognize the author's property rights in his works to the extent that they coincided with the stationer's interest in protecting the work against piracy or rival publishers, and stationers did generally acknowledge their duty to obtain the author's permission to publish his work before acquiring copyright.[44] Both epistles, however, rather than straightforward reflections of the conditions of publication, are persuasive fictions that are designed to act upon the publishing process in order to clarify and to transform the relationship between stationer and author. These fictions are carefully constructed. Wither's initial reluctance to publish *Faire-Virtue* because of the lightness of this early work draws on the conventional 'stigma of print' and the association of poetry with prodigality which tend to distance the author from the print trade. Within this narrative, these earlier negative responses to print are overcome by a professional interest in seeing the work through the press and, in particular, guarding his intellectual property against unauthorized printing and so co-operating with the stationer to achieve this end. Wither in these epistles was effectively constructing a publishing history in which the author takes on a new professional agency.

[43] *Fair-Virtue*, A3r.
[44] Patterson, *Copyright in an Historical Perspective*, 9–12, 67–76.

These 'stationer's' epistles before *Fidelia* and *Faire-Virtue* in many ways replaced the dedication to the patron. Wither's primary relationship in these epistles was not to a patron but to his printer. In this sense, his position is similar to that of the hack writer, in the words of Loewenstein, 'the man who means to live as the beneficiary not of a patron but of a printer assured of a wide popular readership, the author with a genuine economic interest in his printed works'.[45] His recourse to the 'stigma of print' in these epistles does appear anomalous, and yet it seems to function to record his social status as a gentleman and so lend this economic interest a respectability that is reinforced by his humanist insistence that he is acting in the public interest. Wither had an economic and ideological investment in the printed text. He does not seem to have circulated his texts in manuscript as was the fashion amongst his Inns of Court contemporaries but relied primarily on the channels of print.[46]

Wither's concern with the author's role in the publishing process was in part stimulated by the 'unauthorized' publication of the 1619 edition of *Fidelia*, printed by Edward Griffin for Thomas Walkley. This edition advertised that it was 'Newly corrected and augmented', although this was not the case and probably was a merchandizing ploy designed to sell further copies. This text was incorporated in *The workes of Master George Wither*, put out by Walkley in 1620, and did in this case include a new poem, 'Hence away thou Syren leaue me', which was later reprinted in *Faire-Virtue*.[47] It is this edition of *Fidelia* that is the subject of 'The Stationers Postscript' to *Fair-Virtue*:

There bee three or foure Songs in this Poeme *aforegoing which were stollen from the Authour, and heretofore impertinently imprinted in an imperfect and erronious Copie, foolishly intituled* His Workes; *which the* Stationer *hath there falsely affirmed to bee Corrected and Augmented for his owne Aduantage; and without the said Authours knowledge, or respect to his credit.* (P8r)

---

[45] Joseph Loewenstein, 'For a History of Literary Property: John Wolfe's Reformation', *English Literary Renaissance*, 18 (1988), 410–11.

[46] See Peter Beal's section on Wither in his *Index of Literary Manuscripts*, ii (London and New York: Mansell, 1993).

[47] *The workes of Master George Wither, of Lincolns-Inne, Gentleman* (London, 1620), STC 25890.

Kirschbaum has argued that Walkley's so-called 'unauthorized' publication of the *Workes* was not an act of piracy since no action was taken against him by the Stationers' Company which suggests that he obtained the copies legally from Norton, the previous publisher, and in any case it was not illegal to print poems without the author's permission, and so he concludes that the argument of this postscript is 'illogical'.[48] Yet, this line of argument misses the point of the postscript. Like the other 'stationer's' epistles, it is inventing a rhetorical formula that enabled the author to codify his relationship to the press in general and to the printed text in particular. In these epistles, the printed text was viewed almost exclusively as the author's intellectual property whatever the realities of the stationers' copyright. Wither once more speaks through the stationer John Marriot in the postscript to *Fair Virtue*. Piracy is invoked to focus on the way that his authorial rights have been infringed and to insist that the stationer has a responsibility to the author. This means that the agreement of the author is privileged over copyright when determining who owns the printed text. Through these 'stationer's' epistles, Wither begins to formulate a model of literary property that will be codified in the 1709 Statute of Anne which located ownership of copyright in the author as the creator of the text.[49]

Wither's imprisonment in 1614 played a central role in shaping his relationship to print culture. While it certainly caused him financial hardship, in professional terms it was remarkably productive and provided the subject for not only two of his own works in that year, his prison eclogues *The Shepherds Hunting* and his defence *A satyre: dedicated to the Kings most excellent maiestie*, but also Browne's *The Shepheards Pipe*. Even the epistle to *Fidelia*, published in the following year, advertised that the author had recently been

---

[48] Leo Kirschbaum, 'Walkley's Supposed Piracy of Wither's *Workes* in 1620', *The Library*, 19 (1938–9), 342–6. This article responds to Percy Simpson's 'Walkley's Piracy of Wither's Poems in 1620', *The Library*, 6 (1925), 273–4. See also Kirschbaum's *Shakespeare and the Stationers* (Columbus: Ohio State University Press, 1955), 120–1. This edition includes *The Shepheards Pipe* also previously published by Norton which supports Kirschbaum's thesis that Walkley obtained the copies from Norton.

[49] See Loewenstein's study of the relationship between piracy and the definition of literary property in his 'History of Literary Property' (389–412); Patterson, *Copyright in Historical Perspective*, 14–15.

imprisoned. Imprisonment made his reputation amongst his contemporaries and he appeared in both print and manuscript as a prison poet. Since his verses rarely appeared in manuscript, it is significant that most of these were prison poems attributed to him.[50] His fame as a prison poet was established to the extent that Henry Fitzgeffrey could satirize it in his *Certaine Elegies, done by svndrie Excellent Wits* (1618):

> *Felo*) that lately kist the Gaole, hath got
> A smacke of *Poetry*! yea more then that!
> Hee will maintaine none can be truely said
> A *Poet*, that was neere *Imprisoned*.[51]

Abuses stript, and whipt was probably brought to the attention of the authorities through a case of piracy; a testimony to the popularity of the text which went into eight editions between 1613 and 1617, five of those in the first year. On 20 February 1614, Raffe Mabb, William Bladdon, George Gibbons, and Francis Constable were fined for infringing Francis Burton's copyright.[52] Wither was arrested a month later. Although the available records do not give the nature of the offence, he claimed to have been arrested for libelling a peer and the available evidence also suggests that this was the case. He complained in a new passage incorporated into the 1615 edition of *Abuses stript, and whipt* of the popularity of 'libellous' readings of his satire that had led to his downfall:

> . . . heere's the reason they my labour like,
> *They thinke I meane him they suppose I strike.*
> So shall my well-meant lines become to be
> A wrong to others, and a plague to me.
> Heauen shield me from such monsters: for their breath
> Is worse than blasting, and their praise is death.[53]

---

[50] Beal, *Index of Literary Manuscripts*, ii.

[51] Henry Fitzgeffrey, *Certain Elegies, done by Svndrie Excellent Wits. With Satyres and Epigrames* (London, 1618), D4r–v.

[52] William A. Jackson (ed.), *Records of the Stationers' Company, 1602 to 1640* (London: The Bibliographical Society, 1957), 73, and 'Counterfeit Printing in Jacobean Times', *The Library*, 15 (1934–5), 364–6.

[53] *Abuses stript, and whipt* (London, 1615), STC 25896, 45. Pritchard takes Wither at his word and suggests that he 'may have suffered as much from the enthusiasm of admirers who persisted in reading personal satire on Northampton into *Abuses* and thus gave the word a dangerous reputation' ('Wither's Imprisonment', 345).

Wither, however, was not as innocent as he protested in these lines and published his own 'cause' through texts such The *Shepherds Hunting* and *A satyre* which appeared in the months following his release from the Marshalsea.[54] In *A satyre*, he gained comfort from the knowledge that he had a '*cause* so knowne, and knowne oo iust | . . . But all suppos'd me wrong'd that heare my troubles'.[55] Both texts were popular: *The Shepherds Hunting* went into three editions in 1615, while *A satyre* went into four editions between 1614 and 1616.[56]

Wither equated libel laws with censorship and saw censorship as the cultural condition that arose when an arbitrary government set itself against the principle of freedom of speech. In doing so, he developed a cultural model in which meaning is contested and various groups compete for control over discourse. Censorship, accordingly, shaped his model of authorial agency and his relationship to print.[57] Lindsay Kaplan's study, *The Culture of Slander in Early Modern England*, argues that censorship was a sub-category of the laws on defamation in this period and, as a result, wants to replace censorship with slander as the model for studying the power relations between poets and the state.[58] However, this shift in focus is ultimately counterproductive and rather than marginalizing censorship perhaps we need to understand censorship differently. The reason why Kaplan wants to replace censorship with slander is because available models of censorship often assume a degree of control over the press that is only possible in a centralized and highly efficient state bureaucracy. One response to this model has been to minimize censorship and to argue that press control had

---

[54] Allan Pritchard argues that 'Wither may have suffered as much from the enthusiasm of admirers who persisted in reading personal satire on Northampton in *Abuses* and thus gave the work a dangerous reputation, as from the suspiciousness of the earl's own nature' ('*Abuses stript, and whipt* and Wither's Imprisonment', *Review of English Studies*, 56 (1963), 345).

[55] *A satyre: dedicated to his most excellent Maiestie* (London, 1614), STC 25916, B1r.

[56] *The shepherds hunting*, STC 25920–2; *A satyre*, STC 25916–18.

[57] I will be using the term libel rather than the more general term defamation as, although the Common Law did not clearly distinguish between written and spoken defamation, libel was emerging as a separate, albeit ill-defined category of words that were actionable because they were widely disseminated and so the term raises particular issues in relation to the printed word.

[58] M. Lindsay Kaplan, *The Culture of Slander in Early Modern England* (Cambridge: Cambridge University Press, 1997), 1–10.

more to do with economics and the regulation of the book trade than with an ideologically coherent government policy.[59] These critics have a point, but if this is the case then perhaps censorship was more diffuse and operated through other mechanisms alongside the licensing system. This is the implication of Cyndia Clegg's recent work which describes censorship as 'a crazy quilt of proclamations, patents, trade regulations, judicial decrees, and privy council and parliamentary actions patched together by sometimes common and sometimes competing threads of religious, economic, political and private interests'. It is because censorship practices were heterogenous and, to quote Clegg again, more a matter of 'contradictions, violations, and liberties' that attempts to control public discourse were contested by writers such as George Wither.[60]

The particular charge levelled at Wither seems to have been that of *scandalum magnatum*—slandering or libelling a peer or great officer of state. Henry Howard, Earl of Northampton was particularly sensitive to personal attacks in this period from 1612 to 1614 and had brought a number of defamation cases before the Star Chamber according to the statute of *scandalum magnatum* which enabled actions to be brought by peers who had been defamed.[61] The frequency and vehemence with which he brought these cases was noted by contemporaries: Chamberlain commented that the 'world doth mervayle how such a matter shold be taken so hainously', while Henry Wotton thought that he 'hath been moved, besides his own nature and (as some think also) beside his wisdom, to call these things into public discourse' and gave a quote from Tacitus's *Annals* (iv. 34), '*quae spreta exolescunt*' which referred to the unjust

---

[59] See, for example, Sheila Lambert, 'The Printers and the Government, 1604–1637' (in Robin Myers and Michael Harris (eds.), *Aspects of Printing from 1600* (Oxford Polytechnic Press, 1987), 1–29). Lambert criticizes the arguments of Patterson and Hill as 'based on a mistaken premise for there never was any intention or attempt on the part of James I and Charles I to 'suppress all criticism'. However, this not only overstates and oversimplifies their arguments but this quote in the context of the sentence is misleading as it does not come from either Patterson or Hill but from a 1939 article by Godfrey Davis.

[60] Cyndia Susan Clegg, *Press Censorship in Elizabethan England* (Cambridge: Cambridge University Press, 1997), 4–5.

[61] J. H. Baker, *An Introduction to English Legal History*, 3rd edn. (London: Butterworth, 1990), 496; 'T.G.' alludes to the danger of '*Magnatum scandalum*' in response to passages in *Wither's Motto* that refer to his earlier imprisonment (*An Answer to Wither's Motto*, C4r).

prosecution of Cremutius Cordus for treason, instigated by clients of Sejanus, 'upon the novel and till then unheard-of charge of publishing a history, eulogizing Brutus and styling Cassius the last of the Romans'.[62] This analogy suggests that Northampton was seen to be manipulating the law by using *scandalum magnatum* in a novel and arbitrary way to further his own agenda. His use of this law was closely related to his sympathies with Continental absolutism. *Scandalum magnatum* was part of the rhetoric of divine magistracy since the ability of ministers to imprison at will was an extension of the royal prerogative.[63] One of Wither's complaints was that he was not given a fair trial: his case does not seem to have been brought before the Star Chamber and may instead have been tried before the Privy Council which had the power to act as a court. This could have been due to Northampton's failure to secure a prosecution against Sir Stephen Proctor in the month before Wither's arrest: the judges were divided over sentencing, with the Archbishop of Canterbury, the Bishop of London, Lord Ellesmere, and Sir Julius Caesar clearing Proctor of the charge of slander, which led Northampton to protest that 'he neded not to have ben so nice, having precedents of some great persons that have geven sentence in causes that concerned themselves'.[64] The warrant for Wither's arrest was issued from Northampton House on 20 March 1614. The Earl was extremely ill by this period and a number of meetings of the Privy Council from late February into March were held at Northampton House—his signature last appeared on a Privy Council order on 30 March and he died on 15 June.[65] In *The Shepherds Hunting*, Wither says he was brought before a court of virtuous noblemen who were misled by his accusers into believing the false charges against him.

Laws relating to criminal and private cases of defamation

---

[62] Chamberlain, *Letters*, i. 394; Logan Pearsall Smith (ed.), *The Life and Letters of Sir Henry Wotton*, 2 vols. (Oxford: Clarendon Press, 1907), ii. 23; Tacitus, *The Annals*, 5 vols. (Cambridge, Mass.: Harvard University Press (Loeb); London: Heinemann, 1910), iv. 59–60.

[63] Baker, *English Legal History*, 537–8; Linda Levy Peck, *Northampton: Patronage and Policy at the Court of James I* (London: George Allen and Unwin, 1982), 83.

[64] Chamberlain, *Letters*, i. 508–9.

[65] Peck, *Northampton*, 207–8; *Acts of the Privy Council of England, 1613–1614* (London, 1921), xxxiii. 391.

were relatively new and these forms of defamation were treated differently, creating certain inconsistencies. The Criminal defamation, such as *scandalum magnatum*, was defined broadly by the Common Law courts and the Star Chamber. Truth was not a defence and the law was not concerned with intent but rather with the effect of the words particularly in relation to the status of the 'victim'. Words were actionable if they imputed a criminal or disgraceful act, degraded the character of peers or officers, or touched on their dignity or honour in some way.[66] Yet, the scope of *scandalum magnatum*, as suggested by Northampton's insistence that peers could give sentence in cases that concerned themselves, potentially placed it in tension with the common law principle that no free man could be imprisoned except through the due process of the law as was the case in the 1630s when the king and his ministers were increasingly claiming the right to imprison at will. *Scandalum magnatum* also operated differently to private actions for defamation which from the early 1600s did, as Helmholz has pointed out, increasingly take intent into account.[67]

In *A satyre*, Wither anticipated the 1630s debates over arbitrary imprisonment when he complained that *scandalum magnatum* is being used to attack the liberty of the subject. His complaint 'Doe not I know a great mans *Power* and *Might*, | In spight of *Innocence* can smother *Right*?', suggested that this law, which was originally developed to maintain public order, was being used to further peers' own private interests. The law is described in its absolute form in *A satyre*: royal justice 'being fram'd in *Reasons* mould' (B2r) is dictated by the laws of nature and hence immutable. Yet this concept of absolute justice is itself destabilized in the poem as can be seen in the very form of *A satyre: dedicated to his most excellent Maiestie* which, as its title suggests, is both a petition to the king that recognized the absolute truth of royal justice and a complaint that the law in

[66] Thomas Starkie, *A Treatise on the Law of Slander and Libel, and incidentally of Malicious Prosecutions*, 2nd edn. (London: J. & W. T. Clarke, 1830), 175–84; W. S. Holdsworth, 'Defamation in the Sixteenth and Seventeenth Centuries', *Law Quarterly Review*, 159 (1924), 302–15; Baker, *English Legal History*, 496–507.

[67] Baker, *English Legal History*, 537–9; R. H. Helmholz, 'Civil Trials and the Limits of Responsible Speech', in R. H. Helmholz and Thomas Green, *Juries, Libels, and Justice: The Role of English Juries in Seventeenth- and Eighteenth-Century Trials for Libel and Slander* (Los Angeles: William Andrews Clarke Memorial Library, University of California, 1984), 4–6.

his case is unjust, arbitrary, and corrupt. Wither called on the concept of equity, pointing out that the king's 'owne *Lawes* ... | Cannot be fram'd so well to your intent, | But some there be will erre from what you meant' (D2v). Since the written word cannot fully capture the intent of the lawmaker, then the law cannot be absolute and individual circumstances must be taken into account.[68] Wither, an Inns of Court man, pleaded for mitigating circumstances in his own case and introduced forms of excusing facts that were increasingly being used by defendants in private actions on slander to make words less blameworthy and to raise points of law.[69] These are largely expressed in generic terms, based on the traditional distinction between libel and satire, and these generic conventions are in turn transformed through the particularity of Wither's situation. He argued that his satire was not malicious but rather corrective in the most laudible humanist sense and so turned attention to the supposed 'victim's' guilt to imply that it was not he but his accusors who were acting maliciously. The introduction of a concept of equity, however, has a wider transformative function in the poem in that it facilitates an opposition between issues of individual conscience and arbitrary rule and, in the process, enables the introduction of a concept of authorial agency. Like other writers before him, he made intent key to the definition of libel and attempted to stabilize the generic distinction between libel and satire in these terms. Intent is predicated upon the privileging of reason and the individual's ability to govern his actions and foresee their consequences. In this way, intent becomes the key element of the civic virtues that qualify the poet to act as counsellor—intent characterizes the poet's individual capacity for participation in rule, and it is this that secures for the poet the privilege of freedom of speech. The current libel laws act as the instruments of a vaguely-defined corrupt court that wants to restrict this 'ancient' privilege of poets. Libel is thus being used to describe a political environment in which the civic role of poet and the accompanying concept of a public sphere is being contested and, through this process, clarified and defined.

A satyre may be addressed to James, yet the speaker in the

---

[68] Baker, *English Legal History*, 232.
[69] Helmholz, 'Civil Trials and the Limits of Responsible Speech', 11.

opening lines places himself outside the court and refuses to participate in a patronage economy that is associated with bribery and corruption. In this way, the printed text and the genre of satire itself become the only modes of redress for one who is outside the sphere of royal favour, as the speaker reminds the reader, "*Tis a hard thing not to write Satyres*, now' (A6v). Wither once again adopted the role of the Juvenalian satirist, popular in the satirical journalism of the 1590s, preferring his free-spoken, irreverent, and biting invective to the moderate and temperate Horatian style favoured by Jonson. Juvenalian satire provided Wither with a language to 'taxe these *Times*' (B3r) and gives the impression that the poet is speaking his mind despite constraints. His imprisonment figures a broader political crisis and the satire promises its reader insight into political machinations at court through the speaker's attempts to comprehend the causes of his own imprisonment. At the same time, while he boldly speaks his mind, he also leaves the impression that more could be said if the times were freer. The speaker tantalizingly claims that he has engaged in a form of self-censorship, a 'fore-seeing warinesse' (B4v), and curbed his satire, otherwise 'I had told *Truth* enough to haue vndone me' (B4r). These rhetorical sleights of hand are designed to appeal to a readership educated in deciphering encrypted political verse satires and libels.

Wither may have opposed libel to counsel, but in his satires public debate is frequently expressed through a libellous poetics. The market for libel provided new structures and opportunities for political debate that writers such as Wither were keen to exploit. The distinction that he drew between libel and satire, as he was keen to point out, has a literary legacy. The 1599 satires suppressed by the Bishop's Ban constantly invoked this distinction to deny that their satires were libels but in a manner which invites such speculation and becomes a trigger to a libellous reading.[70] Wither similarly placed pressure on the distinction between satire and libel in such a way as to suggest that there is an interpretive ambiguity built into satire that makes libellous readings possible and even desirable. His defence of his satire against those who have slanderously misread it, taken 'That which I haue enstil'd a *Man-like* Monster, |

---

[70] Clegg, *Press Censorship*, 210–12.

To meane some priuate person in the state' (B5r), effectively
promoted just such a libellous reading by directing the reader to
relevant passages in the offending satire, *Abuses stript, and
whipt*, where they would find that his '*Man-like* Monster'
personified vice in such a way as to invite speculation. Such
reading practices associated with libellous satire are formalized
in the extensive hypothetical case that he offered in his defence:

> But say I grant that I had an intent
> To haue it so (as he interprets) meant,
> And let my gracious *Liege*, suppose there were
> One whom the *State* may haue some cause to feare,[71]
> Or thinke there were a man (and great in *Court*)
> That had more faults then I could well report,
> Suppose I knew him, and had gone about
> By some particular markes to point him out,
> That *he* best knowing his owne faults might see,
> He was the *Man* I would should noted be:
> Imagine now such doings in this *Age*,
> And that *this man* so pointed at should rage,
> Call me in question, and by his much threatning,
> By long imprisonment, and ill intreating
> Vrge a *Confession*; wert not a mad part
> For me to tell *him* what lay in my heart?
> Doe not I know a great mans *Power* and *Might*,
> In spight of *Innocence*, can smother *Right*.   (B5v–6r)

This hypothetical case operates in a similar manner to
Patterson's 'functional ambiguity': a formalized textual strategy
whereby writers and readers exploited the indeterminacy of
language to address potentially sensitive issues in public 'without directly provoking or confronting the authorities'.[72] In this
passage, conjecture is used to secure the guilt of his accusers.
His defence is conducted in terms of a concept of authorial
intent, 'But say, (I grant) that I had an intent | To haue it so (as
he interprets) meant', and yet it simultaneously exploits the
indeterminacy of language, and hence intent, to produce a
formula that enables libellous readings. It is precisely the way

---

[71] In the 1622 edition of *A satyre* in his *Juvenilia*, published following his second
imprisonment, he will strengthen the sense of culpability by changing 'some cause'
to 'iust cause' (*Juvenilia* (London, 1622), STC 25911, Dd5v).

[72] Annabel Patterson, *Censorship and Interpretation: The Conditions of Writing
and Reading in Early Modern England* (Madison, Wis.: University of Wisconsin
Press, 1984), 11–18.

that his satire is open, in his words, to 'Diuers constructions' that it has a value amongst a readership educated in libellous material. This passage ends with the warning that if there were such a man he would expose him and endure imprisonment, moving from conjecture to threat in a manner that is reminiscent of the Martin Marprelate pamphlets. In *An epistle*, Marprelate challenged the authorities to prove 'my book to be a libell' and boasted that he had 'prevented you of that advantage in lawe, both in bringing in nothing but matters of fact, which may easily be prooved, if you dare denie them: and also in setting my name to my booke'.[73] Both Marprelate and Wither were not the passive subjects of the law but actively interpreted libel laws to provoke public debate.

Libels were, in many ways, constitutive of a market for news. Although theoretically before 1660 there was no distinction between slander and libel, libel was treated differently due to the fact that it was written and therefore raised particular issues in relation to its dissemination within a wider public domain.[74] By 1621, Wither was making an explicit connection between the laws on libel and censorship in *Wither's Motto*. His response to the 1620 proclamation 'Against excesse of Lavish and Licentious Speech of Matters of State' in his *Motto* was primarily conducted in terms of these 1614 debates on libel. He complained that libel laws were being used to undermine freedom of speech particularly in relation to the printed text since whatever he published someone shall 'a libell make it' (A5v). More attention was paid to verse libels in periods of political instability such as in 1614 and in the early 1620s.[75] The opening section of *Wither's Motto* criticizes this tendency on the part of the authorities to see libel in any form of complaint or satire thus restricting what can be said publicly:

> For now, these guilty Times so captious be
> That such, as loue in speaking to be free;
> May for their freedome, to their cost be shent,
> How harmlesse er'e they be, in their intent:
> And such as of their future peace haue care,
> Vnto the *Times* a little seruile are.   (A6r)

[73] Quoted in Clegg, *Press Censorship*, 189.
[74] Baker, *English Legal History*, 506.
[75] Bellany, 'Libellous Politics in Early Stuart England', 292–3.

This passage gains an added political resonance when viewed in relation to the February Commons debates on the principle of freedom of speech. Three months prior to Wither's first attempt to publish his *Motto*, a number of MPs expressed their uneasiness that the December proclamation could be used to undermine the House's privilege of freedom of speech.

The resulting debates over freedom of speech sought to clarify the role of parliament in the state and, in particular, to define its status as a consiliar institution able to advise on and so participate in formulating policy. Similarly, Wither's defence of his 'free-borne lines' (A5r) set up a tension between restrictive libel laws and a concept of counsel in order to define a sphere of public debate that was identified with the principle of free speech. The very terminology that is used invoked the rights and liberties of the freeborn Englishman enshrined in the ancient constitution which in turn were extended to the printed text. At the same time, *Wither's Motto* gives public voice to a citizen able to participate actively within a public sphere. The current restrictions on free speech paradoxically serve to authorize this voice and the text describes an embattled realm of public debate that is given a legitimacy through its identification with the principles of free speech. The reader was encouraged to read *Wither's Motto* in the context of the December proclamation and it is this that gave the poem its provocative topicality. The epistle 'To anybody' challenges the 'hostile' reader to find anything in his poem that can be used against him since they 'may know, I am too well aduised, to write any thing, which they shall iustly be able to interpret, either to my hinderance, or disparagement' (A2v). Wither's reputation as a writer of topical satires is constantly to the fore and he is worth reading because he himself is 'Newes', as he had Cuddy remind the reader in *The Shepherds Hunting*. The speaker boasts that if he wished he could have easily produced a satire along the lines of his *Abuses stript, and whipt*, that touched such a sensitive political nerve in 1614, if he had wanted 'To play againe, the sharpe-fangd Satyrist', and he teases the reader with the ambiguity of his *Motto* in a manner reminscent of *A satyre*:

> I say, it is my *Motto*; and it is.
> I'le haue it so: For, if it please not me;
> It shall not be a *Satyr*, though it be. (A7r)

This strategy of indirection is built into his *Motto*'s rhetoric of negative definition: 'I have not, want not, care not.'

The speaker keeps current issues in view of the reader by claiming that he will not pass satiric judgement because of the current restrictions:

> You are deceiu'd, if the *Bohemian* state
> You thinke I touch; or the *Palatinate*:
> Or that, this ought of *Eighty-eight* containes;
> The *Pouder-plot*, or any thing of *Spaines*:
> That their *Ambassador* neede question me,
> Or bring me iustly for it on my knee.
> The state of those Occurences I know
> Too well; my Raptures that way to bestow.   (A6v)

The poem sets up certain expectations that it refuses to fulfil in a way that directs the reader to the gaps and silences in the text. The conflation of recent and past events—the invasion of the Palatinate, the defeat of the Spanish Armada, the Gunpowder Plot, and the reference to the power of the Spanish ambassador, Gondomar—mirrors the style of the pro-Palatinate pamphlets of Thomas Scott and Thomas Gainsford which warned of a Spanish conspiracy to overthrow the state. The nature of the reference to Gondomar, given that Gainsford had been imprisoned in November 1620 for his attack on the Spanish ambassador in his pamphlet 'Vox Spiritus or Sir Walter Rawleigh's Ghost', implies that he is behind the crown's efforts to silence 'patriots'.[76] Wither's provocative reference to the power of the Spanish ambassador over the freeborn Englishman gives voice to popular resentment that the December proclamation signalled increasing toleration for recusants at the expense of Patriots. Brooke, Wither's fellow Spenserian, had complained in the 1621 parliament of the 'insolency in Papists, who I protest . . . are more easily discovered by theyr ill speaking of the King and Queen of Bohemia then by not receiving the Communion'.[77]

---

[76] I am using 'patriot' in this context according to Thomas Cogswell's sense of the term as those 'dedicated to a war of behalf of the Palatine exiles' (*The Blessed Revolution: English Politics and the Coming of the War, 1621–24* (Cambridge: Cambridge University Press, 1989), 1); L. B. Wright, 'Propaganda against James I's "Appeasement" of Spain', *Huntington Library Quarterly*, 6 (1943), 149–72.

[77] Wallace Notestein *et al.* (eds.), *Commons Debates 1621*, 7 vols. (New Haven: Yale University Press; Oxford: Oxford University Press, 1935), iii. 142.

Wither's motives in publishing his *Motto* in 1621 combined the ideological with the economic. The anonymous author of a 'Letter to George Wither in answere to a late Pamphlet partly imprinted by George Wood', written around 1625, accused Wither of playing the market for controversial material and seeking to profit from its illegality:

Concerning your Motto, of which my knowledge you had five peeces of the Stac[i]oner before it came forth, w[hi]ch was more, then euer would haue bene gotten, if it had come forth orderly; But it had noe license, and was afterwardes forbidden, which put some life into it; you were in some trouble and soe was the Stationer, and lost his Bookes, But you were on the surer side, for you had your Money before hand.[78]

Wither's Motto proved to be a profitable venture, going into at least eight editions in 1621.[79] There was a great deal of co-operation between Wither and the stationers in the printing of his *Motto*. All had an eye to the profit to be made from unlicensed printing in the political climate of the 1620s and this seems to have outweighed the risks, given that those involved in its printing were fined and imprisoned. He first attempted to publish the work on 14 May, when the stationer, Weaver, tried to enter the copy in the Register but was refused a licence until he obtained 'further aucthority'.[80] Wither then sold the copy to the stationers Marriot and Grismond and, according to his testimony, he told them that the text had already been refused a licence, although Marriot and Grismond claimed at their examination that they did not know that it had been called in question.[81] Marriot and Grismond rushed the text into print since the first edition was published with a letter-press title-page

---

[78] A transcript of this letter is provided by Alan Pritchard in his article 'George Wither's Quarrel with the Stationers: An Anonymous Reply to *The Schollers Purgatory*', *Studies in Bibliography*, 14 (1963), 40–2. According to Wither's testimony at his examination, he did receive this amount for his text.

[79] For a list of editions, see appendix.

[80] Edward Arber (ed.), *A Transcript of the Registers of the Company of Stationers of London, 1554–1640*, 5 vols. (London, 1875–94), iv. 15. See also Jocelyn Creigh's discussion of the printing of the *Motto* ('George Wither and the Stationers: Facts and Fiction', *Papers of the Bibliographical Society of America*, 74 (1980), 50–1).

[81] *State Papers, Domestic*, 14/121/132, 122/12–13. See appendix for the transcripts of the examinations of Wither and the stationers. On Okes's career, see: P. W. M. Blayney, *The Texts of King Lear and their Origins, Volume I: Nicholas Okes and the First Quarto* (Cambridge: Cambridge University Press, 1982).

rather than the engraved title-page used in subsequent editions. Marriot claimed at his examination that the book was not called into question until after this first edition, and he had then taken it to the senior stationer Taverner to be licensed on 16 June, when it was censored and 'then lycenced soe corrected', although he admitted that he did not print this censored version. Okes somehow obtained the second edition of the work printed for Marriot, probably knowing that it was not licensed, although he also claimed otherwise, and printed at least one edition before 4 June when Marriot, Grismond, their printer, Matthews, and Okes were called before the Stationers' Company and prosecuted for printing the book without a licence.[82] Prosecution did not stop the printing of the book, moreover, senior members of the Stationers' Company attempted to profit from this case of unlicensed printing. Both Grismond and Thomas Trussell later testified that Okes had often boasted that he had the protection and encouragement of senior members of the Company in his pirating of the book. The main culprit appears to have been Lownes, a Warden of the Company who had actually prosecuted Marriot, Grismond, and Mathews for printing the work without a licence. Throughout June and early July, it was reported that Lownes was buying copies from Grismond 'daylie' and selling them at his shop.[83]

The popularity of his satires, in general, educated Wither in the power of the press and he sought to give his *Motto* a further topical edge by appending a postscript which he claimed was written just twenty days after the first edition left the press, possibly when the book was just coming to the attention of the authorities with the fining of Marriot and Grismond. The postscript opens with a vivid peripatetic image of the *Motto* circulating 'through this *Iland*' and describes a lively public exchange taking place in print and on the London streets that gives the impression that it is being printed as events take place, which in a way it was, and that it has effectively created a politicized national audience.[84] Once more, Wither is himself news and the postscript situates the *Motto* at the centre of a controversy so that its reception becomes paradigmatic of the current crisis.

[82] *Records of the Stationers' Company, 1602 to 1640*, ed. W. A. Jackson (London: The Bibliographical Society, 1957), 135.
[83] See appendix, *State Papers, Domestic* 14/122/13–14, 18.
[84] *Wither's Motto*, STC 25927, F3r.

His *Motto* has divided society along political lines and is generating further debate both in its defence and from those who oppose it. Opposition is largely coming from the tavern 'clubs' and he refers, in particular, to 'the *Brotherhood*' that 'Will lend their wits, to make the Quarrell good' (F4v). In early 1623, Jonson satirized Wither as Chronomastix, the Whipper of the Times, in his masque *Time Vindicated To Himselfe, and To his Honors* and it is possible that he was rehearsing this satire amongst the 'Tribe of Ben' soon after the publication of the *Motto*.

Wither eagerly directed his readers to watch out for a pamphlet responding to his *Motto*, 'For, yet ere night (tis thought) it will come out' (F4v). It is possible that this pamphlet was T.G.'s *An Answer to Wither's Motto* which was not published until 1625. The author claimed that this delay was due to Wither 'who sought to smoother mee in my birth', but it is unlikely that he had this power and more probable that it was kept out of print due to continued sensitivity over the *Motto*, noticeable in the response to Jonson's *Time Vindicated*. Tellingly, when the stationer tried to obtain a licence for the work in September 1624 it was withheld.[85] 'T.G.' has been identified with Thomas Gainsford, who was imprisoned for his 'Vox Spiritus' in November 1620, and edited pro-Palatine corantos for Nathaniel Butter in the 1620s.[86] The author of *An Answer to Wither's Motto* has an interest in the news and speaks of 'the dispersed newes, | Which either *Pauls*, or our exchange doe vse' (E3r). He is critical of gallants and wits who traffic in oral news and therefore debase public debate, but he defends news in general as a means of educating the public, to 'rectifie their ignorance', praising the godly, and condemning corruption in the commonwealth so that with 'The Countreys carpet lay abroad to view, | . . . they mistake not, what is false or true' (E4r). News enables the citizen to take on an active role

[85] T. G. *An Answer to Wither's Motto*, A2r; *Transcript of the Stationers' Register*, iv. 86.

[86] Gainsford died in 1624 the year before *An Answer* was published. On Gainsford, see: W. H. Phelps, 'Thomas Gainsford (1556–1624), the "Grandfather of English Editors" ', *Publications of the Bibliographical Society of America*, 73 (1979), 84–5; Mark Eccles, 'Thomas Gainsford, "Captain Pamphlet" ', *Huntington Library Quarterly*, 45 (1982), 259–70; S. L. Adams, 'Captain Thomas Gainsford, the 'Vox Spiritus' and the *Vox Populi*', *Bulletin of the Institute of Historical Research*, 49 (1976), 141–4.

in the commonwealth and it is given legitimacy in classical republican terms: 'T.G.' points out that ''tis no new thing to harke after newes | For the *Athenians* still the same did vse' (E4r). Yet, despite these affinities with Wither, 'T.G.' was not a wholly sympathetic reader and largely adopted a critical tone. *An Answer to Wither's Motto* is, as its title suggests, a point by point response to *Wither's Motto*. 'T.G.' read the *Motto* on a number of levels: as a 'book of the self', in relation to Protestant orthodoxy, and as a political satire. The majority of the text, and his criticisms, were in response to these first two aspects and he corrected Wither on matters of religion, particularly the dangers of vanity and presuming election, and pointed out the contradictions in Wither's claim to have not, want not, care not.

'T.G.' also responded to Wither as a writer with a reputation for contemporary satire and an assured popular readership. When he does read the *Motto* politically, it becomes the basis for his own critique. The passages that he draws attention to are in line with Gainsford's interests and can broadly be described as 'patriot'. He praised the passage in 'Nec Habeo' that addresses 'Common-wealths, or Kings', claiming that readers 'haue long'd to know | The owner of that place', but refuses to go into detail so 'that none may finde this out | Of your good meaning, to raise any doubt' (C4v). Although the allusion is deliberately and tantalizingly vague, he seems to be referring to the passage in the *Motto* where the speaker says that he 'can see | A Princes loue may oft abused be' (B6v). 'T.G.' seems to read this as an allusion to James's disgraced favourite, the Earl of Somerset, and *An Answer* continually reiterates the *Motto*'s concern with corruption and unworthy favourites, teasing Wither that his wife cannot compare with Sir Thomas Overbury's *A Wife*—Gainsford had contributed an elegy to the 1616 edition of this text along with Browne and Brooke. Similarly, he criticized Wither for claiming not to care 'that great men doe amisse, | And not be greiued, how the gouernment | Concussion suffers' (E6v) when 'you doe; | And so, and more, doth euerie good man too' (E7v). The greatest danger comes from 'certaine *Aspes*' (E7v) who 'poison men' and he called on the king to crush 'such polluted men' (E8r). The Overbury scandal functions in both texts to crystallize concern over court morality to the extent that it becomes a form of shorthand for the threat of subversion from within the court and conspiracies to undermine the commonwealth, that gained a new energy in the 1620s with the Palatine crisis and rumours of courtiers in the pay of Spain.

An Answer like *Wither's Motto* continually returned to current restrictions on public political debate. 'T.G.' warned Wither of the dangers of courting martyrdom and suggested that his insistence on the innocence of his intent is disingenuous since 'If you had thought so to displease the King, | You would haue sure forborne such rimes to sing' (C4r). Wither, 'T.G.' advises, was also particularly foolhardy in a 'dangerous passage' (F5r) towards the close of '*Nec Curo*' which effectively points the reader to the passage in the *Motto* where Wither recalled his imprisonment in 1614 and boasted that he had lived to see his enemies fall, 'hurled downe to shame, and beggery, | In one twelue hours' (E7r)—this was also one of the passages that particularly interested the authorities at Wither's examination. 'T.G.' warned that 'man must not proclaime all that he doth know | —For when the Frog did with the Bullocke swell, | He dash't his braines out, and so dead he fell' (F5r) and ended by reminding Wither to take 'heed of such a *Monarches* rage' (F6r). 'T.G.' clearly read *Wither's Motto* as an oppositional text and his image of Wither is that of a writer who willingly or, more properly, wilfully took risks to get controversial material into print.

Wither was examined before the House of Lords on 27 June 1621. In response to questioning, he insisted that he had not read the proclamation and that his *Motto* did not 'toucheth the State or Gouernement', yet the date that he gave for its composition, Christmas, coincides with issuing of the proclamation on 24 December. The examiners were interested in discovering how the text came to be printed without a licence, who else apart from the stationers knew of the book, whether Wither knew it infringed the proclamation, and, more specifically, whether certain passages 'wherein he wrighteth he had seen . . . the downfall of those that were his enemyes' were libellous. In response to this last question, Wither claimed he meant the 'late Earle Northampton'.[87] Wither's arrest closely followed the imprisonment of the Earls of Southampton and Oxford, Sandys,

[87] See Appendix, *State Papers, Domestic*, 14/121/132/245–6.

and John Selden after the last sitting of the first session of the
1621 parliament. Southampton was imprisoned for his inter-
ventions in support of the Palatine cause, while Selden, although
not an MP, was imprisoned for supporting the jurisdiction of
the Commons in the Floyd case. The arrests, alongside those of
Gainsford and outspoken clergymen, were designed to break up
centres of opposition and to contain public debate.[88] Wither
was not released until 15 March 1622, two months after the
dissolution of the 1621 parliament.

1621 marked a new phase in Wither's relationship with print.
It has been suggested that he had a hand in a 1621 petition to
parliament which set out the grievances of poor freemen and
journeymen printers against the monopolies held by the Master
and Wardens of the Stationers' Company.[89] His involvement in
this dispute may have resulted from the obstacles that he had
faced in getting his translation of the psalms into print due to
the strict monopoly of the Stationers' Company on the English
metrical psalter—a monopoly which provided senior members
of the Company with a lucrative income.[90] Yet, the type of
militant engagement in the affairs of the Stationers' Company
suggested by the petition would seem to go beyond self-interest
to indicate a wider professional interest in the operation and
regulation of the book trade. The postscript to *Wither's Motto*
had depicted the Stationers' Company, 'that *Corporation*', as
part of a repressive regime seeking to victimize Wither, to 'plot
and practice for my overthrow' (F4v). While the earlier model
of cultural conflict favoured by Wither had tended to focus on
the court, from 1621 it widens to incorporate the Stationers'
Company thereby enabling him to address issues to do with the
regulation of the book trade and their impact on the writer.
Wither was also in the process of developing his own economic
role in the book trade and in 1623 was granted a royal patent
by James which required his *Hymns and Songs of the Church* to
be bound with every copy of the English Psalter. The patent was
resisted by the Stationers' Company and Wither's attempts to

---

[88] S. L. Adams, 'The Protestant Cause: Religious Alliance with the West
European Protestant Communities as a Political Issue in England, 1585–1630',
D.Phil. thesis (Oxford, 1972), 315–19; Cogswell, *Blessed Revolution*, 32–4.

[89] Lambert, 'The Printers and the Government', 12.

[90] James Doelman, 'George Wither, the Stationers Company and the English
Psalter', *Studies in Philology*, 90 (1993), 74–82.

enforce it resulted in a long and bitter dispute.[91] His defence
of this patent in *The Schollers Purgatory* (1625) led him to
develop a materialist account of the author's rights over his
intellectual labour. *The Schollers Purgatory* was printed
illegally by George Wood and Wither was once more called
before the authorities. Wither's recourse to such methods of
publication is indicative of his awareness of the polemical
power of print. His career demonstrates that various attempts at
censorship and regulation of the press generated texts, provoked rather than stifled debates over issues such as freedom of
speech, and helped to forge new working relationships between
writers and printers.

[91] On this dispute, see: Pritchard, 'Wither's Quarrel with the Stationers', 27–42;
Norman E. Carlson, 'Wither and the Stationers', *Studies in Bibliography*, 19 (1966),
210–15; Creigh, 'George Wither and the Stationers', 49–57; Doelman, 'Wither, the
Stationers Company and the English Psalter', 74–82.

5
The 'evill time'; Spenserian Community in the 1620s

THE Bohemian crisis intensified political feeling in the 1620s and efforts to find a solution to the crisis dominated English politics for the next decade. The Spanish occupation of the Palatinate not only provoked but concentrated widespread anti-Spanish and anti-Catholic sentiment. The court was not immune from criticism. James's pursuit of a marriage between Charles and a Spanish infanta in the hope of bringing the crisis to a peaceful resolution was attributed by many to the influence of those at court in the pay of Spain. The language of politics became polarized and polarizing and conflict over policy was largely understood 'in the black-and-white terms of good and evil counsel, protestant zeal and crypto-popery'.[1] Widespread public interest in events at home and on the Continent stimulated an expansion of the public sphere. It has been argued that this decade saw 'a revolution in the dissemination of the news'. The first newspapers or corantos produced for an English market were printed in the Netherlands in 1620 and 1621, while the first newspapers published in England appeared in 1621.[2] The Bohemian crisis politicized a range of media: news was not confined to the newspaper and newsbook but also disseminated through plays, poems, pamphlets, sermons, and ballads. Jerzy Limon has demonstrated that in the theatrical season of 1623/24 there was a 'constant attempt to use drama and the theatre as a means of disseminating news' that was occasioned by the return of Prince Charles and Buckingham from Spain and the resulting collapse of negotiations for a Spanish match.[3] Concepts of the public were simultaneously

---

[1] Peter Lake, 'Constitutional Consensus and Puritan Opposition in the 1620s: Thomas Scott and the Spanish Match', *The Historical Journal*, 25 (1982), 818.
[2] Jerzy Limon, *Dangerous Matter: English Drama and Politics in 1623/24* (Cambridge: Cambridge University Press, 1986), 3.
[3] Limon, *Dangerous Matter*, 4.

undergoing a transformation. The pamphlets of Thomas Scott, Thomas Gainsford, and John Reynolds sought to mobilize public opinion and, in doing so, projected an idealized sphere of public debate in which citizens came together to discuss the current crisis and its solutions.

This expansion of the public sphere and the increasingly sophisticated discourses of citizenship that accompanied it was paradoxically stimulated in part by new restrictions on public political debate. Thomas Scott's *Vox Populi*, published in 1620, gave offence to the Spanish ambassador Gondomar and threatened to destabilize James's plans for a peaceful resolution to the Bohemian crisis through a Spanish marriage. James responded to such criticisms of his policies by reaffirming the sanctity of the *arcana imperii* and issued a royal proclamation on 24 December 1620 restricting public discussion of domestic and foreign policy. This proclamation was reissued on 26 July 1621 and was followed by regulations against disorderly printing on 25 September 1623. These restrictions seem to have had the effect of heightening interest in the concept of public debate and politicizing both print and manuscript cultures. Even in 1620, Scott was portraying a battle in print with liberty given to the Catholic press while the Protestant press in England was being suppressed through the influence of Spain.[4] *Vox Populi: or Newes from Spayne*, itself, purported to derive from these Spanish presses and offered its readers an insight into the imperial intent of Spanish foreign policy.

This is the context of the second major Spenserian revival in the early 1620s. In this period, the type of political critique that Browne, Brooke, and Wither had been developing in the mid-1610s came into its own. Pamphlets, such as those produced by Scott, and plays, such as Thomas Drue's *The Life of the Duchess of Suffolk*, Philip Massinger's *The Bondman*, and Middleton's *Game at Chesse*, blamed the Jacobean peace for fostering corruption and effeminizing the state so that it was vulnerable to the machinations of Spain through their agents at the English court and they advocated a return to the confessional style of politics and aristocratic martialism that was associated with Elizabethan courtiers, such as Essex and

---

[4] Thomas Scott, *Vox Populi: or Newes from Spayne, translated according to the Spanish coppie* (London, 1620), C3v.

Raleigh. The political neo-Elizabethanism that had characterized Spenserian poetry in the previous decades becomes one
of the dominant political languages.[5] Browne, Brooke, and
Wither returned to these forms to give their own responses to
the current crisis and there is a sense in their writings that an
earlier Spenserian poetic has been reinvigorated. The Spenserian
concept of community was also being revitalized and reconfigured. The earlier 1614 community increasingly took on more
abstract forms that often had a national character. This transition was already noticeable in Browne's community of 'English
shepherds' in Book II of *Britannia's Pastorals* (1616). In the
texts of Wither and Brooke, the concept of community was
extended to incorporate an incipient political nation through
the structures of counsel that were, in turn, modelled on parliament. Parliament, within a legal humanist tradition, was one of
the chief structures of counsel whereby the citizen participated
in the political life of the commonwealth.[6] Meetings of parliament served to crystallize issues to do with counsel and to open
issues of state to public debate.

'*I CARE NOT* WHEN THERE COMES A *PARLIAMENT*'

It was hoped that the 1621 parliament would result in a
solution to the Bohemian crisis and reconcile the king and his
people. Brooke, in the early sessions of this parliament, spoke of
reports 'among foreign nations that there is a distaste between
the King and his people, and therefore they less fear us than
heretofore' and so hoped for a new affection between the king
and Commons in this parliament.[7] He was expressing a widespread concern that the channels of counsel between the king
and his subjects had become blocked. These blockages could be

[5] There is a difference between a political neo-Elizabethanism, which views
Elizabeth through her male courtiers, Sidney, Essex, and Raleigh, and her naval
heroes, and Elizabeth's policies, particularly given that an Anglo-Spanish alliance
was initiated in her last parliament. On Elizabethan nostalgia in the 1620s, see
Thomas Cogswell, *The Blessed Revolution: English Politics and the Coming of The
War, 1621–24* (Cambridge: Cambridge University Press, 1989), 12–13; 94–9.

[6] J. G. A. Pocock, *The Machiavellian Moment: Florentine Political Thought and
the Atlantic Republican Tradition* (Princeton: Princeton University Press, 1975),
340.

[7] *Commons Debates 1621*, ii. 86.

traced to the 1614 'addled' parliament which was thought to
have failed because of the machinations of Catholic Spain
through its English agents who, as Thomas Scott had claimed in
his *Vox Populi*, had worked 'such a dislike betwist the King and
the lower house . . . as the King will never indure Parliament
againe'.[8] While MPs, such as Brooke, sought to reinstate these
channels of counsel between the king and the Commons, there
was also a concern that they were threatened by the king himself. The recent December proclamation was perceived to have
the potential to undermine the parliamentary privilege of freedom of speech and so severely limit the House's ability to debate
freely key areas of policy, such as the implications of providing
supply for the relief of the Palatine. When defending this privilege in the debates over the liberty of speech which dominated
the first session of the 1621 parliament, Sir Robert Phelips drew
attention to the arrest of MPs following the dissolution of the
1614 parliament as a breach of this privilege and warned that
'the Prerogatives of Princes grow daily, but the Liberties of
Subjects stand at Stay, if once lost, in danger never to be
regained'.[9] The 1614 'addled' parliament seems to have educated MPs and other interested parties in the ideological importance of parliament. Scott, for example, characterized the
dissolution of this parliament in terms of an ideologically
charged conflict between 'some free mindes . . . who preserve
the privilege of subjects against foreign invasion, (and) call for
the course of the common lawe (a lawe proper to their nation)'
and those in the pay of Spain who 'cry the lawes down and cry
up the prerogative, whereby they prey upo[n] the subject by
suites and exactions'.[10] Ideally parliaments would for Scott
'create an open arena', in the words of Lake, 'in which policy
should be formulated and discussed "in public"'.[11]

Such an 'open arena' was emerging in this period through the
increasingly widespread circulation of political separates.
Proceedings in parliament, such as declarations, speeches, sets
of grievances, were taken down and then entered the wider
public domain through a process of copying either by indi-

[8] Scott, *Vox Populi*, B3r.

[9] Christopher Thompson, *The Debate on the Freedom of Speech in the House of Commons in February 1621* (Orsett, Essex: The Orchard Press, 1985), 2–3, 9–16.

[10] Scott, *Vox Populi*, B3v.

[11] Lake, 'Constitutional Consensus and Puritan Opposition in the 1620s', 824.

viduals or by professional scriveners and booksellers around the Inns of Court who traded in legal manuscripts and books. This practice seems to date from the middle of Elizabeth's reign. Since there is a marked increase in the number of separates that have survived from parliaments after 1610, it is possible that the trade grew following the troubled 1614 parliament. Notestein and Relf have argued that the increasing production and circulation of separates arose out of the 'desire on the part of members for greater publicity', itself a reaction against the practice of parliamentary secrecy. This practice was associated with the *arcana imperii*, the secrecy of the King's Council.[12] It is possible that the increasing interest in making parliamentary proceedings public following the 1614 parliament was associated with the perceived need to ensure the survival of parliaments and to define its role as a consiliar institution. In broader terms, the circulation of political separates did enable the expansion of the public political sphere in the 1620s.

This is the political environment of *Wither's Motto*, as I have suggested in the previous chapter, and Brooke's poems of the 1620s, *A Poem on the Late Massacre in Virginia* and his unpublished elegy for Sir Arthur Chichester. There are many similarities between *Wither's Motto* and Scott's *Vox Populi*. Both texts can be described as 'public polemical performances' that construct themselves as expressions of public opinion.[13] Although it would seem that personal opinion dominates *Wither's Motto*, expressed through 'I have not, want not, care not', it consistently assumes a national, public character. The public, in both texts, is that of the elect nation, populated by moderate Protestants, and now threatened, and in the process unified by the plots of Catholic Spain. Scott and Wither promote an ideal of active citizenship that merges evangelical Protestantism with classical humanism and republicanism.[14] *Wither's Motto* not only expresses an ideal of active citizenship,

[12] Wallace Notestein and Frances Relf (eds.), *Commons Debates for 1629* (Minneapolis: University of Minnesota Press, 1921), pp. xx–xxiii; Harold Love, *Scribal Publication in Seventeenth-Century England* (Oxford: Clarendon Press, 1993), 15–19.

[13] The phrase is Lake's, see: 'Constitutional Consensus and Puritan Opposition in the 1620s', 808.

[14] On Scott's model of active citizenship, see Markku Peltonen, *Classical Humanism and Republicanism in English Political Thought, 1570–1640* (Cambridge: Cambridge University Press, 1995), 229–64.

it puts it into practice by using the resources of print to make key parliamentary proceedings public. In doing so, he extended the parliamentary privilege of freedom of speech to his own work which becomes, like parliament, an instrument of counsel.

Early sessions of the 1621 parliament were dominated by proceedings against Sir Francis Mitchell, Sir Giles Mompesson, Sir Francis Bacon, Sir Henry Yelverton, and Sir John Bennett on charges of corruption. Later, in his *Schollers Pvrgatory*, Wither will lament that in his *Motto* 'some particulars, not then in season to bee medled withall, were at vnawares so neerely toucht vpon, that I vnhappily fell into the displeasure of the State'.[15] One subject that is 'so neerely toucht vpon' in the *Motto* is these recent proceedings in parliament against monopolists and those charged with abuse of public office:

> *I care not* when there comes a *Parliament*:
> For I am no Proiector, who inuent
> New *Monopolies*, or such *Suites*, as Those,
> Who, wickedly pretending goodly showes,
> *Abuses* to reforme; engender more:
> And farre lesse tollerable, then before.
> Abusing *Prince*, and *State*, and *Common-weale*;
> Their (iust deserurd) beggeries to heale:
> Or, that their ill-got profit, may aduance,
> To some Great Place, their Pride, and Ignorance.
> No[r] by Extortion, nor through Bribery,
> To any Seat of Iustice, climb'd am I.   (D8r)

This is too close to the current corruption trials and, in particular, the case against Bacon, the Lord Chancellor, which began on 15 March, 1621, for this passage to have been composed in December 1620 as Wither claimed at his examination. He first tried to have his *Motto* published just over a week after Bacon was impeached on 3 May, and copies of the book were available during the last sitting of the parliamentary session in late May and early June. Bacon was convicted of taking bribes from litigants to facilitate their applications for monopolies and fined, imprisoned, and impeached from public office.[16] The attack on the hypocrisy of those who pretend to reform abuses

---

[15] *The schollers pvrgatory* (London, 1624), STC 25919, 2–3.
[16] T. B. Howell (ed.), *A Complete Collection of State Trials*, 33 vols. (London, 1809–28), ii. 1113.

in the passage would accord with Bacon's earlier role, before his own conviction, in the prosecution of a monopolist, Sir Giles Mompesson, the patentee for inns, the manufacture of gold and silver thread, and concealed crown lands. Bacon had argued that the prosecution of Mompesson was necessary 'to clear the king's honour' since 'the authority granted by the king, was much abused . . . to the intolerable grievance of the subject'.[17]

Corruption tended to be laid at the door of 'evil counsellors', such as Bacon, who were perceived to be the primary blockages in the channels of counsel between the king and his people. The proceedings against Bacon in the 1621 parliament looked like they would finally remove these blockages and bring about a wider change in royal policy.[18] Hope in *Wither's Motto* is offered in the apocalyptic vision of the crushing of those 'damned Instruments' of 'Vice and *falsehood's* Tyranny' so that truth can emerge out of oppression to 'on the ruines of those *Tyrants* tread' (D2v). On March 26, James had delivered a speech condemning corruption in high office and co-operated with parliament in the pursuit of monopolists by moving the monopolies bill on the royal initiative.[19] The fact that James had summoned parliament had raised hopes that he was preparing to intervene in the Palatinate to restore Frederick to his title. Wither may have been willing to risk the publication of his *Motto* despite the proclamation because of James's apparent receptiveness to reform in these early parliamentary sessions. However, Wither's treatment of corruption was miscalculated and touched a sensitive political nerve. Joseph Meade wrote to Sir Martin Stuteville that 'Withers, for his motto, is in the Marshalsea; the king threatening to pare his whelp's claws.'[20] Despite James's co-operation with parliament, he only permitted the investigations to go so far and protected those closest to his authority, particularly his favourite. Buckingham was implicated in the proceedings against Mompesson, his cousin, and through his brother, Sir Edward Villiers, who also had a hand in the patent for the manufacture of gold and

---

[17] *State Trials*, ii. 1122.

[18] Lake, 'Constitutional Consensus and Puritan Opposition in the 1620s', 816–17.

[19] *State trials*, ii, 1128–9; Conrad Russell, *Parliaments and English Politics, 1621–1629* (Oxford: Clarendon Press, 1979), 110.

[20] J. M. French, 'George Wither in Prison', *PMLA* 45 (1930), 961.

silver thread. Pembroke and Southampton, who were investigating the case, hoped to use the prosecution of Mompesson to undermine Buckingham's influence at court, but were thwarted by James's intervention on his favourite's behalf.[21] Accusations against Buckingham resurfaced in proceedings against the Attorney General, Sir Henry Yelverton, who had been imprisoned for his involvement along with Mompesson in bribery and corruption. At his trial, a month prior to the first attempt to enter the *Motto* in the Register, Yelverton made extensive accusations against Buckingham and provocatively compared his influence to that of the favourite Piers Gaveston over Edward II. Buckingham had Yelverton imprisoned in the Tower, despite the protests of Southampton, for his 'treasonous' suggestions that the king had allowed his prerogative to be usurped by a subject.[22]

Wither's extensive description of the way that princes can be betrayed by their favourites in his *Motto* echoes Yelverton's accusations against Buckingham:

> Yet, Princes (by experience) we haue seene,
> By those they loue, haue greatly wronged beene.
> Their too much trust, doth often danger breed,
> And Serpents in their Royall bosoms feed.
> For, all the fauours, guifts, and places, which
> Should honour them; doe but these men enrich.
> With those, they further their owne priuate end:
> Their faction strengthen, gratifie their friends:
> Gaine new Associates, daily to their parts,
> And from their Soueraigne, steale away the hearts,
> Of such as are about them; For those be
> Their Creatures; and rarely thankes hath He,
> Because the Grants of *Pension*, and of *Place*;
> Are taken as Their fauors, not *His* grace.   (D5r)[23]

Unworthy favourites such as Buckingham, and Somerset before him, have corrupted not just the patronage system but, by extension, royal authority itself. They abused the offices

[21] Russell, *Parliaments and English Politics*, 106–7, 111.

[22] *State Trials*, ii. 1131–2; S. R. Gardiner, *History of England from the Accession of James I to the Outbreak of the Civil War, 1603–1642*, 10 vols., 3rd edn. (London, 1889–94), iv. 112–13.

[23] See also the passage beginning '*I haue not* so much heedlesnes of thinges' in *Wither's Motto*, B6v.

bestowed on them by the king for private gain and exploited their positions as patronage brokers to create their own power base. In the proceedings in the 1621 parliaments, corruption was depicted as a disease spreading throughout the body politic and Wither similarly portrays corruption as endemic to public office as 'Great-men' seek to gain wealth and 'nought ashamed are, | In vile, and rascall Suites to haue a share' (B4r). His repeated warnings of the dangers posed by royal favourites too closely touch on the king's honour: favourites falsely appropriate 'the Kings Prerogatiue' (D5r) so that the king becomes 'the Patron of their Villany', and by acting in 'Vertue of his *Name*' they are able to 'abuse the State; | His truer-hearted Seruants, they displace' in favour of their own 'debauched Followers' (D5v). Most dangerously, the recent actions of favourites have made the people suspicious of James:

> The true affections of his people loose him:
> And make those hearts (which did in him beleeue,
> All matchlesse Vertues) to suspect, and grieue.   (D5v)

Wither was not anti-monarchical, but he had a strong sense of the poet's responsibility to counsel his prince and dangerously suggested that the king had allowed his royal prerogative to be abused and usurped by a subject.

Christopher Brooke had retained his seat in the 1621 parliament and took a prominent role in debates and on committees in this session, particularly those in relation to the prosecution of monopolists. He advocated a policy of co-operating with the king. Parliamentary business should not be held up and bills should continue to be passed for fear that James would once again dissolve parliament.[24] His overriding interest was the survival of parliament and to this end the Commons' co-operation with James had to be balanced against the defence of its privileges and procedures. He maintained the right of the lower house to act as a high court in the prosecution of Mompesson, arguing against attempts by the Lords to limit its powers, 'That the house of Comons is like the grand Jury for the whole comonwealth, which is to receaue evidence and to give verdict.'[25] In particular, he was concerned to keep the channels between king and Commons open so that Commons would be

---

[24] *Commons Debates 1621*, iii. 329–30, 362.
[25] *Commons Debates 1621*, vi. 70.

able 'to consult and advise touching matter of war'.[26] The following year Brooke returned to print after a gap of eight years with his *A Poem on the Late Massacre in Virginia*. The poem was the Virginia Company's official expression of mourning for the massacre of the Virginian colonists and its leaders, Captains Powle, Maycock, and Berkeley. The poem can tell us much about contemporary attitudes towards native Americans.[27] Yet, it can also tell us about Brooke's response to the Bohemian crisis. The native Americans in the poem become interchangeable with Spain in that both are committed to the overthrow of the Protestant empire. The massacre is viewed apocalyptically as symptomatic of the forces of the ungodly that were mustering in an attack on Protestantism and this enables Brooke to present the massacre as further justification for a war in defence of Frederick and Elizabeth. The poem praises George Sandys, the Company's treasurer, in enthusiastic terms. His brother, Sir Edwin, was one of Brooke's associates in the 1621 parliament and had been imprisoned along with Southampton, another member of the Company, following the close of the first parliamentary session for pro-Bohemian activity. The 1620s were also a period of increasing tension between the Company and the crown which culminated in the Privy Council demanding the surrender of the Company's patent in 1623 and it was finally dissolved in 1624. Given the aggressive anti-Spanish tone of the poem it is probable that Brooke, like others such as Thomas Scott, saw these attacks on the Company as part of a court-based Spanish conspiracy to bring to an end the extension of the Protestant empire into the New World.

While the poem violently condemns the actions of the Indians, it is also critical of the colonists who, like the Israelites, brought the massacre on themselves by incurring God's wrath:

> But when they once began t'idolatrize,
> And in excesse to glut, and wantonize,
> Turning to fond Securitie his *Grace*,
> *Mercy* was gon, and *Iustice* came in place.[28]

---

[26] *Commons Debates 1621*, ii, 494.

[27] For a reading of the poem in relation to colonialism, see my Oxford 1993 D.Phil. thesis, 'Three Jacobean Spenserians: William Browne, George Wither, and Christopher Brooke', 306–8.

[28] Brooke, *A Poem on the Late Massacre in Virginia* (London, 1622), STC 3830.5, B1v.

Idolatrous faith in the security of peace was a common theme in Spenserian critiques of Jacobean foreign policy and the pamphlets of the 1620s:

> *Securitie*; the Calme, before a Storme,
> That hugs a fearefull Ruine in her Arme;
> *Security*; boading to States most harmes,
> In softned spirits, and disuse of Armes.   (B2r)

Brooke had used the metaphor of the storm in his defence of the second petition in the 1621 parliament, which included advice to the king on the Spanish match, the dangers of recusants, and the need for a war against Spain to restore the Palatinate to Frederick. For Brooke, the petition exemplified the vigilance of the Commons:

I was glad to hear of this petition that posterity might see we were not asleep but foresaw the storm. We do not prescribe anything to the King. We only present a humble petition desiring his Majesty to think of the fittest course, less than which we cannot do. The Prince is a public person and every man hath his interest in him.[29]

Brooke insisted on the Commons' right to provide counsel even in relation to the levying of wars which fell within the ambit of the absolute powers of the king, and gave precedents of parliaments that had been called to advise on war. The concept that the 'Prince is a public person and every man hath his interest in him' runs contrary to the notion of the *arcana imperii* and rather rests on the legal humanist assumption that parliament as a conciliar body has a collective wisdom and responsibility that allows them to act independently in the interest of the king and, by analogy, the nation.[30] Brooke, along with his fellow MPs such as Phelips, was effectively strengthening the institutional role of the Commons and using the principle of freedom of speech to do so. James responded with anger at this perceived encroachment on his prerogative. Later in the December session, Brooke again defended the consiliar role of the Commons and pointed to other, more pressing dangers to the state from recusants and Spanish ambassadors:

---

[29] *Commons Debates 1621*, ii. 494.
[30] Patrick Collinson, 'The Monarchical Republic of Queen Elizabeth I', in his *Elizabethan Essays* (London and Rio Grande: Hambledon Press, 1994), 42.

in the petition we had care on religion for our souls, not our bodies, as the insolencies and seducing of us by the ambassadors and their servants. There was no arguments about the marriage used. I think we did well and are not faulty.[31]

James maintained his right to restrict the Commons' ability to debate issues of state that he perceived to be within his absolute prerogative and, since he was prepared to forego supply, the situation escalated into a dispute that led to the eventual dissolution of this parliament.[32]

Brooke's *Poem on the Great Massacre* is framed within similar terms to the Commons debates on the principle of freedom of speech and maintains the right of the poet-MP to counsel his prince on issues to do with the safety of the commonwealth. The closing section, '*My Apologie*', addresses the rights and responsibilities of the poet in the context of the current restrictions on discussion of state affairs. The poet apologizes to his monarch if he has unwittingly breached the 'mysteries and depth of State designes' (C3v) but defends his action in terms of his loyalty to king and commonwealth. The frame of reference is once more extended from the Virginian to the English situation as the poet exercises his right to provide counsel on state affairs:

> Though I might instance Histories of Time,
> T'haue branded greater States, with self-same Crime,
> Who well might be reproacht for too much trust;
> In which they haue betooke their Armes to rust:
> Who (credulous of Leagues) haue beene deceiu'd;
> In their once plumed Caskes; there haue been twisters
> Spinning for them, as fatall as the *Sisters*.   (C3v)

An explicit connection is made between the fate of the colonists and the dangers posed by James's policy of appeasement, epitomized by the Spanish marriage negotiations, and his refusal to head an international Protestant league in a war against Spain. The image of the spiders' webs that now line soldiers' helmets links the decay of nation, represented by its declining military strength, with a Spanish conspiracy against Protestant England. The following question, 'They couenanted a League of Faith

---

[31] *Commons Debates 1621*, ii. 504.
[32] Thompson, *Debate on Freedom of Speech*, 17.

and Peace | But meant to seal't with bloud of mens decease?'
(C4r) sets up an association between the bloody breakdown of
the treaty between the colonists and the Indians in Virginia and
the breach of the Anglo-Spanish alliance with the invasion
of the Palatinate by Habsburg armies. The verse closes with a
violent call to arms:

> Yet now graue Counsels (to preuent more flawes
> Such Massacres may make) prepare supply
> Of Men, Munition, and Artillery;
> The Ribs of Ships emboweld are with Force,
> Fatall to th'*Indians*, as the *Troian* Horse.   (C4r)

Brooke once again insists on the Commons' consiliar role and
parliament, in this passage, stands in for an absent godly Prince
through its vigilance, foresight, and willingness to grant supply
in support of just causes.

In 1624, there was a dramatic reversal of foreign policy as
James abandoned a strategy of appeasement and summoned a
parliament in order to vote supplies for a war with Spain. This
parliament was dissolved by the death of James on 27 March
1625 and Charles called a new parliament in June. In early
1625, Brooke attempted to publish a funeral poem in memory
of Sir Arthur Chichester, Earl of Belfast, who had died on 19
February, 1625. The elegy takes a 'patriot' pro-war tone, celebrating Elizabethan militarism. Chichester was an ideal 'patriot'
subject: he had fought against the Spanish Armada, had been
knighted by Henry IV after he was wounded at Amiens, served
in the Low Countries and with Essex in Ireland, in 1603 was
appointed lord deputy of Ireland, and in 1622 was called out of
retirement to supervise forces in defence of Frederick.[33] On his
return he was made a member of the Privy Council and later in
1624 a member of the Council of War. At court, he was aligned
with the Bedford–Pembroke circle and highly suspicious of
Buckingham; in January 1624 he joined with Pembroke in
abstaining on a crucial vote brought by Buckingham in an
attempt to prevent parliamentary discussion of his involvement
in the Spanish negotiations.[34] Brooke dedicated the poem to the

---

[33] Gardiner, *History of England*, iv. 303, 315–18, 362–3.
[34] S. L. Adams, 'Foreign Policy and the Parliaments of 1621 and 1624', in Kevin
Sharpe (ed.), *Faction and Parliament: Essays on Early Stuart history* (Oxford:
Oxford University Press, 1978; London: Methuen, 1985), 144, 156.

Secretary for State for Ireland, Sir Francis Annesley, not only a close friend of Chichester, but a firm opponent of the current lord deputy of Ireland, Buckingham's client, Viscount Falkland.[35]

There may have been an attempt to suppress Brooke's poem since it was prepared for printing but not published, and its fate constrasts instructively with the successful publication of Alexander Spicer's *An elegie on the death of Sir Arthur Chichester* in 1625.[36] Spicer's dedicatory verse deferentially submitted the work to Buckingham's inspection.[37] His elegy draws attention away from Chichester to James who is extensively praised as the 'Royal *Salamon*' (11). By contrast, Brooke's elegy expresses the anxieties of 'patriots' in 1624 and 1625 and Chichester's death represents the end of an Elizabethan generation:

> What *wreck of *Noblesse*, and what *rape* of *honor*,
> Hath laboring Tyme brought forth (to humane dearth)
> Whose Womb, a Tomb; whose Byrth, a liveles Earth.
>   What *Howse*, or rather hospitable *Court*
> (Erewhile a Receptable for resort
>   Of all Estate) is that wh^{ch} seemes so vast
> Wth desolation, emptines, and wast?   (ff. 6–7 (204–5))

*This may import the late death of many of the Nobility

During 1624 and 1625, the Earls of Southampton, Oxford, Nottingham, Lord Zouche (Browne's early patron), the Marquis of Hamilton, and the Lennox brothers died, leaving Pembroke as the sole surviving Elizabethan on the Privy Council. This left the government with a lack of military expertise and 'patriot' suspicion of Buckingham's war strategy deepened this sense of crisis. Such experience and leadership were crucial since the 1624 parliament had voted a war subsidy, yet no declaration of war against Spain had been issued by the

[35] *DNB* ii. 3–4.

[36] See the 'Directions for the Printer', British Library, Egerton MS. 2405, f. 1. The poem is in Grosart's edition of Brooke's *Poems* (iv. 195–221) and references to this edition will be provided in brackets after quotes. Brydges has argued unconvincingly that its publication was suspended because Spicer published his elegy first (Sir Edward Brydges and J. Haslewood, *The British Bibliographer*, 4 vols. (London, 1810–14), ii. 237–8). Also see Norbrook's discussion of this poem (*Poetry and Politics in the English Renaissance*, 228).

[37] Alexander Spicer, *An elegie on the death of Sir Arthur Chichester* (London, 1625), STC 23100, A1r.

time the 1625 parliament opened, and Buckingham had appropriated supply to finance the Mansfeldt expedition.[38]

Brooke's poem was not only prepared for the printer, it was
also, in a sense, prepared for the censor. The epistle 'To the
Gentleman that shall licence this poem for the Presse' provocatively points out lines in the body of the poem for the censor's
pen:

> The worthles *Knights* that now and then are made;
> Some Fooles, some Clownes, some Yeomen, some of Trade;
> That when wee speake of them (as t'were in scoffe)
> It may be ask't what Trade the Knight is of:
> Theise parcell-guilt ones, Counterfetts, that fly,
> And dare not stand the Test of *Gentrie*
> Our Heroe scorn'd; compar'd wth hym no better
> Then empty Ciphers, or a flourish't Letter.
> Tytles are Cyphers; Honor but a blast
> That want existent parts to stand and last.   (ff. 15–16 (213))

These lines would have found a suitable referent in the current
favourite: Buckingham had been made duke in 1623, the first
non-royal duke since 1572. Brooke tells the licenser that the
'first 4 lynes' of this passage 'may be razed and left out' but the
rest left as 'being voyd of all offence or scruple, because it may
concerne other Kingdomes as well as our' (f. 25 (223)). The
licenser does not seem to have heeded this advice and a line has
been drawn through the first eight lines in the manuscript. The
provocative style of the epistle shows signs of Wither's
influence, borne out by the commendatory verse that he
contributed to the poem. He had been called before the
Ecclesiastical courts in September of the previous year for the
illegal printing of his *Schollers Pvrgatory*, an attack on the
Stationers' Company. The licenser therefore would have been
suspicious of any text that he had a hand in. Yet, since his verse
could have been removed, it still leaves the question of why
Brooke's poem remained unprinted. It may suggest that the
licenser found the elegy as a whole too sensitive and so it was
refused a licence, or that Brooke decided to publish the poem
through other channels and circulated the poem in manuscript,
with the passages uncensored, amongst his Inns of Court and

[38] Cogswell, *The Blessed Revolution*, 317; Adams, 'Foreign Policy and the Parliaments of 1621 and 1624', 170–1.

parliamentary associates. In this form and environment, the poem with its provocative letter to the licenser would stand as testimony to the encroachments on freedom of speech, while demonstrating the right and ability of the poet to debate matters of state despite the current restrictions.

The poems of Wither and Brooke in the early 1620s rely on a readership with an intense interest in events at home and abroad. The politicization of a wide range of media in the 1620s both stimulated and responded to this interest in the news and helped to shape a public arena through which individuals and communities could participate in these events. The language of corruption that is prevalent in the 1620s enabled contemporaries to relate the Jacobean peace, the aggressive use of the prerogative, and attacks on freedom of speech to a Spanish conspiracy conducted through sympathizers at the English court.[39] As a language for talking about differences over policy and comprehending events, it offered a polarized view of political culture divided between evil and good counsellors, the unregenerate and the godly, and ultimately court and country. This polarizing discourse enabled individuals in the 1620s to imagine an incipient political nation united through an anti-Spanish and anti-papist consensus.[40]

'TO MY NOBLE FRIEND MASTER WILLIAM BROWNE, OF THE EVILL TIME'

Textual friendships amongst the poets once involved in *The Shepheards Pipe* did continue into the 1620s, although there was not a return to the cohesiveness of the print community represented by the 1614 communal eclogues. This was partly because the earlier textual community had its social basis in the Inns of Court. By the 1620s, Wither and Browne had moved away from this environment of their youth: Wither looked to a flourishing print culture, and Browne to scribal communities at Exeter College, Oxford, and the country houses of the Herbert

[39] On this view of politics, see: Malcolm Smuts, 'Court-Centred Politics and Roman Historians', in Sharpe and Lake, *Culture and Politics*, 21–43.

[40] See also Lake, 'Constitutional Consensus and Puritan Opposition in the 1620s', 823–5.

family, although he still maintained his London contacts. Brooke, as a practising lawyer-MP kept up his associations with parliamentary groupings and his Inn, acting as Keeper of the Black Book from 1620 to 1621, and treasurer to Lincoln's Inn from 1623 to 1624.[41] Textual exchanges, however, did persist amongst these writers and continue to be politically motivated, with poets joining together to defend a just cause. The earlier 1614 community takes on a symbolic function to evoke an earlier period of tyranny that has returned in these 'evill times', while the characteristic rhetoric of a 'court'/'country' conflict is redeployed as a language for comprehending the current crisis and for representing a society divided along sharp cultural and political lines. The model of community deployed by these poets is frequently conflated with the 'country' and thereby becomes representative of the nation as a whole.

The earlier Spenserian community is reconfigured through other textual communities. Wither and Browne, in particular, had close ties with Drayton in the 1620s. Both, along with John Reynolds, contributed verses before the second part of Drayton's *Poly-Olbion* in 1622. Wither was once more in prison in late 1621 and the first half of 1622 during which time *Poly-Olbion* was entered in the Stationers' Register. Circumstances were very similar to those of 1614 and his presence adds a topical edge to the volume, aligning it with popular discontent over the Palatinate crisis, and testifies to Drayton's support for Wither's 'cause'. Drayton may also have been eager to capitalize on Wither's notoriety as a 'Whipper of the Times'. And indeed, he had some involvement in the publication of *Wither's Motto*: when examined by the authorities, Wither said that he had shown the manuscript to Drayton and his advice presumably was to publish. The lively and skilful peripatetic verse that Wither contributed to *Poly-Olbion* relies upon this familiarity with Drayton and he, at least, claimed to have read the book from cover to cover in four days:

> FROM CORNWAL'S Foreland *to the* Cliffs *of* DOVER,
> O're hilly CAMBRIA, *and all* ENGLAND *over,*
> Thy Muse *hath borne me; and (in foure dayes) showne*

---

[41] W. P. Bailden (ed.), *The Records of the Honorable Society of Lincoln's Inn: The Black Books, Vol. II 1586–1660* (London: Lincoln's Inn, 1898), 218, 246.

More goodly Prospects, *then I could have knowne*
In foure yeares Travailes.[42]

Wither constantly draws attention to his imprisonment and the restrictions on public debate: no matter what he writes and *'Though I to no mans wrong had gone astray, | I had been pounded on the* Kings *hye way'* (ll. 45–6). Although he often distances himself from the pamphleteer in this period, preferring the company of the Muses, this image of the 'Kings *hye way'* evokes the current highly profitable but dangerous traffic in the news and is reminiscent of the opening lines of the postscript to *Wither's Motto*: 'Qvite through this *Iland* hath my *Motto* rung; | And twenty daies are past since vp I hung | My bold *Impreza'* (F3r). Wither turned the conventional compliment to the author's poetic skills into another opportunity to advertise his cause and he praised Drayton for finding a way to judge *'this Age'* and *'so to write, | That scape thou mayst, the clutches of Despight'* (ll. 37–8).

Wither was keen to reassure his friend that although *'these* Times' will not *'value thy Heroick* Rymes', he may take comfort from the knowledge that future times will. This theme of 'fit audience, though few' is also to be found in Browne's commendatory poem and Drayton's prefatory epistle to the volume, 'To any that will read it', which is structured around an analogy between the fate of Drayton's book and that of the nation, so that its poor reception becomes symptomatic of the current national malaise, these times of 'barbarous Ignorance and base Detraction' (iv. 391). Royal inertia over the Palatinate is translated into imperial decline and heroic failure. Cogswell has described the second part of *Poly-Olbion* as 'a monument to what the poet dubbed "the evill time" of Jacobean neutrality'.[43] England is losing its national character and is no longer receptive to heroic, nationalistic verse, which cannot find a reader amongst its natural audience of the nobility and gentry: Drayton says that he first wrote a chorographical poem because 'there is scarcely any of the Nobilitie, or Gentry of this land, but that he is some way or other, by his Blood interested therein' (391). This absence of a national audience perhaps should be read not so much as a description of a reality, evidence for

---

[42] Drayton, *Works*, iv. 394.
[43] Cogswell, *The Blessed Revolution*, 25.

the poor reception of the first part of *Poly-Olbion*, but as a
rhetorical strategy that styles the poem in terms of an 'epic of
defeat'. This preface is reminiscent of the elegiac tone of Book
II of *Britannia's Pastorals* which similarly lamented the dis-
appearance of an aristocratic martial ethos and community of
honour with the coming of the Jacobean peace. Browne's
own verse before *Poly-Olbion* continues this elegiac note and
honours Drayton as the sole survivor of a glorious generation of
Elizabethan poets who had flourished under Elizabeth. The
failure of the times to provide an heroic subject worthy of
Drayton is likened to a town under siege; an image which
evokes the endless conflicts of civil war and, like the allegory of
famine in Book II of *Britannia Pastorals*, carries a critique of
Stuart imperialism. Nostalgia, in this sense, is a position of resistance from where the poet can produce alternative accounts.
Drayton finds his ideal readers in the embattled community
represented by the commendatory verses of Browne, Wither,
and John Reynolds, a chaplain to the dedicatee, Prince Charles,
who in two years would be imprisoned for his pro-Palatine
pamphlets, *Votivae Angliae* and *Vox Coeli*.

The names of Browne and Drayton were frequently coupled
in this period. Samuel Austin in 1629 urged Browne and
Drayton to join him and turn their talents to divine poetry
rather than secular amatory and pastoral verse.[44] Drayton
addressed an epistle to Browne on the subject of 'the evill time'
in the volume, *The Battaile of Agincourt* (1627). This Caroline
pro-war volume works on a number of seemingly contradictory
levels: it both served as propaganda for Buckingham's expedition to the Île de Ré, and revived an anti-Jacobean, Spenserian-
style community in the elegies that appeared at the end of the
volume. Not one of these Spenserian poets had recorded James's
death and Browne, in particular, made his own position clear at
the end of an ode he addressed to Drayton: 'And if my Muse to
Spenser's glory come, | No king shall own my verses for his
tomb.'[45] Drayton's verse epistles are thought to date from the
early 1620s and are uniformly bitter and hostile in tone and
sharply critical of the times. The verse letters to his friends are

[44] Samuel Austin, *Austins Urania or, the heavenly muse* (London, 1628), STC
971, A7r; David Norbrook, *Poetry and Politics in the English Renaissance* (London:
Routledge and Kegan Paul, 1984), 233.　　　　[45] Browne, *Poems*, ii. 213.

interspersed with poems on the deaths of the three sons of Lord Sheffield, Lady Penelope Clifton, Sir Henry Raynsford, Lady Olive Stanhope, and his mistress, which gives an elegiac cast to the community that is characteristically Spenserian. The first verse, 'Of his Ladies not Coming to London', opens with the motif of Homeric exile and the following community of 'exiles' includes: William Browne; George Sandys, 'exiled' in America, who had recently published his translation of Ovid's *Metamorphoses* and was the former treasurer of the Virginia Company, which had been dissolved by the crown in 1624 after a long battle; the poet, Henry Reynolds; and William Jeffreys, chaplain to Sir Walter Aston, the English ambassador in Spain from 1620 to 1625. The epistle to Jeffreys provides an opportunity for Drayton to comment ironically on his inability to 'report | In home-spunne prose, in good plaine honest words | The newes our wofull *England* vs affords' because of the current restrictions which have led him to adopt the coded forms of satire and elegy (216). John Reynolds, who had been imprisoned over his pro-war pamphlets in 1624, contributed a commendatory verse to the volume. Drayton's epistle to Browne sympathized with his friend's decision to leave Book III of *Britannia's Pastorals* unpublished in these 'arsey varsey' times and to 'sit out of the way | Of this ignoble age'.[46] Browne's ode to Drayton, 'Awake, fair Muse', which remained in manuscript, appears to respond to this epistle; while it allows that some may now seek 'Honour by the victorious steel', the times make the poet 'affect (where men no traffic have) | The holy horror of a savage cave'—an allusion to the 'Den of Oblivion' in Book III of *Britannia's Pastorals*.[47] Cogswell is right to insist on the uniformly pro-war tone of the whole of *The Battaile of Agincourt*, however he downplays the significance of both the anti-Jacobean poems gathered towards the end of the volume— *The Shepheards Sirena*, *The Moone-calfe*, and the elegies—and the apparent burlesque of the Caroline court in *Nimphidia, the Court of Fayrie*.[48] *The Battaile of Agincourt* is a very hetero-

[46] *The Battle of Agincovrt* (London, 1627), STC 7190, 191, 193.
[47] Browne, *Poems*, ii. 212.
[48] Thomas Cogswell, 'The Path to Elizium "Lately Discovered": Drayton and the Early Stuart Court', *Huntington Library Quarterly*, 54 (1991), 207–33. It would be difficult to see how Charles could approve of the anti-Jacobean poems, particularly given his views on kingship.

geneous and unsettling volume and may both praise Charles's pursuit of a pro-war policy and warn of the dangers of falling from this path, while *Nimphidia* suggests a highly ambivalent attitude towards Buckingham.

The community of exiles represented by these verse epistles takes on a pastoral form in *The Shepheard's Sirena* in a manner that deliberately recalls the communal Spenserian eclogues of 1614. Tillotson suggested that *The Shepheard's Sirena* was originally composed as a sequel to *The Shepheards Pipe* and *The Shepherds Hunting* but not published at this time because Drayton feared that he would suffer the same fate as Wither.[49] However, since Wither was able to publish *The Shepherds Hunting* soon after he was released, this does not explain the delay and arguably the poem was composed around the time of the elegies in the early 1620s. The theme of exile dominates the opening section of *The Shepheards Sirena*: Dorilus is separated from his mistress, Sirena, by the cold winter and 'wilde waters' (l. 49). Sirena functions on a number of levels: she is the muse who inspires heroic verse; she has been identified with Mary Curzon, wife of Sir Edward Sackville;[50] and in the context of the early 1620s, she also figures the plight of Princess Elizabeth, particularly given the motifs of exile, winter, and separation across water. The last section of Drayton's pastoral has Dorilus called from his lament into action by his shepherd friends, Tom, Ralph, Gill, Rock, and Rollo, who in style if not name closely resemble the earlier 1614 Spenserian community. Drayton is here rewriting the second eclogue of *The Shepheards Pipe* which had ended with the shepherds vowing to rid a swineherd from their plains with the aid of 'some Satiricke reed' (D2r). In Drayton's version, Dorilus's friends seek his aid in chasing invading 'Swinheards', 'beastly Clownes' from 'our Downes'. Olcon is behind this attack because he has opposed this Spenserian community 'Euer since he was out-gone, | Offring Rymes with vs to make'.[51] Jonson adopted the name 'Alkin' in the lost pastoral drama *The May Lord* and this figure reappears in the unfinished *Sad Shepherd*. These plays have affinities with Spenserian pastoral and Jonson was apparently contemplating

[49] Kathleen Tillotson, 'Drayton, Browne, and Wither', *TLS* (27 Nov. 1937), 911.
[50] Drayton, *Works*, v. 208.
[51] Drayton, *Shepheard's Sirena, The Battle of Agincovrt*, 151–2.

works in an effort to outdo Drayton from around 1619. In conversation with Drayton's friend, Drummond, he claimed he had
'ane jntention to perfect ane Epick Poeme jntitled Heroologia of
the Worthies of his Country, rowsed by fame, and was to dedicate it to his Country', a poem that would presumably perfect
Drayton's imperfect *Poly-Olbion* that '(if ⟨he⟩ had performed
what he promised to writte the deeds of all ye Worthies) had
been excellent'.[52]

If the date of *The Shepheards Sirena* is the early 1620s, then
this is the period when Jonson, in his masque *Time Vindicated
to Himselfe, and to his Honors* (1623), satirizes Wither who
had the support of Drayton and Browne. Drayton's pastoral
may allude to some type of politically-charged rivalry at the
tavern 'clubs' between these Spenserian poets and Jonson and
the 'Tribe of Ben'.[53] Both Wither and Browne give the taverns a
formative role in the political culture of the 1620s. Drayton had
celebrated a meeting at the Apollo Room at the Devil and St
Dunstan tavern, also frequented by Jonson and the 'Tribe of
Ben', in his 'The Sacrifice to Apollo' in his *Odes* (1619), and
Browne, in his ode addressed to Drayton, also identified himself
as one of 'Apollo's troop' but complained that he had retired to
a 'savage cave' because of rude 'satyrs'.[54] Jonson's masque *Time
Vindicated* and his *The Staple of News* (1624) were responses
to the royal proclamations restricting public discussion of
affairs of state and the expanding market for news.[55] Jonson
sought to inhabit rather than place himself outside the public
political sphere that was emerging in this period. His response

[52] Jonson, *Works*, i. 132–3. For Jonson's Elizabethanism, see: Anne Barton,
'Harking back to Elizabeth: Ben Jonson and Caroline nostalgia', *English Literary
History*, 48 (1981), 701–31.

[53] Critics have tended to read Drayton's eclogues in terms of poetic competition
between the Spenserians and either the school of Jonson or Donne, see: W. Hebel,
'Drayton's *Sirena*', *PMLA* 39 (1924), 814–26; Raymond Jenkins, 'Drayton's relation to the School of Donne as revealed in the *Shepheard's Sirena*', *PMLA* 38
(1923), 557–87, 'Drayton's *Sirena* Again', *PMLA* 42 (1927), 129–39; Tillotson,
'Drayton, Browne, and Wither', 911, and 'Introduction and Notes: *The Shepheards
Sirena*', Drayton, *Works*, v. 207–8.

[54] Browne, *Poems*, ii. 212.

[55] For a recent rereading of these texts in relation to the news, see: Julie Sanders,
'Print, Popular Culture, Consumption and Commodification in *The Staple of
News*', in Sanders, Kate Chedgzoy and Susan Wiseman (eds.), *Refashioning Ben
Jonson: Gender, Politics, and the Jonsonian Canon* (Basingstoke and London:
Macmillan, 1998), 183–207.

to *Wither's Motto* is indicative of the way that different communities were competing for control over print and the concept of public debate itself. In *Time Vindicated*, Jonson sought to mark out the 'difference 'twixt liberty and licence' and to distinguish between himself and Wither in terms of their relationship to print culture.[56] His characterization of Wither sought to identify him with the debasing commodification of print when separated from humanist imperatives. This is not the authorial image that Wither promoted, in fact, he always insisted on his humanist motives when publishing his work. Jonson wanted to fashion Wither and pamphleteers, such as Scott, in a manner that both dismissed them as popular in a negative sense and partook of that popularity. This strategy seems to have had some success, although not in the way that Jonson would have wished. It appears that his satire was itself too much in the vein of the *Motto*: Chamberlain reported to Carleton that Jonson 'is like to heare of yt on both sides of the head for personating George Withers a poet or poetaster as he termes him, as hunting after fame by beeing a cronomastix . . . which is become so tender an argument that yt must not be touched in either jest or earnest'.[57]

Yet, *The Shepheards Sirena* appears in a volume that is prefaced by 'The Vision of Ben Jonson, on the Muses of His Friend, M. Drayton' which suggests that by 1627 relations may have changed between the two poets. The verse begins with the lines 'It hath been questioned, Michael, if I be | A friend at all; if at all, to thee' (A3r), possibly an allusion to an earlier period of rivalry. Relations between writers were not fixed in stone and could vary according to a range of ideological and personal factors. Attempts to assess Jonson's situation in the 1620s are further complicated by the complex nature of his personal, professional, and ideological affiliations. Cogswell has argued that Jonson and Drayton were allied in 1627 in their support for Charles's pro-war policies and rallied behind Buckingham's expedition.[58] Moreover, in the early 1620s, Jonson was pro-

[56] Ben Jonson, *Works*, ed. C. H. Hereford, Percy Simpson, and Evelyn Simpson, 11 vols. (Oxford: Clarendon Press, 1925–52), vii. 662 line 216. Richard Burt, *Licensed by Authority: Ben Jonson and the Discourses of Censorship* (Ithaca, NY, and London: Cornell University Press, 1993), 128–9.

[57] Chamberlain, *Letters*, ii. 473.

[58] Cogswell, 'The Path to Elizium "Lately Discovered" ', 215.

ducing verse satires that had affinities with the type of political critique developed in Spenserian texts. His 'An Epistle to a Friend, to Persuade Him to the Wars' (*Underwood*, xv, *Works*, viii. 213–16) was written at the beginning of the Bohemian crisis around 1620 in support of the campaign to raise companies of English volunteers to aid Frederick and Elizabeth. 'A Speech according to Horace', composed around 1626, is concerned with the national degeneracy that follows from the security of peace. Yet, despite these affinities, Jonson uses a political vocabulary that differs in significant ways from that of Browne, Brooke, and Wither. Jonson views corruption in these poems in neo-classical terms and it is not specifically identified with the court but rather is a general condition associated with commodification. Although there is a mocking reference to 'Old *Aesope Gundomar*' (5) in 'A Speech according to Horace', it has none of the aggression of Spenserian attacks. Nor does Jonson use the ideologically charged dichotomies of 'court' and 'country' or the language of anti-popery that typifies the work of these writers and the pamphlets circulating in this period. Finally, he seems to have had little sympathy with the ideal of active citizenship and instead mocks 'ciuill Soldierie' (44) in 'A Speech according to Horace'.

It seems likely that *The Shepheards Sirena* was composed around the time of Wither's imprisonment in 1621 and 1622 which would have given an added topicality to this revival of the 1614 community. This earlier textual community had recently reappeared in print in Thomas Walkley's 1620 edition of *The Workes of Master George Wither, of Lincolnes Inne* which took the unusual step of reprinting Browne's *The Shepheards Pipe* alongside Wither's *The Shepherds Hunting*.[59] The volume opens with *A satyre written to the King* and a new note was included on the title-page explaining that it had been written 'when he was Prisoner in the *Marshallsey*, for his first Booke'. Walkley may have envisioned a new market for these works in the heated 1620s. Wither, himself, tactically revives the political pastoralism of these earlier communal volumes in his *Faire-Virtue* (1622), entered in the Stationers' Register when he was once more in the Marshalsea. The characteristic satiric

---

[59] Since both texts were published by Norton, Walkley probably bought the copyrights of both texts.

opposition between 'court' and 'country' predominates and the 'country' stands for a moral and intellectual independence and a native tradition of poetry that finds its authority outside the court:

> See, if any *Palace* yeelds
> Ought more glorious, then the *Fields*.
> And consider well, if we
> May not as high-flying be
> In our thoughts, as you that sing
> In the Chambers of a King.　　(B8v)

This Spenserian 'country' looks forward to a godly common-wealth reformed along Protestant lines which had found a new impetus in the 1620s with the Bohemian crisis.[60]

As in his earlier prison poem, *The Shepherds Hunting*, the poet is once more in exile, but this time, taking his lead from Browne in Book II of his *Britannia's Pastorals*, he has returned to his native land, in Wither's case the 'Ford *of* Arle' (B1v) or Arlesford which is halfway between Winchester and Bentworth, his birthplace. Philarete's exile is the result of a conspiracy against Virtue and her followers '*in these* Vice *abounding dayes*' (B4r).[61] Although *Faire-Virtue* was at first published anony-mously (another issue did appear in the same year with Wither's name on the title-page) there were numerous indications both in style and content that this was the author of *Wither's Motto*, including the phrase that had become his signature '*in a word . . . I am Master of my selfe*' (B5v). In *The Shepherds Hunting*, Wither's visitors in his prison exile had been his fellow poets, but in 1622 his visitors were a '*troupe of Beauties*' famed '*Through all the Plaines of happy* Britany' (B3r). This meeting initially is conducted in terms of a 'court'/'country' opposition, but the grounds are laid for a *rapprochement* when the ladies convince the poet that they come not to mock but in admiration

---

[60] This vision of the 'country' is also able to incorporate traditional rural festivities, apparent in Wither's 'A Christmas Caroll' appended to *Faire-Virtue*, in a way that suggests that these festivities have not been fully appropriated to a royalist ideology. On the Stuart appropriation of traditional customs and festivities, see Leah Marcus, *The Politics of Mirth: Jonson, Herrick, Milton, and Marvell, and The Defense of Holiday Pastimes* (Chicago and London: Chicago University Press, 1986).

[61] Philarete replaces Roget as Wither's pastoral name in the 1622 edition of *Shepherds Hunting* in his *Juvenilia*.

of his mistress, Fair Virtue, and her poet. Wither in this period was seeking reconciliation with the king and sometime after his release wrote a verse petition to Prince Charles thanking him for mediating between himself and James, 'you[r] Meditation [sic] takes effect att last, | And I enlarged from vneasie bandes'.[62] The verse to Charles requests a 'second favour' to help him to restore his finances and this may have borne fruit in the lucrative royal patent on his *Hymnes and Songs of the Church* (1623) which he dedicated, in thanks, to James. The patent was possibly meant to ensure Wither's loyalty and silence during a difficult period for the crown. It certainly kept him occupied since this controversial patent was fiercely resisted by members of the Stationers' Company and equally tenaciously defended by Wither in skirmishes between 1623 and 1635.[63]

Yet, while Wither may have been seeking reconciliation with James in 1622, this does not seem to have precluded his support for the cause of Princess Elizabeth. The figure of Fair Virtue had particular ties with Elizabeth and appeared in plans for a poem in praise of the princess in *A satyre* (1614):

> I'le make her *Name* giue life vnto a *Song*,
> Whose neuer-dying note shall last as long
> As there is either *Riuer*, *Groue*, or *Spring*,
> Or *Downe* for *Sheepe*, or *Shepheards Lad* to sing.
>
> .   .   .   .
>
> And since the world will not haue *Vice* thus showne,
> By blazing *Vertue* I will make it knowne.   (F1v–2r)

The term 'blazing' is associated etymologically with the blazon—a device that effectively structures the main body of the poem in *Faire-Virtue*. While Fair-Virtue is a generalized figure of Protestant femininity, Elizabeth does make a highly politicized appearance in the poem:

[62] Allan Pritchard, 'An Unpublished Poem by George Wither', *Modern Philology*, 61 (1963), 120–1.

[63] For studies of this conflict see Jocelyn Creigh, 'George Wither and the Stationers: Facts and Fiction', *Papers of the Bibliographical Society of America*, 74 (1980), 49–57; Allan Pritchard, 'George Wither's Quarrel with the Stationers: An Anonymous Reply to the *Schollers Purgatory*', *Studies in Bibliography*, 14 (1963), 27–42; N. E. Carlson, 'Wither and the Stationers', *Studies in Bibliography*, 15 (1964), 210–15.

(With esteeme of vertuous) she
Might the *German Empresse* be.
Such my *Mistresse* is; and nought
Shall haue the power to change her thought.   (K1r)

These lines encourage the reader to identify Fair Virtue with Elizabeth. By giving her the title '*German Empresse*', Wither aligns himself with her supporters, particularly the circle that had gathered around the Countess of Bedford and the Earl of Pembroke, who viewed Frederick's acceptance of the Bohemian crown as a prelude to his election as the Holy Roman Emperor and part of an apocalyptic struggle that would result in the overthrow of the papist Habsburg Empire.[64] In the final section of the poem, a melancholy lady emerges as the spokeswoman for this group of aristocratic women and calls on the poet to echo her sorrow in verse. In July 1621, the Countess of Bedford, who was renowned for her piety in later years and was a leading figure amongst supporters of Frederick and Elizabeth, was finally granted permission by James to visit Elizabeth, her childhood friend, at the Hague, although the king continued to place a number of restrictions on the countess which hindered her activities on behalf of Elizabeth in England.[65] The presence of this female 'court' in the Spenserian 'country' suggests that it too is in some form of exile. Elizabeth's plight gives a topical inflection to the opening image of '*Faire* Thetis' leaving '*her father* Neptunes *brackish Court*' to find refuge in the '*sweeter waters*' of '*Cynthia's Bathing place*' (B1r).

These aristocratic women have a great deal of sympathy for the poet and are entertained by his *Abuses stript, and whipt*, a '*Countrey-Dance* thats better knowne: | Nor, hath gain'd a greater commendation, | Mongst those that loue an honest recreation' (M3r). At the end of the poem, they and Wither are joined by

Three men, that by their *Habits* Courtiers seemd:
For (though obscure) by some he is esteemd
Among the greatest: who do not contemne
In his retyred walkes, to visit him.

<hr/>

[64] Adams, 'Foreign Policy and the Parliaments of 1621 and 1624', 143–4, 147–8.
[65] S. L. Adams, 'The Protestant Cause: Religious Alliance with the West European Calvinist Communities as a Political Issue in England, 1585–1630', D.Phil. thesis (Oxford, 1972), 316.

And there they tast those pleasures of the mind,
Which they can nor in *Court*, nor *Cittie* find.   (N4r)

The number of the visitors is precise and could allude to his earlier visitors in *The Shepherds Hunting*, Browne, Brooke, and Ferrars. However, none of these could be accounted courtiers and the figures are unnamed, perhaps in recognition of their superior social status. One of these figures may allude to the Earl of Pembroke who headed the 'patriot' coalition at court which included the Countess of Bedford. In his *Emblemes*, Wither granted Pembroke the honour of securing his release and restoring him to James's favour, and it may be that Charles and Pembroke had acted together on his behalf. Wither turned to the Spenserian language of community in the early 1620s because it provided him with a sophisticated medium for negotiating a position in relation to the court. A satiric opposition between 'court' and 'country' once more functions rhetorically to represent a political culture that is sharply divided rather than united in consensus and enables Wither to invoke the earlier oppositional 1614 community that had gathered around him when he had once before been 'unjustly' imprisoned. This time it is the speaker's aristocratic friends who have joined him in exile in the 'country' in sympathy with his 'cause', itself epitomized by his mistress, Fair Virtue. While in his writings he condemned patronage as a system that fostered corruption and curbed independence, the language of community allowed him to transform patronage relationships in Spenserian terms so that the poet takes on the privileged role of public spokesman for this 'patriot' community.

Browne also had close ties with Pembroke and seems to have found a stable source of patronage in the Herbert family. There is evidence that a literary community gathered around the Sidney and Herbert families continued throughout the Jacobean and early Carolinian period.[66] This community would have included Lady Mary Wroth, her aunt, the Dowager Countess of Pembroke, William, Earl of Pembroke, and his sister-in-law, the Countess of Montgomery. Given Browne's role within the

---

[66] Margaret Hannay, *Philip's Phoenix: Mary Sidney, Countess of Pembroke* (New York and Oxford: Oxford University Press, 1990), 208–10; Mary Ellen Lamb, *Gender and Authorship in the Sidney Circle* (Madison, Wis.: University of Wisconsin Press, 1990), 143–8.

Herbert family, it is likely that he had some contact with this circle. Between 1623 and 1625, he acted as tutor to Robert Dormer, the ward of Philip Herbert, Earl of Montgomery, at Eton and Exeter College, Oxford. Dormer came from a recusant family and the Herberts ensured that he obtained a Calvinist education while at Oxford, engaging John Prideaux, the Calvinist Regius Professor of Divinity, as his tutor in theology.[67] In the 1620s and 1630s, Browne acted as 'the official poet of the Herbert family', producing elegies for Mary Herbert, the Dowager Countess of Pembroke, Susan Vere, Countess of Montgomery, and her son, Charles, Lord Herbert of Cardiff and Shurland, Anne Prideaux, the daughter of John Prideaux, who was Pembroke's client, and Pembroke's chaplain, John Smyth.[68] Browne's numerous elegies tended to be popular amongst an Inns of Court and university audience. However, the elegies for the members of the Herbert family, excluding the epitaph 'On the Countess Dowager of Pembroke', appear to have had a very limited circulation, and may have been confined to the family itself. Manuscript enabled the poet to address a more intimate and socially exclusive community of readers. Browne's epitaph on the Dowager Countess of Pembroke, by contrast, circulated widely in manuscript and appeared in print, and seems to have been the official memorial put out by the Herbert family. It was sent by Chamberlain to Dudley Carleton at the Hague to mark her death, and was first published in the 1623 edition of Camden's *Remaines*, although in both cases the verse was not attributed to Browne.[69] Browne's epitaph and his 'An elegy on the Countess Dowager of Pembroke' appear to have been the only verse commemorations for Mary Herbert. This was probably due to her declining prestige as a patron following the death of her husband; Browne's fellow Spenserian, John Davies of Hereford, was one of the few poets

---

[67] For Prideaux's association with Pembroke and his opposition to Arminianism in the 1620s, see: Nicholas Tyacke, *Anti-Calvinists: The Rise of English Arminianism, 1590–1640* (Oxford: Clarendon Press, 1987), 72–3.

[68] Michael Brennan, 'The Literary Patronage of the Herbert family, Earls of Pembroke, 1550–1640', D.Phil. thesis (Oxford, 1982), 190.

[69] Peter Beal records fifty-one manuscript copies of this verse in his *Index of English Literary Manuscripts* (London and New York: Mansell, 1993: i. BrW, 180–231). *S.P.Dom.* 14/123/30 f. 43; Joan Grundy, 'A New Manuscript of the Countess of Pembroke's Epitaph', *Notes and Queries*, 7 (1960), 63–4; William Camden, *Remaines* (London, 1623) STC 4523, 430.

who continued to dedicate works to her in the early seventeenth century.[70]

Browne's 'An elegy on the Countess Dowager of Pembroke' seems to have been intended for circulation only within the family.[71] The elegy is remarkably personalized given its subject, and unusually there is not any mention of her life, her sons, or the famous Sidney family that would give the elegy a public aspect. There do appear to be a number of personal references, for example, Browne speaks of the ignorance of the French gentry in a way that suggests shared first-hand experience—the Dowager Countess had toured the Continent, including France, from 1614 to 1616 and, as Pembroke had signed a pass for a 'William Browne' to travel on the Continent in 1616, he may have first met the Dowager Countess in Europe.[72] Enjambment is used extensively throughout the elegy to give the impression of a spontaneous outpouring of emotion. It is not surprising that a subsequent reader chose to include this elegy amongst poems attributed to Donne as the elegy echoes his metaphysical, intellectual style, particularly in the extensive meditation on the Dowager Countess's apotheosis. However, the elegy is also characteristically Spenserian in the way that consolation comes from a community brought together by the poet's art. The opening lines of the elegy move from 'we' and 'us' to 'I' as the speaker places himself amongst an intimate community of mourners, 'And I that knewe thee shall noe less cause haue | To sit me downe & weepe beside thy graue.'[73] This community returns at the close of the elegy:

> These lines shall give
> To vs a second life; and we will liue
> To pull the Distaffe from the hands of ffate

---

[70] Hannay, *Philip's Phoenix*, 193–4.

[71] The only recorded copies of this poem are in the Landsdowne MS 777, which was probably transcribed from Browne's own collection of his unpublished verse, and a contemporary manuscript miscellany of poems mainly by Donne that was compiled by Henry Champernowne of Dartington, Devon. The verse appears at the end of the volume, lacks lines 1–52, and follows, without a separate title-page, the poems 'Sir Philip Sidney to Lady Penelope Rich', and 'The Lady Penelope Rich to Sʳ Phillipe Sidney' (Bodleian Library, Oxford, MS Eng. Poet. f. 9, 224–41).

[72] Brennan, 'Literary Patronage of the Herbert family', 189.

[73] British Library, Landsdowne MS 777, f. 44; Browne, *Poems*, ii. 249. Line reference to the Goodwin edition will be included in brackets after the manuscript reference.

And spin our owne thredds for so long a Date
That Death shall never seize vpon your ffame
Till this shall perish in the whole worlds flame.   (f.47 (ll.173–8))

Browne takes over the role of Spenser in his volume of elegies for Sidney, *Astrophel*, as the spokesman for the Sidney–Herbert family since it is the poet's art that gives order to their grief. The elegy becomes the concrete embodiment of a community that is rendered all the more intimate by Browne's choice of manuscript rather than print to commemorate the Dowager Countess.

The edition of poems attributed to the Earl of Pembroke and Benjamin Rudyerd compiled by John Donne the younger in 1660 may shed more light on this Sidney–Herbert scribal community. Attribution of authorship in this volume is highly unreliable and it includes Browne's epitaph on the Dowager Countess and verses by Sir Edward Dyer, Sir Walter Raleigh, and Sir Henry Wotton. However, the volume's unreliability may itself be instructive and give an indication of the type of verses circulating within this scribal community. Donne probably had two main sources for the volume: the personal miscellany of the Countess of Devonshire, a friend of Pembroke, and the song books of Henry Lawes and Nicholas Lanyer. He may have also had access to verses through his friendship with Philip Herbert, Earl of Montgomery, Browne's patron from the 1620s.[74] An interesting feature of the volume is the dominance of the Elizabethan complaint. When Browne returns to work on Book III of *Britannia's Pastorals*, this is also the form that he chooses and it is possible that there was some form of literary exchange between Browne and Pembroke. The love complaint, 'Come saddest thoughts possess my heart', ascribed to Pembroke in Donne's volume, revolves around the themes of love's martyrdom, death, and exile:

> In sable weedes I'le cloathed be,
> And put on sorrowes livery;
> Then to some desart will I go,
> The fittest place to harbor wo;
> Where Owls and Ravens horrid cries
> Shall Eccho forth my miseries.[75]

---

[74] D. Taylor, 'The Third Earl of Pembroke as a Patron of Poetry', *Tulane Studies in English*, 5 (1955), 42–4.

[75] John Donne, the younger (ed.), *Poems, written by the Right Honourable*

The situation of the speaker in this verse is echoed in that of the unnamed shepherd in Book III of *Britannia's Pastorals* who inhabits the 'Den of Oblivion'. The verses that are strewn around the cave and find a sympathetic reader in the shepherd Celadyne symbolize a form of literary exchange that may have a basis in Browne's situation within the Herbert household. The copy of Book III in the library of Salisbury Cathedral appears to be a presentation copy that could have once belonged to the Herbert family as it is written in a fair hand, possibly Browne's, and appended to Books I and II with further leaves for continuing the poem.[76]

Browne was involved with other communities in this period and had attracted a group of younger writers at Exeter College, Oxford. As late as 1635, current and past members of the college produced a series of verses encouraging him to continue Book III of *Britannia's Pastorals* that were inserted in a 1625 edition of the poem which may have been presented to the college by Browne.[77] William Kidley wrote his heroic poem, 'Kidley's Hawkins', at Exeter in 1625 under the guidance of Browne and he called on the older poet to join him in celebrating the Elizabethan naval heroes or at least to 'sit and dictate to my Infant muse'.[78] Browne produced a number of elegies for his Oxford associates, such as Francis Vaux of Broadgate Hall, John Deane of New College, and Richard Turner of St Mary's Hall, later Vicar of Burford. He also continued to maintain London contacts and in 1625 produced an elegy on the merchant Richard Fishbourne, Middleton's patron, who had been importing corantoes from Holland in 1616 and may have continued this trade in the 1620s when it became a

William Earl of Pembroke, Lord Steward of his Majesties Household. Whereof Many of which are answered by way of Repartee, by Sʳ Benjamin Ruddier, Knight. With Several Distinct Poems, written by them Occasionally, and Apart (London, 1660), 102.

[76] Beal claims that the copy is written by a professional scribe, however the librarian at Salisbury Cathedral believes it to be Browne's hand.

[77] These verses are reprinted in Bullen's edition from William Beloe's *Anecdotes of Literature and Scarce Books* (6 vols. (London: Rivington, 1812), vi. 58) who found them in the 1625 edition of *Britannia's Pastorals*: 'I am of the opinion that mine is the copy presented by the poet to his college, as it contains a number of complimentary verses to Browne, by different members of Exeter, in the handwriting of each.' This copy has not been traced.

[78] William Kidley, 'Kidley's Hawkins or a Poetical Relation of the Voyage of Sʳ Richard Hawkins Knight vnto Mare Del^{znc}', BL Sloane MS 2024, f. 8.

means of avoiding the restrictions.[79] Browne may have been acquainted with Fishbourne's partner in the importing of corantoes, John Browne, through his Inner Temple friend, Thomas Gardiner, a cousin of John.[80] Browne's elegy celebrates Fishbourne as an exemplary London citizen whose memory would live on through his endowment of lectureships used to appoint Puritan ministers, 'Whilst a good preacher in them hath a Roome | You liue, and need noe epitaph nor Tombe.'[81]

Whereas it seems that very little of Wither's poetry circulated in manuscript, the majority of Browne's poems were published through scribal channels amongst an Inns of Court, university, and gentry audience. Herendeen has suggested that Browne abandoned public poetry after securing the patronage of the Herbert family because he did not have the financial incentive and, unlike Drayton and Wither, the psychological compulsion of the professional poet to publish his work.[82] While Browne does not seem to have had as strong an economic and ideological investment in print in his later career as these other writers, Herendeen does perhaps assume a rather restrictive view of the role of manuscript in early modern culture. Drayton too had a negative view of manuscript publishing and this may have coloured his view of Browne's 'silence' during the 'evill time' of the early 1620s. Browne in his manuscript verse did not refrain from addressing the current crisis or from responding to the trade in news, on the contrary, in view of the restrictions, manuscript may have given him more freedom to comment on the times given that most radical political material was circulating in this form.[83] Manuscript, moreover, does not necessarily imply an exclusively elite audience. Browne's elegies, in particular, indicate that he was able to address a range of audiences

[79] Margot Heinemann, *Puritanism and Theatre: Thomas Middleton and Opposition Drama under the Early Stuarts* (Cambridge: Cambridge University Press, 1982), 157; Adams, 'The Protestant Cause, 292–3.

[80] Browne, *Poems*, ii. 347.

[81] Landsdowne MS 777, f. 38; Browne, *Poems*, ii. 261. Heinemann, *Puritanism and the Theatre*, 260.

[82] William Herendeen, *From Landscape to Literature: The River and the Myth of Geography* (Pittsburgh: Duquesne University Press, 1986), 317–18.

[83] Cogswell, 'Underground Verse and the Transformation of Early Stuart Political Culture', in Susan D. Amussen and Mark A. Kislansky (eds.), *Political Culture and Cultural Politics in Early Modern England* (Manchester and New York: Manchester University Press, 1995), 278–9.

from the aristocratic Herberts to the London merchant Fishbourne.

THE 'DEN OF OBLIVION'

Browne composed the first two Songs of Book III in the first half
of the 1620s, during the 'evill time'.[84] Book II of *Britannia's
Pastorals* had initiated a complex process of de-forming the
Virgilian epic that simultaneously enabled a critique of Stuart
Augustanism. Book III is similarly generically innovative and
confidently works within the form of the elegiac romance, with
its accompanying poetics of exile, that had structured much of
Book II. This third Book remained unfinished, yet the first two
Songs are highly accomplished. For the first Song, Browne
returned to the Elizabethan lyric which had dominated the
second Song of Book II devoted to the 'English shepherds'. His
mock-heroic vision of the fairy court which closes this Song is
an ingeneous satire on the Jacobean court and James's appeasement of Spain that is also suggestive of the way that the
Virgilian epic is being deconstructed in *Britannia's Pastorals* as
a whole.

The first Song of Book III goes back to the beginning of
Britannia's Pastorals to the story of Marina and Celadyne from
the first Song of Book I. An elegiac tone is dominant and the
poem opens with a community of shepherds lamenting the loss
of Marina. The organizing theme of this Song is exile and
Browne emends the line 'As one in absence cleane bereav'd of
all' to 'As one in exile'.[85] The lost Marina carries a complex set
of associations, bringing together images of the poet's dead
mistress and his exile from his homeland, the memory of
Elizabeth I and the exiled Princess Elizabeth, and a broader
pattern of heroic failure and lost causes. Celadyne's lament for

[84] A date of 1624 to early 1625 for final composition has been fixed on by Joan
Holmer ('Internal Evidence for Dating William Browne's *Britannia's Pastorals*,
Book III', *Papers of the Bibliographical Society of America*, 70 (1976), 362–4) and
by Cedric Brown and Margherita Piva ('William Browne, Marino, France, and the
Third Book of *Britannia's Pastorals*', *Review of English Studies*, 29 (1978),
385–404). However, some of the first Song was probably composed in the early
1620s.

[85] Salisbury Cathedral Library, MS T.2.45, f. 1v. References to Goodwin's
edition of Book III will be included in brackets.

Marina inspires the poet's own farewell to his native soil and
the elegy for his beloved. This verse itself appears to be a
reworking of Daniel's sonnet 53, 'at the Author's beeing in
Italie', from his *Delia* (1592):

> Drawne with th'attractive vertue of her eyes,
> My toucht heart turnes it to that happy coast:
> My joyfull North, where all my fortune lies,
> The jewell of my hopes desired most,
> There where my *Delia* fairer than the Sunne,
> Deckt with her youth whereon the world doth smile.
> Joyes in that honor which her eyes have wonne,
> Th'eternall wonder of our happy Ile.
> Flourish faire *Albion*, glory of the North.
> *Neptunes* best darling, held betweene his armes;
> Divided from the world, as better worth,
> Kept for himselfe, defended from all harmes.
> Still let disarmed peace decke her and thee;
> And Muse-foe *Mars*, abroad farre fostred bee.[86]

For both Daniel and Browne physical exile becomes a means of
identifying desire for the beloved with patriotic longing. In
Daniel's sonnet, the transformation of the body of the beloved
into the nation enables a Virgilian-style identification between
the poet's art and the imperial power of monarchs embodied in
an Augustan 'disarmed peace'.[87] Browne reverses this formula.
The speaker's song begins with his exile from his native land,
'My *Tavy's* flowry shore', and England's 'peopled Cities and
her fertill fields' (f. 2v (28)). Exile coincides with the death of
his mistress so that patriotic longing is incorporated into the
dynamics of selfhood. Unlike Daniel, Browne cannot repossess
the body of his beloved/nation through an imperial trope. Exile
is rather figured as a lack at the centre of the self, as the failure
to possess the body of the beloved and the loss of an imaginary
wholeness, so that the relationship to the homeland is both subjective and transient. In Celadyne's song, 'Vaine dreames', patriotic longing once more takes the form of a desire to behold his
absent mistress.

The relationship between the poet and his mistress/homeland

---

[86] Daniel, *Complete Works*, i. 72.
[87] See Gerald MacLean's reading of this sonnet in his *Time's Witness: Historical
Representation in English Poetry, 1603–1660* (Madison, Wis.: University of
Wisconsin Press, 1990), 73–4).

is structured by a romance deferral and a pervasive sense of the intangible and ineffable nature of the object of desire that refuses to provide the subject with the unified self-image that he desires. Browne's lyricized, subjective nationalism looks forward to the Romantic sense of nostalgia as homesickness, a sickness of the soul.

The unnamed shepherd who appears in the first Song introduces a contemporary political dimension to the theme of exile:

> a gentle swayne, on whose sweet youth
> Fortune had thrown her worst, and all mens ruth,
> Whoe like a *Satyre* now, from mens aboade
> The uncouth pathes of gloomy deserts trode.   (f. 5v (33))

This shepherd turned satyr had previously appeared in the second Song of Book II where a woeful swain disdained by his mistress, a 'braue *Huntresse*', and beset by 'sad misfortune', turns into a wild man. This is itself a reworking of the Timias and Belphoebe episode from Book IV of *The Faerie Queene*. Browne was fascinated by this episode and turned to it again in his 'Fido: Epistle to Fidelia' where he defended Timias's actions against the tyrannically jealous Belphoebe, 'since she for thy thirst noe help would bring, | Thou lawfully mightst seeke another spring'.[88] Spenser had used this episode to figure Raleigh's fall from the Queen's favour for marrying one of her ladies-in-waiting, Elizabeth Throckmorton. Browne's approach to this story would suggest that for him it symbolized the way that the subjects could be sacrificed to the tyrannical passions of monarchs. Raleigh had been executed by James in 1618 for piracy against the Spanish on his ill-fated voyage to Guiana at the request of the Spanish ambassador, Gondomar. In this first Song, however, the unnamed shepherd is by his very nature an allusive figure—he is also a version of the poet—and, in this context, represents the memory of an Elizabethan past in a similar fashion to the ghost narratives of the 1620s, Thomas Gainsford's 'Vox Spiritus: Sir Walter Rawleigh's Ghost', circulating in 1620, and Thomas Scott's *Robert Earle of Essex, his Ghost* (1624) and his *Sir Walter Rawleigh's Ghost* (1626). These pamphlets combine the form of the *Mirror for Magistrates* with the news. The ghosts of Essex and Raleigh

---

[88] Landsdowne MS 777, f. 31; Goodwin, *Browne, Poems*, ii. 237.

return to haunt the present and to offer counsel in a period of national crisis when the monarch has failed to provide effective national leadership. They are simultaneously figures of lost political causes and embody the return of an account of empire that the current regime is attempting to repress. This empire is that of the elect nation which is defined through its opposition to papal Rome and these ghosts tell of their glorious heroic histories which serve as a measure of England's decline as a Protestant imperial power. The remedy that they offer is a revival of a martial culture and war with Spain to restore Elizabeth and Frederick.

The dead Protestant heroes, Essex and Prince Henry, in Books I and II of *Britannia's Pastorals* had symbolized the poet's estrangement from Augustan myths of empire. The unnamed shepherd in Book III performs a similiar function. His sighs are likened to Dido's lament upon learning of her betrayal and abandonment by *'Ilium's Aeneas'* (f. 10v (43)). In Virgil's epic, Dido's abandonment set in motion an imperial destiny that culminated in the *Pax Augustus*. Browne, characteristically, chooses Ovid's version and takes his Dido from the *Heroides* which reclaimed Dido as a figure for alternative voices and histories repressed by an Augustan imperialism.[89] The epistles in the *Heroides* are closely related to the exilic elegies in that both feminize the poetic voice: the poet's desire to return to his homeland echoes the anguished longing of his heroines.[90] To write from exile is 'to write like a woman', as Linda Kauffman has argued, and 'to challenge conventional notions of traditions, of origins, of fathers, of paternity, of authority, of identity'.[91] Exile in *Britannia's Pastorals* enables Browne to dismantle Virgilian forms and, in the process, to create an alternative poetics of subjectivity, exemplified by his exilic lyrics. The poetic voice is similarly feminized in Book III, particularly in the elaborate sestina, 'Listen! ye gentle windes to my sadd mone' (f. 7v (37)). The male poet identifies with the

---

[89] On the relationship between the Dido of Ovid and Virgil, see: John Watkins, *The Specter of Dido: Spenser and the Virgillian Epic* (New Haven and London: Yale University Press, 1995), 31.

[90] Betty Rose Nagle, *Poetics of Exile: Program and Polemic in the 'Tristia' and 'Epistulae ex Ponto' of Ovid* (Brussels: Latomus, 1980), 43.

[91] Linda Kauffman, *Discourse of Desire: Gender, Genre, and Epistolary Fictions* (Ithaca, NY: Cornell University Press, 1986), 61.

nightingale's song and it is possible that this sestina was composed in response to Lady Mary Wroth's sonnets on this theme that appeared in *The Countess of Montgomery's Urania* (1622).[92] The nightingale was often adopted by women poets, such as Lanyer and Wroth, to figure the expressive marginality of the female voice. Browne appropriated the nightingale within a poetics of exile to express his alienation from the times and to figure his turn inward to his own echoic song.

The allusion to Ovid's Dido is immediately followed by the recollection of Drake's fatal shipwreck. This lost Elizabethan hero like the other 1620s ghosts simultaneously embodies England's decline as an imperial power and an alternative Elizabethan vision of empire that has been suppressed by the Jacobean peace. The next set of sonnets sung by the unnamed shepherd change from the earlier love laments into an Essexian style of courtly complaint. The speaker complains of the inconstancy of fortune, the advancement of unworthy favourites and his own neglect, and the marginalizing of a community of honour that combined '*virtue* and true meritt' like 'our ancient blood, | Whose very Names, and Courages well steeld, | Made up an Armye, and could crowne a Field' (f. 12 (46–7)). The poem here is in sympathy with the aristocratic martial ethos of the ghost narratives. The speaker imagines a release from his self-imposed exile if the times:

> Opene the way to merit and to love!
> That we may teach a Cato and a *Dove*
> To heart a Cause and weighe affection deare
> And I will thincke we live, not tarry heere.   (f.12 (47))

This 'cause' that would combine the republican Cato and the dove, the symbol of love, would appear to be that of Princess Elizabeth. The solution that is offered is conceived in aristocratic and not monarchical terms which gives a classical republican edge to Browne's critique of an Augustan imperial ideology.

The unnamed shepherd has found refuge in the 'Den of Oblivion' which, although it is located near Browne's birthplace, Ramsham, near Tavistock, looks remarkably like a

---

[92] Browne also uses the metaphor of the labyrinth of love which structures the 'Crown of Sonnets' in 'Pamphilia to Amphilanthus'.

London tavern. The door is framed by two pillars with mathe-
matical figures inscribed upon them, possibly a reference to a
particular tavern, and is guarded by its resident deities, the
bacchic Lyaeus pouring forth wine and the '*Genius of America*'
who blows out tobacco smoke. Inside is the 'noise of Ballad
makers, Rymers—drinkers'. These figures are typically condemned in contemporary verses, but the speaker places himself
amongst their number—they turn out '*Complaints* and
Sonnetts, . . . | Maye be in such a manner as now I doe'—and
likens them in georgic terms to a 'little Commonwealth of
thrifty Bees' (f. 6v (35)). This commonwealth has a civic form
and these 'yong adventurers' act as citizens through their combined literary labours (f. 7 (36)). These texts are constitutive of
the commonwealth, but since they end up in '*Oblivion*' they
also have the ephemerality of the news. Wither similarly portrayed the taverns as the hub of early 1620s political culture in
his postscript to *Wither's Motto*, raucous meeting places where
current news and rumours were exchanged, pamphlets were
conceived and launched, and new projects formulated. Browne
chooses the taverns as the environment which fosters the
unnamed shepherd's politicized complaints and satire on the
Jacobean court in his poem on the fairy court. The 'Den of
Oblivion', however, is also able to incorporate other types of
community: the lyrics scattered throughout the cave suggest an
aristocratic scribal community along the lines of the Sidney–
Herbert circle.

The relatively positive vision of the 'madd Crewe' (f. 6 (35))
who inhabit the tavern-like 'Den of Oblivion' imagines a sphere
of public debate not solely in the usual sober civic humanist
terms of the Spenserians but also through a carnivalesque
language of the marketplace. This is part of a change in style in
Book III that is also noticeable in Drayton's 1620s poems, such
as *The Moone-calfe* and *Nimphidia, the Court of Fairy*, both of
which appeared in the 1627 *Battaile of Agincourt* and depict a
world turned 'arsey-varsey', in the words of his epistle to
Browne. They are probably part of the literary exchange that
Browne refers to at the end of his fairy poem when he claims
that it was produced in collaboration with 'others, to whom
heaven infused breath | When raignd our glorious dear
Elizabeth' (f. 17 (60)). The satiric vision of Oberon's fairy court

at the end of the first Song is 'on the winges of Rumor blowne' (f. 13 (50)), an image which returns to the riotous world of the tavern. De Lattre points to a 'distinct change' in fairy poetry that occurred in the 1620s with the poems of Browne and Drayton when a mock-heroic tone was introduced.[93] Their fairy poems have a precedent in Elizabethan satirical journalism, which combined burlesque and the grotesque with a lively topicality. The changing form of the fairy poem represented by the satires of Browne and Drayton can therefore be seen in terms of the expanding market for topical satires in the 1620s— a market that was symbolized by the tavern.[94] Browne's fairy court is a mock-heroic representation of the Jacobean peace that looks forward to Swift's Lilliputia. The particular subject of satire is the Spanish match and perhaps, more specifically, the collapse of these negotiations following Charles and Buckingham's own 'mock-heroic' quest to claim the Spanish Infanta in 1623.[95] The tone of the satire is aggressively anti-Spanish, echoing popular hispanophobia, and there are a number of references to Gondomar, 'one of Spaines graue Grandis' (f. 14 (27)). The style of the fairy poem is neo-Elizabethan: the presence of 'learned Spenser' at edges of the fairy banquet ironically contrasts the Fairy Queen/Elizabeth with the fairy prince Oberon/James. Burlesque in these fairy poems is more than a satiric tool and works at the level of genre and ideology to open classical and courtly ceremonial forms to new disruptive and popular energies. The princely dignity of Oberon is belittled by his dress: 'Their mighty king; a *Prince* of subtill powre | Cladd in a sute of speckled Gilliflowre' (f. 15 (54)). The use of minute, exquisite detail in the description of the fairy banquet derides royal ceremony and the king's notorious obsession with hunting is specifically parodied in mock-heroic terms. The 'brave discourse' of Oberon and his courtiers concerns their 'hawks and Sporte': their hawks, the royal bird of prey, are wagtails, their quarry are butterflies, and their mounts are a squirrel, a weasel, a rat, a stoat, a hare, and a cat (ff. 15–16 (55–7)).

[93] F. De Lattre, *English Fairy Poetry. From the Origins to the Seventeenth Century* (London: Henry Frowde; Paris: Henri Didier, 1912), 146, 150.

[94] Neil Rhodes, *Elizabethan Grotesque* (London, Boston and Henley: Routledge and Kegan Paul, 1980), 21–8.

[95] Brown and Piva, 'Browne, Marino, and France', 398.

The mock-heroic vision of the fairy court ends with Browne's vigorous defence of the reputation of the Elizabethan martialist, Sir Richard Grenville, a cousin of Raleigh.[96] As others have noted, Browne was probably responding to William Monson's *Naval Tracts*, written in 1624, which accused Grenville of foolishly engaging Spanish ships and then running away.[97] Monson, a Catholic and hispanophile, was a client of the Howards, and had been responsible for the capture of Arabella Stuart after her escape from the Tower, and implicated in the poisoning of Overbury. In the 1620s and 1630s, he was employed as a government consultant on the navy and his *Naval Tracts* were almost a manifesto for an Anglo-Spanish alliance.[98] The essay on 'The Queen's Death and the Advantages of Peace that ensued above War in her Time' condemned the interventionist foreign policy championed by the pro-war 'patriots' at court and in the Commons.[99] Browne's recuperation of Grenville's memory asserts the necessity of intervention on the Continent and reform at court to defend the nation against the ambitions of Spain. The slandered Grenville in Book III is a marker of the way that England has fallen away from her imperial destiny and points towards the means of its revival. Like the other ghosts of Elizabethan heroes in *Britannia's Pastorals* and the pamphlets of Scott, he registers the national decline under the Jacobean peace and symbolizes an alternative political vision that can be achieved through the agency of an independent and martial aristocracy.

The unfinished second Song of Book III is similarly implicated in the mid 1620 debates over foreign policy. This Song closely imitates Marino's *L'Adone*, composed at the French court of Maria de Medici in 1623 probably in honour of Henrietta Maria, and Browne may have intended this Song as a celebration of the marriage of Henrietta Maria and Charles.[100] Browne along with Dormer contributed epithalamia in honour

[96] Raleigh had defended Grenville in his *A Report of the truth of the fight about the Isle of Acores, this last summer, betwixt the 'Revenge', one of her Majesty's Ships, and an Armada of the King of Spain* (London, 1591).

[97] Holmer, 'Internal Evidence for Dating Book III', 352–5; Brown and Piva, 'Browne, Marino, France', 399.

[98] Sir William Monson, *The Naval Tracts in Six Books*, ed. M. Oppenheim (Navy Records Society, 1902), i. p. li.

[99] Monson, *Naval Tracts*, ii. 289.

[100] Brown and Piva, 'Browne, Marino, France', 401–4.

of the marriage to *Epithalamia Oxoniensia*. A journey to France provides the occasion for his poem of exile in the first Song and Browne would have accompanied Dormer on his Grand Tour after his marriage to Montgomery's daughter, Anna Sophia, in February 1625; the tour may have been organized in conjunction with Montgomery's journey to the French court in May, 1625 to escort Henrietta Maria to England for her marriage.[101] Browne probably had sympathies with a French alliance as part of a grand alliance against the Habsburgs. Although there were fears that a Catholic French bride would raise the same religious problems as a Spanish infanta, Charles's public declaration that he would not 'marry a Catholic on terms prejudicial to English law' had relieved some of these anxieties.[102]

Browne did not complete this second Song and if it began as an epithalamia for Charles and Henrietta Maria, then it ends as a poem for the poet's mistress, Caelia, and there are no closing references to the royal couple, as one might expect. Book III itself remained unfinished and unpublished and it seems that Browne in the 1630s and 1640s was exploring other possibilities. There are signs that Book III is already in the process of changing and fragmenting into other forms. Most of the songs assigned to Celadyne and the unnamed shepherd circulated separately as lyrics, for example, the first song 'Marina's gone, and now sit I' also appears in contemporary verse miscellanies as 'Caelia is gone'.[103] These exilic lyrics provide an alternative to the epic and initiate a form of subjective nationalism. They are related to romance which itself is conducive to such a move inward, and yet romance also holds out other political possibilities. Browne maintained his interest in the form and began translating Gomberville's *History of Polexandre* sometime after 1638 and continued working on the volume until his death in 1645 when Philip Herbert, the fourth Earl of Pembroke, took responsibility for publishing the volume that he had sponsored. The fourth Earl of Pembroke was a patron of the chivalric

---

[101] Ibid. 401; Linda Levy Peck, *Patronage and Corruption in Early Stuart England* (Boston: Unwin Hyman, 1990), 84. It may have been on his Grand Tour that Dormer met Elizabeth and Frederick as by 1632 he was a firm favourite of the couple (M. A. E. Green, *et al.* (eds.), *Calendar of State Papers, Domestic Series, 1631–33*, 81 vols. (London: Longman, 1857–1947), 418).

[102] Cogswell, *The Blessed Revolution*, 156.

[103] Landsdowne MS 777, f. 22r–v; Bodleian Library, Oxford, MS Juels-Jenson Drayton e.2, ff. 4–5.

prose romance and the baronial politics that this genre could foster informed his allegiance to the parliamentarian cause in the 1640s.[104] The fact that *Britannia's Pastorals* remained unfinished is in many ways in keeping with the radical energies of romance. Romance imagines a history that is open-ended and *Britannia's Pastorals*, as a whole, often sets up a multitude of narrative possibilities, giving the poem an air of historical contigency, that speaks to a writer negotiating a period of dramatic change.

[104] M. Le Roy, Sieur de Gomberville, *The History of Polexander: in Five Bookes. Done into English by William Browne, Gent. For the Right Honourable Philip, Earle of Pembroke and Montgomery, &c* (London, 1647), Wing 1025, 1026. J. S. A. Adamson, 'Chivalry and Political Culture in Caroline England', in Kevin Sharpe and Peter Lake (eds.), *Culture and Politics in Early Stuart England* (Basingstoke and London: Macmillan, 1994), 179–80.

Conclusion

TEXTUAL exchanges between Browne, Brooke, and Wither did not continue beyond the 1620s. Brooke was probably of a similar age to his friend, John Donne, and in his fifties in the 1620s. He appears to have had his last seat in the 1625 parliament, although he did not take an active role and he died in February 1628. Browne most likely left the Herbert household in 1628 when he married Timothy Eversfield. In the 1630s, he had an estate at Horsham in Sussex and moved to Dorking in Surrey sometime before his death. Nonetheless, he maintained close ties with Philip Herbert, fourth Earl of Pembroke, who sponsored the posthumous publication of his translation of Gomberville's *Polexandre*. Aside from this translation, one of the last records that we have of Browne is his letter to Benjamin Rudyerd on 29 November 1640. In this letter, Browne enthused over Rudyerd's 'late speech in Parliament, wherein they believe the spirit which inspired the Reformation and the genius which dictated the Magna Charta possessed you' and he prayed 'for more such members in the Commonwealth'.[1] His wife's family were parliamentarians during the Civil War and similar political sympathies are suggested by this letter.[2] Writing soon after the Long Parliament met, Browne appears to express his support for MPs' attack on Charles's policy of Spanish appeasement and Laudian ecclesiastical innovations, and their introduction of measures which limited the king's powers. Wither was both long-lived and prolific and continued writing and publishing his poetry until his death in 1667. An extended consideration of his later career lies outside the scope of this study.[3] For much of the 1630s, Wither struggled with the Stationers' Company over his patent and this curbed his ability to get his

---

[1] Bodleian Library, Ashmole MS 830, f. 288.

[2] Edwin Stuart Briggs, 'Browne of Tavistock: A Biographical and Critical Study', Ph.D. thesis (Harvard, 1956).

[3] On his later career, see: Charles Hensley, *The Later Career of George Wither* (The Hague and Paris: Mouton, 1969); David Norbrook, *Writing the English Republic: Poetry, Rhetoric and Politics 1627–1660* (Cambridge: Cambridge University Press, 1999).

works printed in England. In the 1640s, like Browne, his sympathies were with the parliamentarians and he fought for their cause when war broke out. His pamphleteering and military career were the culmination of his self-portrait as the godly citizen in his *Motto* and he played a central role in the formation of a republican literary culture.

Chronologically I have tended to divide this study of the textual exchanges between these poets into two distinct periods—1614 and the early 1620s. There are differences in the nature of these exchanges over this period which demonstrate that this particular textual community was not a static entity. These differences argue for a conceptual model which does not insist on an absolute identification between the actual friendships of writers, which have a very specific spatial and historical location, and the fictions of community they employ, but instead is able to recognize the way these fictions can become loosened from their original context. The relationship between actual social networks and fictions of community in 1614 was extremely close and the result was a very cohesive literary community. This was due to a range of factors. In personal terms, Browne and Wither were at an early stage in their careers; they were young men eager to make their mark and the Inns of Court provided an environment in which these energies could be channelled into collaborative projects. It was through this environment that they met Brooke. The particular form that this textual community took in 1614 was the product of the complex interaction of prior discursive models, events, ideology, and print. All three poets had produced elegies for Prince Henry and his death had reinvigorated a Spenserian model of community. Wither's imprisonment during the run up to the 1614 parliament created a dynamic that brought issues of counsel into sharp focus. Their responses to the events of 1614 were expressed through a Protestant humanist language of citizenship whereby the concept of a community began to modulate into that of a public. The importance of print to this expression of publicness cannot be underestimated. These writers made innovative use of print to give material manifestation to a textual community represented by the volumes of collaborative eclogues, *The Shepheards Pipe* and *The Shepherds Hunting*. This community did gain its cohesiveness through the

Inns of Court, yet it was print that gave the localized and relatively transient social relationships supported by this environment a material and permanent expression. Through print, this Spenserian community entered into wider public circulation whereby Brathwaite in 1615 could confidently invoke this group of poets to make a point to his readers about the state of culture in this period. Similarly, the stationer Thomas Walkley thought it worthwhile printing *The Shepherds Hunting* together with its companion volume, Browne's *The Shepheards Pipe*, in a volume of Wither's works possibly to attract the politicized readership that was emerging in the 1620s.

Textual exchanges between these poets were more diffuse in the 1620s to the extent that the value of considering their works in terms of the earlier model of community may be questioned. The importance of 1614, however, largely resides in the way that it provided an education in the ideological uses of print and the possibilities for public debate and each of these writers took a commitment to a civic concept of the public sphere into the 1620s. In comparison to 1614, the arena of public political debate in the 1620s had expanded considerably providing more of an opportunity for these writers to add their voice to a broader and highly politicized 'patriot' community. The Bohemian crisis had a unifying effect in that there was an assumption of a consensus of Protestant opinion opposed to Catholic Spain. Writers, such as Thomas Scott, were invoking an incipient political nation and developing tbe concept of a public opinion that could be mobilized when this nation came under threat. The 1614 print community did return in the 1620s in a politically charged symbolic form. *The Shepheards Pipe* and *The Shepherds Hunting* were, in many ways, remarkable volumes. These writers developed a concept of community not only to intervene in Jacobean political culture, but also to imagine a civic space that would make such an intervention possible. Print had also meant that this 1614 model of community was no longer necessarily dependent on actual ongoing social relationships but could take on a degree of autonomy to operate in a more abstract, universalizing form. Hence, in the 1620s, Wither's *Fair-Virtue*, Book III of Browne's *Britannia's Pastorals*, the second part of Drayton's *Poly-Olbion* and his elegies gathered in *The Battaile of Agincourt*, were able to invoke this earlier community to give shape to a wider political and national community. Political culture in the decades following the 1620s underwent a series of rapid and profound transformations. When viewed retrospectively, this early seventeenth-century textual community can look relatively primitive and limited. However, it was innovative and did have a formative role in generating new discourses of citizenship and publicness that would be realized later in the century.

I have been using the term 'oppositional' to describe these poets collectively. They were consistently hostile to royal policies that favoured the interests of Spain and to an aggressive use of the prerogative against the subjects' liberties. I am not, however, using the term in the sense of a dichotomy between the court and a unified and ideologically coherent opposition. I have argued that the court was relatively heterogeneous under James. By this I do not mean that it was a quasi-liberal institution able to accommodate differences within an overarching consensus.[4] Rather, it was heterogeneous in the sense of competing interest groups which could not fully be contained by the court. Tensions between different groupings had the potential to become divisive when differences were given focus, such as in 1614 and in the 1620s. In order to consider the nature of these poets' responses to James's policies, we need to integrate a concept of opposition into a model of counsel. When these poets produced critiques of royal policy they saw themselves as providing counsel and they tended to attribute differences over policy to the influence of evil counsellors. This model of court corruption, however, ultimately drew attention to a weak monarchical government which had prevented genuine counsel and was therefore in need of thoroughgoing reform. Remedy was to be found through parliament and the collective actions of godly citizens. In their writings, they do not distinguish between political models drawn from humanism and from the common law but move easily between the two in a way that begins to translate the liberty of the subject in terms of a Protestant humanist ideal of active citizenship. It is possible that the constitutional model of a mixed government was able to

---

[4] See Richard Burt's qualification of the arguments of Smut and Sharpe for the 'liberalizing' heterogeneity of the early Stuart court in his *Licensed by Authority: Ben Jonson and the Discourses of Censorship* (Ithaca, NY, and London: Cornell University Press, 1993), 14–15.

incorporate an unstable and yet productive dynamic between the common law and humanism, and between the monarchy and a public political sphere.

One way of characterizing these poets as an oppositional literary community has been to set them in competition with Jonson in his role as the representative of a court poetic. This cultural model does need reconsidering given '*th*' Exchange *of* Letters', in the words of Jonson to Browne, between members of this Spenserian literary community and Jonson. Jonson is a difficult figure to place in Jacobean political culture since he had a habit of circulating between diverse and often competing communities.[5] Throughout this study, I have drawn attention to points of contact between Jonson and these poets in order to develop a picture of a fluid and vigorous culture that was energized by these types of exchanges. This concentration on the relations between writers rather than their relationship to the centre has the effect of turning boundaries between communities into zones of contact and lines of communication. Although I have been arguing that this particular grouping of poets constituted a distinctive textual community, I do not want to give the impression that it was closed to other individuals and communities. Rather, I see this community as part of a complex network and involved in an ongoing dialogue with other individuals and communities both past and present. That said, it is possible and necessary to draw distinctions between the various textual communities. Jonson and this group of Spenserian poets were distinguished both by their relationship to the centre and to an expanding literary marketplace. His view of the literary marketplace was more hierarchical and exclusive than that of Browne, Brooke, and, in particular, Wither. These poets also engaged in exclusionary strategies but their view of a public sphere was that of an open arena in which state affairs were discussed in public. A similar vision was offered by 'T.G.' in his *An Answer to Wither's Motto* at a national level when he spoke of the 'Countreys carpet lay abroad to view' through the availability of news so that its citizens 'mistake not, what is false or true' (E4r). Jonson and Browne and Brooke did engage in an 'Exchange *of* Letters' but ultimately, along with Wither, they

---

[5] Burt, *Licensed by Authority*, 18.

had a different conception of what a public sphere might look like.

A model of multiple and competing textual communities offers a way of thinking about the pluralization of the public sphere in the early modern period. These multiple publics are wider than Habermas's bourgeois public sphere as they allow for nonliberal and nonbourgeois public spheres.[6] This study has concentrated on a textual community that was developing a language of citizenship and a model of publicness that does appear to anticipate the concept of a bourgeois public sphere. However, I have also attempted to suggest that there were other models of the public available in the period and, relatedly, other forms of textual community. Further analysis of these other textual communities is necessary to develop our picture of early modern culture. In contrast to models of patronage, the concept of textual communities offers an angle on early modern culture that looks at social and cultural relations both horizontally and vertically. Such a perspective can draw attention to the emergence of an intellectual profession that claimed autonomy from the church and the court and was instead validated by its own internal relations, qualifications, and practices, but nonetheless was part of the social structure of the period. Browne, Brooke, and Wither identified themselves collectively as an intellectual community that was independent from the dominant political order. By appropriating a magisterial model of counsel to validate the role of the poet, they asserted the historical and collective agency of the humanist intellectual. Their characteristic appeal to their 'freeborne muse' or their 'free-borne lines' draws on the language of the liberties of the freeborn Englishman to give a radical edge to this language of intellectual freedom. This language does idealize this community and turn it into a literary utopia. However, this itself is a function of the way that this community begins to transform loose relational networks into professional relationships. As such, this particular textual community represents an important stage in the historical transformation from a patronage system to a literary public sphere.

---

[6] See also Nancy Fraser, 'Rethinking the Public Sphere: A Contribution to the Critique of Actually Existing Democracy', in Craig Calhoun (ed.), *Habermas and the Public Sphere* (Cambridge, Mass.: MIT Press, 1992), 115–16.

Transcripts of the Examinations of Wither and the Stationers State Papers, Domestic

14/121/132 ff. 245–6
The examination of George Withers taken the 27th of Iune 1621 at Whit[e]hall.

He confesseth that the booke entituled Withers Motto is of his making, and that he made it about Christmas last.

He sayth that since that time he shewed it to Mr. Tauernor and desired his warrant for the printing which he refused. And that afterwards, this examenant bringing the sayd booke unto a stationers shopp called Grismand (and Marriott being present) and there reading some part of it, they ⟨thereby⟩ desired to buy it, that they might print it, to which he consented but told the stationers that Mr. Tauernor had denyed him licence to print it before.

He sayth that they gaue him fiue peeces for the copye.

That the booke was printed about five or sixe weekes since.

Being asked whether he acquaynted any of his freinds with the copy before the printing, he awnsweareth that he did acquaynt diuers of his freinds with it. as namely Mr. Drayton, and some others whose names he remembreth not.

Being put in mind of his ma^{tys} proclamation published before the parliament, restrayning the licentious speaking or wrighting in matters concerning state, or gouernment, he sayth he did not read the proclamation. Neither he thinke there is any thing in his booke that toucheth the state or gouernement.

Being told of passages in his booke, wherein wrighteth he had seen ⟨nigh⟩ the downfall of those that were his enemyes, or words to that purpose. And being asked whom he meaneth by those words he sayth he meane the late Earle Northampton.

14/122/12 f. 15
The examinac[i]on of John Marriott taken the 10 of July 1621.

Beinge demaunded what moued him to vndertake the printing of Withers Motto, after the said Booke was called in question: he sayth that to his knowledge, the said Booke was never called in question vpon the first impression, but after it was vndertaken by the Ex[amenan]t to be printed by a proued impression it was then questioned before that Impression was out.

Whereupon the Ex[amenan]t went to Mr.Tauernor intreatinge him to lycence the Booke, wch hee refused to doe, but puttinge out of it what hee thought fitt, hee then lycenced soe corrected; ⟨we.eth..⟩ it was never printed by this Exam[enan]t, nor did this Exam[enan]t ever sell anie of those Bookes since that time.

Beinge demaunded whoe printed the thre Impressions that came out since, Hee sayeth they were printed by one Nicholas Oakes wthout the priuitie, consent, or knowledge of this Ex[amenan]t. although his name was still vsed in the Bookes by the said Okes.

Beinge demaunded whoe printed the first coppie, Hee sayeth that it was printed by this Ex[amenan]t appointed by one Mathewes a poore man dwellinge in Bridelane: And that this Ex[amenan]t vpon the Complaint of the Stationers to the Lo: Archbishop of Cant. was comitted by his Grace vpon the second Impression of the Booke, and fyned by the Stationers in Compound.

Jo: Marriott

Examined by:
Clement Edmondes.

14/122/13 f. 16
[The examination of John Grismond, stationer July 10 1621]

Was questioned. Hee sayeth that the second Impression was printed before it was questioned and as for what hee knoweth, it was questioned only because it was printed wthout lycence, wch was a Contempt to theire Companies, and vpon the Companies Complaint to the Lo: Archbishop of Canterburie Marriott was com[m]itted to prison, and a fyne imposed both vpon him, and the said Ex[amenan]t.

Hee further sayeth that after the said Imprisonment, and ffyne, one Oakes a printer, notwithstanding hee knew of the said fyne and Imprisonment printed first 3000 of the Bookes, and afterwards 3000 more. And sayth that Trussell the Messinger hath affirmed before witnes, that Oakes told him: the Company had willed him not to bee out of way in case hee should be sent for, and they would beare him out for printinge the said Booke.

John Grismond

Examined by:
Edmondes

14/122/14 f. 17
(Note by Thomas Trussell)

Vpon Satterday being 7th of this instant July, Mr. Oakes the printer told me that he had don nothing about Withers his booke, but by the Consent of the Company of Stationers, and that the master of the Company, bad him send them word how it went with him, and if he were comitted, they wold gett him discharged, also he said that the master of the Company had sent to the Clarke of the Company to goe along with him, these & the like speeches did he vse once or twise, the same day.

Tho: Trussell

14/122/18 f. 21
The Examinac[i]on of Nicholas Oakes Printer taken the 12 of Iuly 1621

Beinge demaunded what lycence hee had to print a Booke called Withers motto. Hee sayth hee had a printed Coppie w[c]h was lycenced for ought hee knoweth. Hee sayeth hee was not the first that printed it by twoe seuerall Impressions. Hee sayeth that the Impression w[c]h hee made was donn w[th]out the priuitie or knowledge of Marriott that first printed it.

Beinge demaunded why hee vsed Marriotts name in the Booke: Hee sayeth hee brought the Title readie printed, and soe fixed it to the Booke to make it p[er]fect.

Beinge demaunded whether this Impression w[c]h hee made was donn before hee knew the Booke was questioned and that Marriott had ben punished for printing it. Hee sayeth that the Impression was donn before it was questioned in the Stationers Hall, or els where for ought hee knew: and that hee was fyned the same day that Marriott was.

Beinge demaunded whether Lounds late Warden of the Companie did not sell some of the Bookes after they were prohibited. Hee sayeth that this Ex[amenan]t neuer sould anie one Booke to Lounds, nor knoweth that hee sould anie after the prohibic[i]on: but hee thinketh some were sould here and there, but cannot accuse anie one man.

Mr. Nicholas Okes

Examined by:
Edmondes

14/122/19 f. 22
The Examinac[i]on of John Grismond taken the 12 of Iuly 1621

Beinge demaunded whether hee hath sould anie of the Bookes called Withers Motto, since hee was questioned for it, and that Marriott was committed by the Lo: Archb: of Canterburie and fyned in the Stationers Hall. Hee sayth that hee hath since that time soulde diuers of the said Bookes, and amongst others hee sold them at sundrey and severall times to Lounds then Warden of the Companie, who com-playned of this Exam[enan]t and ⟨Marriot⟩ to the Lo: Archbishop, was p[re]sent when Marriott was com[m]itted for printinge the said Booke, and yet neuertheles after all this was donn the said Lounds did daylie send to this Ex[amenan]t for the said Bookes, and sould them againe in his Shoppe.

John Grismond

Examined by:
Edmondes

Editions of *Wither's Motto* (1621)

Editions of *Wither's Motto* (1621).

STC 25925   *Wither's Motto*. A. Mathews f. Marriot and
              Grismond.
              Ends F2v with '*FINIS*'.
              This issue has a letter-press title-page.

     25925.5 Anr. issue. Letter-press title-page cancelled and
              replaced by a bifolium with an engraved title-page.

     25926   Anr. ed. N. Okes.
              Ends F2v with '*FINIS*'.

     25926.5 Anr. ed. Mathews f. Marriot.
              Ends F2v with '*FINIS*'.

     25927   Anr. ed. N. Okes.
              F2v has catchword: '*A Post-*'.
              Includes 'Postscript.'

     25928   Anr. ed. Mathews f. Marriot,
              Postscript begins on F2v.

     [25928.1 Anr. ed. according to the annotated Bodleian STC
              catalogue
              [Shelf-mark: Mason AA 105]
              Mathews f. Marriot.
              Postscript begins on F3r.]

     25928.3 Anr. ed. Mathews f. Marriot.
              Postscript begins on F2v.

     25928.5 Anr. issue. Mathews f. Marriot.
              Postscript begins on F2v.

     25928.7 Anr. ed. Mathews f. Marriot.
              Postscript begins on F2v.

Bibliography

I MANUSCRIPTS

Bodleian Library, Oxford, MS Arch Selden Supra 53.
Bodleian Library, Oxford, MS Ashmole 40.
Bodleian Library, Oxford, MS Ashmole 45.
Bodleian Library, Oxford, MS Ashmole 46.
Bodleian Library, Oxford, MS Ashmole 59.
Bodleian Library, Oxford, MS Ashmole 767.
Bodleian Library, Oxford, MS Ashmole 830.
Bodleian Library, Oxford, MS Eng. Poet. f. 9.
Bodleian Library, Oxford, Malone MS 483.
Bodleian Library, Oxford, MS Rawlinson poet.154.

British Library, Additional MS 4149.
British Library, Additional MSS 14,824–26.
British Library, Additional MS 23,147.
British Library, Additional MS 23,299.
British Library, Additional MS 23,399.
British Library, Additional MS 34,360.
British Library, Additional MS 35,298.
British Library, MS Egerton 2045.
British Library, Landsdowne MS 777.
British Library, MS Sloane 2024.
British Library, MS Stowe 68.
British Library, MS Stowe 952.
British Library, MS Stowe 962.

University of Durham, MS Cosin V III. 9.
Public Record Office, State Papers Series, Domestic, James I, 14/121–123.
Salisbury Cathedral Library, MS T.2.45.

II PRINTED BOOKS

Acts of the Privy Council of England, 1613–1614 (London, 1921).
AUSTIN, SAMUEL. *Austins Urania, or, the heavenly muse* (London, 1628), STC 971.

BACON, FRANCIS. *The Essays,* ed. John Pitcher (London: Penguin, 1985).

BIRCH, THOMAS (ed.). *The Court and Times of James the First,* 2 vols. (London: Henry Colburn, 1848).

BRATHWAITE, RICHARD. *A Strappado for the Diuell. Epigrams and Satyres alluding to the time, with diuers measures of no lesse Delight* (London, 1615), STC 3588.

BROOKE, CHRISTOPHER. *The ghost of Richard the third* (London, 1614), STC 3830.

—— *A Poem on the Late Massacre in Virginia* (London, 1622), STC 3830.5.

—— *The poems,* ed. A. B. Grosart, *The Miscellanies of the Fuller Worthies Library,* 4 vols. (1872–76), vol. iv.

—— and BROWNE, WILLIAM. *Two Elegies, consecrated to the neuer-dying memorie of the most worthily admyred; most hartily loued; and generally bewayled Prince; Henry Prince of Wales* (London, 1613), STC 3831.

BROWNE, WILLIAM. *Britannia's Pastorals* (London, 1613), STC 3914.

—— *The Shepheards Pipe* (London, 1614), STC 3917.

—— *Britannia's Pastorals. The second booke* (London, 1616), STC 3915.5.

—— *The Whole Works of William Browne, of Tavistock, and of the Inner Temple; Now first collected and edited, with a memoir of the poet and notes,* ed. W. Carew Hazlitt, 2 vols. (Roxburghe Library, 1868).

—— *The Poems,* ed. George Goodwin, intr. A. H. Bullen, 2 vols. (London: George Routledge & Sons; New York: Dutton, 1894).

BUCK, SIR GEORGE. *The History of King Richard the Third (1619),* ed. A. N. Kincaid (Gloucester: Alan Sutton, 1979).

BURTON, ROBERT. *The Anatomy of Melancholy,* ed. Holbrook Jackson, 3 vols. (London and Toronto: Dent; New York: Dutton, 1932).

CAMDEN, WILLIAM. *Remaines* (London, 1623), STC 4523.

CAMPBELL, L. B. (ed.), *The Mirror for Magistrates* (Cambridge: Cambridge University Press, 1938).

CARPENTER, NATHANIEL. *Geographie Delineated Forth in two Bookes. Containing the Sphericall and Topicall parts thereof,* 2nd edn. (Oxford, 1635), STC 4677.

CHAMBERLAIN, JOHN. *The Letters,* ed. Norman E. McClure, 2 vols. (Philadelphia: The American Philosophical Society, 1939).

CLAPHAM, HENOCH. *Errour on the Left Hand through Frozen Securitie* (London, 1608).

CORNWALLIS, SIR WILLIAM (the younger). *The Encomium of Richard*

244 *Bibliography*

III, ed. A. N. Kincaid (London: Turner and Devereaux, 1977).

DANIEL, SAMUEL. *The Complete Works in Verse and Prose*, ed. A. B. Grosart, 5 vols. (London, 1885–96).

DAVIES OF HEREFORD, JOHN. *Microcosmos. The discovery of the little world, with the government thereof* (Oxford, 1603), STC 6333.

—— *The Scourge of Folly* (London, 1611), STC 6341.

—— *The Muses Sacrifice* (London, 1612).

DEKKER, THOMAS. *The Dramatic Works*, ed. Fredson Bowers, 5 vols. (Cambridge: Cambridge University Press, 1953–61).

DE VERE, EDWARD, and DEVEREUX, ROBERT. *The Poems of Edward De Vere, Seventeenth Earl of Oxford and of Robert Devereux, Second Earl of Essex*, ed. Stephen May, *Studies in Philology*, 77 (1980), 5–132.

DOD, JOHN, and CLEAVER, ROBERT. *A Godly Forme of Householde Governement: For the Ordering of Private Families, according to the direction of Gods Word* (London, 1614), STC 5387.

DONNE, JOHN (the younger). *Poems, written by the Right Honorable William Earl of Pembroke, Lord Steward of his Majesties Household. Whereof Many of which are answered by way of repartee, by Sr Benjamin Ruddier, knight. With several distinct poems, written by them occasionally, and apart* (London, 1660).

DOWLAND, JOHN. *The Third and Last Book of Songs or Airs, An English Garner*, ed. Edward Arber (1882).

DU BARTAS, GUILLAUME DE SALUSTE SIEUR. *The Divine Weeks and Works Translated by Josuah Sylvester*, ed. Susan Snyder, 2 vols. (Oxford: Clarendon Press, 1979).

DRAYTON, MICHAEL. *Poemes. Lyrick and pastorall* (London, 1606). STC 7225.5.

—— *The Battaile of Agincovrt* (London, 1627), STC 7190.

—— *The Works*, ed. J. Hebel. 5 vols. (Oxford: Basil Blackwell, 1941).

—— *Englands Helicon, or, the muses harmony* (London, 1614), STC 3192.

FELLOWES, E. H., *et al.* (eds.) *English Madrigal Verse, 1588–1632*, rev. and enlarged F. W. Sternfield and D. Greer (Oxford: Clarendon Press, 1967).

FITZGEFFREY, CHARLES. *Sir Francis Drake his Honorable lifes commendation and his Tragicall deathes lamentation* (Oxford, 1596), STC 10944.

FITZGEFFREY, HENRY. *Certain Elegies, done by Svndrie Excellent Wits. With Satyres and Epigrames* (London, 1618), STC 10945.3.

FOSTER, ELIZABETH READ (ed.). *Proceedings in Parliament, 1610*, 2 vols. (New Haven and London: Yale University Press, 1966).

G., T. *An Answer to Wither's Motto* (Oxford, 1625), STC 11509.

GREEN, M. A. E., *et al.* (eds.) *Calendar of State Papers, Domestic Series*, 81 vols. (London: Longman, 1857–1947).

GOMBERVILLE, M. LE ROY, SIEUR DE. *The History of Polexander: in Five Bookes. Done into English by William Browne, Gent. For the Right Honourable Philip, Earle of Pembroke and Montgomery, &c* (London, 1647), Wing 1025, 1026.

GREVILLE, FULKE. *The Tragedy of Mvstapha* (London, 1609), STC 12362.

GUARINI, *Il Pastor Fido: Or The faithfull Shepheard. Translated out of Italian into English* (London, 1602), STC 12415.

HARBERT, WILLIAM. *Englands sorrowe or, a farewell to Essex* (London, 1606), STC 12582.

HOCCLEVE, THOMAS. *Works*, ed. F. J. Furnivall, 3 vols. *English Early Text Society* (London: Kegan Paul, Trench, and Trubner, 1892–7).

—— *The Minor Poems*, ed. F. J. Furnivall and I. Gollancz; rev. J. Mitchell and A. I. Doyle (Oxford: Oxford University Press, 1970).

HOWELL, T. B. (ed.). *A Complete Collection of State Trials*, 33 vols. (London: 1809–28).

HUNTER, WILLIAM B. (ed.). *The English Spenserians: The Poetry of Giles Fletcher, George Wither, Michael Drayton, Phineas Fletcher, and Henry More* (Utah: University of Utah Press, 1977).

JANSSON, MAIJA (ed.). *Proceedings in Parliament 1614 (House of Commons)* (Philadelphia: American Philosophical Society, 1988).

JONSON, BEN. *Works*, ed. C. H. Hereford, Percy Simpson, and Evelyn Simpson, 11 vols. (Oxford: Clarendon Press, 1925–52).

—— *Ben Jonson*, ed. Ian Donaldson (Oxford: Oxford University Press, 1985).

JOSEPHUS. *The Famous and Memorable Workes*, trans. Thomas Lodge (London, 1609), STC 14810.

LANCASHIRE, ANNE (ed.). *The Second Maiden's Tragedy* (Manchester: Manchester University Press, 1978).

LINDLEY, DAVID (ed.). *Court Masques: Jacobean and Caroline Entertainments* (Oxford and New York: Oxford University Press, 1995).

LOK, HENRY. *Ecclesiastes: abridged and dilated in English poesie* (London, 1597), STC 16696.

MARKHAM, FRANCIS. *Fiue decades of epistles of warre* (London, 1622), STC 17332.

MARKHAM, GERVASE. *The most Honorable Tragedy of Sir Richard Grinville, knight* (London, 1595). STC 17385.

MIDDLETON, THOMAS. *The Works*, ed. A. H. Bullen, 8 vols. (London, 1886).

MILTON, JOHN. *The Works*, ed. T. O. Mabbot and J. M. French, 18 vols. (New York: Columbia University Press, 1931–8).

—— *Paradise Lost*, ed. Alistair Fowler (Essex and New York: Longman, 1986).

MONSON, SIR WILLIAM. *The Naval Tracts in Six Books*, ed. M. Oppenheim (Navy Records Society, 1902).

MONTAIGNE, MICHEL DE. *The essayes, or morall, politike discourses: done into English by J. Florio* (London, 1603), STC 18041.

MORE, SIR THOMAS. *The History of* King *Richard III*, in *The Complete Works*, ed. R. S. Sylvester, 15 vols. (New Haven and London: Yale University Press, 1963), vol ii.

NICCOLS, RICHARD. *A Mirour for Magistrates* (London, 1610), STC 13446.

—— *Londons Artillery* (London, 1616).

NOTESTEIN, WALLACE, *et al.* (eds.). *Commons Debates 1621*, 7 vols. (New Haven: Yale University Press; Oxford: Oxford University Press, 1935).

—— and RELF, FRANCES (ed.). *Commons Debates for 1629* (Minneapolis: University of Minnesota, 1921).

OVERBURY, SIR THOMAS. *Sir Thomas Ouerburie His Wife with new Elegies vpon his (now knowne) vntimely death* (London, 1616), STC 18910.

—— *The Miscellaneous Works in Prose and Verse*, ed. Edward Rimbault (London: John Russell Smith, 1856).

—— *The 'Conceited Newes' of Sir Thomas Overbury and his Friends*, ed. James E. Savage (Florida: Scholars' Facsimiles and Reprints, 1968).

—— *The Plough-mans Tale. Shewing by the doctrine and liues of the Romish Clergie, that the Pope is Antichrist and they his Ministers* (London, 1606).

RISDON, TRISTRAM. *The Chorographical Description, or, Survey of the County of Devon* (London, 1714).

SANNAZARO, JACOPO. *Arcadia and Piscatorial Eclogues*, trans. R. Nash (Detroit: State University Press, 1966).

SCOTT, THOMAS. *Vox Populi: or Newes from Spayne, translated according to the Spanish coppie* (London, 1620).

SPICER, ALEXANDER. *An elegie on the death of Sir Arthur Chichester* (London, 1625), STC 23100.

SMITH, LOGAN PEARSALL (ed.). *The Life and Letters of Sir Henry Wotton*, 2 vols. (Oxford: Clarendon Press, 1907).

SPENSER, EDMUND. *Poetical Works*, ed. J. C. Smith and E. De Selincourt (Oxford and New York: Oxford University Press, 1912; 23rd edn. 1969).

—— *The Faerie Qveene*, ed. A. C. Hamilton (London and New York: Longman, 1977).

TACITUS, *The Ende of Nero and Beginning of Galba. Fower Bookes of the Histories of Cornelius Tacitvs. The Life of Agricola*, trans. Henry Saville (London, 1591).

—— *The Annals*, 5 vols. (Cambridge, Mass.: Harvard University Press (Loeb); London: Heinemann, 1910).

TAYLOR, JOHN. *Taylors Vrania, or His Heauenly Muse with a briefe Narration of the thirteen sieges, and sixe Sackings of the famous Cittie of Ierusalem* (London, 1615), STC 23806.

—— *The pennyles pilgrimage, or the money-less perambulation of J. Taylor*.

—— *From London to Edenborough* (London, 1618), STC 23784.

—— *A new discovery by sea, with a wherry from London to Salisbury* (London, 1623), STC 23778.

THORPE, M. J. (ed.). *Calendar of State Papers, the Scottish Series, 1509–1603*, 2 vols. (London, 1858).

VIRGIL, *Virgil*, trans. H. Rushton, rev. edn. (Cambridge, Mass.: Harvard University Press (Loeb); London: William Heinemann, 1967).

WEEVER, JOHN. *Epigrammes in the oldest cut, and newest fashion* (London, 1599).

WESTCOTE, THOMAS. *View of Devonshire in MDCXXX, with a Pedigree of Most of its Gentry*, ed. Rev. G. Oliver and Pitman Jones (Exeter, 1845).

WHARTON, JOHN. *Whartons Dreame* (London, 1578).

WITHER, GEORGE. *Epithalamia: or Nuptiall Poemes* (London, 1612), STC 5901.

—— *Abuses stript, and whipt. Or satirical essayes* (London, 1613), STC 25891; (London, 1615), STC 25896.

—— *Prince Henries obsequies, or, mournefvll elegies vpon his death* (London, 1613), STC 25915.

—— *A satyre: dedicated to his most excellent Maiestie* (London, 1614), STC 25916.

—— *The Shepherds Hunting. being, certaine eglogs written during the time of the authors imprisonment in the Marshalsey* (London, 1615), STC 25920.

—— *Fidelia* (London, 1615), STC 25905; (London, 1617), STC 25906; (London, 1619), STC 25907.

—— *The workes of Master George Wither, of Lincolns-Inne, Gentleman* (London, 1620), STC 25890.

—— *Wither's motto* (London, 1621), STC 25927.

—— *Faire-Vertue, the mistresse of Phil'Arete* (London, 1622), STC 25903.

WITHER, GEORGE. *Juuenilia* (London, 1622), STC 25911.
—— *The schollers pvrgatory* (London, 1624), STC 25919.
ZOUCHE, RICHARD. *The Dove* (London, 1613), STC 26130.

III SECONDARY MATERIAL

ADAMS, S. L. 'Captain Thomas Gainsford, the "Vox Spiritus" and the Vox Populi', *Bulletin of the Institute for Historical Research*, 49 (1976), 141–4.
—— 'Foreign Policy and the Parliaments of 1621 and 1624', in Kevin Sharpe (ed.), *Faction and Parliament: Essays on Early Stuart History* (Oxford: Oxford University Press, 1978; London: Methuen, 1985), 139–71.
—— 'Spain or the Netherlands? The Dilemmas of Early Stuart Foreign Policy', in Howard Tomlinson (ed.), *Before the English Civil War: Essays on Early Stuart Politics and Government* (London: Macmillan, 1983), 79–101.
ADAMSON, J. S. A. 'Chivalry and Political Culture in Caroline England', in Kevin Sharpe and Peter Lake (eds.), *Culture and Politics in Early Stuart England* (Basingstoke and London: Macmillan, 1994), 161–97.
ALPERS, PAUL. 'Spenser's Late Pastorals', *English Literary History*, 56 (1989), 797–817.
AMUSSEN, SUSAN D. *An Ordered Society: Gender and Class in Early Modern England* (Oxford: Basil Blackwell, 1988).
—— 'Gender, Family and the Social Order, 1560–1725', in Anthony Fletcher and John Stevenson (eds.), *Order and Disorder in Early Modern England* (Cambridge: Cambridge University Press, 1985), 196–217.
ANDERSON, BENEDICT. *Imagined Communities: Reflections on the Origin and Spread of Nationalism* (London: Verso, 1983).
ARBER, EDWARD (ed.). *A Transcript of the Registers of the Company of Stationers of London, 1554–1640*, 5 vols. (London, 1875–94).
BAILDEN, W. P. (ed.). *The Records of the Honorable Society of Lincoln's Inn. The Black Books, Vol II 1586–1660* (London, 1898).
Baker, J. H. *An Introduction to English Legal History*, 3rd edn. (London: Butterworth, 1990).
BAKHTIN, M. M. *Speech Genres and Other Late Essays*, ed. Caryl Emerson and Michael Holquist, trans. Vernon W. McGee (Austin: University of Texas Press, 1996).
BALD, R. C. *John Donne: A Life* (Oxford: Clarendon Press, 1970).
BARKAN, LEONARD. *The Gods Made Flesh: Metamorphosis and the*

Pursuit of Paganism (New Haven and London: Yale University Press, 1986).

BARKER, FRANCIS. *The Tremulous Private Body: Essays on Subjection* (London: Methuen, 1984).

BARROLL, LEEDS. 'The Court of the First Stuart Queen', in Linda Levy Peck (ed.), *The Mental World of the Jacobean Court* (Cambridge: Cambridge University Press, 1991), 191–208.

BARTON, ANNE. 'Harking back to Elizabeth: Ben Jonson and Caroline nostalgia', *English Literary History*, 48 (1981), 701–31.

BEAL, PETER. *Index of English Literary Manuscripts*, 2 vols. (London and New York: Mansell, 1980–93).

BELLANY, ALASTAIR. ' "Raylinge Rymes and Vaunting Verse": Libellous Politics in Early Stuart England, 1603–28', in Kevin Sharpe and Peter Lake (eds.), *Culture and Politics in Early Stuart England* (Basingstoke and London: Macmillan, 1994), 285–310.

BELOE, WILLIAM. *Anecdotes of Literature and Scarce Books*, 6 vols. (London: Rivington, 1812).

BELSEY, CATHERINE. *The Subject of Tragedy: Identity and Difference in Renaissance Drama* (London and New York: Methuen, 1985).

BERGERON, DAVID. *Shakespeare's Romances and the Royal Family* (Kansas: University Press of Kansas, 1985).

BERKOWITZ, DAVID. *John Selden's Formative Years: Politics and Society in Seventeenth-Century England* (Washington: Folger Books, 1998).

BLACK, W. H. *A Descriptive, Analytical, and Critical Catalogue of the Manuscripts Bequeathed unto the University of Oxford by Elias Ashmole* (Oxford: Oxford University Press, 1845).

BLAYNEY, P. W. M. *The Texts of King Lear and their Origins*. i: *Nicholas Okes and the First Quarto* (Cambridge: Cambridge University Press, 1982).

BORISH, M. E. 'A Second Version of John Day's *Peregrinatio Scholastica*', *Modern Language Notes*, 55 (1940), 35–9.

BRAUNMULLER, A. R. 'Robert Carr, Earl of Somerset, as Collector and Patron', in Linda Levy Peck (ed.), *The Mental World of the Jacobean Court* (Cambridge: Cambridge University Press, 1991), 230–50.

BRAY, A. E. *A Description of the part of Devonshire bordering on the Tamar and Tavy*, 3 vols. (London: John Murray, 1836).

BRAY, ALAN. 'Homosexuality and the Signs of Male Friendship in Elizabethan England', *History Workshop Journal*, 29 (1990), 1–19.

BRENNAN, MICHAEL. *Literary Patronage in the English Renaissance: The Pembroke Family* (London: Routledge, 1988).

BRENNAN, TIMOTHY. 'The National Longing for Form', in Homi

Bhabha (ed.), *Nation and Narration* (London, 1990), 44–70.

BRIOIST, PASCAL. 'Que de choses avons nous vues et véçues à la Sirène', *Histoire et Civilisation*, 4 (1991), 89–132.

BROWN, CEDRIC, and PIVA, MARGHERITA. 'William Browne, Marino, France, and the Third Book of *Britannia's Pastorals*', *Review of English Studies*, 29 (1978), 385–404.

BRYDGES, SIR EDWARD, and HASLEWOOD, J. *The British Bibliographer*, 4 vols. (London, 1810–14).

BURGESS, GLENN. *The Politics of the Ancient Constitution: An Introduction to English Political Thought, 1603–1642* (London and Basingstoke: Macmillan, 1992).

—— *Absolute Monarchy and the Stuart Constitution* (New Haven and London: Yale University Press, 1996).

BURKE, PETER. 'Tacitism, Scepticism, and Reason of State', in J. H. Burns and Mark Goldie (eds.), *The Cambridge History of Political Thought, 1450–1700* (Cambridge: Cambridge University Press, 1991), 479–98.

BURROW, COLIN. 'Original Fictions: Metamorphosis in *The Faerie Queene*', in Charles Martindale (ed.), *Ovid Renewed: Ovidian Influences on Literature and Art from the Middle Ages to the Twentieth Century* (Cambridge: Cambridge University Press, 1988), 99–119.

—— *Epic Romance: Homer to Milton* (Oxford: Clarendon Press, 1993).

BURT, RICHARD. *Licensed by Authority: Ben Jonson and the Discourses of Censorship* (Ithaca, NY, and London: Cornell University Press, 1993).

BUTLER, MARTIN. 'Ben Jonson's *Pan's Anniversary* and the Politics of Early Stuart Pastoral', *English Literary Renaissance*, 22 (1992), 369–404.

—— 'Ben Jonson and the Limits of Courtly Panegyric', in Kevin Sharpe and Peter Lake (eds.), *Culture and Politics in Early Stuart England* (Basingstoke and London: Macmillan, 1994), 91–115.

—— and LINDLEY, DAVID. 'Restoring Astraea: Jonson's Masque for the Fall of Somerset', *English Literary History*, 61 (1994), 807–27.

CALHOUN, CRAIG (ed.), *Habermas and the Public Sphere* (Cambridge, Mass.: MIT Press, 1992).

CALHOUN, THOMAS O. 'George Wither: Origins and Consequences of a Loose Poetics', *Texas Studies in Language and Literature*, 16 (1974), 263–79.

CAPP, BERNARD. *The World of John Taylor the Water Poet* (Oxford: Clarendon Press, 1994).

CARLSON, N. E. 'Wither and the Stationers', *Studies in Bibliography*,

15 (1964), 210–15.

CAVE, TERENCE. *The Cornucopian Text: Problems of Writing in the French Renaissance* (Oxford: Clarendon Press, 1979).

CHARTIER, ROGER (ed.). *The Culture of Print: Power and the Uses of Print in Early Modern Europe*, trans. Lydia G. Cochrane (Princeton, Princeton University Press, 1989).

CHAUDHURI, SUKANTA. *Renaissance Pastoral and its English Developments* (Oxford: Clarendon Press, 1989).

CHRISTIANSON, PAUL. 'Young John Selden and the Ancient Constitution, 1610–18', *Proceedings of the American Philosophical Society*, 128 (1984), 271–86.

CLARK, PETER. *English Provincial Society from the Reformation to Revolution: Religion, Politics, and Society in Kent 1500–1640* (Sussex: Harvester Press, 1977).

CLEGG, CYNDIA SUSAN. *Press Censorship in Elizabethan England* (Cambridge: Cambridge University Press, 1997).

CLUCAS, STEVEN. ' "Noble virtue in extremes": Henry Percy, ninth Earl of Northumberland, Patronage, and Stoic Consolation', *Renaissance Studies*, 9 (1995), 273–87.

COGSWELL, THOMAS. *The Blessed Revolution: English Politics and the Coming of the War, 1621–24* (Cambridge: Cambridge University Press, 1989).

—— 'The Path to Elizium "Lately Discovered": Drayton and the Early Stuart Court', *Huntington Library Quarterly*, 54 (1991), 207–33.

—— 'Underground Verse and the Transformation of Early Stuart Political Culture', in Susan D. Amussen and Mark A. Kislansky (eds.), *Political Culture and Cultural Politics in Early Modern England* (Manchester and New York: Manchester University Press, 1995), 277–300.

COLLINSON, PATRICK. *The Birthpangs of Protestant England: Religious and Cultural Change in the Sixteenth and Seventeenth Centuries* (London: Macmillan, 1988).

—— 'The Monarchical Republic of Queen Elizabeth I', in *Elizabethan Essays* (London and Rio Grande: Hambledon Press, 1994).

COOPER, HELEN. *Pastoral: Mediaeval into Renaissance* (Ipswich: D. S. Brewer; Totowa: Rowman and Littlefield, 1977).

COPE, SIR WILLIAM. *Bramshill: Its History and Architecture* (London: H. J. Infield, 1883).

CREIGH, JOCELYN. 'George Wither and the Stationers: Facts and Fiction', *Papers of the Bibliographical Society of America*, 74 (1980), 49–57.

CROFT, PAULINE. 'Fresh Light on Bate's Case', *The Historical Journal*, 30 (1987), 523–39.

252   *Bibliography*

CROFT, PAULINE. 'The Reputation of Robert Cecil: Libels, Political Opinion and Popular Awareness in the Early Seventeenth Century', *Transactions of the Royal Historical Society*, 1 (1991), 43–69.

CUDDY, NEIL. 'The Revival of the Entourage: the Bedchamber of James I, 1603–25', in David Starkey *et al.* (eds.), *The English Court: from the Wars of the Roses to Civil* War (London and New York: Longman, 1987), 173–225.

CUST, RICHARD. 'News and Politics in Early Seventeenth-Century England', *Past and Present*, 112 (1986), 60–90.

——and HUGHES, ANN. (eds.) *Conflict in Early Stuart England: Studies in Religion and Politics, 1603–1642* (London and New York: Longman, 1989).

DALY, JAMES. 'The Idea of Absolute Monarchy in Seventeenth-Century England', *The Historical Journal*, 21 (1978), 227–50.

DAVIES, BERNARD. 'The Text of Spenser's *Complaints*', *Modern Language Review*, 20 (1925), 21–2.

DEAN, DAVID. 'Pressure Groups and Lobbies in the Elizabethan and Early Jacobaean Parliaments', *Parliaments, Estates and Representation*, 11 (1991), 139–52.

DE LATTRE, F. *English Fairy Poetry. From the Origins to the Seventeenth Century* (London: Henry Frowde; Paris: Henri Didier, 1912).

DOBELL, PERCY. 'Note on Sales', *TLS* (22 Sept. 1921), 616.

DOELMAN, JAMES. 'George Wither, the Stationers Company and the English Psalter', *Studies in Philology*, 90 (1993), 74–82.

DUBROW, HEATHER. *A Happier Eden: The Politics of Marriage in the Stuart Epithalamium* (Ithaca, NY, and London: Cornell University Press, 1990).

——'"The Sun in Water": Donne's Somerset Epithalamium and the Poetics of Patronage', in Heather Dubrow and Richard Strier (eds.), *The Historical Renaissance: New Essays on Tudor and Stuart Literature and Culture* (Chicago and London: University of Chicago Press, 1988), 197–219.

ECCLES, MARK. 'Thomas Gainsford, "Captain Pamphlet"', *Huntington Library Quarterly*, 45 (1982), 259–70.

EDWARDS, ROBERT. 'Exile, Self, and Society', in Maria-Ines Lagos-Pope (ed.), *Exile in Literature* (1988), 15–31.

EISENSTEIN, ELIZABETH. *The Printing Press as an Agent of Change: Communications and Cultural Transformations in Early Modern Europe*, 2 vols. (Cambridge: Cambridge University Press, 1979).

GEOFFREY ELEY, 'Nations, Publics, and Political Cultures: Placing Habermas in the Nineteenth Century', in Craig Calhoun (ed.), *Habermas and the Public Sphere* (Cambridge, Mass.: MIT Press, 1992), 303–6.

ELSKY, MARTIN. *Authorizing Words: Speech, Writing, and Print in the English Renaissance* (Ithaca, NY, and London: Cornell University Press, 1989).

ETTIN, ANDREW. *Literature and the Pastoral* (New Haven and London: Yale University Press, 1984).

EVANS, JOAN. A *History of the Society of Antiquaries* (Oxford: Oxford University Press, 1956).

FENLON, DERMOT. 'Thomas More and Tyranny', *Journal of Ecclesiastical History*, 32 (1981), 453–76.

FERGUSON, ARTHUR B. *The Articulate Citizen and the English Renaissance* (Durham, NC: Duke University Press, 1965).

FERGUSON, MARGARET W. ' "The Afflatus of Ruin": Meditations on Rome by Du Bellay, Spenser, and Stevens', in Annabel Patterson (ed.), *Roman Images* (Baltimore and London: The Johns Hopkins University Press, 1982), 23–50.

FINKELPEARL, PHILIP. *John Marston of the Middle Temple: An Elizabethan Dramatist and his Social Setting* (Cambridge, Mass.: Harvard University Press, 1969).

FIRTH, C. H. 'The British Empire', *The Scottish Historical Review*, 15 (1918), 185–89.

FITTER, CHRIS. *Poetry, Space, Landscape: Towards a New Theory* (Cambridge: Cambridge University Press, 1995).

FOUCAULT, MICHEL. 'What is an Author?', in Josué V. Harari (ed.), *Textual Strategies: Perspectives in Post-structuralist Criticism* (London: Methuen, 1979), 141–60.

FRASER, NANCY. 'Rethinking the Public Sphere: A Contribution to the Critique of Actually Existing Democracy', in Craig Calhoun (ed.), *Habermas and the Public Sphere* (Cambridge, Mass.: MIT Press, 1992), 109–42.

FRENCH, J. M. 'George Wither in Prison', *PMLA* 45 (1930): 959–66.

GALLOWAY, BRUCE. *The Union of England and Scotland, 1603–1608* (Edinburgh: John Donald, 1986).

GARDINER, S. R. *History of England from the Accession of James I to the Outbreak of the Civil War, 1603–1642*, 10 vols., 3rd edn. (London, 1889–94).

GOSSE, EDMUND. *The Jacobean Poets* (London: John Murray, 1894).

GOTTFRIED, RUDOLF B. 'Spenser and the Italian Myth of Locality', *Studies in Philology*, 34 (1937), 107–25.

GREENBLATT, STEPHEN. 'Sidney's *Arcadia* and the Mixed Mode', *Studies in Philology*, 70 (1973), 269–78.

—— *Renaissance Self-fashioning: From More to Shakespeare* (Chicago and London: Chicago University Press, 1980).

GREENE, ROLAND. 'The *Shepheardes Calender*, Dialogue, and

254   Bibliography

Periphrasis', *Spenser Studies*, 8 (1987), 1–33.

GREG, W. W. *Pastoral Poetry and Pastoral Drama: A Literary Inquiry with Special Reference to the Pre-Restoration Stage in England* (London: A. H. Bullen, 1906).

GRUNDY, JOAN. 'William Browne and the Italian Pastoral', *Review of English Studies*, 16 (1953), 305–16.

——'Keats and William Browne', *Review of English Studies*, 21 (1955), 44–52.

——'A New Manuscript of the Countess of Pembroke's Epitaph', *Notes and Queries*, 7 (1960), 63–64.

—— *The Spenserian Poets: A Study in Elizabethan and Jacobean Poetry* (London: Edward Arnold, 1969).

HABERMAS, JÜRGEN. *The Structural Transformation of the Public Sphere: An Inquiry into a Category of Bourgeois Society*, trans. Thomas Burger and Frederick Lawrence (Cambridge, Mass.: MIT Press, 1989).

——'Further Reflections on the Public Sphere', in Craig Calhoun (ed.), *Habermas and the Public Sphere* (Cambridge, Mass.: MIT Press, 1992), 421–61.

HADFIELD, ANDREW. *Literature, Politics and National Identity: Reformation to Renaissance* (Cambridge: Cambridge University Press, 1994).

HAMMOND, PAUL. 'The Language of the Hive: Political Discourse in Seventeenth-Century England', *The Seventeenth-Century*, 9 (1994), 119–33.

HANFORD, J. H. 'The Pastoral Elegy and Milton's *Lycidas*', in Charles Patrides (ed.), *Milton's 'Lycidas': The Tradition and the Poem* (New York: Holt, Rinehart, Wilson, 1961), 27–55.

HANNAY, MARGARET. *Philip's Phoenix: Mary Sidney, Countess of Pembroke* (New York and Oxford: Oxford University Press, 1990).

HANSEN, MELANIE. 'Identity and Ownership: Narratives of the Land in the English Renaissance', in William Zunder and Suzanne Trill (eds.), *Writing and the English Renaissance* (London and New York: Longman, 1996), 87–105.

HARDIN, RICHARD. *Michael Drayton and the Passing of Elizabethan England* (Lawrence, Manhattan: The University Press of Kansas, 1973).

HARTMAN, GEOFFREY. *Saving the Text: Literature/Derrida/Philosophy* (Baltimore and London: The Johns Hopkins University Press, 1981).

HARVEY, ELIZABETH D., and MAUS, KATHERINE E. *Soliciting Interpretation: Literary Theory and Seventeenth-Century Poetry* (Chicago and London: University of Chicago Press, 1990).

HEBEL, W. 'Drayton's *Sirena*', *PMLA* 39 (1924), 814–26.

HEINEMANN, MARGOT. *Puritanism and Theatre: Thomas Middleton and Opposition Drama under the Early Stuarts* (Cambridge: Cambridge University Press, 1982).

HELGERSON, RICHARD. *Self-Crown'd Laureates: Spenser, Jonson, Milton, and the Literary System* (Berkeley and Los Angeles: University of California Press, 1983).

——*Forms of Nationhood: The Elizabethan Writing of England* (Chicago and London: University of Chicago Press, 1992).

HELMHOLZ, R. H. 'Civil Trials and the Limits of Responsible Speech', in R. H. Helmholz and Thomas Green, *Juries, Libels, and Justice: The Role of English Juries in Seventeenth- and Eighteenth-Century Trials for Libel and Slander* (Los Angeles: William Andrews Clarke Memorial Library, University of California, 1984).

HENINGER JR, S. K. 'The Renaissance Perversion of Pastoral', *Journal of the History of Ideas*, 22 (1961), 254–61.

HENSLEY, CHARLES. *The Later Career of George Wither* (The Hague and Paris: Mouton, 1969).

HERENDEEN, WILLIAM. *From Landscape to Literature: The River and the Myth of Geography* (Pittsburgh: Duquesne University Press, 1986).

HOBSBAWN, ERIC. 'Inventing Traditions', in Eric Hobsbawn and Terence Ranger (eds.), *The Invention of Traditions*, 2nd edn. (Cambridge: Canto, 1992), 1–14.

HOLDERNESS, GRAHAM, et al. *Shakespeare: Out of Court Dramatizations of Court Society* (Basingstoke and London: Macmillan, 1990).

HOLDSWORTH, W. S. 'Defamation in the Sixteenth and Seventeenth Centuries', *Law Quarterly Review*, 159 (1924), 302–15.

HOLMER, JOAN. 'Internal Evidence for Dating William Browne's *Britannia's Pastorals*, Book III', *Papers of the Bibliographical Society of America*, 70 (1976), 347–64.

HOTINE, MARGARET. '*Richard III* and *Macbeth*—Studies in Tudor Tyranny?' *Notes and Queries*, 236 (1991), 480–6.

HUNT, WILLIAM. 'Spectral Origins of the English Revolution: Legitimation Crisis in Early Stuart England', in Geoff Eley and William Hunt (eds.), *Reviving the English Revolution: Reflections and Elaborations on the Work of Christopher Hill* (London and New York: Verso, 1988), 305–32.

HUTSON, LORNA. *Thomas Nashe in context* (Oxford: Clarendon Press, 1989).

HUTTER, HORST. *Politics as Friendship: The Origins of Classical Notions of Politics in the Theory and Practice of Friendship* (Waterloo, Ont.: Wilfred Laurier University Press, 1978).

HYATTE, REGINALD. *The Arts of Friendship: The Idealization of*

Friendship in Medieval and Renaissance Literature (Leiden, New York, Cologne: E. J. Brill, 1994).

INGRAM, MARTIN. *Church Courts, Sex and Marriage in England, 1570–1640* (Cambridge: Cambridge University Press, 1987).

JACK, R. D. S. *The Italian Influence on Scottish Literature* (Edinburgh: Edinburgh University Press, 1972).

JACKSON, WILLIAM A. (ed.), *Records of the Stationers' Company, 1602 to 1640* (London: The Bibliographical Society, 1957).

—— 'Counterfeit Printing in Jacobean Times', *The Library*, 15 (1934–5), 364–76.

JAMES, MERVYN. 'English Politics and the Concept of Honour, 1485–1642', *Past and Present*, Suppl. 3 (1978).

JARDINE, LISA. *Erasmus, Man of Letters: the Construction of Charisma in Print* (Princeton: Princeton University Press, 1993).

JENKINS, RAYMOND. 'Drayton's Relation to the School of Donne as Revealed in the *Shepheards Sirena*', *PMLA* 38 (1923), 557–87.

—— 'Drayton's *Sirena* Again', *PMLA* 42 (1927), 129–39.

JOHNSON, A. FORBES. *A Catalogue of Engraved and Etched English Title-Pages* (Oxford: Oxford University Press, 1934).

JONAS, LEAH. *The Divine Science: the Aesthetic of some Representative Seventeenth-Century English Poets* (New York: Columbia University Press, 1940).

KAUFFMAN, LINDA. *Discourse of Desire: Gender, Genre, and Epistolary Fictions* (Ithaca, NY: Cornell University Press, 1986).

KAPLAN, M. LINDSAY. *The Culture of Slander in Early Modern England* (Cambridge: Cambridge University Press, 1997).

KAY, DENNIS. *Melodious Tears: The English Funeral Elegy from Spenser to Milton* (Oxford: Clarendon Press, 1990).

KEACH, WILLIAM. *Elizabethan Erotic Narratives: Irony and Pathos in the Ovidian Poetry of Shakespeare, Marlowe and their Contemporaries* (Sussex: Harvester, 1977).

KENNEDY, WILLIAM. *Jacopo Sannazaro and the Uses of the Pastoral* (Hanover and London: University Press of New England, 1983).

KENNER, HUGH (ed.). *Seventeenth-Century Poetry: The Schools of Donne and Jonson* (New York: Holt, Rinehart and Winston, 1964).

KING, JOHN N. 'Spenser's *Shepheardes Calender* and Protestant Pastoral Satire', in Barbara Keifer Lewalski (ed.), *Renaissance Genres: Essays on Theory, History, and Interpretation* (Cambridge, Mass. and London: Harvard University Press, 1986), 369–98.

—— *Spenser's Poetry and the Reformation Tradition* (Princeton: Princeton University Press, 1990).

KINNEY, CLARE REGAN. *Strategies of Poetic Narrative: Chaucer,*

Spenser, Milton, Eliot (Cambridge: Cambridge University Press, 1992).

KIRSCHBAUM, LEO. 'Walkley's Supposed Piracy of Wither's *Workes* in 1620', *Library*, 19 (1938–9), 339–46.

—— 'Author's Copyright in England before 1640', *Papers of the Bibliographical Society of America*, 40 (1946), 43–80.

—— *Shakespeare and the Stationers* (Columbus: Ohio State University Press, 1955).

KNOTT, JOHN. *Discourses of Martyrdom in English Literature, 1563–1694* (Cambridge: Cambridge University Press, 1993).

LAKE, PETER. 'Constitutional Consensus and Puritan Opposition in the 1620s: Thomas Scott and the Spanish Match', *The Historical Journal*, 25 (1982), 805–25.

—— 'Anti-Popery: the Structure of a Prejudice', in Richard Cust and Ann Hughes (eds.), *Conflict in Early Stuart England* (London and New York: Longman, 1994), 72–106.

LAMB, CHARLES. 'On the Poetical Works of George Wither', in *The Prose Works*, 3 vols. (London: Edward Moxon, 1836), i. 218–26.

LAMB, MARY ELLEN. *Gender and Authorship in the Sidney Circle* (Wisconsin: University of Wisconsin Press, 1990).

LAMBERT, SHEILA. 'The Printers and the Government, 1604–1637', in Robin Myers and Michael Harris (eds.), *Aspects of Printing from 1600* (Oxford Polytechnic Press, 1987), 1–29.

LERNER, LAWRENCE. 'Ovid and the Elizabethans', in Charles Martindale (ed.), *Ovid Renewed: Ovidian Influences on Literature and Art from the Middle Ages to the Twentieth Century* (Cambridge: Cambridge University Press, 1988), 121–35.

LEVACK, BRIAN. *The Formation of the British State: England, Scotland, and the Union* (Oxford: Clarendon Press, 1987).

LIMON, JERZY. *Dangerous Matter: English Drama and Politics in 1623/24* (Cambridge: Cambridge University Press, 1986).

LINDENBAUM, PETER. 'John Milton and the Republican Mode of Literary Production', *Yearbook of English Studies*, 21 (1991), 121–36.

LINDLEY, DAVID. 'Embarrassing Ben: The Masques for Frances Howard', *English Literary Renaissance*, 16 (1986), 343–59.

—— *The Trials of Frances Howard* (London: Macmillan, 1996).

LOEWENSTEIN, JOSEPH. *Responsive Readings: Versions of Echo in Pastoral, Epic, and the Jonsonian Masque* (New Haven and London: Yale University Press, 1984).

—— 'Guarini and the Presence of Genre', in Nancy Klein Maguire (ed.), *Renaissance Tragicomedy: Explorations in Genre and Politics* (New York: AMS Press, 1987), 33–55.

—— 'For a History of Literary Property: John Wolfe's Reformation',

English Literary Renaissance, 18 (1988), 389–421.
LOFTIE, W. J. *The Inns of Court and Chancery* (Southampton: Ashford Press, 1985).
LOOMIE, ALBERT J. (ed.). *Spain and the Jacobean Catholics*, 2 vols. (Catholic Record Society, 1973).
LOVE, HAROLD. *Scribal Publication in Seventeenth-Century England* (Oxford: Clarendon Press, 1993).
LUPTON, JULIA REINHARD. 'Mapping mutability: or, Spenser's Irish plot', in Brendan Bradshaw *et al.* (eds.), *Representing Ireland* (Cambridge: Cambridge University Press, 1994), 93–115.
—— 'Home-Making in Ireland: Virgil's Eclogue I and Book VI of *The Faerie Queene*', *Spenser Studies*, 7 (1990), 119–27.
LYON, J. H. *A Study of the Newe Metamorphosis, written by J. M., Gent, 1600* (New York: Columbia University Press, 1919).
McCLENNEN, J. 'William Browne as a Satirist', *Papers of the Michigan Academy of Science, Arts and Letters*, 33 (1947), 355–62.
McEACHERN, CLAIRE. *The Poetics of Nationhood, 1590–1612* (Cambridge: Cambridge University Press, 1996).
MACFIE, PAMELA ROYSTON. 'Text and *Textura*: Spenser's Arachnean Art', in D. Allen and R. White (eds.), *Traditions and Innovations: Essays on British Literature of the Middle Ages and the Renaissance* (Newark: University of Delaware Press, 1990), 88–96.
—— 'Ovid, Arachne, and the Poetics of Paradise', in Rachel Jacoff and Jeffrey T. Schnapp (eds.), *The Poetry of Allusion: Virgil and Ovid in Dante's 'Commedia'* (Stanford: Stanford University Press, 1991), 159–72.
MacLEAN, GERALD. *Time's Witness: Historical Representation in English Poetry, 1603–1660* (Wisconsin: University of Wisconsin Press, 1990).
McMULLAN, GORDON. *The Politics of Unease in the Plays of John Fletcher* (Amherst: The University of Massachusetts Press, 1994).
—— and HOPE, JONATHAN (eds.), *The Politics of Tragicomedy: Shakespeare and After* (London: Routledge, 1992).
MacPHAIL, ERIC. 'Friendship as a Political Ideal in Montaigne's *Essais*', *Montaigne Studies*, 1 (1989), 177–87.
McRAE, ANDREW. 'Husbandry Manuals and the Language of Agrarian Improvement', in Michael Leslie and Timothy Raylor (eds.), *Culture and Cultivation in Early Modern England* (Leicester and London: Leicester University Press, 1992), 35–62.
MAGUIRE, NANCY KLEIN (ed.). *Renaissance Tragicomedy: Explorations in Genre and Politics* (New York: AMS Press, 1987).
MALLETTE, RICHARD. *Spenser, Milton and Renaissance Pastoral* (Lewisburg: Bucknell University Press, 1981).

MARCUS, LEAH. *The Politics of Mirth: Jonson, Herrick, Milton, and Marvell, and the Defense of Holiday Pastimes* (Chicago and London: University of Chicago Press, 1986).

—— *Puzzling Shakespeare: Local Reading and its Discontents* (Berkeley, Los Angeles, and London: University of California Press, 1988).

—— 'Politics and Pastoral: Writing the Court on the Countryside', in Kevin Sharpe and Peter Lake (eds.), *Culture and Politics in Early Stuart England* (Basingstoke and London: Macmillan, 1994), 139–59.

MAROTTI, ARTHUR F. *Manuscript, Print, and the English Renaissance Lyric* (Ithaca, NY, and London: Cornell University Press, 1995).

MARTIN, HENRI-JEAN. *The History and Power of Writing*, trans. Lydia G. Cochrane (Chicago and London: University of Chicago Press, 1988).

MARTIN, JULIAN. *Francis Bacon, the State, and the Reform of Natural Philosophy* (Cambridge: Cambridge University Press, 1992).

MARTINDALE, CHARLES. *Ovid Renewed: Ovidian Influences on Literature and Art from the Middle Ages to the Twentieth Century* (Cambridge: Cambridge University Press, 1988).

MAYCOCK, A. L. *Nicholas Ferrar of Little Gidding* (Michigan: Eerdams, 1980).

MAYER, T. F. 'Tournai and Tyranny: Imperial Kingship and Critical Humanism', *The Historical Journal*, 36 (1991), 257–77.

MILLER, NANCY. 'Arachnologies: The Woman, the Text, and the Critic', in Nancy Miller (ed.), *The Poetics of Gender* (New York: Columbia University Press, 1986), 270–95.

MILTON, ANTHONY. 'Thomas Wentworth and the Political Thought of the Personal Rule', in J. F. Merritt (ed.), *The Political World of Thomas Wentworth, Earl of Strafford, 1621–24* (Cambridge: Cambridge University Press, 1996).

MAIR, THOMAS. *The Addled Parliament of 1614* (Oxford: Oxford University Press, 1958).

MONTROSE, LOUIS ADRIAN. 'Of Gentlemen and Shepherds: The Politics of Elizabethan Pastoral Form', *English Literary History*, 50 (1983), 415–59.

MOORMAN, F. W. *William Browne. His Britannia's Pastorals and the Pastoral Poetry of the Elizabethan Age* (Strassburg: Trubner, 1897).

NAGLE, BETTY ROSE. *The Poetics of Exile: Program and Polemic in the 'Tristia' and 'Expistulae ex Ponto' of Ovid* (Brussels: Latomus, 1980).

NORBROOK, DAVID. *Poetry and Politics in the English Renaissance* (London: Routledge and Kegan Paul, 1984).

NORBROOK, DAVID. ' "The Masque of Truth": Court Entertainments and International Protestant Politics in the Early Stuart Period', *The Seventeenth Century*, 1 (1986), 81–110.

—— 'The Monarchy of Wit and the Republic of Letters: Donne's Politics', in Elizabeth. D. Harvey and Katherine Eisaman Maus (eds.), *Soliciting Interpretation: Literary Theory and Seventeenth-Century English Poetry* (Chicago and London: University of Chicago Press, 1990), 3–36.

—— ' "What Cares these Roarers for the Name of King?": Language and Utopia in *The Tempest*', in Gordon McMullan and Jonathan Hope (eds.), *The Politics of Tragicomedy: Shakespeare and After* (London: Routledge, 1992), 21–54.

—— 'Levelling Poetry: George Wither and the English Revolution, 1642–1649', *English Literary Renaissance*, 21 (1991), 217–56.

—— 'Rhetoric, Ideology and the Elizabethan World Picture', in Peter Mack (ed.), *Renaissance Rhetoric* (London and Basingstoke: Macmillan, 1994).

—— *Writing the English Republic: Poetry, Rhetoric and Politics 1627–1660* (Cambridge: Cambridge University Press, 1999).

O'CALLAGHAN, MICHELLE. ' "Talking Politics": Tyranny, Parliament, and Christopher Brooke's *The ghost of Richard the third* (1614)', *The Historical Journal*, 41 (1998), 97–120.

ORBISON, T. (ed.). *The Middle Temple Documents Relating to George Chapman's 'The Memorable Masque'*, The Malone Society (Oxford: Oxford University Press, 1983).

OTIS, BROOK. *Ovid as an Epic Poet*, 2nd edn. (Cambridge: Cambridge University Press, 1970).

PAGE, J. W. (ed.). *The Rivers of Devon from Source to Sea* (London: Seeley & Co., 1893).

PAGE, WILLIAM. *A History of Hampshire and the Isle of Wight* (London: Constable and Co., 1961 (*Victoria History of the Counties of England*, vol. iv)).

PARKER, PATRICIA. *Inescapable Romance: Studies in the Poetics of a Mode* (Princeton: Princeton University Press, 1979).

PARKER, ROSZICA. *The Subversive Stitch: Embroidery and the Making of the Feminine* (London: The Women's Press, 1984).

PARRY, GRAHAM. *The Golden Age Restor'd: The Culture of the Stuart Court, 1603–42* (Manchester: Manchester University Press, 1981).

PARSONS, LEILA. 'Prince Henry (1594–1612) as a Patron of Literature', *Modern Language Review*, 47 (1952), 503–7.

PATTERSON, ANNABEL. *Censorship and Interpretation: The Conditions of Writing and Reading in Early Modern England* (Wisconsin: University of Wisconsin Press, 1984).

—— *Pastoral and Ideology. Virgil to Valery* (Oxford: Clarendon Press, 1988).

—— 'All Donne', in Elizabeth D. Harvey and Katherine E. Maus (eds.), *Soliciting Interpretation: Literary Theory and Seventeenth-Century English Poetry* (Chicago and London: University of Chicago Press, 1990), 37–67.

—— 'John Donne, Kingsman?', in Linda Levy Peck (ed.), *The Mental World of the Jacobean Court* (Cambridge: Cambridge University Press, 1991), 251–72.

—— *Reading between the lines* (London: Routledge, 1993).

PATTERSON, L. R. *Copyright in an Historical Perspective* (Nashville: Vanderbilt University Press, 1968).

PECK, LINDA LEVY. *Northampton: Patronage and Policy at the Court of James I* (London: George Allen and Unwin, 1982).

—— *Court Patronage and Corruption in Early Stuart England* (Boston: Unwin Hyman, 1990).

—— 'The Mentality of a Jacobean Grandee', in Linda Levy Peck (ed.), *The Mental World of the Jacobean Court* (Cambridge: Cambridge University Press, 1991), 148–68.

—— (ed.). *The Mental World of the Jacobean Court* (Cambridge: Cambridge University Press, 1991).

PELTONEN, MARKKU. *Classical Humanism and Republicanism in English Political Thought, 1570–1640* (Cambridge: Cambridge University Press, 1995).

PENN, C. D. *The Navy under the Early Stuarts and its influence on English History* (London: Cornmarket Press, 1970).

PERSELS, JEFFREY C. 'Charting Poetic Identity in Exile: Entering Du Bellay's *Regrets*', *Romance Notes*, 28 (1988), 195–202.

PHELPS, W. H. 'Thomas Gainsford (1556–1624), the "Grandfather of English Editors"' *Publications of the Bibliographical Society of America*, 73 (1979), 79–85.

PITCHER, JOHN. *Samuel Daniel: The Brotherton Manuscript* (Leeds: University of Leeds, 1981).

—— '"In those figures which they seeme": Samuel Daniel's *Tethys' Festival*', in David Lindley (ed.), *The Court Masque* (Manchester: Manchester University Press, 1984), 33–59.

POCOCK, J. G. A. *The Machiavellian Moment: Florentine Political Thought and the Atlantic Republican Tradition* (Princeton: Princeton University Press, 1975).

POGGIOLI, RENATO. *The Oaten Flute: Essays on Pastoral Poetry and the Pastoral Ideal* (Cambridge, Mass.: Harvard University Press, 1975).

POLLOCK, LINDA. ' "Teach her to live under obedience": The Making of Women in the Upper Ranks of Early Modern England', *Continuity and Change*, 2 (1989), 231–58.

PRESCOTT, ANNE LAKE. 'The Reception of Du Bartas in England', *Studies in the Renaissance*, 15 (1968), 144–73.

—— 'Evil Tongues at the Court of Saul: The Renaissance David as a Slandered Courtier', *Journal of Medieval and Renaissance Studies*, 2 (1991), 163–86.

—— 'Marginal Discourses: Drayton's Muse and Selden's "Story"', *Studies in Philology*, 88 (1991), 307–28.

PRESTWICH, MENNA. *Cranfield: Politics and Profit under the Early Stuarts* (Oxford: Clarendon Press, 1966).

PRITCHARD, ALLAN. '*Abuses Stript and Whipt* and Wither's imprisonment', *Review of English Studies*, 14 (1963), 337–45.

—— 'An Unpublished Poem by George Wither', *Modern Philology*, 61 (1963), 120–1.

—— 'George Wither's Quarrel with the Stationers: An Anonymous Reply to *The Schollers Purgatory*', *Studies in Bibliography*, 14 (1963), 27–42.

PROCTER, JOHANNA. '*The Queenes Arcadia (1606)* and *Hymens Triumph (1615)*: Samuel Daniel's Court Pastoral Plays', in J. Salmons and W. Moretti (eds.), *The Renaissance in Ferrara and its European Horizons* (Cardiff: University of Wales Press; Ravenna: Mario Lapucci Edizioni del Girasole, 1984), 83–109.

QUINT, DAVID. *Epic and Empire: Politics and Generic Form from Virgil to Milton* (Princeton: Princeton University Press, 1993).

RAYLOR, TIMOTHY. *Cavaliers, Clubs, and Literary Culture: Sir John Menzies, James Smith, and the Order of Fancy* (Newark: University of Delaware Press; London, and Toronto: Associated University Presses, 1994).

REBHOLZ, R. A. *The Life of Fulke Greville, First Lord Brooke* (Oxford: Clarendon Press, 1971).

RHODES, NEIL. *Elizabethan Grotesque* (London, Boston, and Henley: Routledge and Kegan Paul, 1980).

RIDDELL, JAMES A., and STEWART, STANLEY. *Jonson's Spenser: Evidence and Historical Criticism* (Pittsburgh: Duquesne University Press, 1995).

RIVERS, ISABEL. *The Poetry of Conservatism, 1600–1745: A Study of Poets and Public Affairs from Jonson to Pope* (Cambridge: Rivers Press, 1973).

ROBERTS, CLAYTON, and DUNCAN, OWEN. 'The Parliamentary Undertaking of 1614', *English Historical Review*, 93 (1978): 481–98.

RUFF, LILLIAN, and WILSON, D. ARNOLD. 'The Madrigal, the Lute Song, and Elizabethan Politics', *Past and Present*, 44 (1969), 3–51.

RUSSELL, CONRAD. *Parliaments and English Politics 1621–1629* (Oxford: Oxford University Press, 1978).

—— *The Addled Parliament of 1614: The Limits of Revision* (University of Reading, 1992).

SACKS, D. H. 'Searching for "Culture" in the English Renaissance', *Shakespeare Quarterly*, 39 (1988), 465–88.

SALMON, J. M. H. 'Seneca and Tacitus in Jacobean England' in Linda Levy Peck (ed.), *The Mental World of the Jacobean Court* (Cambridge: Cambridge University Press, 1991), 169–88.

SANDERS, JULIE. 'Print, Popular Culture, Consumption and Commodification in *The Staple of News*' in Kate Chedgzoy Sanders and Susan Wiseman (eds.), *Refashioning Ben Jonson: Gender, Politics and the Jonsonian Canon* (Basingstoke and London: Macmillan, 1998), 183–207.

SCOTT, JONATHAN. *Algernon Sidney and the English Republic, 1623–1677* (Cambridge: Cambridge University Press, 1988).

SEDDON, P. R. 'Robert Carr, Earl of Somerset', *Renaissance and Modern Studies*, 14 (1970), 48–68.

SEYMOUR, M. C. 'The Manuscripts of Hoccleve's *Regiment of Princes*', *Edinburgh Bibliographical Society Transactions*, 4 (1974), 253–85.

SHAPIRO, I. A. 'The "Mermaid Club"', *Modern Language Review*, 45 (1950), 6–17.

SHARPE, KEVIN. *Sir Robert Cotton 1586–1631, History and Politics in Early Modern England* (Oxford: Oxford University Press, 1979).

—— *Criticism and Compliment: The Politics of Literature in the England of Charles I* (Cambridge: Cambridge University Press, 1987).

—— and LAKE, PETER (eds.), *Culture and Politics in Early Stuart England* (Basingstoke and London: Macmillan, 1994).

SHEEN ERICA. ' "The Agent for his Master": Political Service and Professional Liberty in *Cymbeline*', in Gordon McMullan and Jonathan Hope (eds.), *The Politics of Tragicomedy: Shakespeare and After* (London: Routledge, 1992), 55–76.

SIMPSON, PERCY. 'Walkley's Piracy of Wither's Poems in 1620', *The Library*, 6 (1925), 273–7.

SMUTS, MALCOLM. *Court Culture and the Origins of a Royalist Tradition in Early Stuart England* (Philadelphia: University of Pennsylvania Press, 1987).

—— 'Court-Centred Politics and Roman Historians', in Kevin Sharpe and Peter Lake (eds.), *Culture and Politics in Early Stuart England* (Basingstoke and London: Macmillan, 1994), 21–43.

SOMMERVILLE, JOHANN. *Politics and Ideology in England, 1603–1640*

(London and New York: Longman, 1986).

—— 'James I and the Divine Right of Kings: English Politics and Continental Theory', in Linda Levy Peck (ed.), *The Mental World of the Jacobean Court* (Cambridge: Cambridge University Press, 1991), 55–70.

—— 'English and European Political Ideas in the Early Seventeenth Century: Revisionism and the Case of Absolutism', *Journal of British Studies*, 15 (1996), 168–94.

STACHNIEWSKI, JOHN. *The Persecutory Imagination: English Puritanism and the Literature of Religious Despair* (Oxford: Clarendon Press, 1991).

STARKIE, THOMAS. *A Treatise on the Law of Slander and Libel, and incidentally of Malicious Prosecutions*, 2nd edn. (London: J. & W. T. Clarke, 1830).

STEEN, S. J. 'Fashioning an Acceptable Self: Arbella Stuart', *English Literary Renaissance*, 18 (1988), 78–95.

STRONG, ROY. *Henry, Prince of Wales and England's Lost Renaissance* (London: Thames & Hudson, 1986).

TAYLOR, D. 'The Third Earl of Pembroke as a Patron of Poetry', *Tulane Studies in English* 5 (1955), 41–67.

TESKEY, GORDON. 'Mutability, Genealogy, and the Authority of Forms', *Representations*, 41 (1993), 104–22.

THIRSK, JOAN. *The Agrarian History of England and Wales*. iv. *1500–1640* (Cambridge: Cambridge University Press, 1967).

THOMPSON, CHRISTOPHER. *The Debate on the Freedom of Speech in the House of Commons in February 1621* (Essex: The Orchard Press, 1985).

TILLOT, P. M. (ed.). *A History of Yorkshire, The City of York* (London: Oxford University Press, 1961).

TILLOTSON, KATHLEEN. 'Drayton, Browne, and Wither', *TLS* (27 Nov. 1937), 911.

TUFTE, VIRGINIA. *The Poetry of Marriage: The Epithalamium in Europe and Its Development in England* (Los Angeles: Tinnon Brown, 1970).

TURNER, JAMES. *The Politics of Landscape: Rural Scenery and Society in English Poetry, 1630–1660* (Oxford: Basil Blackwell, 1979).

TUVE, ROSEMUND. 'Ancients, Moderns, and Saxons', *English Literary History*, 6 (1939), 166–82.

TYACKE, NICHOLAS. *Anti-Calvinism: The Rise of English Arminianism, 1590–1640* (Oxford: Clarendon Press, 1987).

TYLUS, JANE. 'Jacobean Poetry and Lyric Disappointment', in Elizabeth D. Harvey and Katherine E. Maus (eds.), *Soliciting Interpretation: Literary Theory and Seventeenth-Century English*

Poetry (Chicago and London: University of Chicago Press, 1990), 174–98.

WATKINS, JOHN. *The Specter of Dido: Spenser and the Virgilian Epic* (New Haven and London: Yale University Press, 1995).

WEITZMANN, FRANCIS WHITE. 'Notes on the Elizabethan Elegie', *PMLA* 50 (1935), 435–43.

WERNHAM, R. B. 'The Public Records in the Sixteenth and Seventeenth Centuries', in Levi Fox (ed.), *English Historical Scholarship in the Sixteenth and Seventeenth Centuries* (London and New York: Oxford University Press, 1956).

WHITLOCK, BAIRD. *John Hoskyns, Serjeant-at-Law* (Washington: University Press of America, 1982).

WILKES, G. A. 'The "Humours Heav'n on Earth" of John Davies of Hereford, and a Suppressed Poem', *Notes and Queries*, 6 (1959), 209–10.

WILLIAMS, PENRY. *The Council in the Marches of Wales under Elizabeth I* (Cardiff: University of Wales Press, 1958).

WILLIAMS, S. 'Two Seventeenth-Century Semi-Dramatic Allegories of Truth the Daughter of Time', *The Guildhall Miscellany*, 11 (1963), 207–20.

WORDEN, BLAIR. 'Classical Republicanism and the Puritan Revolution', in Hugh Lloyd-Jones *et al.* (eds.), *History and Imagination: Essays in Honour of H. R. Trevor-Roper* (London: Duckworth, 1981), 182–200.

WORMALD, JENNY. 'James VI and I, *Basilikon Doron* and *The Trew Law of Free Monarchies:* The Scottish Context and the English Translation', in Linda Levy Peck (ed.), *The Mental World of the Jacobean Court* (Cambridge: Cambridge University Press, 1991), 43–54.

WRIGHT, L. B. 'Propaganda against James I's "Appeasement" of Spain', *Huntington Library Quarterly*, 6 (1943), 149–72.

YATES, FRANCES. *Shakespeare's Last Plays: A New Approach* (London: Routledge and Kegan Paul, 1975).

YOCH, JAMES D. 'The Renaissance Dramatization of Temperance: The Italian Revival of Tragicomedy and *The Faithful Shepherdess*', in Nancy Klein Maguire (ed.), *Renaissance Tragicomedy: Explorations in Genre and Politics* (New York: AMS Press, 1987), 115–38.

ZAGORIN, PEREZ. *The Court and the Country: The Beginnings of the English Revolution* (London: Routledge and Kegan Paul, 1969).

UNPUBLISHED THESES

ADAMS, S. L. 'The Protestant Cause: Religious Alliance with the West European Calvinist Communities as a Political Issue in England, 1585–1630', D.Phil. thesis (Oxford, 1972).

BRENNAN, MICHAEL. 'The Literary Patronage of the Herbert Family, Earls of Pembroke, 1550–1640', D.Phil. thesis (Oxford, 1982).

BRIGGS, EDWIN STUART. 'Browne of Tavistock: A Biographical and Critical Study', Ph.D. thesis (Harvard, 1956).

FRENCH, J. M. 'George Wither', Ph.D. thesis (Harvard, 1928).

KAY, DENNIS. 'The English Funeral Elegy in the reigns of Elizabeth I and James I, with Special Reference to Poems on the Death of Prince Henry (1612)', D.Phil. thesis (Oxford, 1982).

LAING, ROSEMARY. 'The Disintegration of Pastoral: Studies in Seventeenth-Century Theory and Practice', D.Phil. thesis (Oxford, 1982).

MARSHALL, CAROL. 'William Browne and *Britannia's Pastorals*', Ph.D. thesis (Radcliffe College, 1951).

NORBROOK, DAVID. 'Panegyric of the Monarch and Its Social Context under Elizabeth I and James I', D.Phil. thesis (Oxford, 1978).

O'CALLAGHAN, MICHELLE. 'Three Jacobean Spenserians: William Browne, George Wither, and Christopher Brooke', D.Phil. thesis (Oxford, 1993).

TILLOTSON, GEORGE. 'William Browne of Tavistock: His Life and Pastorals', B.Litt. thesis (Oxford, 1930).

TYLUS, JANE. 'The Myth of Enclosure: Renaissance Pastoral from Sannazzaro to Shakespeare', Ph.D. thesis (Johns Hopkins University, 1985).

WILKS, T. V. 'The Court Culture of Prince Henry and his Circle, 1603–1613', 2 vols., D.Phil. thesis (Oxford, 1987).

WOOLF, DANIEL. 'Change and Continuity in English Historical Thought, c.1590–1640', D. Phil. thesis (Oxford, 1983).

Index